*The Birth Control Movement
and American Society*

The Birth Control Movement and American Society

From Private Vice to Public Virtue

With a New Preface on
the Relationship between Historical
Scholarship and Feminist Issues

JAMES REED

Princeton University Press / Princeton, N.J.

Published by Princeton University Press,
41 William Street, Princeton, New Jersey 08540
In the United Kingdom: Princeton University Press,
Guildford, Surrey

First Basic Books edition, 1978
First Princeton Paperback printing, 1984
LCC 83-60459
ISBN 0-691-09404-7 / ISBN 0-691-02830-3 (pbk.)

The author wishes to thank the following for permission to quote from the sources
listed: Houghton Library, American Birth Control League Papers; Richard Gamble
and Countway Library, Clarence J. Gamble Papers; Dorothy Dickinson Barbour and
Countway Library, Robert L. Dickinson Papers; Sophia Smith Collection, Margaret
Sanger Papers and Dorothy Brush Papers; Countway Library, Norman Himes
Papers; the Schlesinger Library, Transcript of Interviews with Emily H. Mudd;
Alfred A. Knopf, Inc., Emma Goldman, *Living My Life* © 1934; Harcourt Brace
Jovanovich, Inc., Mary McCarthy, *The Group* © 1954; T. S. Eliot, "Difficulties of a
Statesman" in *Collected Poems, 1909-1962*, © 1936 by Harcourt Brace Jovanovich, Inc.;
© 1963, 1964 by T. S. Eliot. Reprinted with permission of the publishers.

Clothbound editions of Princeton University Press books
are printed on acid-free paper, and binding materials
are chosen for strength and durability.
Paperbacks, while satisfactory for personal collections,
are not usually suitable for library rebinding.

Printed in the United States of America by
Princeton University Press, Princeton, New Jersey

TEXT DESIGNED BY VINCENT TORRE
Original title: *From Private Vice to Public Virtue:
The Birth Control Movement and American Society Since 1830*

Contents

PART I
BIRTH CONTROL BEFORE MARGARET SANGER

PART II
THE WOMAN REBEL: MARGARET SANGER AND THE
STRUGGLE FOR CLINICS

PART III
ROBERT L. DICKINSON AND THE COMMITTEE ON
MATERNAL HEALTH

PART VIII
THE TROUBLE WITH FAMILY PLANNING

Preface

I set out to write a history of the birth control movement in the United States but had to make hard choices about what should be included. *From Private Vice to Public Virtue* describes the efforts of a small group of Americans to spread the practice of contraception, first in the United States, then in the rest of the world. Given the complexity of the problem of changing human reproductive behavior, birth controllers inevitably disagreed over strategy. This study focuses on those individuals who at any given time represented innovation or change in the birth control movement. I have neglected the internal history of the Planned Parenthood Federation of America and of state and local birth control leagues in order to concentrate on the role of key individuals and their relationship to American society. They worked through a variety of institutions, ranging from the anarchist journal *Mother Earth* to the relatively conservative Population Council. They ranged in political values from socialists to capitalists, but for all of them the separation of sex from procreation had revolutionary implications. Birth control was a metaphor for individual responsibility, an essential first step in the effort to achieve self-direction.

The desire to control fertility, as old as human society, has found expression in a startling variety of means. The Egyptian recipe for a contraceptive suppository of crocodile dung (1850 B.C.), described by Norman Himes in *Medical History of Contraception* (1936), was but one of many such devices which could be culled from the literature of ancient cultures. Anthropologists studying human reproduction in premodern cultures have found that the desire for children is not an innate human drive but an acquired motive which must be reinforced by social rewards and punishments sufficient to overcome the wish to avoid the pain of childbirth and the burdens of parenthood. There have never been any happy savages reproducing with ease. Rather, conflict between the social need to preserve the species and the individual desire to escape the burdens of childbearing is a universal part of the human experience. Societies that survive necessarily develop pronatal values that support the process of reproduction.

The Europeans who founded American society in the seventeenth century came from an expanding culture that had developed a powerful rationale for parenthood. Woman's main social role was to bear many children in order to guarantee the growth and eventual worldwide triumph of the Christian faith.

Social needs or goals are often at odds, however, with the aspirations of individuals. Eighteenth century Americans inherited and built upon a manipulative attitude toward nature. Some men and women perceived an advantage in having fewer children and began seeking ways to control family size, despite values inherited from the past that imposed a burden of guilt for failure to accept society's version of what was natural. By the turn of the nineteenth century, the fertility of American women had begun a long secular trend downward. Infant mortality remained murderously high. Yet generation after generation of American women had fewer children than their mothers, despite the wails of social leaders that they were shirking their patriotic duty, committing "race suicide," sinning against Nature. Part I of this study analyzes how and why socially ambitious Americans began to limit their families and examines the changes in values, in attitudes toward women, children, and sex, that made possible the demographic transition to small families in a nation dedicated to peopling a continent with good Christian republicans, a nation where Malthus was irrelevant.

The desire of socially ambitious Americans to control their fertility provided a market for numerous "little books" that described birth control methods. These nineteenth century marriage manuals testify to the fact that Americans possessed the technology and knowledge of the process of conception necessary to develop effective and safe contraceptives, but, beginning in the 1870s, birth control information was suppressed by federal and state legislation. The majority of American men feared both the dissatisfaction of middle-class women with traditional roles and the high fertility of the foreign born in comparison with those from genteel background. For social leaders, male and female, the desire to have fewer children was associated with hedonism and the decline of the Protestant values of self-sacrifice and hard work. Thus, contraception remained a furtive private practice until the twentieth century.

There were three motives for wanting to make birth control available to everyone. Parts II, III, and V are devoted to analysis of the efforts of Margaret Sanger, Robert Dickinson, and Clarence Gamble to justify and to spread contraceptive practice. These three "birth controllers" articulated the concerns of large numbers of Americans, but each came to the cause of birth control from a different background and each found in it a means of expressing a personal animus. Sanger gave expression to a feminist impulse, the desire to give women control over their bodies. Dickinson believed that the main threat to stable family life sprang from poor sexual adjustment and championed birth control as a means of strengthening the family. Gamble was concerned over the fact that the poor had more children than their social betters and feared that this differential fertility between classes would lead to the welfare state or worse. These three motives, autonomy for women, better marital sex adjustment, and concern over differential fertility, provided the impetus for the emergence of the birth control movement in the 1920s and 1930s.

I have provided separate treatment for each of these three leaders of the movement because their goals and reform styles should not be confused. Dickinson and Sanger approached the problem of establishing clinical studies of contraception with different assumptions and used contrasting strategies. His attempt to organize clinical study failed; hers succeeded. His failure illustrates the barriers to medical research and needs to be analyzed separately from her successful effort to overcome legal and medical obstacles to research. While Dickinson was most concerned with lobbying among fellow professionals, Gamble resented the high cost of delivering birth control through doctors and devoted a great deal of energy to a search for doctor-less contraceptives. Sanger, Dickinson, and Gamble cooperated with one another, but their coalitions were fragile, pragmatic attempts to maximize one's influence in the belief that the spread of contraceptive practice would promote one's goals, even if motives had to be disguised.

From World War I to World War II, Sanger, Dickinson, and Gamble achieved a great deal. Sanger led a successful drive to establish a nationwide system of birth control clinics where women could obtain reliable contraceptive advice. Dickinson, through skillful lobbying among fellow physicians, managed to convince organized medicine that contraception should be a recognized medical service. Gamble organized several programs in mass distribution of contraceptives and convinced the surgeon general that faulty condoms ought to be taken off the market. Yet birth controllers did not win a place for contraception in federal public health programs or gain wide acceptance for their goal of "every child a wanted child." They labored in a society where the birth rate was approaching the replacement level, a phenomenon which alarmed some social scientists, as we shall describe in Part IV. They associated birth control with low fertility among the middle classes, economic stagnation, and the specter of an end to population growth. The "population problem" was a dearth of people of the right kind. Birth controllers lacked a commanding rationalization or social purpose strong enough to overcome public indifference, fear of immorality, the opposition of the Roman Catholic hierarchy, and the pronatalist values of a society in which growth was equated with progress.

The discovery of the population explosion in the Third World after World War II provided new justification for birth control. Demographers associated with the Princeton Office of Population Research, who had been primarily concerned with problems of differential fertility between classes and declining population growth rates during the 1930s, began in the late 1940s to call attention to the threat posed by rapid population growth to the economic development and political stability of the Third World. Part VI describes the frustration experienced by Americans in their efforts to aid the less developed nations to develop effective population control programs. These failures stimulated contraceptive research that led to the development of the plastic intrauterine devices.

The new rationale for birth control was also a key factor in the successful search for an oral contraceptive. Part VII describes how Margaret Sanger and her feminist ally Katharine McCormick were finally able, after years of searching, to realize their dream of a physiological contraceptive that was completely divorced from coitus. McCormick provided the biologist Gregory Pincus with money and with social justification, *but* he was willing to cooperate with her only *because* of the new respectability provided for contraceptive research by the threat of demographic catastrophe.

By 1975, contraception, once shunned as a vice practiced by the selfish, had become a public virtue, a moral imperative in a crowded world. Population watchers debated whether or not society could afford to allow individual freedom of choice in the matter of parenthood. Part VIII analyzes the debate between those who believe that voluntary family planning can control population growth and those who advocate more coercive policies. The history of the American birth control movement points to the fact that birth control is mainly a question of social values and human motives. The successes of birth control advocates were limited by the social context in which they worked rather than by lack of technology or mistaken strategies of change. American sexual norms changed radically between 1830 and 1975 in response to pressures generated by economic and social development, and American birth rates in the 1970s provide evidence that new sexual values are emerging appropriate to a society in which well-being will no longer be associated with large size, conspicuous consumption, and continuous growth.

Preface to the Princeton Edition

When I began work on this book in 1970, Norman Himes' *Medical History of Contraception* (1936) headed my list of background reading. It was one of the X-catalogued books that had to be retrieved from a locked room in Harvard's Widener Library, and I was ashamed to be so embarrassed as I went through the ritual of obtaining my first officially designated dirty book.

Suppressing the urge to go wash my hands, I began taking notes on the monograph that taught me how tedious sex research could be. Finally, lunch time arrived, followed by browsing in the university bookstore, where I discovered a new paperback edition of Himes' book, purchased two copies, and seldom again had to ask for any item from the Widener X room.

Himes was a sociologist, but his book was labeled a "medical history" in order to avoid prosecution under the Comstock Acts. The rapid changes in sexual values that made possible a cheap paperback edition of Himes' book, only thirty-four years after its original publication as a "for doctors only" monograph, led many historians to such topics as sexual reform, gender, and family. If nothing else, historical research over the last decade has proven relevant to basic questions of both public policy and personal politics. I am delighted by the rich discourse that has answered many of the questions posed by scholars during the 1970s and raised many more. The question of whether professional historians should deal with sexuality has been definitively answered, and my original sense that other historians did not quite accept the legitimacy of my topic has been replaced by regret that it is impossible to read all of the interesting work being published on sexual reform.

Some of the questions that informed this book now seem settled (yes, nineteenth-century birth control methods worked well enough; the attitudes of doctors toward birth control had less to do with technology and professionalism than with their desire to defend "civilized morality"), while time and further thought have raised new concerns and revealed to me ignored opportunities.[1]

The most critical reviews of my work came from Marxist-Feminists seeking to vindicate Linda Gordon, whose *Woman's Body, Woman's*

Right: A Social History of Birth Control in America (1976) had received rough treatment in some professional journals.[2] I did not have an opportunity to review Gordon's book, and, as she acknowledges in her citations, I provided her with my draft manuscript and with documents uncovered in my research that were of particular interest to her.[3] Nevertheless, I was denounced during a session at the meeting of the Organization of American Historians in 1978 for participating in Gordon's martyrdom. Similarly, *Feminist Studies* devoted fifteen pages to a comparison of our works in which dozens of phrases or opinions were attributed to me but not a single page reference was provided, although the authors of that article gave a traditional note to their single quotation from Engels—"We make history ourselves, but . . . under very definite antecedents and conditions." Marxist-Feminists were alleged to have a special understanding of this truism, while "liberal reformist" "idealists" like myself were blind to the realities of class, gender, domination, and exploitation. The most serious problem with my work was my failure to provide an adequate understanding of contemporary political economy. Gordon was supposed to provide a more useful history in terms of strategies for defending and promoting the interests of women in the face of onslaughts from the Moral Majority and other reactionary groups.[4]

I hope to answer this criticism in the course of explaining the assumptions and historical context that influenced this book, and I will conclude with thoughts on how I might have done better. Probably the greatest influence on me before I began research for this book was a tradition of scholarship that captured my imagination and made me want to be an historian—work that was narrative in form, highly empirical, and spoke to the present; examples include Perry Miller's *The New England Mind: From Colony to Province* (1953) and Charles Rosenberg's *The Cholera Years* (1962). Even flattering reviewers noted the demands that I made on readers, and one, whom I suspect of wanting to throw the book on the floor, perfectly captured my intent: "This book is long, serious, and resolutely empirical. Mr. Reed has mastered an awesome amount of material. . . . That sort of research requires patience—more than five years from him, many hours from his readers. Because he wants to be fair, both to his historical subjects and to the truth, Mr. Reed methodically assembles the evidence before drawing conclusions and making judgments."[5]

Because I believed the subject of this book to be as important as most that got historians' attention, I had the same responsibility as a political or diplomatic historian to pay attention to tedious details that might, collectively, shift "the weight of the evidence." There was a need in an underdeveloped field for monographs and surveys that might serve as benchmarks for further research. And, as the first person to work through the archives that should provide much of the evidence for a history of the birth control movement, I felt that I had a right to make demands on my readers. Also, one of my responsibilities was to bring to their attention materials that would not be readily available or apparent to them.

Although my historical models and methods fairly can be described as conventional, I selected the topic of birth control because of a pressing sense that sexual values, including my own, needed rethinking. Like the characters in this book, I worked in a particular social context that now seems remote. I was influenced by contemporary events that made an entire generation conscious of the decline of the American pronatalist consensus and of the rebellion of women who were no longer willing to accept the social status quo.

Between 1965 and the completion of this book in 1976, a series of federal court decisions, legislative acts, and apparent changes in public opinion led me to believe that women were gaining unprecedented civil liberties, and I welcomed these events. In 1965 the Supreme Court declared unconstitutional a Connecticut law that prohibited contraceptive practice by anyone, married or single, adolescent or adult. In 1967 Congress amended the Social Security Acts to include budgets for contraceptives in domestic maternal health programs and removed contraceptives from the list of items that could not be purchased with foreign aid funds (these actions marked the practical inclusion of family planning in federal welfare policy). In 1970 Congress finally removed contraceptive devices from the list of obscenities banned by the federal Comstock laws; in 1972 *Eisenstadt v. Baird* established that the unmarried should have the same access to birth control as the married; and in 1973 "non-therapeutic" abortion was legalized by judicial decision.[6]

During this period—when the right of individuals to control their fertility was first recognized by government—there were other changes, ranging from the renewal of feminism to the sexual desegregation of college dormitories that seemed to promise liberation from some of the traditional tyrannies of gender. This was the period of the Civil Rights movement, of Lyndon Johnson's War on Poverty (remember the Office of Economic Opportunity!), and finally of the debacle in

Vietnam. There was much discussion of "the population explosion" and the threat of "ecocatastrophe." It became common for young adults to live together openly without getting married, and many of the newly married suddenly felt free to declare their intention to remain childless.

These changes raised as many new issues as they resolved, but in the mid-1970s there seemed good reason to hope that women were finally beginning to be recognized as citizens who had a right to share expectations raised by the traditional American ideals of individual autonomy, equality before the law, and equality of opportunity (or life, liberty, and the pursuit of happiness). The contrast between those liberal promises and the fate of large numbers of Americans has inspired some of the best contemporary work by historians, but most of those who exposed the contradictions and described the tragic struggles to realize democratic ideals had a firm sense of our society's accomplishments as well as its failures. In short, this book was written before the alleged "death of liberalism" and was influenced by faith both in the value of scholarship and in political traditions of pluralism, compromise, and coalition building.

Today a counteroffensive is being waged against "liberal" reforms, including the victories for reproductive self-determination that I have listed. It should be noted, however, that the debate in 1983 centers around such questions as whether federal funding will continue for 5,000 birth control clinics and for abortions. While there is real danger that many women will be forced back into what Margaret Sanger called "the misery and breeding pen"—and many have never escaped it—we should not forget the important accomplishments of the recent past nor denigrate the successful strategies that helped to bring about significant changes in public policy regarding access to contraception and abortion.

In order to provide perspective on current policy debates, let me point to an experiment in population control described in this book (see pp. 247-52). During the late 1930s a coalition of social scientists and birth control advocates organized a project in rural Logan County, West Virginia, to find out if birth rates among the poor could be lowered through door-to-door distribution of contraceptive jelly. The men who conceived this project were interested in such social "problems" as rural poverty and were insensitive to feminist issues or even to elementary questions concerning the rights of human subjects in social experiments. Nevertheless, many women were eager to have the free contraceptive jelly and their birth rates declined by over forty percent. Although the jelly-users expressed strong interest in other birth control methods and wanted to continue contraceptive practice, the sponsors abandoned the project because of its annual cost of less than $6 per woman. In 1938 the state of West Virginia spent less than $1.25 per rural family on public health, and birth control services seemed an extravagance beyond the means of private philanthropy or government.

In January of 1975 I recorded the "oral history" of Louise Hutchins, M.D., of Berea, Kentucky.[7] Her work provides a startling contrast to the 1930s. Dr. Hutchins traveled from county to county in a state-sponsored public health van dispensing contraceptive services in areas where there were formerly no medical services at all. Unlike the would-be social engineers of the 1930s, she wanted to liberate women from male tyranny as well as from bad health and unwanted pregnancies. By the 1970s there had been an enormous improvement in the level of medical services available to the women of Kentucky and West Virginia. The poor still lacked equal access to health care, but no woman any longer was being denied access to contraceptive advice by the law or poverty—and both the number of women enrolled in medical schools and their feminist self-consciousness were rapidly increasing.

The expansion of the welfare state after World War II, for me symbolized by the passage in 1965 of Medicare and Medicaid, has been a mixed blessing. Horror stories of welfare mothers being involuntarily sterilized should not blind us, however, to the very real benefits that women have gained over the last twenty years. Alliances among diverse groups, including feminists, Planned Parenthood, professional lobbies, and liberal politicians, have been essential to significant political victories. In the current struggle for the right to reproductive self-determination, the cultivation of a "correct line" at the expense of the development of coalitions among interests that differ toward capitalism, meritocracy, professionalism, and the welfare state is, I think, unwise. Those whose lips curl at the mention of the National Organization for Women, the Allan Guttmacher Institute, the Population Council, the Rockefeller Foundation, or Tip O'Neill are unlikely to be able to organize effective campaigns in the interests of women or of social justice.

Let me return to the important question raised by my Marxist-Feminist critics: What kind of history is most useful? I believe that my attempt at an even-handed description of the activities of feminist and non-feminist birth controllers, the founding of the Population Council, the development of the IUD and the pill, and of specific changes in public policy is more useful to those engaged in political struggles for women's rights than a "history" that ignores the accomplishments of nonsympathetic characters and slanders many potential allies. My complaint that Linda Gordon "treated the activities of a large number of organizations and individuals . . . as one vast undifferentiated conspiracy in the service of political repression and American imperialism" and that she allowed "her own ideology to compensate for inadequate research" was not an attempt at red-baiting but a response to her cavalier characterization of those she disliked as exponents of forced population control (see p. 439). It is simply not true, as Gordon claims, that "all the major population-control organizations of the 1970s were born from the Planned Parenthood Federation" or that the Population Council and Planned Parenthood-World Population promoted the idea that "effective population control can never happen voluntarily." It is not true that they "increasingly advocate various kinds of coercion in their programs" or that in the 1960s "receiving any foreign aid usually obligated receiving nations to undertake population control programs in accordance with U.S. State Department specifications."[8] Undocumentable assertions of that kind have no place in historical scholarship—feminist, radical, or bourgeois. They cannot serve as a guide to political action but only as a means of separating the true believers from the compromised majority.

Most of my regrets about my book involve failures to deal more critically with both the ideologies and social strategies of birth controllers. While I tried not to let disagreements with other historians shape my work, I sought to correct some reigning attitudes. These included the condescension toward nineteenth-century sexual standards and toward Margaret Sanger. As a result I emphasized the celebration of mutuality and "companionate marriage" that was a salient part of the nineteenth-century discourse on sex, while I neglected the contradictions. Recent work of historians informed by feminist concerns has led me to a keener appreciation of the realities of inequality and exploitation in the past and today.[9] Similarly, in my efforts to correct the extremely censorious treatment of Margaret Sanger by David Kennedy—to show that her differences with Robert Dickinson

and other professionals should be understood as legitimate policy
disputes and conflicts of value rather than as examples of Sanger's
egotism and irrationality—I failed to provide the critical commentary
on Sanger that she deserves as an important figure in modern history
(see pp. 441-42).[10]

My second thoughts on Sanger involve her fascination with wealth
and her decreasing concern with large issues of social justice; on the
question of her effectiveness as a lobbyist for birth control, I remain
her defender. Some recent criticism of Sanger for the "medicalization"
of the birth control movement seems misconceived. First, Sanger was
a vigorous exponent of self-help, and she turned to the idea of the
physician-staffed birth control advice center (or "clinic") only after a
1918 court decision that upheld the closing of her Brownsville clinic
but left the door open for contraceptive advice by doctors for "therapeutic" reasons.[11] Second, the primary advocates of birth control
without doctors have been those with the least concern for civil liberties of women and the poor. Clarence Gamble and Alvin Kaufman
promoted simple methods because they feared the growth of the
welfare state and wanted to reverse the differential birth rate between
classes without resort to medical socialism. Such liberals and feminists
as Hannah Stone and Helena Wright believed that every woman
deserved access to the best contraceptive technology available, and
before 1960 that was a diaphragm fitted by a physician. More importantly, they hoped that birth control clinics would serve as general
health screening centers where a wide range of physical and psychological needs could be identified.[12] The glib assumption by some scholars that coalitions with professionals could not have been in the best
interest of women illustrates the point that judgments about the birth
control movement require careful attention to the day-to-day problems of historical figures working in particular contexts.[13] We simply
play tricks on the dead when we judge them by our current concerns
without sufficient attention to theirs. We also cheat ourselves by pos-
tulating defective solutions to our problems based on bad history.

In retrospect, I find my book least satisfying in those areas where
current headlines and living informants most shaped my interpretation. My greatest regret is that I did not treat more analytically the
post World War II effort to redefine "the population problem." While
I believe that my narrative still serves as a useful introduction, all of
Part VI, "Propagandists Turned to Prophets," suffers from my failure

to show how the events I describe were part of an attempt to cope with a changing international political economy amid an escalating Cold War.

The "population explosion" discovered by American social scientists was real enough, but their response to this event was shaped by their commitment to the national interests of the United States and to what used to be called the free enterprise system. Beginning in the 1920s, American demographers had developed a sophisticated theory of demographic transition, in which birth rates were viewed as largely determined by socio-economic factors, in contrast to the biological determinism of previous population watchers, who assumed that changes in fecundity or biological capacity were the major causes of variation in birth rates.[14] In response to events following World War II, however, some American demographers (Frank Notestein was the most important) began to argue that human reproductive patterns could be changed through the introduction of family planning programs—wholesale social change need not precede demographic transition from a vital economy of high death rates and high birth rates to a vital economy of low death rates and low birth rates. This was a remarkable change of opinion and deserved greater critical scrutiny than I provided.[15] As I have grown to understand the poverty of modernization theory, I have also regretted the paucity of my imagination in Part VI.

Despite these weaknesses, I hope that our understanding of the birth control movement was well served by this book, which I wanted to be useful to the widest possible audience of interested citizens. I remain hopeful that others with different questions and sensibilities will find much to do in this area, and that this book will serve them as a reliable introduction.

New Brunswick, New Jersey
March 1983

Notes

1. On birth control in the nineteenth century, Part I of this book should be read in conjunction with James C. Mohr, *Abortion in America: The Origins and Evolution of National Policy* (New Haven, 1978) and Angus McLaren, *Birth Control in Nineteenth Century England* (New York, 1978). For additional analysis of the attitudes of physicians toward contraception, see Reed, "Doctors, Birth Control, and Social Values: 1830-1970" in *The Therapeutic Revolution: Essays in the Social History of*

American Medicine, edited Morris Vogel and Charles Rosenberg (Philadelphia, 1979), pp. 109-33 and the works by Harrison and Soloway cited in note 13 below.

2. For review of Gordon's reviews, see Elizabeth Fox-Genovese, "Comment on the Reviews of *Woman's Body, Woman's Right*," *Signs* (Summer 1979), 804-8; Sarah Elbert and Sander Kelman, "Reply to Shorter on *Woman's Body, Woman's Right*," *Journal of Social History* 12 (Fall 1978), 173-77.

For critical comparison of my book with Gordon's from the Marxist-Feminist perspective, see Elizabeth Fee and Michael Wallace, "The History and Politics of Birth Control," *Feminist Studies* 5 (Spring 1979), 201-15; Ann J. Lane, "The Politics of Birth Control," *Marxist Perspectives* (Fall 1979), 160-69.

3. Gordon, pp. 425, 442, 443, 447.

4. Fee and Wallace, pp. 202, 206, 208, 213-14.

5. Peter Filene, "The Birth of Birth Control," *New York Times Book Review* (February 26, 1978), p. 37.

6. For a detailed chronicle of events, see Phyllis T. Piotrow, *World Population Crisis: The United States Response* (New York, 1973).

7. The Hutchins interview is one of a series sponsored by The Schlesinger Library, Cambridge, Mass. They are available to interested scholars at the library.

8. Gordon, pp. 397-98, 393.

9. I am particularly impressed by Suzanne Lebsock, *The Free Women of Petersburg: Status and Culture in a Southern Town, 1784-1860* (New York, 1983), a work of mature feminist scholarship that shows there need be no conflict between standards of scholarship and self-conscious ethical commitment.

10. David Kennedy, *Birth Control in America: The Career of Margaret Sanger* (New Haven, 1970).

11. For a perceptive analysis of changes in Sanger's writing in relation to the political environment of this period, see Joan M. Jensen, "The Evolution of Margaret Sanger's *Family Limitation* Pamphlet, 1914-1921," *Signs* 6 (Spring 1981), 548-67.

12. On Gamble and Kaufman, see chs. 16-20 and 23 of this book. Gamble's conflict with Dr. Helena Wright is described on pp. 297-300.

For criticism of the "medicalization" of the birth control movement, see Gordon, ch. 10 and Sheila Rothman, *Woman's Proper Place: A History of Changing Ideals and Practices; 1870 to the Present* (New York, 1978), pp. 200-9, 281-90.

13. For similar conclusions, see Brian Harrison, "Women's Health and the Women's Movement in Britain: 1840-1940" in *Biology, Medicine, and Society: 1840-1940*, ed. Charles Webster (Cambridge, England, 1981), pp. 66-71; Richard A. Soloway, *Birth Control and the Population Question in England, 1877-1930* (Chapel Hill, 1982), chs. 10-14.

14. See in this book ch. 14, "Birth Control in American Social Science: 1870-1940" and especially the description of Raymond Pearl's work, pp. 205-6.

15. On this subject see, Dennis G. Hodgson, "Demographic Transition Theory and the Family Planning Perspective: The Evolution of Theory within American Demography" (Ph.D. dissertation, Cornell University, 1976); William Petersen, "Demographic 'Theory' and Public Policy," paper presented to workshop, Historical Perspectives on the Scientific Study of Fertility, American Academy of Arts and Sciences, Boston, May 5-6, 1978.

Acknowledgments

I am indebted to a large number of individuals and institutions for assistance and support. My research began in the Countway Library of Medicine, where Richard Wolfe provided many valuable leads as well as free access to manuscript collections and rare books. Mary-Elizabeth Murdock and the staff of the Sophia Smith Collection were also particularly gracious. The first draft was completed during two years as Rockefeller Research Fellow in The Schlesinger Library, where Jeannette Cheek and Pat King made it a pleasure to combine work for The Schlesinger-Rockefeller Oral History Project with my own research.

Greer Williams and Marguerite Zapoleon allowed me to read their manuscript biographies of Clarence Gamble and of Edith Campbell. Paul Gebhard and Alan Johnson of the Institute for Sex Research provided unpublished data on contraceptive practice from the sex histories collected by Alfred Kinsey and his fellow researchers. Paul Neuthaler of Basic Books supported my desire to publish a large book and provided crucial support at several times.

Helpful comments on the manuscript were provided by Sarah Alpern, Gary Daily, Carl Degler, Philip Greven, Gerald Grob, Linda Henry, R. Christian Johnson, James H. Jones, Regina Morantz, William O'Neill, David Rothman, Alan Sweezy, Maris Vinovskis, Mary Walsh, Donald Weinstein, Greer Williams, Elin Wolfe, and Richard Wolfe. Barbara Sicherman suggested the title in her comments.

I am especially grateful to Ellen Chesler Mallow, who is also working on the history of the American birth control movement. I benefited greatly from her careful reading and from many conversations.

My principal intellectual debt is to Donald Fleming, who encouraged me to undertake this project and provided invaluable advice and criticism. His example as a scholar and a teacher sustained me when I might have quit.

I have tried to use as much as possible of the criticism offered by my readers and suspect that none of them will be completely satisfied. My only defense of the form and substance of this work is that it answers the questions that most interested me when I began studying the history of the American birth control movement. I hope that others with different questions and sensibilities will find much to do in this area and that *From Private Vice to Public Virtue* will serve them as a reliable introduction.

Finally, I would like to acknowledge the sacrifices made by my wife Diane and our children Kim and Chris so that this book could be written. They endured, and for that I am most grateful.

PART I

BIRTH CONTROL
BEFORE
MARGARET SANGER

CHAPTER **1**   # Contraceptive Technology in the Nineteenth Century

A DEMOGRAPHIC revolution took place in the United States between 1800 and 1940. The high birth rates and high mortality characteristic of a premodern society were replaced by a new vital economy of fewer births and fewer deaths. The course of the demographic transition in the United States greatly differed, however, from the model developed by demographers intent on discovering the dynamics of economic development in the Third World. Americans began having fewer children before large-scale industrialization or urbanization took place, and dramatic declines in fertility preceded by at least a century the late nineteenth century advances in public health that gave the infant a good chance of surviving childhood. Thus, Americans began having smaller families in the absence of two factors that social scientists have often assumed to be determining—rapid industrialization and declining infant mortality.[1]

In 1800, American white women were having many more children than the women of Western Europe; by 1900 they were relatively infertile compared with their European sisters. Although early nineteenth century birth rates must be constructed from inadequate sources, the projections available indicate that in 1800 American women were bearing an average of 7.04 children; 5.21 in 1860; and 3.56 in 1900.[2] This downward secular trend would continue until the 1930s, when the birth rate briefly fell below the level required to maintain the existing population. The low fertility of the 1930s is often viewed as a result of the Great Depression, but it should be seen as the culmination of a trend that had begun by 1800. More than half of the decline in fertility between 1800 and 1940 occurred during the nineteenth century, and a considerable part before 1860.[3]

The decline in fertility began before any large proportion of the population lived in urban areas or was engaged in nonagricultural work. Throughout the nineteenth century the drop in the birth rate of the rural population more than kept pace with that of the urban population. While fertility was generally higher in rural and more recently settled areas, the shifts in fertility in each region of the United States followed a similar downward pattern. A study of Indiana in 1820 found differences in fertility among villages when compared to farming areas and among agricultural as compared to nonagricultural households. Because of the pervasiveness of the fertility decline, however, it cannot be explained simply as a function of industrialization or of urbanization.[4]

Richard D. Brown has argued that a "modern personality" emerged in the United States before industrialization got under way and that the prior existence of new attitudes was an important factor in the development of the American economy. Apparently the decline in fertility and economic development were both part of a larger process, the transition from a traditional to a modern society. Profound changes in social values were both cause and effect of that process.[5] Maris Vinovskis, in a study of "socioeconomic determinants" of fertility in 1850 and 1860, found that low levels of fertility at the state level were most highly correlated with such measures of education as literacy and school attendance.[6] Although a majority of Americans still lived on farms or in rural towns during the first half of the nineteenth century, they were increasingly better educated, read more newspapers and books, participated more in the political process, had more faith in material progress, and were more confident than their fathers of the individual's ability to control nature and his own life.

Given that the decline in fertility was one result of changing attitudes toward human ability to manipulate the environment, we still need to know how the desire to have fewer children was realized. What birth control methods were available in the nineteenth century? What role did they play in the transition from the seven to the less-than-four-child family?

Many historians, noting a lack of "scientific" methods of family limitation, have concluded that contraceptive practice "could have made but a small contribution to the declining birth rate of the nineteenth century. The most eulogized method of birth limitation was indirect, sexual abstinence, enforced by a model of female asexuality."[7] Late marriage was a form of abstinence, and one scholar, using sparse and scattered marriage records in five states, argued that later and fewer marriages were a significant cause of declining fertility, an hypothesis that has been cast in doubt by recent demographic studies.[8] Nineteenth century observers blamed corsets, physical degeneracy caused by lack of proper nutrition and physical activity, the spread of venereal disease, and even female education for the trend toward smaller families. Arthur Calhoun recorded samples of this spectrum of complaint in his *Social History of the American Family* (1917–19), but rejected the idea that social change had made Americans less fecund. He thought that the trend toward fewer children had resulted from conscious decisions made by married couples who had used abortion and contraception to limit the size of their families.[9]

Perhaps Calhoun erred in not giving more attention to the possible role of decreased frequency of coitus as a method of family limitation. Evaluation of the relative parts played by sexual repression, abortion, and contraception in the fertility decline depends on an understanding of the effectiveness and "psychological availability" of nineteenth century birth control methods. If the available methods did not significantly reduce the fertility of consistent users, they could not have made much difference. Even if effective contraceptive regimens were available, the problem remains of whether or not significant numbers of nineteenth century Americans used them rather than abstinence or abortion.

Historians have often noted the sexually repressive tone of many of the marriage manuals written by nineteenth century physicians and have usually assumed that reliable contraceptive advice was not available. Advertisements for "electromagnetic prevention machines," a great variety of secret drugs, and other quackery were prominent in medical tracts. The rabid medical sectarianism of the time was especially virulent in the sex advice field, and most authors unfortunately spent more time denouncing their competitors' methods than explaining their own.

Not all of the advice was bad however. It could be argued that there were no fundamental advances in contraceptive technology from the middle of the nineteenth century until the marketing of the birth control pill in 1960. By 1865 various physicians had publicly endorsed withdrawal (*coitus interruptus*), spermicidal douches, the vaginal diaphragm or pessary, rubber condoms, and periodic abstinence. These birth control methods were effective by nineteenth century medical standards. Most nineteenth century birth control advocates intended their advice for married couples who sought only the means to limit their children to a manageable three or four. Sufficient contraceptive means were available to achieve that end. To dismiss these methods as "unscientific" is to apply modern and seldom achieved therapeutic standards to nineteenth century conditions.

English reformers inspired the first American tracts on birth control. During the early 1820s, Francis Place and a small band of freethinking radicals included family limitation among their proposals to improve the position of labor. At the age of seventeen, John Stuart Mill spent several days in jail for distributing Place's "diabolical handbills," which urged workers to practice *coitus interruptus* and described how to use a vaginal sponge as a contraceptive. For years it was believed that Robert Owen, the manufacturer, utopian socialist, and chief theorist of the cooperative movement, had written the handbills; this belief was false, although it was true that Owen's

6

son, Robert Dale Owen (1801–77), wrote the first important American tract on birth control.[10]

Robert Owen spent his life in a vain effort to banish religious superstition and to reestablish the sense of community that he believed had been destroyed by the rise of capitalism. He lost most of his fortune in an attempt to build a working model of his ideals at New Harmony, Indiana. Robert Dale Owen labored in his father's experimental colony as superintendent of schools and as editor of the New Harmony *Gazette*. After the experiment failed he edited *The Free Enquirer* in New York, turning it into America's leading free-thought journal, in which the reform of everything from grammar to sexual morality received careful attention. When an employee printed an unauthorized prospectus for *Every Woman's Book,* an English tract that included contraceptive advice, on Owen's press, he felt compelled to explain his own view of the work, and he cautiously recommended it. Rivals for leadership of the New York labor movement accused Owen of immorality. This charge prodded Owen into writing a book on birth control.[11]

Moral Physiology; or, A Brief and Plain Treatise on the Population Question (1831) was an essay in social science, with a brief discussion of birth control methods included almost as an afterthought. In the first three American editions, all published in 1831, Owen recommended *coitus interruptus,* while arguing that the vaginal sponge was ineffective and the skin condom expensive and unaesthetic. Later the nonapproved methods were relegated to a footnote. The booklet caused Owen some embarrassment during his successful 1836 campaign for the Indiana assembly until it was distributed to voters so that they could see what Owen's opponents were talking about. Ironically, it won approval of the local clergy. The tract sold well for the rest of the century, but without further promotion by Owen.[12]

Moral Physiology changed the life of Charles Knowlton (1800–50), a Yankee from the Berkshire country of western Massachusetts, who in 1832 published the first popular tract on birth control by a physician, *Fruits of Philosophy; or, The Private Companion of Young Married People.* Knowlton, an 1824 graduate of New Hampshire Medical Institution (now Dartmouth Medical School), a militant freethinker, and ne'er-do-well father of three, had hoped to win fame and fortune with the publication of *Elements of Modern Materialism* in 1829. His ponderous exposition of the principles of agnosticism did not sell, the cost of its publication left him heavily in debt, and clerical opposition to his religious views sabotaged several attempts to establish practice in rural towns. On a trip to promote *Elements* in the spring of 1830, Knowlton was invited by Owen to speak at the Hall of Science, the social center for Manhattan's freethinkers. Owen agreed to try to sell *Elements*, giving Knowlton his own books in return. [13]

After reading *Moral Physiology* Knowlton decided that a better method than *coitus interruptus*, one that demanded less sacrifice of pleasure, would have to be invented if Owen's vision of fewer and better nurtured children was to be realized. Knowlton set out to release mankind from its shackles and to win wealth and fame by finding the ideal birth control method. In 1839, anxious to prove the originality of his contribution to contraceptive knowledge because of numerous works that recommended his method without giving him credit or royalty, he described the process by which he sought to discover "some sure, cheap, convenient, and harmless method, which should not in any way interfere with enjoyment."

> Strange as it now seems to me, and must seem to others, I spent days and nights in close reflection on this point, before I arrived at my present mature idea. A first thought that glanced through my mind, was to wash out the semen with the syringe; but then it occurred to me, that this would not answer, because almost certainly there would be a trifle of semen lodged among the folds and ridges of the vagina that would not be washed away, and this trifle would be enough to cause conception. So this idea was dismissed; but it at length occurred to me, to add something to the water that should not hurt the woman, but yet kill the little tender animalcules, or in other words, destroy the fecundating property of the semen. . . .

Knowlton was not absolutely sure of his method, and delayed publishing *Fruits* for four months, until an old friend "agreeably surprised me, by assuring me that my plan would 'carry,' as he well knew from ten years experience in his own family." [14]

8

In the next five years, Knowlton sold 7,000 copies of *Fruits* at from fifty cents to one dollar, the price deliberately kept a little steep to keep it out of the hands of the immature. Though he complained that the success of his book was limited by plagiarized editions, the publication of *Fruits* marked a turning point in his medical career. Six months after he published the first edition, he settled permanently in the Berkshire village of Ashfield, where his practice began to prosper.[15]

Despite his religious views and the hostility of the local clergy, Knowlton was not a social outcast. He always claimed that his enemies were inspired by his freethinking rather than by his proselytizing for birth control. Knowlton's sale of *Fruits* led to three prosecutions under the Massachusetts common law obscenity statute. The first time he was fined fifty dollars in Taunton, and his feelings were hurt when another physician testified, probably correctly, that there was nothing new in the book. According to Knowlton's account of the trial, one juror tried to console him. "Well, we brought you in guilty—we did not see how we could well get rid of it, still I like your book, and you must let me have one of them." The judge subscribed for the next edition, and the prosecuting attorney returned his share of the costs to Knowlton.[16]

On the complaint of a Lowell physician, who had received only a prospectus of *Fruits,* Knowlton was prosecuted a second time, and, owing, he claimed, to a poorly managed defense, he did three months at hard labor in the East Cambridge jail. A third prosecution at Greenfield was *nol prossed* after two juries failed to reach a verdict.[17]

It is significant that Knowlton's practice prospered after he published *Fruits.* The Congregationalist minister of Ashfield, who had inspired the Greenfield prosecution, was dismissed in July 1835, after his attacks on Knowlton had caused a bitter division in his congregation.[18] Knowlton became a respected member of the Massachusetts Medical Society, published regularly in the *Boston Medical and Surgical Journal* (now *New England Journal of Medicine*), where his autobiography was published in 1851, and was a staunch defender of orthodox practice against quackery.[19] Despite respectability Knowlton continued to sell *Fruits* and remained an outspoken freethinker. After Knowlton died of heart disease in 1850, his son

Lorenzo, also a physician, was invited by a committee of leading citizens to take his father's place. When the English free-thinkers Charles Bradlaugh and Annie Besant were prosecuted for reprinting *Fruits* in 1877, their highly publicized trial did more than any other event in the nineteenth century to spread the good news that sex and procreation could be separated.[20]

No competent physician would recommend douching as a means of contraception today, but douching does reduce the fertility of women who conscientiously use it. A 1955 survey of several thousand representative married women in Indianapolis found that 20 percent of those practicing contraception still used the douche. Douching reduced the risk of conception by over 80 percent for those who used it faithfully. Moreover, those who denied using any contraceptive method, but admitted to "douching for cleanliness only" soon after intercourse, more than doubled the intervals between their pregnancies compared with those women who did nothing at all.[21] The persistence of douching as a contraceptive means and the lowered fertility of women who denied any contraceptive intent in the practice reflected the attractiveness of a birth control method that could be disguised as simple personal cleanliness and involved the purchase of no overtly contraceptive devices. Feminine syringes were common articles in nineteenth century apothecary shops.[22]

In defending himself against the charge that a widespread knowledge of douching would promote promiscuity, Knowlton argued that there already existed a knowledge of *coitus interruptus*, "which common sense . . . teaches everyone, and by which all mischief can surely be avoided." This fact proved his point that feminine virtue rested on more than fear of pregnancy. Although the desire to promote his book prevented Knowlton from admitting it, the main advantages of his method over withdrawal were not a matter of effectiveness, but of less interference with pleasure for the male and the placing of control in the hands of the woman, "where," he claimed, "for good reasons it ought to be."[23]

Social scientists have confirmed Knowlton's belief that *coitus interruptus* is autochthonous or entirely natural. Premodern populations in a wide range of places and times have adopted the practice.[24] The success of Knowlton's book depended on the increasingly manipulative attitude toward nature, the impatience with obstacles to convenience and material well-being, that was becoming a salient characteristic of the American. His advocacy of a mechanical device (the vaginal syringe) over a method that required nothing except human effort might also be viewed as a male strategy for placing the responsibility for contraception with the female. In terms of simple effectiveness, withdrawal is a more efficient method than douching.[25] Knowlton's work did not lessen the popularity of Owen's *Moral Physiology*, which went through nine authorized editions in its first five years. Perhaps the continuing demand for Owen's work was partly due to his advocacy of a simple male method. As late as 1876, Eliza Duffey, feminist and author of popular advice book for brides, though she could not discuss contraception openly, placed great emphasis on the ideal of mutuality in sexual relations and the need for self-control, and then referred the reader to *Moral Physiology* for further instruction.[26]

Moral Physiology and *Fruits of Philosophy* were more than birth control tracts. Both provided lengthy philosophical defenses of family limitation within the context of a utilitarian world view. These books read quite well in comparison with the tortured exegeses provided by many twentieth century compilers of "medical indications" for "therapeutic contraception." In addition to a dose of philosophy, Knowlton provided his readers with a general description of their sexual anatomies. Apparently this information was a factor in the popularity of *Fruits* because soon Frederick Hollick (1818–1900), another young physician who drew inspiration from Robert Dale Owen, was doing a booming business as a sex educator.

Hollick claimed to have studied in Edinburgh, but there is no record of his having received a degree.[27] His works do reflect a thorough knowledge of the best medical literature. While Knowlton believed that sperm reached the ovum through absorption by the walls of the vagina, Hollick rejected this theory and explained that "the Animalcules can pass into the Womb themselves, by their own motions . . . , one of them creeps in, and thus effects impregnation."[28]

Hollick claimed that his interest in sex education began when experience in his practice convinced him that "the prevailing ignorance in regard to sexual matters" was a source of much disease and unnecessary suffering. In the spring of 1844, he began lecturing to female audiences in New York on woman's diseases. He soon expanded his repertoire of lectures to include general anatomy, as well as the functions and diseases of the male and female sexual organs. The success of his lectures was guaranteed by the novel visual aids he used. During a trip to France he had purchased a set of "wonderful models of the human body, made of *papier-mâché*, full-sized, and formed and colored to life—so exact, in fact, that it might be difficult to distinguish the model from the real body." Included were male and female sexual anatomies, "which could be taken to pieces, and shown part by part, externally and internally, all molded and colored to nature . . . with a complete series showing the development of the new being in the womb at every stage." After several months of packed audiences in New York, Hollick moved on to Philadelphia "where my success was even greater, upwards of *four hundred ladies* having attended in one day!"[29]

Success of the lecture circuit was followed by publication of a series of popular illustrated advice books. In the 1870s, Hollick had given up lecturing for practice and writing in New York. By then his *Marriage Guide or Natural History of Generation* had gone through dozens of editions, and he proudly quoted one of his western agents, who wrote him that his books had become, "over a large part of the country, *household books*, so that not a house, cabin, nor miner's camp can be found without them for hundreds of miles."[30]

Before the passage of the Comstock Act in 1873, Hollick freely discussed the problem of family limitation. He did not approve of withdrawal, douching, vaginal tampons, or condoms, although he sometimes described these methods and noted their widespread use, but he had calculated a natural or rhythm system of contraception based on periodic abstinence. Hollick explained that women with regular menstrual cycles could enjoy a week or more of sex every month without fear of conception. In most cases:

. . . the egg reaches the Womb some time between the second and tenth day after the Menstrual flow has stopped, and . . . it then remains there from two to six days at the utmost, but after that it passes away. Consequently, *Conception is possible as long as sixteen days after every monthly flow has stopped, but after that time it is impossible!* In fact, it is hardly ever the case that it can take place so long as sixteen days after, because the egg is seldom more than two days in reaching the Womb, and if it remains six, as an extreme limit, *eight days* is probably about the average. If the truth be ascertained, I have no doubt that nine out of every ten females have conceived within the first seven days after the flow, and impregnation would not follow connection after the Tenth day once out of fifty times, but still it is requisite to state the latest possible time and that is sixteen days.[31]

Hollick's knowledge of the menstrual cycle was crude by modern standards, but a woman with regular cycles who followed his advice would be unlikely to conceive.[32] Unfortunately, the French biologist Felix Pouchet published inaccurate estimates of the timing of human ovulation that were based on studies of female dogs. Bogus claims like Pouchet's led to misunderstanding of the human menstrual cycle, and physicians in the English-speaking world became increasingly confused on the question of when conception occurred.[33] Still, Hollick's sound advice was repeated by Francis Low Nichols in *Esoteric Anthropology* (1853), by William Alcott in *The Physiology of Marriage* (1855), and "limiting intercourse to the period from the sixteenth day after menstruation to the twenty-fifth" was listed as one among many methods in an 1898 medical symposium.[34]

Although the history of the safe period during the nineteenth century is a sad example of increasing confusion, the midcentury development of modern rubber manufacturing provided a substance that made inexpensive condoms and flexible vaginal diaphragms possible. In 1837, Charles Goodyear (1800–60), a Connecticut Yankee and the son of the inventor of the spring steel hay and manure fork, succeeded in vulcanizing rubber by combining raw latex with sulfur at high temperature, thereby creating a durable new material upon which countless industries would be based. The failures of previous inventors who had tried to vulcanize rubber made it difficult to raise capital for rubber manufacturing, but by the mid-1840s Goodyear's process had been copied and improved by well-financed manufacturers in America and Britain. Fi-

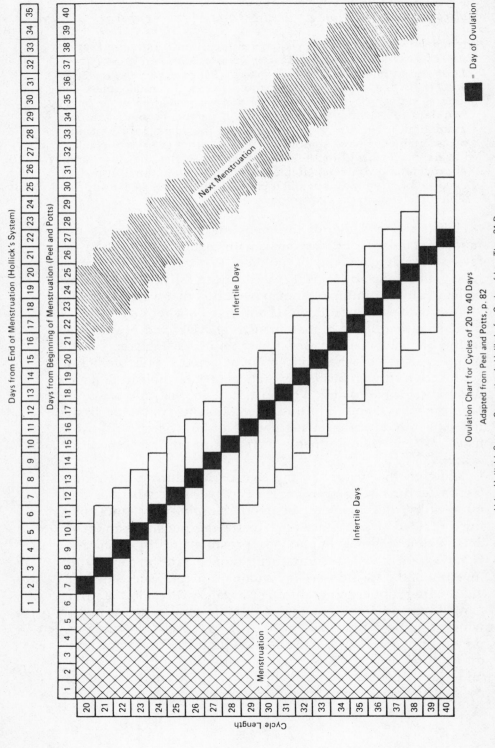

Days from End of Menstruation (Hollick's System)

| 1 | 2 | 3 | 4 | 5 | 6 | 7 | 8 | 9 | 10 | 11 | 12 | 13 | 14 | 15 | 16 | 17 | 18 | 19 | 20 | 21 | 22 | 23 | 24 | 25 | 26 | 27 | 28 | 29 | 30 | 31 | 32 | 33 | 34 | 35 |

Days from Beginning of Menstruation (Peel and Potts)

Next Menstruation

Infertile Days

Infertile Days

Menstruation

Cycle Length

= Day of Ovulation

Ovulation Chart for Cycles of 20 to 40 Days
Adapted from Peel and Potts, p. 82
Using Hollick's System, Conception Is Unlikely for Cycles of Less Than 31 Days

nally, in 1846, Alexander Parkes, a British chemist, developed the "cold cure" process by which rubber could be vulcanized instantaneously by treatment in a solution of sulfur chloride in carbon bisulfide. Parkes' discovery was important in the development of contraceptive devices because the one remaining problem in rubber manufacturing had been the handling of thin, delicate articles, and cold vulcanization minimized this problem.[35]

By the 1850s all the basic processes of rubber manufacturing had been worked out, and the business of manufacturing "questionable rubber goods" was booming in the United States. Previously the only condoms available were expensive, made from the ceca of sheep or other animals, and imported from Europe. In the 1890s one observer of the condom trade complained that while there were factories equipped with the best machinery, "where the business is looked upon as legitimate and done in a straightforward business-like manner" and the "out put sold for medicinal purposes only," the profitability of the trade and the lack of any sane regulation attracted many unscrupulous manufacturers who sold shoddy goods. This competition "hammered prices down so that there is but little profit and consequently small temptation now to engage in the business. Indeed, competition has come nearer to closing the factories of the makers of these goods than have the efforts of any individuals interested in seeing them shut up."[36] In 1938, Norman Himes still recommended to readers of *Practical Birth Control Methods* that they test their condoms for defects by blowing them up like balloons before use.[37] Despite the problems posed for ethical manufacturers and for consumers by the lack of quality controls, thin rubber condoms were readily available at low prices in the United States before the Civil War, and they provided a large part of the "Damnable Rubber Devices" confiscated by late nineteenth century anti-vice crusaders.

Although Charles Goodyear published thick catalogs intended to increase the use of rubber, he never listed condoms among the hundreds of items best made from his product. He did include pessaries, devices worn in the vagina to support the uterus or to apply medication to it.[38] The physiology of conception was well enough understood so that the possible contraceptive usefulness of the pessary was a matter of common sense to some physicians. In 1864, Edward Bliss Foote (1829–1906), an 1858 graduate of Pennsylvania Medical University and former journalist, published another edition of his *Medical Common Sense,* a small volume for the layman, "written in language strictly mundane," and first published in 1858. Foote complained, "The country is flooded with quack nostrums, injurious and unreliable 'recipes,' etc., all of which have been produced . . . because there is an actual demand for some reliable prevention." Among the methods he rejected was douching, which had apparently become quite prevalent. "Many a lady who is suffering under the most aggravated forms of leucorrhoea [purulent vaginal discharge] can trace its origin directly to their application." Foote also condemned the widespread use of *coitus interruptus* as injurious to mental health. Worst of all, he claimed, was the practice of abortion, "now so prevalent among married people." [39]

Foote's solutions to the problem of family limitation were the condom or a "womb veil." The womb veil he explained:

> consists of an India-rubber contrivance which the female easily adjusts in the vagina before copulation, and which spreads a thin tissue of the rubber before the mouth of the womb so as to prevent the seminal aura from entering. . . . Its application is easy and accomplished in a moment, without the aid of a light. It places conception entirely under the control of the wife, to whom it naturally belongs; for it is for her to say at what time and under what circumstances she will become the mother and the moral, religious, and physical instructress of offspring. [40]

Foote's son later claimed that his father invented the womb veil. In 1836, Friedrich A. Wilde, a German gynecologist, had described a cervical cap molded to fit each patient. Foote's device was not a cervical cap, but a true vaginal diaphragm designed to fit longitudinally in the vagina, the forward end under the pubic bone, the back end in the posterior fornix, as in the modern device. [41] Whether or not Foote invented the vaginal diaphragm, the necessary knowledge of female anatomy and of the process of conception, along with reliable materials, was readily available to any physician with imagination and the will to prevent conception.

Lack of imagination was not a fault of American physicians.

In 1866 the president of the New Hampshire State Medical Society complained about what he called "A Raid on the Uterus":

> A distinguished surgeon in New York city, twenty-five years ago, said, when Dupuytren's operation for relaxation of the *sphincter ani* was in vogue, every young man who came from Paris found every other individual's anus too large, and proceeded to pucker it up. The result was that New York anuses looked like gimlet-holes in a piece of pork. It seems to me that just such a raid is being made upon the uterus at this time. It is a harmless, unoffensive little organ, stowed away in a quiet place. Simply a muscular organ, having no function to perform save at certain periods of life, but furnishing a capital field for surgical operations, and is now-a-days subject to all sorts of barbarity from surgeons anxious for notoriety. Had Dame Nature forseen this, she would have made it iron-clad. What with burning and cauterizing, cutting and slashing, and gouging, and splitting, and skewering, and pessarying, the old-fashioned womb will cease to exist, except in history. The *Transactions* of the National Medical Association for 1864 has figured [*sic*] one hundred and twenty-three different kinds of pessaries, embracing every variety, from a simple plug to a patent threshing machine, which can only be worn with the largest hoops. They look like the drawings of turbine water wheels, or a leaf from a work on entomology. Pessaries, I suppose, are sometimes useful, but there are more than there is any necessity for. I do think this filling the vagina with such traps, making a Chinese toyshop of it, is outrageous. . . . Our grandmothers never knew they had wombs only as they were reminded of it by the struggle of a healthy fetus; which, by the by, they always held on to. Now-a-days, even our young women must have their wombs shored up, and if a baby accidentally gets in by the side of the machinery, and finds a lodgment in the uterus, it may, perchance, have a knitting needle stuck in its eyes before it has any.[42]

It seemed to another disapproving observer that the United States had become the leader among civilized nations in both the "destruction of unborn life" and in the "arts of prevention." "Methods that have long been employed in France have become not only well understood here, but improved upon by Yankee skill and ingenuity."[43] In 1880 only France among all the nations of Western Europe had a lower ratio of children to women of child-bearing age than the United States.[44]

Although would-be contraceptors were faced with a puzzling variety of advice, the soundness of which depended upon whose book one bought, information on numerous imperfect, but not ineffective, birth control methods was available. In comparison with the failure rate of most drugs and procedures prescribed by nineteenth century doctors, birth control methods were effective. The psychological availability of birth control methods or the ability of nineteenth century married couples to use contraceptive technology effectively, not the lack of "scientific" contraceptives, is the crucial factor that must be evaluated in order to estimate the impact of contraceptive practice on nineteenth century birth rates.

CHAPTER 2   # The Rise of the Companionate Family

PUBLICATION of Robert Dale Owen's *Moral Physiology* in 1831 marked the beginning of a national debate over the morality and safety of contraceptive practice. In an age that proclaimed the ability of every person to save his soul and to get rich, Americans began consuming self-help books in great quantity. The marriage manual, a part of this new literature, became a staple of American culture during the middle decades of the nineteenth century and provided a forum for discussion not only of family limitation but of the proper relationship between the family and society, as well as the role of man and woman within the family. Marital advice books found an audience among couples who either lacked or were dissatisfied with traditional sources of information provided by family and community. Thus, the intense interest in birth control was part of a larger concern with the future of the family in a world of economic change and social uncertainty.[1]

The most influential nineteenth century domestic advisers were moralists and educators who denounced the hedonism and individualism that they believed were responsible for the social disorder of the new republic, but they also tried to provide their readers with family ideals and gender roles appropriate to the needs of a socially ambitious and geographically

19

mobile middle class. These writers, along with some twentieth century social scientists, often eulogized an older social order that never existed, "the classical family of Western nostalgia."[2] Work by historical demographers has shown that family structure has not changed a great deal in the United States since the seventeenth century. Most of the newly married have established separate households and a nuclear family structure has been normative.[3] Although the "extended family" never existed on a large scale, relatives have always provided important economic and psychological support for newly formed families. By 1800, however, important changes were taking place in the quality of kinship relations and in the functions of the family. The timing of these changes varied by region, class, and ethnic group, but they had become a general part of the experience of the middle classes by the early nineteenth century and led to a widespread sense of crisis that found expression in the literature of domestic instruction.[4]

The search for economic opportunity was leading the young away from their communities of origin. Geographical mobility weakened kinship ties and forced the newly married to be more dependent on their own consciences or internalized standards of conduct in ordering their lives. Economic change was also altering the roles of men and women within the family. As traditional tasks like the manufacture of cloth were transferred from home to factory, middle-class women lost their role as economic producers. Since only the poor woman worked outside the home, respectable women were expected to stay inside it. Thus, while middle-class women escaped some of the drudgery of preindustrial domesticity, their social roles were limited, at least in theory, to the domestic sphere.[5]

Marriage manuals were in part an attempt to explain and rationalize the new context of family life. The family was presented as a private enclave rather than a part of a larger community in which the boundary between the family and the rest of the world was vaguely defined. Domestic advisers told their women readers that the circumscribed world of the home was a better and safer place for its separation from the male economy—a place where children could be nurtured safe from the world's corruption. If the wife was no longer her husband's partner in work, her responsibility for his spiritual welfare was increased. Men ought to marry because they needed the civilizing influence of women in a viciously competitive world, and women deserved protection and respect as the conservators of religious values and the nurturers of children and men. Domestic advisers placed great emphasis on mutuality in family relationships. While women were urged to submit to their husband's authority, husbands were reminded that they needed the guidance of woman's superior intuitive insight and should confer with her on domestic decisions. Husbands were urged to spend all of their free time at home, and one author reprimanded the absent husband with the query: "Did he marry for a housekeeper and a mother for his children or did he seek companionship for life?"[6]

The literature of domesticity depicted marriage as an intense, private, child-centered relationship between equals with differing natural abilities. The Puritan emphasis on marital companionship developed into a celebration of romantic love as *the* justification for marriage. The eighteenth century redefinition of the child as a malleable product of its environment became the doctrine of Christian nurture, the idea that children were not innately depraved but could be shaped into free moral individuals by loving but firm parents. Alexis de Tocqueville echoed the spirit of the new domestic ideology when he noted that in the United States the concept of two spheres of activity determined by gender did not represent a devaluation of woman's status but the application to the family of "the great principle of political economy which governs the manufacturers of our age, by carefully dividing the duties of man from those of woman in order that the great work of society may be better carried on."[7] The ideal of the home as a private retreat from the tension and disorder of public life provided a mobile, restless people with an image of domestic stability, order, and bliss that endured with relatively few modifications for over a century and found fullest expression in the surburban sprawl of the middle twentieth century.

In separating human activity into two spheres, the home and the world of business, domestic advisers were in part simply acknowledging a result of economic development, but they also viewed the home as a theater for reform. America in the process of industrialization seemed to antebellum moralists to be "given over without reservation to the pursuit of wealth." The well-ordered home might provide an essential moral balance. Women isolated would also be quarantined from the rampant selfishness and individualism of a laissez-faire economy. And they would provide a core of common values in a population fragmented by regional, class, and ethnic differences.

William Alcott, Catharine Beecher, and other "household divinities" laid most of the burden for perfecting the world squarely on the shoulders of wives. Only "domestic reform" could eradicate the causes of social disorder, and women of necessity would play the crucial role in the rearing of new generations of free moral individuals because economic change dictated that men would be away from home during most of the child's wakeful hours.[8]

One of the most difficult questions faced by marriage theorists and their clientele was the problem of reconciling marriages based on romantic love with a manageable number of children. Studies by social scientists of Hutterite communities in North America indicate that healthy women bear an average of ten to thirteen children when neither contraception, induced abortion, nor sexual abstinence are used to control fertility.[9] Large families posed a threat to the social ambitions of many nineteenth century Americans because children were seldom an economic asset in a commercial or industrial economy except among the very poor who did not expect to educate their children and thus could put them to work as soon as possible. If parents were to give their children the careful supervision demanded by moral reformers or the education and financial aid required in the struggle for higher economic status, they would have to limit their number.

Domestic advisers differed in their solution to the problem of family limitation. Some championed abstention from coitus except when children were wanted; others advocated contraceptive practice. The majority of writers had an ambiguous view of the subject. They counseled self-control while describing contraceptive practices, often in the process of denouncing them. These marriage counselors valued sexual expression so long as it contributed to stable family life but feared sensuality, or sex as recreation, as a form of self-indulgence that might undermine the Protestant ideals of moral earnestness, austerity, and self-control. Thus, the most salient aspect of the debate over birth control was the ambiguity with which the subject was treated.

The writings of William A. Alcott, M.D. (1798–1859), illustrate this ambiguity. Alcott, who shared an interest in educational reform with his cousin Bronson Alcott, poured his hopes for the regeneration of American society into a series of popular marriage manuals. As a physician Alcott felt a great obligation to provide his readers with reliable sex advice, and, as a careful student of the "laws of health," he could hardly ignore sex.

Sexual attraction, in Alcott's view, was God's way of controlling the reckless independence of young adults. ". . . a time arrives when the education of the family almost ceases. Boys, if not girls, in their fancied wisdom and strength, grow impatient of parental restraint, and are more or less ungovernable." But just as young people escaped home and the humanizing influence of mother and sisters, the desire to mate led to the "renewal of family love" and the ultimate socialization provided by marriage. "Bad as the world is now," he wrote, "how much worse would it be but for matrimony," the means by which each generation of young adults was taught the need for discipline and compromise and to think of others first.[10]

No one valued more than Alcott the joys of marital companionship and the outlet provided by the home for the precious energies that might otherwise be squandered on vice. Still, if the marriage bed became no more than an outlet for unbridled lust, then energy needed for the world's work would be wasted and the discipline of family life evaded. Alcott was concerned by the cost of establishing a proper household. Children required intensive nurture and should only be brought into the world when they could be properly cared for. Marriage was necessary to social order, but how could a man afford it? The solution he proposed was a compromise on the part of both husband and wife. She, denouncing luxury, had to dedicate herself to efficient frugality, and he "must be contented to deny himself that which is admitted to be of inferior value, for the sake of what is of greater worth." Idealized companionship, then, rather than the pursuit of fashion or the complete satisfaction of sexual desire, was the key to happy marriage and social order.[11]

Sex was a precious force, to be conserved and used wisely. In Alcott's view, even "the far-famed and very far hated, Sylvester Graham" had not gone too far when he advised that sexual intercourse be limited to once a week at most, and ideally to once a month. "This doctrine . . . so utterly at war with the general habits and feelings of mankind" was the real source of hostility to Graham. ". . . while the public odium was ostensibly directed against his anti-fine flour and anti-flesh eating doctrines, it was his anti-sexual indulgence doctrines, in reality, which excited the public hatred and rendered his name a by-word of reproach."[12] Alcott leaned toward Graham's position, but he was a reasonable man and wanted to be heard. Competition was fierce in the sex advice field, and abstinence had to be justified rather than simply prescribed.

In Alcott's view, sex, like eating, was more fun if not indulged in too often, and the sensation would last longer too. ". . . the pleasures of love, no less than the strength of the orgasm, are enhanced by their infrequency." Also, the strength of progeny was a function of the vitality and zest of parents. Feeble children were invariably born to tired, satiated parents. Finally, disease struck when vital forces were depleted, and industrious men and women had but little of these energies to spare.[13]

Alcott knew that his readers were tempted by other voices such as that of Charles Knowlton, "a physician of much greater practical skill than strict integrity." Knowlton's book had wide circulation. "I have found it in nearly every part of our widespread country." Copies of *Fruits of Philosophy* were "highly prized," and those who used Knowlton's "chemical lotion" "usually regard it as entirely certain in its effects; though I have reason to doubt the soundness of this conclusion." Love of pleasure, "a regard to economy," "the fear of absolute poverty," and "a regard to each other's feelings and convenience" were all poor excuses offered for contraceptive practice, and even abortion was justified on similar reasoning.[14]

Alcott believed that there were legitimate reasons for preventing conception, especially in cases of "tendencies to disease." "We have no right with our eyes open, to propagate a race with every reasonable prospect of it being a sickly one." Withdrawal was not as bad as masturbation. Another alternative was the "well known physiological law that conception cannot take place at every period of female life between the ca-tamenial discharges; but only during the first fortnight, or as some say, the first eight days which immediately follow the cessation of the menses. If, therefore, we deny ourselves, during a full fortnight as above mentioned, no subsequent intercourse, up to the commencement of the next catamenial discharge, can possibly be productive." Alcott urged right-thinking young people, however, to try complete abstinence as a means of family limitation. "It will be said," Alcott admonished, "that I require a degree of abstinence which human nature cannot bear," but "since God is the author of human nature, it is but reasonable presumption that he has not so arranged things as to require of his creatures what is almost an impossibility." Besides, even if a woman had a child every two years, and abstained from sexual intercourse during pregnancy and lactation, that would leave nine months of every two years for sexual indulgence, or a grand total of at least ninety months between the ages of twenty-two and forty-five. Not even counting the golden years after forty-five, "much greater license is given us, than is given to the beasts that perish."[15]

Alcott's views on sex were very close to the positions taken by other physicians who might be considered more liberal. Thomas Low Nichols expounded a doctrine of "free love" in *Esoteric Anthropology* (1853), but he argued not for freer sexual expression but for monogamous relations based solely on spiritualized passion rather than lust or social convention.[16] Charles Knowlton and Frederick Hollick both justified their works as efforts to replace hypocrisy and vice with greater mutuality in marriage. John Cowan, whose *The Science of a New Life* (1874) was endorsed by both Henry Ward Beecher and Elizabeth Cady Stanton, believed the future of the race depended on the kind of children that could only be born to willing mothers.[17] All of these writers sought to preserve and improve marriage by basing it on a higher affection rather than mere sexual or economic need. All agreed that women were too often treated as sex objects and their finer sensibilities damaged by the callousness of ignorant or idealless husbands. Cowan denounced men who used their wives "simply as chattels" who lay "passive and motionless" during intercourse. "As to the possible pleasure to him of such a union, he might as well practice solitary indulgence, for the one could not possibly do him more harm than the other." [18]

The complexity of the sources of tension in American homes escaped all of these writers. Except for Nichols, whose wife was a teacher and feminist, they assumed that husband, home, and children were the only desire of right-thinking women. Moreover, the American perfectionist impulse nowhere found more abstract expression than in the expectations Alcott and Cowan tried to create about the degree of efficiency and total contentment that could be achieved by a conscientious woman within her sphere. Women were expected to play an increasingly complex role in the nurture of children, keep spotlessly clean homes, cook scientifically planned meals, and serve as lover and confessor to busy husbands. Most women had to meet these expectations alone, without the aid of mothers, aunts, sisters, servants, or the fabulous gadgetry of the twentieth century. The future of not only their own families but of the nation as well depended on perfect order and rejuvenating sublimity at home. [19] Since so much depended on the well-ordered family, the problem of reconciling emotional fulfillment in marriage with a manageable number of children could not be ignored. Many medical advisers gave sympathetic attention to the question of family limitation.

John Cowan argued that the solution was a higher standard of conduct for men. "The pains, the troubles, the heart burnings, the sickness, the danger of premature death, that woman has to experience through man's lust is beyond all comprehension, and if there is one direction more than another in which 'Woman's Rights' should assert itself, it is in this one choice of time for sexual congress." The ideal solution was restriction of sexual intercourse to those golden moments when a child was desired and both partners were in perfect health. Cowan devoted two chapters to description of how to prepare for perfect mating—time, weather, location, mood, all were crucial if *"a child of genius, beauty, and strength should be created."* [20]

There was a certain defensiveness, even futility, in the discussions of sex by Cowan, Alcott, and other advisers. Cowan had to discuss contraception, and he devoted a chapter to it. But in denouncing the use of *coitus reservatus,* withdrawal, the condom, douching, and "sponge or rubber pads, placed against the mouth of the womb, to prevent the entrance of the sperm," Cowan also described these methods. Apparently he assumed that these practices were generally known, and, therefore, there was no risk of injuring the pure-minded for whom *The Science of a New Life* was intended. William Alcott complained that some young people laughed at his sexual ideals as totally out of touch with reality, but, like Cowan, he described birth control methods in his marriage manual.[21]

Alcott and Cowan were moral perfectionists who insisted that sexual drives be subordinated to higher ends. While they were radical in their demands that Americans live up to the highest possible standards of sexual conduct, they were conservatives in that the norms they championed provided no alternative to heroic domesticity for women or sober monogamy for men. Their models had meaning only in contrast to the disorder of everyday life. Young people bought their books because they were uncertain about how to behave in the face of the breakdown of traditional expectations in a rapidly changing society. Both this literature and the pursuit of pleasure and fashion so often denounced in it were reflections of the fluidity of the social order and the relative freedom of individuals to order their lives for themselves.

American society rewarded individual initiative and self-control. Despite the usual equation of birth control with lack of self-control in nineteenth century literature, contraceptive practice depended on precisely the self-discipline and other habits of mind characteristic of a society in which "I calculate" had become a synonym for "I believe" or "I think."[22] The need for consultation between married mates was a central theme of marital advice literature, and the fertility of American women was declining. Sufficient contraceptive means existed to account for this decline, but the perils of overindulgence of "animal" appetites and the need to control sexual desire were part of the conventional wisdom of the age. The historian then is faced with an ambiguous array of evidence, in part reflecting the wide range of advice offered in the domestic literature.

Contraceptive information existed, but could the average American couple get hold of it? Having obtained it, could they use it? Did sexual repression or contraceptive practice play the key role in the nineteenth century fertility decline?

In the case of Frederick Hollick's safe period, sexual repression and contraception were not mutually exclusive categories. Rather, family planning depended on a couple's ability to limit intercourse to approximately one week of every month. The bogus safe periods described by some physicians have misled several historians into claiming that all nineteenth century writers misunderstood the female fertility cycle,[23] but it seems reasonable to suppose that among some of Hollick's thousands of readers periodic abstinence was a workable alternative to no coitus at all. In some marriages economic need or respect for the wife's well-being undoubtedly led men to question traditional male sexual prerogatives. In such cases self-control might have taken the form of *coitus interruptus* or use of condoms.

Apparently women were turning to physicians in unprecedented numbers for a variety of vague complaints that in part reflected a desire for help in controlling their fertility. Some of the new specialists in women's diseases undoubtedly provided abortions under the guise of treating uterine disease, as Dr. Buck charged in "A Raid on the Uterus." Medical reformers joined with other citizens who were alarmed by the growing popularity of abortion in lobbying campaigns that led to the passage of a series of state laws prohibiting a practice that had been allowed under the common law, at least until it became increasingly common.[24]

The majority of American doctors had little interest in helping women avoid pregnancy. They shared the prevailing sexual ideology which viewed all healthy women as willing mothers, and, if they specialized in gynecology, they devoted themselves to repairing birth injuries and helping women to conceive.[25] The career of James Marion Sims (1813–83), the most honored nineteenth century American gynecologist, illustrates the close relationship between the social attitudes of medical leaders and the services that they offered. Sims gained international fame in the 1850s by developing an operation for repair of tears in the bladder (vesicovaginal fistula), a common childbirth injury that had formerly doomed thousands of women to live out their lives continuously soaked with urine. He devoted a large part of his practice, however, to the treatment of sterility and most of his classic *Clinical Notes on Uterine Surgery* described the dozens of elaborate, ingenious, and sometimes painful methods that he developed to help women conceive. In an age when hysterectomy was a high-risk procedure, even the great surgeons like Sims relied heavily on pessaries in the treatment of uterine prolapse, and Sims described dozens of pessaries for various purposes, including a spring-loaded rubber ring that resembled in all but contraceptive intent the vaginal diaphragms used in twentieth century birth control clinics. Female readers of Edward Foote learned of contraceptive womb veils, but Sims, like most specialists in women's diseases, devoted himself solely to helping women become mothers, leaving contraception to the second-rate or the quack.[26]

The physicians who did discuss contraception in print during the nineteenth century were more interested in influencing behavior than in describing it. The prescriptive literature clearly reflects a deeply felt need to control fertility, but it does not provide the historian with any sure indicators of how individuals actually behaved. Diaries, letters, and other manuscript sources provide some behavioral insights, but they often raise as many questions as they answer. For example, Thomas Longshore, a philosopher and reformer, wrote in an autobiographical manuscript of the desire he and his wife, Hannah Longshore, M.D. (1819–1901), shared to limit their family to two children, a goal they achieved, but he gave no indication of precisely how they limited their fertility.

> We had resolved in the beginning that we were not strong and healthy enough to raise a large family, and without the necessary supplies, that two children might be more than we could give good constitutions and proper train and educate. We had both often felt what burdens many incompetent parents were assuming in attempting to raise large families. It was a serious subject with us and often engaged our thoughts.
>
> It was a matter of conviction in which we so agreed that we felt it a duty to act so wisely, and be such an example that others should profit by it. We have always thought we acted the part of wisdom in conforming our lives to our judgment.[27]

The Longshores might have limited their family through abstinence, total or periodic, through resort to induced abortion, or by using condoms, douching, or other mechanical contraceptives. They might have used some combination of these practices. Hannah Longshore did not marry until she was thirty-two and had her last child at thirty-six. Since female fecundity declines rapidly in the late thirties, they might have practiced contraception and believed that they were preventing conception, when in fact she simply was no longer fertile.

Lester Frank Ward (1841–1913), the critic of social Darwinism and exponent of government by scientific bureaucracy, left a diary that includes a somewhat more explicit discussion of the means that he and his first wife used to control their fertility.[28] Ward did not share the view of other nineteenth century intellectuals that abstinence was the ideal birth control method, and his description of relations between the sexes in mid-nineteenth century America provides a startling contrast to the sexual ideology championed by William Alcott.

The tenth child of a millwright who followed the work provided by canal construction, Ward was self-supporting at the age of sixteen. At nineteen he was working at odd jobs in northern Pennsylvania, while trying to save enough money to go to school. Ward's diary covers the period 1860–70 and reveals an ambitious, hard-working, self-directed young man on the make—exceptional only in that his yearnings for a better life were expressed in an insatiable desire for book learning.

Ward began courting his future wife, Lizzie Vought, in May 1860. His diary reveals that they were allowed a surprising amount of time alone together. Heavy letter writing was followed by heavy petting. After Ward had been going steady with Miss Vought for about six months, he noted:

> Friday evening the girl and I had a very sweet time. I kissed her on her soft breasts, and took many liberties with her sweet person, and we are going to stop. It is a very fascinating practice and fills us with very sweet, tender and familiar sentiments, and consequently makes us happy. But the difficulty is that we might become so addicted in that direction that we might go too deep and possibly confound ourselves by the standards of virtue.[29]

One month later Ward showed Lizzie the copy of Frederick Hollick's *Physiology* that he had been studying, and coitus followed after eight more months of intense courtship (October 1861).[30] They got married in August 1862, and Ward joined the Union Army.

Ward apparently viewed joining the army not only as an act of patriotism but also as an employment opportunity for a young husband who could not afford to establish a household. After Ward was wounded in action, he obtained a hospital job in Washington and permission to have his wife join him. They still did not want a child, since they were both committed to obtaining college educations. In March 1864, Ward wrote that his wife had been ill:

> The truth is that she was going to have a child, but she took an effective remedy which she had secured from Mrs. Gee. It did its work and she is out of danger.[31]

Three months later Ward and several of his friends were forced to call on Mrs. Gee after he discovered that she was spreading "false and abusive rumors" about his wife.[32]

In October, Ward ordered some contraceptive pills but did not "trust them overmuch," so he sent off to Syracuse for an "instrument" advertised in a book and noted: "We have not tried it much, but I trust it a little more." When the device failed, Ward consulted a doctor, who "gave me useful instruction which I plan to put into practice."[33]

After Ward was established as a clerk in the Washington bureaucracy, he and Lizzie had a son whom they apparently wanted, but the child died in infancy. Apparently the Wards resumed contraceptive practice after the birth of their son. In September 1867, Ward noted, "I bought a fine syringe with India rubber tubes for my wife." Four months later they were concerned that she might be pregnant. "On Monday my wife, who had passed her period three entire weeks, so that we commenced to give up all hope, finally became sick, which turned our solicitude to joy."[34] Ward's ten-year diary ends in 1870 without further clear reference to birth control.

Ward wrote his diary in French, and the anonymity provided by a foreign language may have encouraged the striking candor of his entries, but even in this remarkable personal document much is left unsaid or revealed only in vague language. Ward's diary does show, however, that he and his wife were capable of taking the knowledge that they desired from books such as Frederick Hollick's *Physiology* while discarding the moral prescriptions that they did not want (Hollick recommended only his "safe period" and denounced other contraceptive regimens as unaesthetic or unsafe).

The sexual histories collected by Celia Duel Mosher, M.D. (1863–1940), provide another contrast between literature and behavior.[35] Mosher, a faculty member at Stanford and medical adviser to women students, designed a long questionnaire on sexual experiences and attitudes and recruited forty-five married women acquaintances for subjects. Seventy percent (33) of these women were born before 1870 and all but one before 1890.[36] Eighty-two percent (37) reported using mechanical methods of birth control.[37] These women and their husbands were able to limit their fertility despite the difficulty of obtaining reliable birth control information. For example, one subject listed two methods, "rubber cap over uterus" and "cundum" (condom) and noted that she experienced no ill effects from contraceptive practice.[38]

The ubiquity of descriptions of contraceptive practices in nineteenth century medical advice books, even in those by authors who denounced birth control, indicates that domestic counselors understood that many book buyers were more interested in facts than in moral prescriptions. As Eliza Duffey pointed out in 1876, even the critics of contraception often exploited the public hunger for knowledge. Duffey wrote, ". . . when they give public utterance to their opinions, they join in the general denunciation of preventives to conception, shrewdly twisting [them so] that their readers may receive the necessary knowledge through the very means they take to condemn."[39]

Historical demographers have viewed dramatic declines in marital fertility as clear evidence that some form of family limitation was being employed on a large scale.[40] One has argued that the nineteenth century American fertility decline is evidence for an increase of female power within the family that made it possible for women to challenge traditional male sexual prerogatives successfully.[41] Since few records of behavior have survived, the social historian can only define the options that were available to nineteenth century married couples.

Both abstinence and contraception were possible solutions to a central problem of the companionate marriage based on romantic love, the need to reconcile celebration of passion with the necessity of fewer and better nurtured children. The choice of means to this end probably varied from couple to couple, with some abstaining from coitus and others experimenting with one or more contraceptive regimens. By the early twentieth century Americans increasingly viewed abstinence as an unacceptable option. During the nineteenth century, however, the leading interpreters of American morals prescribed sexual repression or self-control, and contraception remained a semilicit compromise chosen by those who believed that a good marriage depended on physical as well as spiritual communication.

CHAPTER 3   # The Suppression of Contraceptive Information

IN 1900, despite widespread discussion of contraception in print during the middle decades of the nineteenth century, the law, respectable opinion, and organized medicine were united in condemning contraceptive practice. Federal law defined the mailing of birth control information as an obscene act and a felony. A Connecticut statute outlawed the practice of family limitation, although no state investigators were hired to snoop out wrongdoers.[1]

The systematic suppression of birth control information began in the 1870s as a small part of a great crusade to make America live up to its sexual ideals. The main thrust of antebellum moral reform eventually had focused on the fight against slavery, but after the Civil War former abolitionists and their descendents, both literal and spiritual, led campaigns to make American cities safe for middle-class families through the suppression of commercial vice.[2]

Many women abolitionists had become self-conscious feminists in the 1840s when they were told that they had no right to divert their energies from their proper roles as homemakers, even to work for the destruction of slavery. America's first generation of professional women led the post–Civil War purity movement. Elizabeth Blackwell, Antoinette Brown Blackwell, and Frances Willard drew inspiration for their careers in medicine, the ministry, and social reform from the suffering of other women whose interests as mothers and homemakers were threatened by social evil. To protect the sanctity of woman's sphere, some women would have to leave it.[3]

The thousands of women who enlisted in the purity crusade believed that justice required a single standard of sexual morality for both sexes. They associated freer sexuality with the selfish appetites of men who lacked respect for women. Campaigns against prostitution, alcohol, and pornography, while directed against real social problems, also provided one way for women to strike out against the injustices imposed on their sex in a man's world. Prostitution symbolized the degradation of woman through the separation of sex from both love and procreation. The immoral trade in female bodies posed a very real danger to the health of wives and of future generations. The husband who patronized prostitutes might bring venereal disease and rotting degeneration into the home. Pornography and alcohol threatened accepted standards of conduct since men inflamed by drink and dirty pictures were likely to demand sexual favors from their wives to which they had no right. The men who committed such crimes were poor fathers, poor citizens, and a danger to innocent wives and infants who might become infected with syphilis or gonorrhea. A just society in which healthy mothers could flourish depended on the suppression of male vice.[4]

The male tendency to relax standards of sexual conduct received a sharp rebuke when leaders of American medicine tried to deal with the problem of venereal disease through the regulation of prostitution. In America's cities prostitution and venereal disease were everyday problems for the police and for doctors. Some of these male professionals responded with proposals to legalize and to regulate prostitution. They believed that the first step in the control of venereal disease was to identify and to treat the people who had it. Help would only be accepted when some of the shame was removed from infection and venereal diseases could be "treated as other diseases."[5] In March 1867 the New York Police Department asked the metropolitan health commissioner to formulate a plan for medical inspection of prostitutes. Susan B. Anthony organized a successful campaign against this proposal. Women, she argued,

35

were not chattel to be exploited to satisfy male lust. Similar episodes were reenacted repeatedly during the next thirty years
in almost every American city.[6]

In 1874, James Marion Sims, who was then the president of
the American Medical Association, recommended a national
system of regulation for prostitution and control of venereal
disease that included the cooperation of American physicians
with international organizations in the field. An effort was
begun to use the medical profession as a lobby for regulation
throughout the nation. Aaron Powell, Elizabeth Blackwell,
Frances Willard, and other purity reformers responded with a
crusade to defeat regulation. They wrote articles for medical
journals and lobbied tirelessly at the conventions of the American Public Health Association and in local legislatures. Advocates of women's rights and social purity gained strength
from these struggles, and regulationists such as Sims suffered
humiliating defeats.[7]

Organized medicine was forced to abandon regulation and
to accept views compatible with the ideal of one high standard
of sexual morality for all. Medical men learned that the integrity of their profession depended on the support of public
opinion. It was their duty to defend the highest moral standards of the community. Prostitution was, after all, not a necessary social evil but the result of a double standard of morality
and the exploitation of one sex by another. The campaign
against the legalization of prostitution had been won by 1886,
when a member of the New York Academy of Medicine explained to his colleagues that the control of venereal disease
depended on the recognition of prostitution as a moral problem, not a physical one. Reform required the emancipation
and elevation of woman, a proper education in the sanctity of
marriage, the threat of social ostracism for moral transgressors,
and the creation of public opinion favorable to a higher, spiritualized man-woman relationship. In 1894 the president of the
New York Academy endorsed efforts to collect physicians' signatures on a petition stating that chastity was in accord with
the laws of health and an 1894 editorial in the *Journal of the
American Medical Association* entitled "Scientific Cookery" welcomed the coming transformation of society promised by an
expansion of domestic reform. According to the AMA's *Jour-*

nal, the increasing purity and efficiency of American women would lead to reduced infant mortality; decrease of contagious disease; less divorce, insanity, and pauperism; and greater harmony between the sexes.[8]

While the "new abolitionists" were impressing upon the public the necessity of treating sexual matters with great seriousness, Anthony Comstock (1844–1915), a young veteran of the Grand Army of the Republic, had begun a campaign to strengthen the obscenity laws. Like many rural New Englanders before him, Comstock had moved to New York in search of opportunity. There he became active in the Young Men's Christian Association, which had been founded to provide emigrants from rural America with a place to go other than the saloon or bawdy house. The devout and literal-minded Comstock was especially outraged by the exploitation of his kind by the city's vice merchants. Those who could not stand the loneliness or boredom of boardinghouse rooms often fell victim to the temptation of drink, gambling, and fornication. In Comstock's view, once a young man lost the habits of thrift, sobriety, and chaste thought, a downhill course into ruin was inevitable.[9]

Morris Jesup, Samuel Colgate, and other financial angels of the YMCA shared Comstock's desire to clean up the city. Comstock solicited the support of these substantial men of affairs for a campaign against commercial vice.[10] Their financial backing allowed him to leave his job as a dry-goods salesman and to devote full time to lobbying for stronger obscenity laws. In March 1873, Comstock pushed a bill through Congress that closed many loopholes in the 1872 act which prohibited the mailing of obscene matter. The new bill explicitly defined for the first time information on "the prevention of conception" as obscene. The passage of a series of state laws modeled on the federal statute followed. Congress also appointed Comstock to the position of special agent of the Post Office Department with authority to arrest those who used the mails in violation of the law.[11] The works of Owen, Knowlton, Hollick, and Foote, as well as some by Alcott, were branded as smut.

Comstock's extreme zealousness in the pursuit of evildoers unnerved even some of his supporters in the YMCA and led to the incorporation of the New York Society for the Suppression of Vice as a separate organization with Comstock as director. Comstock was relentless. By January 1874 he had traveled 23,500 miles by rail on his inspector's pass, had made fifty-five arrests and secured twenty convictions under the federal law, and had seized 60,300 obscene rubber articles. [12]

Comstock could not imagine anyone giving birth control information for a legitimate reason. He equated birth control with abortion. In his book *Frauds Exposed* (1880), Comstock quoted a Baptist minister who had written a letter to the New York *Times* denouncing the federal law of 1873.

> I protest against the laws and proceedings under them of Anthony Comstock, wherein he attempts to regulate and prohibit the sale of certain things hitherto commended by prudent physicians as harmless and yet invaluable to sick and over-burdened mothers. I am aware of the fact that some of those who have favored these prohibitions buy and use what they denounce. Common sense is a jewel, and there ought to be laws, if we are going to invade the privacy of homes, to discourage the bringing into existence of weaklings; also to guard the mothers from burdens that prevent them from caring for the children they have.

Comstock's reply to this reasonable criticism was libelous.

> The laws he protests against prevent the abortionist selling or sending his vile incentives to crime through the mails. . . . Evidently this pastor is either crazy, stupidly ignorant, a very bad man at heart, or else he has a very poor way of expressing himself so as to make people understand his meaning. [13]

Comstock used decoy letters, false signatures, and appeals to the sympathy of physicians in order to entrap them. He arrested one reputable woman doctor for selling him a female syringe identical to those available in any drugstore. Some of Comstock's victims were people of standing. Dr. Charles Mansfield of Boston outraged Comstock when he secured a member of the YMCA for counsel after his arrest. President Grant pardoned another alleged "abortionist" who had been practicing in Albany for seven years. When Comstock ran out of birth controllers, he turned to prosecuting gamblers, idealistic free lovers, and publishers of anticlerical tracts. It had become dangerous to discuss contraception in print, and the subject was omitted from post-1873 editions of many books in which it had originally been given space.[14]

Moral reformers responded to the alien environment of the city with a broad campaign of social control that included the suppression of birth control information. Prudery, rather than the secret of family limitation, was the city's gift to the village. For the urban middle classes born in the last quarter of the nineteenth century, "the facts of life" were no longer given by experience but learned from books, or not learned at all. The suppression of birth control information exacerbated tensions in the companionate family and made living in industrial America a more difficult experience. Attempts to protect the family were making it a less workable institution.

The repressive nature of reform in part reflected a pragmatic response to real dangers. Neither syphilis nor gonorrhea could be controlled through regulation of prostitution because they were hard to diagnose and there were no means to cure them. (Penicillin was not available until 1942, and even salvarsan, an arsenical drug with serious side effects and limited effectiveness used in the treatment of syphilis, was not available until 1910).[15] The purity crusaders correctly pointed out that the prospects for controlling venereal disease depended on higher standards of sexual conduct. The double standard of sexual morality was the basic problem, and chastity the only effective prophylaxis available. Men who contracted venereal disease before marriage could not be cured, and even after the passage of many years they ran the risk of infecting their wives, who would become sterile or bear blind or deformed infants. The double standard of morality that sanctioned prostitution was an abomination by any standard of judgment. Unfortunately, purity crusaders associated contraception with prostitution, in part, because "vice emporiums" served as retail outlets for birth control devices. As one physician explained, condoms were "suggestive of licentiousness and the brothel, and their employment degrades to bestiality the true feelings of manhood and the holy state of matrimony."[16]

Medical leaders might have recognized that contraception could be divorced from licentiousness and used to improve sex in marriage, but they had little interest in the subject and were intent on establishing themselves as guardians of public morality. They were concerned, however, over the declining birth rate among the middle classes. When Henry Maudsley, one of the founders of British psychotherapy, surveyed the American medical literature on sex in 1874, he found that American doctors were devoting a great deal of attention to the effects of educational opportunity and social freedom on the attitudes of young women toward childbearing.[17] They claimed that American women were losing their biological capacity to breed. Harvard's Edward Clarke blamed these apparent changes on female college education and warned, "If these causes should continue for the next half-century, and increase in the same ratio as they have for the last fifty years, it requires no prophet to foretell that the wives who are to be mothers in our republic must be drawn from transatlantic homes."[18] An observer of the American scene more sympathetic to change explained that the medical profession "in the United States is arrayed in a very ill-tempered opposition on assumed physiological grounds, to the higher education of women."[19] The men whose fears found expression in these jeremiads were fervent believers in the crucial role women played in the maintenance and progress of civilization through the superior moral influence they alone could exert on men and children in the home. In the flux of change the moral superiority of women, protected from the brutalizing effects of industrial society by the selflessness of domesticity, seemed to offer the one uncontaminated source of human decency.

Doctors instinctively used the threat of disease and the jargon of science to reinforce traditional definitions of proper female behavior. Alexander Skene, the author of an influential textbook on the diseases of women and professor of gynecology in the Long Island College Hospital, lent his authority to those who feared that the health of American women was being undermined by too much freedom in his *Education and Culture as Related to the Health and Diseases of Women.*[20] Skene had little sympathy for those who maintained that man was naturally superior to woman in character, willpower, intelligence, or creativity. Equally erroneous, he argued, was the feminist doctrine of the natural equality of the sexes. Women were unique, not inferior. A whole generation of students at

40

Long Island College Hospital learned that gynecology was a very special calling because it provided biological insights into woman's unique capacities and functions that were fundamental to any sound plan of education for her.[21]

In Skene's view, woman's social role was determined by her biological role as breeder. Her monthly ability to conceive and foster a new life revealed Nature's intent that "to be a wife and mother" was "the chief end and object of woman's life." Skene admitted that "The pale, care-worn mother, exhausted by frequent child-bearing and prolonged lactation, whose nervous system is rebelling against overtaxation, may be seen every day." But, he argued, these tragedies could be ameliorated by the advance of medical science and public education. "The fulfillment of the injunction 'to multiply' " remained "the highest earthly function of woman." He warned his readers of the dangers of family limitation:

> The woman who willingly tries to reverse the order of her physical being in the hope of gratifying some fancy or ambition, is almost sure to suffer sooner or later from disappointment and ill-health. Doctors make fortunes (small ones) by trying to restore health and peace of mind to those who violate the laws of morals and health in their efforts to prevent reproduction. In such cases, the relations [physiological processes] are deranged by perverted mind influence. Disease of the maltreated organ follows, and revenges their [sic] wrong by torturing the brain and nervous system.[22]

Skene's *Education and Culture* provided anxious parents with a classic exposition of the cult of domesticity. The primary source of neurosis among young women, he explained, was their refusal to accept biological fate.

> The home is woman's kingdom. There she rules or should rule, with an unseen hand. . . . She governs by the kindness of her heart, which is far more potent than the intrigues of the head which kings and statesmen employ. If she possesses health and vigor of body and mind when she takes her place at home, she will ever find her duties pleasant and agreeable. . . . It is the feeble and diseased mind that becomes wretched under ordinary cares.[23]

Thus, "the ideal life of woman" would be realized not by perverted attempts to thwart nature, but by the progressive ability of medical science to make woman's burdens easier to bear.

In 1908, M. Carey Thomas, the president of Bryn Mawr College, recalled the awful doubts raised by medical jeremiads against higher education for women that her generation had to overcome. As a girl, she remembered, "I was terror-struck lest I, and every other woman with me, were doomed to live as pathological invalids in a universe merciless to woman as a sex." Time and experience had taught "that it is not we, but the man who believes such things about us, who is himself pathological, blinded by neurotic mists of sex."[24] President Thomas and Dr. Skene shared some sexual values, however. Feminists, purity crusaders, and medical sex counselors all sought to link sexuality to a moral idealism. They would have considered atavistic the modern impulse to separate sex from love and to celebrate sex as simply liberating passion. The stereotype of the late nineteenth century as an era of sexual ignorance and hypocrisy, which "tabooed" sexual subjects, is not wholly accurate. The concern of medical men over female discontent and neurosis inspired widespread debate and provided one motive for the first attempts to apply empirical methods to the study of sex problems.[25]

While Skene and other conservatives opposed greater social opportunities for women, they did not necessarily view them as lacking in sexual desire or incapable of sexual fulfillment.[26] Rather, poor sexual adjustment in marriage seemed to pose a threat to stable family life, and they did not always blame women for their unhappiness. In 1898 the Physicians Club of Chicago sponsored a symposium on "sexual hygiene" in order to provide a forum for a frank exchange of information that would help local doctors to become better marriage counselors. One of the participants explained, "Outside the medical profession it is taken for granted that the doctor knows all about these things [sex]. But within our ranks we are aware that this is not true. The text-books omit this department." The public increasingly turned to physicians instead of the clergy for sex advice, but some of them were willing to admit, at least among themselves, that they had insufficient knowledge of the subject. An edited transcript of the symposium was published as a "for doctors only" handbook titled *Sexual Hygiene* in an effort to meet the need for information.[27]

The editors of *Sexual Hygiene* believed that husbands bore

the major share of the blame for the marital unhappiness that seemed to be reaching epidemic proportions. Too many of them were ignorant of, or ignored, the sexual needs of their wives. Husbands had to be taught "that the God-given relation is two-sided, and that without harmony and mutual enjoyment it becomes a mere masturbation to the body and mind of the one who alone is gratified."[28] Married women needed and had a right to the experience of orgasm. Better marital sex would lower the divorce rate and keep both husbands and wives at home, where they belonged.

One chapter of *Sexual Hygiene* was devoted to contraception. The contributing physicians viewed birth control as a necessary means in some cases of reconciling the economic and personal interests of husbands and wives, and they knew of numerous methods. But contraceptive advice had to be given with discretion. There were situations in which birth control information should be kept from patients. "We all know perfectly the difference between the dragged-out woman on the verge of consumption . . . and the society belle who mistakenly thinks she does not want babies when every fiber of her being is crying out for this means of bringing her back to healthy thought."[29]

This ambiguous attitude toward birth control was most strikingly revealed in a long discussion of contraceptive methods. The strong-willed might try "limiting intercourse to the period from the sixteenth day after menstruation to the twenty-fifth." Men could practice withdrawal or use condoms. The condom was very effective "if the best are used, but we all know that rubber is a non-conductor of electricity, and this is a factor that I think should not be lost sight of. They are not the easiest thing in the world to put on either."[30]

While a highly effective and safe contraceptive was mocked because it interfered with male pleasure, female methods received indiscriminate endorsement. "The little sponge in a silk net with string attached is a familiar sight in drug stores. If this is moistened with some acid or antiseptic solution before use and rightly placed, it is very safe and harmless." In addition to the sponge, would-be female contraceptors might chose either douching, or "a vaginal suppository of cocoa butter and ten per cent of boric and tannic acids," or "the womb veil with

eighty grams of quinine mutate to an ounce of petrolatum."
All seemed to work well enough. The chief complaint against
intrauterine stem pessaries was that "there are many women
who cannot place them." A final bit of advice was offered for
the woman who wanted to avoid having children without
good reason. "Get a divorce and vacate the position for some
other woman, who is able and willing to fulfill all a wife's
duties as well as to enjoy her privileges."[31]

Although the participants in the Chicago symposium knew
of many female methods, they expressed no concern with
making distinctions between them or for the problems that
women might have in using them. Systematic clinical evaluation of birth control would not begin until the 1920s, when
minor improvements in the "womb veil" or vaginal diaphragm would provide the most effective female method available until the marketing of the anovulant pill in 1960. Serious
study of birth control methods might have begun in the late
nineteenth century, since, as the discussion of birth control
methods in *Sexual Hygiene* makes clear, both the necessary
technology and knowledge of sexual anatomy were available,
but doctors did not make any major efforts to improve contraceptive means. Since the family might be weakened if sex
was too easily separated from procreation, physicians believed
that they had a social obligation to manage carefully the dissemination of birth control. Indeed, in the case of the "society
belle" or other healthy woman who did not want children,
their duty was to force "her back to healthy thought." In this
context doctors were not greatly concerned over the failure
rates of birth control regimens.

Other factors contributed to the reluctance of the medical
profession to provide contraceptive services. Doctors knew
that public support for their profession depended on strict ad-
herence to the highest standards of public morality. As long as
respectable opinion associated contraception with licentiousness, they would be reluctant to deal openly with the subject.
The void left by the reticence of orthodox practitioners was
filled by druggists, patent medicine merchants, and quacks
who made extravagant claims for drugs and devices that were
often ineffective or dangerous. Birth control became associated

44

with quackery and the threat it posed to the social and economic position of the medical profession.

The physician who wanted to provide reliable contraceptive advice faced many practical problems. It was illegal to give information in most states. *Sexual Hygiene* might have been banned from the mails and its publishers arrested if it had come to the attention of Anthony Comstock or some other purity zealot. Because of the failure of medical leaders to engage in contraceptive research, no one knew much about the effectiveness or safety of birth control methods. If a doctor prescribed a birth control method that failed, his patient might demand an abortion. Neither government nor organized medicine provided quality standards or controls for condoms, contraceptive jellies, or pessaries. Diaphragms, when attainable, were hard to fit in the days before the pharmaceutical industry began to provide numerous aids, and medical schools did not teach such techniques. But neither the specter of Comstockery, nor professionalism, nor technical problems were crucial factors. Physicians were proud of their skills as instrument makers and craftsmen at a time when therapeutic means were scarce, and they did not hesitate to experiment with dangerous drugs or surgical procedures in the battle against disease. The fundamental source of medical resistance to contraception sprang from fear that young people might shirk their duty to multiply in stable unions if it became too easy to control fertility. The middle-class birth rate fell decade after decade, while the poor and the foreign born seemed relentlessly fertile. Alarmed over the low fertility among their paying customers and the apparently decreasing ability or desire of young women to become mothers, physicians responded as social conservatives rather than scientists. Medical attitudes toward birth control were shaped less by the pratical or ideological needs of the profession than by the commitment of doctors to the maintenance of social order as they understood it.

CHAPTER 4   **The Anarchists**

DURING the decade before World War I, a few physicians made major efforts to win a recognized place for contraception in regular medical practice. William Robinson (1869–1936), the medical journalist and muckraker, filled his *Critic and Guide* with pleas for sex education, repeal of the Comstock Act, and recognition of the need for family limitation. Robinson convinced Abraham Jacobi, the founder of American pediatrics, to include a word for birth control in his 1912 presidential address to the American Medical Association, but Jacobi's colleagues ignored his request that they take up the problem of birth control, and Robinson, despite his attacks on sexual hypocrisy, left information on how to prevent conception out of his popular advice books because of the Comstock Act.[1] Liberal physicians hesitated to challenge the obscenity laws because association with sexual reform might damage their professional status. For example, in 1916, when Margaret Sanger, a nurse who had been making headlines with her defiance of the Comstock Act, asked Robert L. Dickinson, one of the country's most prominent gynecologists and one of a few physicians who defended contraceptive practice in print, for the names of doctors who might be interested in her cause, he considered including his own on the list he provided. He did not. His wife strongly opposed his involvement at a crucial point in his career. Dickinson retired from active practice at the age of sixty and eventually became the leading medical advocate of contraception. But in 1916 he was not willing to commit professional suicide by associating with the feminists and radicals who were attacking Comstockery.[2]

46

Emma Goldman, a leader of American anarchists, viewed the reticence of liberals like Dickinson and Robinson with contempt. In a review of Robinson's *Fewer and Better Babies* (1916), she noted that there was no practical birth control information in it, and concluded that Robinson was just one in a long line of bourgeois reformers who never accomplished much.[3] Since 1906 she too had been agitating for birth control in her journal *Mother Earth*, but she believed that it was hypocritical to talk about birth control unless you were willing to provide the public with concrete information. On that score she and Dr. Ben Reitman, her lover and manager, could claim priority.

When imprisoned at Blackwell's Island in 1893, Goldman received instruction as a practical nurse. After her release from prison she secured work with the help of a prison doctor, but lack of a nursing degree limited her opportunities. With money borrowed from an old comrade who had become a successful commercial artist, Goldman studied for a year at Vienna's renowned Allgemeine Krankenhaus and received diplomas in nursing and midwifery.[4]

Returning to New York, she began practicing midwifery among the "foreign element." For the first time she came "face to face with the living conditions of the workers," about which, until then, she "had talked and written mostly from theory." Her most compelling experience was exposure to "the fierce, blind struggle of the women of the poor against frequent pregnancies."

> Most of them lived in continual dread of conception; the great mass of the married women submitted helplessly, and when they found themselves pregnant, their alarm and worry would result in the determination to get rid of their expected offspring. It was incredible what fantastic methods despair could invent; jumping off tables, rolling on the floor, massaging the stomach, drinking nauseating concoctions, and using blunt instruments.

Goldman empathized with the plight of these women. Unable to care for the children they had, each new child was "a curse of God," another addition to the flock of "ill-born, ill-kept, and unwanted children who trailed at my feet when I was helping another poor creature into the world." "After such confinements I would return home sick and distressed, hating

47

the men responsible for the frightful condition of their wives and children, hating myself most of all because I did not know how to help them."[5]

The professors in Vienna had stressed the dangers of abortion. Despite pathetic pleas to end pregnancies "for the sake of the poor little ones already here," Goldman could not bring herself to join those doctors who provided abortions for a price. She was sterile because of an inverted womb, but when she sought contraceptive advice for her patients, she was coldly rebuffed. One doctor said, "The poor have only themselves to blame; they indulge their appetites too much." Another "held out the hope of great changes in the near future when women would become more intelligent and independent. 'When she uses her brains more, her productive organs will function less.' "[6]

In 1900, Goldman represented American anarchists at an international congress in Paris. She threatened to leave the meeting when its organizers refused to allow her to read papers on sex problems, such issues being beneath orthodox radical scrutiny. Personal experience had taught her "that women and children carried the heaviest burden of our ruthless economic system," and "it was mockery to expect them to wait until the social revolution . . . in order to right injustice." She did receive a sympathetic hearing from Victor Dave, a member of the First International Workingmen's Association and the last surviving leader of the Paris Commune of 1871. Dave knew of plans to hold a secret Neo-Malthusian Congress in Paris and introduced her to the leaders of the movement. She returned to the United States with a stock of birth control literature and supplies, determined to make open discussion of contraception a reality in the United States.[7]

Goldman's plans were interrupted by her arrest and persecution following the assassination of President McKinley. Eventually, however, American free speech advocates began to support her right to access to public forums. The Manhattan Liberal Club and similar groups took special pride in inviting her to lecture. Among those participating in the cultural ferment associated with Greenwich Village before World War I, Emma Goldman became a heroine and even a model. Goldman's advocacy of "free love," in practice, amounted to a romantic belief that all successful relationships between a man and a woman rested on an essentially private mutual commitment which could not be created or maintained by laws. Her criticism of big business, her hatred for the double standard of sexual morality, her defense of prostitutes and other social outcasts, and her insistence on social equality for women—all of these ideals began to command more attention in the decade before World War I.[8]

During a lecture stop in Chicago in the spring of 1908, Goldman could not rent a hall. Dr. Ben L. Reitman (1879–1942), known to her only as the organizer of a parade for the jobless, offered her the use of a vacant store he had rented for gatherings of homeless men. She fell in love with the fabulous Dr. Reitman at first sight. "A handsome brute" with dark brown eyes, "a mass of black curly hair which evidently had not been washed for some time," and beautiful long hands, Ben Reitman constantly scandalized Goldman's dedicated anarchist comrades who resented the brash Midwesterner's flamboyance, prayer meetings, eye for the ladies, occasional shady dealings, and lack of ideological consistency. Waif, convict, hobo, student, doctor, labor organizer, social worker—Reitman impressed Goldman as a genuine representative of the "have nots," and she clung to him for his primitive vitality as well as for his organizational skills.[9]

Reitman's peddler father had deserted his family while he was an infant. At eight Ben was running errands for Chicago prostitutes; at eleven he was arrested for picking up coal from railroad tracks, the first of more than fifty times he was arrested, "but never as a real criminal . . . always for hoboing and propaganda agitation." Paroled to his mother, he ran away from home to bum around the world before taking a job as a janitor in 1899 at the Chicago Polyclinic. Some of the doctors at the clinic took an interest in the philosopher who mopped up, and with their help Reitman graduated from Loyola Medical College in 1904.[10]

Reitman was trying to settle down to practice medicine among Chicago's "dangerous classes" when he met Emma. After becoming lovers they toured the country fighting dozens of battles for radical causes and for Goldman's right to lecture. Reitman "achieved wonders" in obtaining halls, attracting audiences, and selling literature. For the first time Goldman was able to reach beyond the enclaves of foreign-born radicals to a large general audience of native Americans. In 1910 on one tour she delivered 120 lectures to 25,000 paid admissions in 37 cities, sold 10,000 pieces of literature, and gave away thousands more.[11]

Birth control was one topic among many in Goldman's repertoire. She did not give information on techniques in her talks; she did give "how-to" literature to those who approached her privately, and Ben liberally distributed leaflets. Although often arrested and harassed by the police as radical agitators, neither was sentenced to prison before 1916, and birth control remained a minor part of their program to free mankind from its chains.[12]

In 1914, Margaret Sanger, a nurse who had experience with the abortion problem remarkably similar to Goldman's, founded a new journal, *The Woman Rebel,* dedicated to the proposition that women should raise more hell and fewer babies. Postal authorities declared *Rebel* unmailable. Sanger continued to mail her journal, then fled the country to avoid prosecution. In an effort to learn where Sanger was hiding, an agent for the New York Society for the Suppression of Vice tricked her husband into giving him one of her birth control pamphlets and then arrested Mr. Sanger for obscenity.[13]

Emma Goldman felt conscience-bound to plunge into another free speech fight and began lecturing on birth control techniques and holding meetings to raise money for the Sangers. Goldman was arrested for distributing birth control leaflets in Portland, but she was not prosecuted, and for a time she was more concerned with efforts of her comrades to keep her from lecturing on homosexuality than with the birth control issue. She was arrested again and prosecuted in New York in February 1916. Reitman was also arrested for distributing leaflets at a meeting called to protest Goldman's arrest. He wrote of the irony of being jailed in New York, "the wonderful strange town," for giving away literature that had "been freely and openly distributed in Denver, Los Angeles, Portland, Seattle, San Francisco, Chicago, Cleveland, and nearly all the large cities without the slightest interference from anyone."[14]

Goldman spent fifteen days in Queens County Jail. Reitman

shoveled coal for sixty days on Blackwell's Island and later spent six months in the Warrensville, Ohio, workhouse for distributing leaflets in Cleveland. Goldman and Reitman began to lose interest in birth control, however, because the issue of American entrance into World War I seemed more important. Reitman explained that birth control was "getting to be terribly respectable. The other day in Des Moines, Iowa a judge sentenced a man and woman to study and apply birth control." Goldman and Reitman wrote antiwar and anti-conscription articles for *Mother Earth*. She was convicted of "conspiracy to defeat military registration," was imprisoned for two years, and was deported to Russia upon her release from prison. Reitman returned to Chicago to the social work that made him King of the Hobos, running a traveler's aid society for bums and working on venereal disease control with the Chicago Department of Health.[15]

In 1938, Reitman's memories of Goldman's work for birth control were stirred when he read Norman Himes' *Medical History of Contraception* (1936). Reitman wrote a pseudoepic poem to Himes denouncing his failure in *Medical History* to give proper credit to radicals in the spread of birth control.[16] Reitman also enclosed in his letter one of the pamphlets he had used in his birth control work. Entitled "Why and How the Poor Should Not Have Many Children," this four-page leaflet provided better information on contraceptive technique than could be found in medical journals. Readers learned that the best birth control methods were condoms and womb veils. The fact that womb veils had to be fitted by a doctor made them "somewhat objectionable for general use," since many readers could not afford a physician's services, so instruction in proper douching technique and formulas for contraceptive suppositories were also provided.[17]

In his poem Reitman objected to Himes' interpretation of the history of contraception:

. . . what makes me weep
You have no understanding or appreciation
Of the basis of American or European B.C. Propaganda
You contacted no one in America or Europe in the Radical
    Movements.

Reitman doubted whether Himes was capable of objectivity.

I mean your prejudice against the Radicals
Is so great that you could not give them credit.
Emma Goldman
More than anyone person in America
Popularized B.C. [. . .]

She was Margaret Sanger's INSPIRATION
No that ain't the word.
Margaret imitated her and denied her.
Emma was the first person in America
To lecture on Birth Control
And influence the NEWSPAPERS
To talk about B.C.

The Physicians, Social Scientists, Clergy & etc.
Became interested in B.C.
Only after the Radical had broken the ground.
And gone to jail.

The enclosed pamphlet
Was distributed by the millions
Free.
In hundreds of Cities of America.

It went thru many editors.
Was copied and recopied.
And translated into many languages. . . .
The decline in the Birth Rate
Was influenced by this pamphlet
More than any other piece of literature. . . .
I would say its influence was greater
Than the Birth Control Clinics. . . .

A dozen different Persons. . . .
manufactured tablets, suppositories, jellies, pessaries
And they were sold by the ton.
GET THIS INTO YOUR HEAD
This was all done as part of the radical propaganda
ANTI WAR
ANTI MARRIAGE
ANTI CHILDREN BY ACCIDENT

While it is doubtful that "Why and How" had the impact on
the birth rate that Reitman claimed, he was right on several
points. The American Medical Association did not recognize
contraception as a medical service until 1937, when most

Americans were still learning what they knew of birth control from nonmedical sources. Unlike physicians, the radicals were not inhibited by the need to find medical reasons for prescribing birth control, and they were willing to spread information in anonymous forms. The people did not have to seek them; they sought the people. One of the great shifts in the history of contraception began in the mid-1930s, when conservative physicians, who had originally assumed that contraceptive information should be available only from doctors, began to find merit in Reitman's leafleting methods as it became clear that the available birth control clinics could not reach the deprived millions most in need of help.

Reitman, however, did not understand the factors that limited the impact of radical agitation for birth control. The disassociation of contraception from radicalism was essential to its acceptance by doctors and social workers of professional standing and to the support of state and local health agencies which provided the only medical treatment most of the poor received. The biggest task in winning over the middle-class majority of public opinion was to show that birth control was neither "ANTI MARRIAGE" nor "ANTI CHILDREN" but a means of strengthening marriage in modern society. If contraception was to be changed from a hit-or-miss search for protection into a sure and legitimate service generally available from competent sources, then it would have to be accepted by middle-class opinion, the law, and organized medicine. Changes in medical practice could not precede changes in public opinion or the law. Even if birth control was established as a useful and legal practice, medical acceptance would require clinical evidence of the effectiveness and harmlessness of specific contraceptive methods. That kind of evidence could only come from clinics with thousands of patients, good records, medical supervision, and institutional support.

CHAPTER 5

Permissiveness with Affection: A Sexual Standard for an Affluent Society

To preach a negative and color-less ideal of chastity to young men and women is to neglect the primary duty of awakening their intelligence, their responsibility, their self-reliance and indepen-dence. Once this is established, the matter of chastity will take care of itself.

Margaret Sanger,
The Pivot of Civilization
(1922)

PUBLIC opinion and laws on con-traception would never be changed as long as it remained in-decent to discuss human sexuality in public. Emma Goldman and Ben Reitman operated outside of what genteel America called "civilized morality," the dominant codes of middle-class respectability. During the first decades of the twentieth century, however, not only Greenwich Village folk, but social workers, doctors, and a large part of the educated public per-ceived an accelerating crisis in sexual morality. The recogni-tion that conventional standards of sexual conduct were some-how inadequate was reflected in a decline of reticence about discussing sex matters publicly. Articles on birth control, pros-titution, divorce, psychoanalysis, and sexual morals became standard fare in popular journals in the decade before World War I. A writer in *The Atlantic* complained in 1914 of the "ob-session of sex which has set us all a-babbling about matters once excluded from the amenities of conversation," while *Current Opinion* shouted that "Sex O'Clock" had struck in America.[1]

Physicians and social workers, who were determined to destroy the "conspiracy of silence" surrounding prostitution, venereal disease, and the double standard of sexual morality, initiated the repeal of the taboo against direct reference to sex. Once begun, however, open discussion of sex quickly became widespread, as conservatives had warned all along. Avid public interest revealed a depth of discontent undreamed of by those who accepted official models of thought and conduct. The facts of life were out of tune with American ideals.

Twentieth century critics of "Comstockery" created a popular stereotype of the nineteenth century as an era of cruel and repressive sexual standards. Their attacks on "Puritanism" and "Victorian prudery" often caricatured another age's search for humane ideals that deserves more understanding if not respect. In fact, twentieth century American sexual standards do not represent radical departures so much as continuing attempts to resolve contradictions in the mid-nineteenth century ideal of companionate marriage.

During the nineteenth century rapid social change made Americans increasingly self-conscious about sex and the differences between men and women. While middle-class women were losing many of their former economic functions as the home ceased to be a unit of production, and they thus withdrew from what society defined as "productive labor," their increased economic dependence did not necessarily mean a loss of social status, nor did the role of women in the world outside the home decline. Rather, women began a sustained search for social power through a large number of voluntary associations, including vice-suppression societies and woman suffrage associations. Both the stringent sexual restraint prescribed by "civilized morality" and the new ideology of domesticity enhanced the bargaining position of women in relation to men. The radical decline in marital fertility during the nineteenth century testifies to the increasing ability of women to question male sexual prerogatives.[2] Given the high levels of maternal mortality and morbidity during the nineteenth century, the emphasis in reform literature on the

55

control of male sexuality and on mutuality in the marriage bed should be viewed both as a response to real dangers and as a reflection of the determination of women to gain greater control over their lives. Thus, the separation of human activity into two spheres provided opportunities as well as liabilities for women. At home they could claim to represent the highest moral values of their culture; they argued for better education on the grounds that child rearing and homemaking were too important to be left to the ignorant; and they justified roles in reform as essential to protect their sphere from male corruption.

While American women initiated large-scale conflict with men over their social and legal status for the first time in the nineteenth century, and thus emerged as a distinct interest group, they did not gain equality with men.[3] Entrance of women on a large scale into most occupations, whether elementary education, librarianship, or clerical work, led to the definition of the field as "woman's work," with concurrent low wages and social status.[4] Although the celebration of woman's superior moral and intuitive insights helped some women to claim roles outside the home, ultimately the emphasis on innate biological differences limited the power and the aspirations of women.[5] Advocates of women's rights were able to win property rights for married women, but wives remained at best junior partners to their husbands, dependent on them for economic support even if they believed that their wives had as much right as they to emotional and sexual gratification. A married woman might be her husband's friend rather than his chattel, and she might command his consultation in important matters, but she remained "the better half," one to be consulted and deferred to on occasion but still dependent on him for her privileges.

Alexis de Tocqueville and other European observers argued, however, that the married woman in America commanded somewhat more respect than in Europe. Lacking an aristocracy, America also lacked a hedonistic tradition that sanctioned frivolous relations between the sexes. Sexual standards were set by the dominant bourgeoisie who placed great emphasis on the Protestant virtues of introspection and moral earnestness.[6] Whatever the existential reality in marriage,

Americans at least idealized companionship based on perfect mutuality. The prevailing sexual ideology recognized neither the mistress nor the prostitute as an acceptable outlet for male sexual drives. Thus, the need to reconcile sexual desire with a manageable number of children posed an especially pressing problem for right-thinking Americans.

Nineteenth century writers on sex assumed, however, that sexual expression could be subordinated to higher ends. They equated freedom with spiritual and mental development, not sexual expression. Nothing was impossible to a people committed to moral perfection. Purity in mind would assure chastity before marriage and abstinence within marriage when required.

The generation that popularized this ideal was born between 1790 and 1810 and was still close to the crude realities of a provincial rural society in which genteel values were more often honored than strictly enforced. For those born after midcentury, however, suppression of sexuality was a more salient part of childhood training. Attempts to idealize conduct, expressed in the taboos of childhood and the separation of the sexes in adolescence, made even sexual expression in marriage problematic for many. Contraceptive practice depended on the ability of men and women to discuss sex, to touch their genitals, and to accept their sexual needs as legitimate. For those taught to loathe parts of their bodies and denied the opportunity to know the opposite sex before marriage, abstinence was the only means of family limitation.

Thousands of late nineteenth century couples made their peace with one another and with society, but those who could not cope with the demands of civilized morality—either by successfully internalizing its values or by tacitly ignoring some of its demands—provided the first generation of American psychotherapists with many classic cases of neurosis. And the growth of prostitution as organized commercial vice testified to the increasing inability of American men to marry early or to find sexual satisfaction within marriage.[7]

In the first decades of the twentieth century the ideology of civilized morality began to collapse under the weight of its inherent contradictions. Ironically, the first important challenges came not from radicals but from genteel critics interested only in preserving social order. Prince Albert Morrow, an eminent dermatologist, was haunted by the image of innocent women and children ravaged by syphilis and gonorrhea brought into the home by men. A problem not previously recognized by poorly trained physicians, or at least easier to ignore in the pre-urban age, was perceived now as an intolerable threat to the family. In 1905, Dr. Morrow founded the American Society for Sanitary and Moral Prophylaxis and enlisted other concerned physicians in a campaign to inform the public of the horrors of venereal infection. Although Morrow's efforts were initially opposed by some purity crusaders, by 1913 the interests of preventive medicine and social righteousness were joined in the American Social Hygiene Association. Medical men working in the movement tacitly assumed the necessity of sexual fulfillment in marriage in order to keep husbands away from prostitutes.[8]

Social hygienists found allies among municipal reformers as campaigns against political corruption revealed that organized prostitution was a major industry and an important source of profit to urban political bosses. Sparked by the eloquence of Jane Addams, Lillian Wald, and other female voices of American conscience, prominent philanthropists and social workers led campaigns to outlaw brothels and the white slave trade and, characteristically, to provide rehabilitation for exploited women, many of whom were immigrants. Treatment of "The Traffic in Souls" in the press and the new moving pictures often appalled these humanitarian crusaders, who discovered that they had aroused more interest than they intended. One noted that the treatment of prostitution by the press was:

> a subject which only the student of morbid psychology, I suppose, can illuminate properly . . . and out of all this there arose a new conception of the prostitute quite as grotesque as that which it replaced. She was no longer the ruined and abandoned thing she once was, too vile for any contact with the virtuous and respectable. . . . she became the white-slave, a shanghaied innocent kept under lock and key.[9]

While journalists made prostitution appear mysterious and suggestively sensual, standards of feminine virtue were being undermined by competing models provided by fiction, magazine advertisements, vaudeville, and moving pictures. American business had discovered that the association of a product with leisure, pleasure, and sex sold the goods. Automobiles, telephones, and contact between the sexes at school and work lessened the ability of parents to control the behavior of their children. The University of Pennsylvania economist Simon Patten analyzed the breakdown of traditional mechanisms of social control, and in 1905 he announced the arrival of a new era of abundance in a series of lectures that were published under the title *The New Basis of Civilization.* Patten believed that the Protestant values of hard work and dedicated abstinence were a result of the ancient human struggle against nature for subsistence. These values had supported an economic revolution that, through its unprecedented successes, threatened the restraints of worldly asceticism and traditional morality.[10]

The emerging consumer society of the early twentieth century offered new roles to middle-class women. During the nineteenth century there were few employment opportunities available to those who did not want to lose social status, but the rapid increase in white-collar jobs allowed women from genteel families to enter the job market on a larger scale. Between 1910 and 1920 the proportion of female workers engaged in nonmanual occupations jumped from 17 to 30 percent, and work outside the home became socially acceptable.[11] Women entered the white-collar world at the bottom and sexual discrimination guaranteed that most of them would remain there, but their increased access to the world outside the home altered attitudes toward proper female behavior. The rapid growth of the maternity clothes industry began in 1910 when the fashion house of Lane Bryant brought out a line of moderately priced dresses for street wear. These garments provided women with suitable dress for public activity, testified to their determination to escape the "confinement" that society had imposed on their mothers, and symbolized the new public visibility of women not only as office workers but as shoppers or consumers. In 1911 the New York *Herald* accepted its first advertisement for maternity apparel, and readers learned that, "It is no longer the fashion nor the practice for expectant mothers to stay in seclusion."[12]

Some women even began to question the necessity for pain in childbirth and campaigned for the introduction into America of "Twilight Sleep," a procedure developed by German doctors who used scopolamine, a cerebral depressant that has an amnesiac effect, to inhibit pain during labor. In 1914, Dr. Eliza Ransom, a feminist angered by the reluctance of American doctors to experiment with Twilight Sleep, founded a Twilight Sleep Maternity Hospital in Boston and developed a large following among society women. The new obstetrical practice drew a great deal of attention from publications directed at women, and orthodox practitioners gradually adopted the use of scopolamine as an obstetrical anesthetic, largely because their clientele insisted that they had the right to childbirth with less pain.[13] If women could escape the traditional confinement of pregnancy and the pain of childbirth, then menstruation could not be the debilitating handicap declared by conservative doctors, and in 1920 the Kimberly Clark Company marketed Kotex, the first disposable sanitary napkin, a product that removed one motive for wearing petticoats and reenforced the trend toward less cumbersome clothing.[14] In 1915 a woman writer explained the increasing impatience of young Americans with old attitudes toward the human body in a *Good Housekeeping* article on "The Neglected Psychology of Twilight Sleep." In the past religious values sustained women in childbirth, but a more secular attitude was emerging:

> Today . . . we are all, men and women alike, inclined to think of our bodies, not as instruments of cosmic forces, but as personal possessions of ourselves, tools of our desires—very exalted desires in many cases, but still merely personal. We take care of our bodies, study them, worry about them, treat them, in short, much as one does a favorite horse, and then demand that they service us . . . absolutely . . . to inflict upon [the modern woman] many burdens and sufferings which a cruder type of woman took as a matter of course is unnatural.[15]

Relations between the sexes began to reflect the values of an affluent society. Married companionship in the home had seemed to be the best that the nineteenth century economy could support for its young middle classes. Young men and women in the early twentieth century sought the pleasure of companionship before marriage in the world outside the home. The generous figure of the Gibson girl was replaced in the popular imagination by a creature with slim hips and short hair, who played tennis or swam, danced the fox trot, smoked cigarettes, and necked with men she might not marry. This "new woman" was a comrade in arms with male friends against the sexually segregated adolescence and exaggerated sex roles of their parents. A popular columnist described the "type of girl that the modern young man falls for" in 1915 as a "young woman who can play golf all day and dance all night, and drive a motor car, and give first aid to the injured if anybody gets hurt, and who is in no more danger of swooning than he is." [16]

As youth listened to the appeals of the advertising industry to relax, consume, and enjoy, the traditional values of austerity and sacrifice weakened. Young men found the model of the ascetic businessman or heroic entrepreneur less attractive in an increasingly bureaucratized economy. Corporate success often depended on sociability rather than individual initiative, and the organization man began to find meaning and pleasure in the rewards of the economy of abundance rather than in work itself. [17] As he turned from self-absorbed money making, the "new man" began to cultivate friendships with women, and more intimacy led to profound changes in sexual behavior. Among the four cohorts, or statistical generations, of predominately upper-middle-class women interviewed by Alfred Kinsey in the 1940s, those born between 1900 and 1909 set a pattern of premarital sexual behavior that remained essentially unchanged until after World War II. These women made necking America's favorite pastime, and 36 percent of them engaged in premarital intercourse. Premarital coitus among men born between 1900 and 1909 did not increase, but coitus with prostitutes decreased by over 50 percent, the slack being taken up by friends, two-thirds of whom were fiancées. [18]

The new courting pattern—prolonged heavy petting, often leading to coitus, and usually followed by marriage—did not signal the collapse of monogamy, marriage, or the family. Rather, it reflected the emergence of a single standard of permissiveness with affection. As the sociologist Ira Reiss shrewdly observed, the new standard did not mean frivolous sexuality or acceptance of "body-centered" coitus. Sex as self-centered pleasure was the standard of men who avoided coitus with their fiancées because they were "good girls" and sought relief with prostitutes.[19]

Young people were simply expanding the limits of the nineteenth century ideal of companionate marriage and "person-centered" coitus developed by their parents. Petting provided the opportunity for the sexes to learn to know one another. It was a necessary prelude to mature sexual relationships and an appropriate form of sexual expression for adolescence, the prolonged period of social dependency necessary for the middle classes in an industrial society. Kinsey's study showed a correlation between heavy petting and the ability of women to achieve orgasm in marriage. Sexual compatibility in marriage, in turn, was associated with a low divorce rate.[20]

Both the nineteenth century ideal of companionate marriage and the twentieth century standard of permissiveness with affection were relationships based on mutuality and justified by affection. In the twentieth century version of ideal love between man and woman, sex and procreation could be separated, but sex was still justified by the investment of much psychological capital in a stable relationship. Permissiveness with affection rested even more narrowly on intimate and personal values than the companionate marriage and was thus more dependent on sexual attraction and fulfillment. In retrospect, the emergence between 1915 and 1921 of a movement to legitimize and spread contraceptive practice might be viewed as a logical, if not inevitable, response to one source of tension in the sex lives of socially ambitious Americans. The essential cultural prerequisite for the success of the American birth control movement was the secularization of society or the celebration of material well-being and pleasure exemplified by the growth of the advertising industry. The progressive rationalization of human relationships in an industrial society was leading toward the acceptance of human sexuality as a means of individual expression divorced from any large social necessity or religious purpose. Many Americans, however, were not ready to believe that affection alone justified sex, no matter how they might be conducting their private lives. During the first half of the twentieth century the case for birth control would have to be made in mixed metaphors and twisted analogies that often had a tenuous relationship to the popular appeal of the cause.

PART II

THE WOMAN REBEL: MARGARET SANGER AND THE STRUGGLE FOR CLINICS

CHAPTER 6   **The Burden of Domesticity**

$\mathbf{M}$ARGARET SANGER (1879–1966) led a successful campaign from 1914 to 1937 to remove the stigma of obscenity from contraception and to establish a nationwide system of clinics where women could obtain reliable birth control services. She organized research, recruited manufacturers for birth control devices, and won court battles that modified the Comstock laws and laid the groundwork for the formal acceptance of birth control by organized medicine in 1937. After World War II she played key roles in the rise of an international planned parenthood movement and in the development of the birth control pill. Through these achievements she had a greater impact on the world than any other American woman. In 1909, however, she was a thirty-year-old suburban housewife, raising three children in Hastings-on-Hudson, and waiting for her husband to return home from the nine-to-five grind in the city.

Sanger was drawn into her career as a reformer through a series of vivid personal experiences. "World hunger" and dissatisfaction with life in suburbia drew her to the rebel's paradise of pre–World War I New York. There she sought personal freedom and discovered the plight of the city's poor women. Most important, she found ideas that connected her problems with those of other women and justified rebellion against the father and husband who had dominated her life and whom she blamed for isolating her from the world of experience beyond the home.

Through her public career she realized a personal desire for self-fulfillment free from the burdens imposed on her as a daughter, wife, and mother, but she owed the tremendous success she enjoyed as a reformer to an ability to explain her cause in terms that the general public could understand and accept. Her triumphs symbolized a growing awareness among thousands of Americans that the maintenance of stable families depended on more satisfactory sexual adjustment. Birth control might provide a means of reconciling marital passion with the desire for fewer children, a higher standard of living, and greater personal freedom, but many Americans feared that the easy separation of sex from procreation would undermine public morality and weaken the family. Sanger became the dominant figure in the history of contraception by providing social justification for practices that had once seemed wholly personal and selfish. By dramatizing the suffering of working-class women whose health and hopes for a better life were destroyed by unwanted pregnancies, she forced public recognition of what was already a fact of middle-class behavior. The horrible specter she raised of rampant abortion, high maternal mortality, and the instability of family life among the impoverished helped to define by contrast the strengths of middle-class family life.

The clinics necessary to provide contraceptive services to indigent women also served as centers of education where private practitioners were instructed in contraceptive technique, a subject not taught in medical schools. The thousands of club women who rallied behind Sanger's banner not only helped to free lower-class women from fear of pregnancy but also freed themselves by bringing their own conduct into the open and by providing the means through which doctors in private practice could learn about birth control. Although she drew most of her support from among the privileged, Sanger would have passionately resented any attempt to link her with efforts to preserve the domestic status quo. She hoped that women in control of themselves would become a revolutionary force by choosing to rear children only under the best possible conditions, thereby eliminating not only poverty but mediocrity as well.

The Roman Catholics and medical men who were the most

vehement critics of Sanger's utopian vision argued that she had nothing new to offer. Birth controllers, they said, were simply trying to promote dangerous practices that had been discredited and suppressed in the nineteenth century. Sanger's critics were right when they noted that she had no new technology to offer, but their persistent hostility had little to do with the effectiveness and safety of birth control methods. Vaginal diaphragms, cervical caps, spermicidal compounds, condoms, and a safe period were all known in the nineteenth century. Yet before Sanger no one undertook the systematic evaluation of birth control methods to separate the safe and effective from the unreliable and dangerous. Attitudes toward sex, women, and the family, rather than lack of technical know-how, account for most of the hostility toward birth control. Once birth controllers convinced the public that the separation of sex from procreation was morally safe, if not socially essential, then the limitations of existing birth control methods would be a minor inconvenience rather than a major obstacle to the acceptance of birth control by organized medicine and by government.

Sanger began her reform career as one of many individuals demanding wholesale social change in an era of reform. Her willingness to concentrate on one issue and her changing tactics alienated old comrades. She understood, however, that the fight for acceptance of birth control depended on manipulation of public opinion, victories in court, and skillful lobbying among professional elites. Each audience required a different strategy of change. Thus, she had to disassociate herself from the radicals and medical heretics who were the first to advocate family limitation. She retained many assumptions and attitudes drawn from earlier reformers, but her burning conviction that birth control was *the* most important concrete step that could be taken to improve the quality of life sprang from her own experience as a daughter, wife, nurse, and radical agitator.

Born in the factory town of Corning, New York, in 1879, Sanger was the sixth child and third daughter of Michael Higgins, a straight-backed, outspoken Irishman who had joined the Union Army at fifteen to fight slavery, was decorated for bravery, and kept things lively in drab Corning by advocating the ideas of the socialist Henry George and the atheist Robert Ingersoll. Higgins was a good stonecutter and might have had a profitable business. "However," one son remembered, "he was more interested in making speeches, introducing someone who was discussing socialism, et cetera. Many a time one of us would have to come down the street to Clark's Shoe Store and yank him out of an argument or discussion to come back to his place and sell a monument to a waiting customer." [1]

Although a loving husband and father, Higgins was too engrossed in his own ideals to give much thought to his family's need for comfort and security. According to Margaret, doors were never locked, bums never turned away without a meal. "If it happened to be pay day they could count on a quarter as well as a meal." Thieves that he refused to notice had to be chased out of his chicken coop by neighbors. Money set aside for winter coal went for a banquet for fifty in honor of Henry George, and a Catholic boycott of his monument business followed sponsorship of a lecture by Robert Ingersoll. [2]

Anne Higgins' devotion to her husband never wavered and was symbolized by the birth of eleven children, "all ten-pounders or more." Margaret helped deliver a fourteen-and-a-half pound boy when she was eight and remembered that her mother always had a cough. Anne Higgins died of tuberculosis in her forties. Michael Higgins lived to be eighty-four. His daughter Margaret never got over the contrast. [3]

The Higgins children had enough to eat, but they seldom had anything beyond necessities. The older children left home as soon as they could. Margaret resented their deprivation in comparison with the white-collar workers in Corning.

> Corning was not on the whole a pleasant town. Along the river flats lived the factory workers, chiefly Irish; on the heights above the rolling clouds of smoke that belched from the chimneys lived the owners and executives. The tiny yards of the former were a-sprawl with children; in the gardens on the hills only two or three played. This contrast made a track in my mind. Large families were associated with poverty, toil, unemployment, drunkenness, cruelty, fighting, jails; the small ones with cleanliness, leisure, freedom, light, space, sunshine.

Michael Higgins' indifference to money matters and a succession of new Higgins babies often threatened to bring the family down to the river-shanty standard of living.[4]

Margaret's two older sisters had wanted something better, but the family was too dependent on their wages for them to hope for much for themselves. They helped their younger sister escape their fate by paying her way to Claverack College in Hudson, New York, one of the first coeducational preparatory schools in the United States. Margaret had to work for her room and board, and she "did not have the money to do things the other girls did," but washing dishes at Claverack was far easier than the work at home, and she never wanted to go back.[5]

Margaret became the belle of Claverack, learned to love the world portrayed in the novels of George Eliot, and played the leading feminine roles in school plays, but gave up her ambition to be an actress when the drama school to which she applied asked for her measurements. "I had expected to have to account for the quality of my voice, for my ability to sing, to play, for grace, agility, character, and morals." On graduation from Claverack she took a job teaching first grade to eighty-four immigrant children in a southern New Jersey public school. The school year had barely begun when she was called home to nurse her mother through the terminal stages of pulmonary tuberculosis.[6]

Having tasted the freedom of boarding school and of working for herself, Margaret resented the burdens of managing her father's household, his failures as a provider, and his assumption that she should obey him as if she were his dependent. She loved her father, however, as "a philosopher, a rebel, and an artist." He had always treated her like a friend with whom he discussed the great and small issues of the time with complete openness. She remembered his physical strength and courage when she clung to his hand as he stood up to an angry crowd to assert Robert Ingersoll's right to speak in Corning. When the death of an infant son left Anne prostrate with grief, Michael had enlisted his daughter's aid in digging up the boy's coffin and making a death mask from which he made a bust of the infant for his wife. He was an ardent supporter of woman's suffrage and an advocate of Amelia Bloomer's trousers, "though his wife and daughters never wore them," and he sent a steady stream of letters to Margaret when she was at Claverack "filled with ammunition about the historical background of the importance of women." Yet, after his wife's death, he expected his daughter to assume the role of obedient drudge. His own example was the main reason that she refused to play the part.[7]

While caring for her mother, Margaret borrowed medical books from the family physician and decided to become an M.D. When she told the doctor of her ambition, he "smiled tolerantly, 'You'll probably get over it.' " Nursing was the closest practical alternative. After her father locked her out of the house for returning home from a dance past his ten o'clock curfew, Margaret escaped home a second time by entering the new nursing school at White Plains Hospital, one year after her mother's death.[8]

The long hours and backbreaking drudgery of nursing school in the nineteenth century were aggravated for her by a series of operations for tubercular glands, a condition that she believed she had contracted while nursing her mother. The disease persistently reappeared for twenty-three years in the glands of the neck, breast, and armpits and in spots in the lungs, until the removal of infected tonsils in 1920. Despite poor health and hard work, she was a willing student. Anything was better than Corning. She was completing her training at Manhattan Eye and Ear Hospital and looking forward to earning a decent living, when she met the next man in her life.[9]

Stories differ on how William Sanger met Margaret Higgins. In one version he came to the hospital to have an object removed from his eye. In her autobiography, Margaret met Bill when he came to show a doctor friend house plans that he had been commissioned to draw. By all accounts, he immediately fell in love with the petite redhead. An architect by profession but "pure artist by temperament," Bill Sanger courted the student nurse with an overwhelming insistence. Eight years older, established professionally, informed about all the exciting things going on in New York, Sanger confided "his dream of eventually being able to leave architecture behind and devote himself to painting. . . . Some day we were going to be married, and as soon as we had saved enough money we would go to Paris, whither the inspiration of the great French painters was summoning artists from all over the world."[10]

Miss Higgins did not want to get married. She had debts, needed clothes, and was reluctant to trade her education for domesticity. She explained to her sister,

> . . . when I think of all the hard work—the bitter tears I shed night after night for the old training—the lonesome nights I passed waiting for some old tramp to die—then when it is finished—without a laurel to get married—then I want to stop it all—I would love one year of private nursing—and get some money—and then if anyone wants me all right.[11]

Bill insisted that they be married immediately. "He was selfish, afraid the precious article would be lost to him," especially jealous of two of Margaret's doctor friends, and even resented the time she spent with a girl friend from Claverack. He arranged for a minister and witnesses without Margaret's knowledge, and, she explained to her sister,

> . . . he made me marry him, now or never he said. I only had two hours off duty—and we drove around the Park arguing on the subject until four o'clock—then he turned in and made me get out—and we were married at ten minutes past—and I was due here [at the hospital] at four thirty. I vow I will not live with such a beast of a man. I can not give up my training. . . .

A steady stream of books, flowers, and endearing notes finally persuaded Margaret that further resistance was futile. "I am very sorry to have had this thing occur but yet I am very, very, happy."[12]

Mrs. Sanger was pregnant six months after her marriage, and the tuberculosis became worse. Spending her confinement at a sanatorium in the Adirondacks, she returned to New York for the particularly difficult delivery of a son. Sent back to the mountains by a doctor and a husband who feared she might not survive, she found life as a twenty-five-year-old invalid intolerable; developed a hysterical revulsion against the creosote-tablet, raw-egg, and rest therapy; and fled back to New York, determined to lead a normal life no matter what the consequences.

Her health improved after her abrupt return to Manhattan, and the Sangers planned to build a home in Westchester County as a symbol of her refusal to become an invalid. They hoped to settle down to a comfortable suburban existence. Another son was born and a daughter soon after. The tuberculosis cropped up again and the doctor advised against more children. Margaret filled her life with "the momentous problems of servants, gardens, . . . schools," and the activities of the new ladies literary club. [13]

She had been drawn to Bill by qualities of idealism and enthusiasm that he shared with her father. Unfortunately, he also shared her father's lack of concern for money matters. Opera tickets and orchids were plentiful, but household bills went unpaid. Bill got more work as a draftsman than as an architect. Their new home burned the night they moved into it after Bill stirred up a roaring fire in the furnace and overheated as yet uninsulated pipes. Although they rebuilt, the smell of smoke lingered as dreams of Paris faded. Life with Bill was beginning to resemble life with father. [14]

Increasingly Margaret felt trapped in the house her husband had built for her. Years later, when she visited Ibsen's grave, she "stood there in silent tribute" and "had the feeling he had understood women and the ties they had been loosening. To my mind Nora never went back to the 'doll's house'. . . . Or, if she did return, she entered by another door." Margaret sought diversion in writing for her children and their friends. Bill supported her by volunteering to wash dishes, but she recalled that he drew the shades first, "so that nobody could see him."

Labor literature received from the foreman of a gang working in the neighborhood reawakened Margaret's memories of her father's ideals. Bill came home to find her excited about a cause in which he was taking part as a follower of Eugene Debs and a member of Manhattan's Branch Five of the Socialist Party of America. The Sangers attended a socialist lecture in Yonkers in 1910. Bill later associated that meeting with "Margaret's awakening."

Suddenly she was transformed. She devoured every article and book that she could lay her capable hands on—she attended meet-

74

ings and lectures—she got to know the leaders of the Social and Radical Labor movements—she plunged into welfare work. Gone forever was the conservative Irish girl I had married: a new woman, forceful, intelligent, hungry for facts, tireless, ambitious and cool, had miraculously come into being.[15]

That new woman took less and less interest in husband, children, and home. Hutchins Hapgood, the chronicler of Greenwich Village life, remembered her as "a pretty woman" who "seemed to grant little value to her husband," "a sweet gentle painter who lacked ego and ambition."[16]

In 1913 the International Exhibition of Modern Art marked the debut of modernism in the arts in America. Inspired by the works of the French impressionists and by his wife's desire to escape "the tame domesticity . . . bordering on stagnation" of suburban life, Bill decided to devote more time to painting. His wife had already resolved "to resume nursing in order to earn my share." Renting the house at Hastings-on-Hudson, they found an uptown Manhattan apartment and "plunged back into the rushing stream of New York life."[17]

The Sanger apartment became a gathering place for other refugees from the tedium of ordinary life. Warm debates between advocates of bread-and-butter unionism and direct-action general strikers were followed by hot dog and beer suppers. All paid their share and helped to clean up. Bill's mother provided free baby-sitting, liberating Margaret for private nursing and political activity.

Among the competing personalities she met, Margaret was attracted to spokesmen for untrammeled individual expression. Alexander Berkman, the anarchist editor of *Mother Earth,* William D. Haywood, a leader of the syndicalist International Workers of the World, and John Reed, the poet of revolution from Harvard, found her an avid listener. They became her intimate friends. The one unquestioned article of faith held by citizens of the new American bohemia was the necessity of destroying the "Puritanical" chains that bound them. Wage slavery and sexual oppression, the twin ghouls of capitalist society, could not be destroyed by votes for women or craft-oriented labor unions. The transformation of society, they argued, depended on the spread of cultural radicalism that would inspire progressive individuals to renounce the tyranny of both the bourgeois family and regimented work.[18]

Berkman, Haywood, and Reed seemed willing to accept women as equals. Most radicals, Margaret Sanger found,

> are stirred by the Socialist call to the workers to revolt from wage-slavery, but they are unmoved by the Socialist call to women to revolt from sex-slavery. They are still too oversexed, too tainted with the sins of their fathers, to be able to look upon woman's claims as upon their own. The class-consciousness is not yet perfect enough to have wiped out their inherited sex-consciousness.[19]

Elizabeth Cady Stanton and Charlotte Perkins Gilman, as well as more conservative advocates of women's rights, had long complained about "sex slavery."[20] Margaret Sanger shared their conviction that men had to recognize woman's right to complete control of her body, but she wanted more than the right not to marry or the right to refuse to participate in "sexual indulgence" in marriage. She wanted the right to behave as her conscience dictated, free of the code of female propriety shared by reformer and conservative. She saw no reason why personal independence should require the sacrifice of sexual satisfaction. The conventional formulas of female protest could not justify her growing desire to escape the suffocating bounds of marriage and to participate fully in the exciting revolt against the smug gentility of Victorian America.[21]

Sanger began a piecemeal apprenticeship in radical activism, borrowing ideas that fitted her situation and shaping an outlook of her own. In April 1912, "Miss Margaret Sanger, of New York, the International Workers of the World organizer" was arrested twice in three days in Hazelton, Pennsylvania, where strikers were trying to shut down the Duplan Silk Mill. Her first arrest was for attempting to keep workers from entering the plant. Her second arrest, however, reflected more personal outrage than socialist commitment. One of the Hazelton town officials named McKelvey explained that,

> he had made a remark about the woman as she passed him and she immediately asked Officer Brobst to arrest him, she claiming McKelvey had insulted her. The officer responded that he had not seen or heard it and hence could not act. . . . the Sanger woman then said 'I'll slap his face' and moved at him. McKelvey stood still

and as she swung at him, caught her arm and turned her over to the police.

Before the judge could dismiss the case, Sanger managed to testify that she believed in direct action because justice could not be obtained through laws and courts.[22]

Despite her lack of success in Hazelton, Sanger made important contributions to the radical labor movement during the strikes by textile workers in Lawrence, Massachusetts, and Paterson, New Jersey, in 1912 and 1913. The Socialist Party of America's Local Five, to which both Margaret and William Sanger belonged, had been responsible for bringing William Haywood, the spokesman for militant western miners, east to debate the issue of industrial sabotage with Morris Hillquit, the leader of those who believed in conventional trade unionism, at Cooper Union in early 1912. When a spontaneous strike broke out in Lawrence over a wage cut, Haywood rushed to provide radical leadership to the strikers, who were divided by ethnic origin and by competing labor philosophies and organizations.[23]

The Lawrence strike succeeded because of the tremendous sympathy aroused for the workers' children. Haywood picked Sanger to lead the women's committee of the Socialist Party in evacuating the strikers' children to foster homes in New York and Philadelphia because, as a nurse, mother, and native American, she commanded greater public sympathy than most other radicals. The medical examinations that Sanger insisted on before taking responsibility for the children revealed the ravages of malnutrition, poor clothing, and lack of medical care. Lawrence police responded to growing national attention by arresting mothers of a new group of refugee children gathered at the railroad station. A congressional hearing resulted, and Sanger effectively countered claims by the mill owners that the children were being exploited for publicity with factual testimony on enlarged tonsils and rotting teeth. The strike was won, and the city fathers of Lawrence began a publicity campaign to redeem the city's reputation.[24]

Catapulted into a position of national importance by the Lawrence success, Big Bill Haywood next tried to gain members for the International Workers of the World in the textile town of Paterson, New Jersey, where a strike had begun in January 1913. As the struggle lasted through the summer and talk began of compromise with management, John Reed decided to organize a pageant in New York to dramatize the plight of the workers and to win public opinion for their cause. Reed and his lover, Mabel Dodge, "called a meeting at Margaret Sanger's house and got all the people interested who were good workers." The Lawrence pageant, staged in Madison Square Garden, attracted the enthusiastic support of Manhattan intellectuals and drew 15,000 paying spectators; but the pageant lost money, drew strikers away from the picket line, and created jealousies between those who took part and those who stayed in Paterson. The strike was lost; Reed left with Dodge for her Florence villa; Haywood was a shattered man; and Sanger began to differentiate her concerns from those of other radicals.[25]

"Thoroughly despondent after the Paterson debacle," Sanger increasingly found fault with her radical comrades. Her husband, bitterly resentful of her friendship with Haywood, argued that he was simply using the rhetoric of revolution as an excuse for gaining access to another man's wife. She began to detect callousness in her fellow radicals toward the personal concerns of laboring women. Another woman IWW organizer remembered her addressing a meeting of women strikers on woman's right to limit her family.

> She received a hearty response. Immediately afterward, William Haywood got up to speak. He drew a rosy picture of the economic commonwealth of the future, one of the glories of which was to be that 'they could have without fear of want *all the babies they pleased'*. Needless to say, his promise elicited no response whatever. I have never forgotten the incident because I was aghast at it and it seemed to me actually insulting both to the previous speaker and to the women listening. I suppose it was just insensitiveness on his part.[26]

Margaret Sanger was appalled by the misery of the wives and children of the strikers. She was even more upset, however, by the indifference of the male leaders of the labor movement to the special needs of women. While male strikers were intent on winning a little more money and shorter hours, "The women really cared for neither of these. Dominating each was the relationship between her husband, her children, and herself." The prospect of higher wages offered some hope to these women, but gnawing fear of pregnancy and dim awareness that wages would never be adequate unless family size could be controlled were ever present sources of anxiety. She claimed that labor radicals were petty tyrants in their own homes, where a combination of scarcity and unwanted pregnancies placed the real burden of industrial warfare on their wives. "Women and their requirements were not being taken into account in reconstructing this new world about which all were talking. They were failing to consider the quality of life itself." [27]

In reaction to the "purely masculine reasoning" of most radicals, Sanger was "driven to ask" whether the uncontrolled fecundity of workers "was not at least partially responsbile, along with industrial injustice, for the widespread misery of the world." She found, however, that such talk was heresy among orthodox socialists. Everywhere there was "the same insistence upon the purely economic phases of human nature, the same belief that if the problem of hunger were solved, the question of women and children would take care of itself." These were flattering dogmas since they taught the poor laborer "that all the fault is with someone else, that he is the victim of circumstances, and not even a partner in the creation of his own and his children's misery." [28]

The Higgins children had never been allowed to view themselves as victims of circumstances. Losers were losers and nothing more. Poverty and suffering were not redeeming, were too real to be glorified. Most of all, weakness and incompetence were contemptible. Michael Higgins treated his children like adults. Father was never physically intimidated by anyone; his sons could fight and hunt. When Margaret "went out into the world and observed men, otherwise admirable, who could not pound a nail or use a saw, pick, shovel, or ax, I was dumbfounded. I had always taken for granted that any man could make things with his hands." "I expected this even of women." [29]

The image of the crucified Christ had no appeal to Margaret Higgins. Her heroes refused the hemlock and went to the gallows kicking. Father taught that "subjection to any church was a reflection on strength and character. You should be able to get from yourself what you had to go to church for." Self-sufficiency, stoicism, and "eugenic pride" were part of the rebel creed of Michael Higgins, along with uncompromising resentment of industrial plutocrats. One of Margaret's brothers became an all-American end at Penn State, was a successful coach there, and is enshrined in the Football Hall of Fame. In her own search for models of rebellion, she was drawn "towards the individualist, anarchist philosophy," and she was never really comfortable with philosophies of collectivism or of paternalism, although she considered herself a follower of Norman Thomas, and supported him for president, except when a Roman Catholic was running. Then the future of the Republic demanded her vote for the non-Catholic with the best chance of winning.[30]

While she hated "the wretchedness and hopelessness of the poor," Sanger "never experienced that satisfaction in working among them so many noble women have found." She found in the anarchism of Alexander Berkman a congenial "credo of pure individualism—to stand on your own and be yourself, never to have one person dictate to another, even parent to child." She had ambivalent feelings about industrial sabotage, general strikes, and even legislation as remedies for the woes of labor but was unequivocally committed to autonomy for women. The one reform that she could make her own was the task of giving woman control over her body, the essential first step toward personal independence. Revolution was to begin at home.[31]

Personal resentments and firsthand witness of the suffering of strikers' wives had led her to question the dogmas of other radicals, but two specific experiences—a brush with the Comstock laws and an abortion tragedy—helped her to find her unique mission as a reformer. By 1912, while continuing to work as a nurse, she had established herself as a writer and speaker in socialist circles. The scandal of prostitution, the ravages of venereal disease, and their common source in the wage system were popular themes in socialist literature. As a nurse, she often spoke to working women's groups on sexual hygiene. Beginning in November 1912, *The Call*, New York's socialist daily, published a series of her Sunday supplement articles on female sexuality. The series ran until February 9, 1913, when the Post Office ruled that an article on syphilis was unmailable under the Comstock Act.[32]

If women could not read the plain truth about venereal disease, a recognized social evil, then they certainly would never be allowed knowledge of contraception, an essential in any practical plan of liberation. Emma Goldman had advocated family limitation since her experience of nursing among Manhattan's poor in the 1890s. Her exploits were legend among cultural rebels, but birth control was a minor feature of Goldman's revolutionary platform. Infuriated by censorship of her *Call* articles, Sanger turned the reluctance of doctors to provide contraceptive information into a symbol of oppression and thus defined a cause for her own.

During her student nursing days Sanger had been called out on maternity cases. Sometimes the doctor did not arrive in time, and the nurse had to assist the delivery. The close relationship with the patient created by shared experience was rewarding. Mutual confidence sometimes gave the patient courage to ask a question she feared to put to a man. "Miss Higgins, what should I do not to have another baby right away?" When the nurse asked the doctor, the usual answer was, "She ought to be ashamed of herself to talk to a young girl about things like that."[33]

In 1912, Sanger was not "a young girl" but a mother of three who knew that the middle classes used condoms and withdrawal. Many of her patients were poor. Sex was one of the few luxuries their husbands had, and these men refused to limit their own enjoyment. Too many children meant crowding, lack of proper nurture, and a vicious cycle of poverty spawned by the ignorance and helplessness of women. The Lower East Side of Manhattan seemed like a hell where the wretched "were beyond the scope of organized charity or religion." Pregnancy was a chronic condition among the women of this district. On Saturday nights Sanger saw lines of fifty to one hundred women who stood "with their shawls over their heads waiting outside the office of the five-dollar abortionist." Constantly the nurse heard pleas for the "secret rich people have" to stop the babies from coming and "the story told a thousand times of death from abortion and children going into institutions."[34]

Both Sanger and Goldman witnessed deaths from induced abortions. A 1917 study by a physician of 464 indigent women who received care in the dispensaries of New York's Department of Health revealed the stark reality of the frequency of resort to abortion among the poor. Of the 192 of these women who never used contraceptives, 104 had a history of abortions. There were 202 abortions, or an average of almost two apiece.[35]

Sanger claimed that the death of one of her patients from a second self-induced abortion was the traumatic event that made her a "Woman Rebel." Sadie Sachs was the wife of a truck driver and the mother of three small children. Her tiny apartment reflected industry and desire to raise her family properly despite slum conditions. Called in to nurse Mrs. Sachs through an infection following a self-induced abortion, Sanger spent three weeks of backbreaking work in the heat of a tenement where every drop of water had to be carried up three flights of stairs. Mrs. Sachs lived to beg to be told how to prevent another pregnancy. The doctor was "a kindly man . . . but such incidents had become so familiar to him that he had long since lost whatever delicacy he might once have had." "Tell Jake to sleep on the roof."

Several months later Sanger was called back to the Sachs apartment to find Sadie in a coma following another abortion. For Sanger her death symbolized the blindness of father, husband, male doctors, and fellow radicals to the needs of women. She resolved never "to go back to merely keeping alive" and to do something to change "the destiny of mothers whose miseries were as vast as the sky."[36]

Sanger used the Sachs story with great effect in her campaigns for birth control. One historian has suggested that the story represents "a common autobiographical ploy of reformers," a self-justifying myth that often obscures complex motivation.[37] Whether or not Sadie Sachs actually existed, or her story represented a composite of several experiences, some of them perhaps borrowed from other nurses, is beyond proof. The abortion problem was real, and Sanger's portrayal of the attitude of physicians toward contraception was accurate, although there were a few doctors who argued that the poor wanted and could effectively use contraceptive information. Sanger's intense reaction to the abortion problem sprang, in part, from her belief that many of her contemporaries, although sympathetic toward the poor, were indifferent to the special plight of women. Her description of tenement life contrasts with the picture drawn by the journalist Hutchins Hapgood in *Spirit of the Ghetto* (1902). Hapgood described a colorful, aspiring, and self-reliant people on the way up, whose rich culture and religious values not only made tenement life endurable but reflected a redeeming sense of community lacking in American culture. He made no mention of lines of women queued up in front of abortion mills.

On the Lower East Side both hope and social mobility were realities, as were defeat and despair. But the contrast between the Sanger and the Hapgood visions of life in the Jewish ghetto helps to explain the uncompromising resentment Sanger felt toward other reformers who were less concerned about the plight of women. Thirty-four and the tubercular mother of three, Sanger's feeling of having been trapped by marriage made the suffering of tenement mothers her own. There seemed to be no justice for these women, whose "weary misshapen bodies, always ailing, never failing, were destined to be thrown on the scrap heap before they were thirty-five." Neither the radical nor liberal imagination envisioned a basically different situation for women. A distinctively female voice was needed. Women "had to be made aware of how they were being shackled, and roused to mutiny." [38]

Raising the female consciousness of working women would only lead to frustration, Sanger believed, unless effective contraceptive means were available. She decided that her first task was to find an effective birth control method that depended entirely on the woman. Douching, spermicidal mixtures, tampons, and cervical caps all found advocates in the nineteenth century, but these methods had never been studied systematically, and even middle-class women had great difficulty in obtaining reliable contraceptive information. Better information on contraception could be obtained from an anarchist leaflet than from a medical journal. [39]

Sanger claimed to have spent almost a year searching without success in American libraries for the birth control method she needed. There was no clinically tested, medically recognized, easily available female method. Bill Haywood suggested that she continue her search in France and offered to introduce her to Victor Dave, the hero of French syndicalism who had helped Emma Goldman in 1901. Sanger had already resolved to ask her husband for a divorce. He wanted to paint in Paris, and this experiment provided a gentle way of gaining a separation. Selling the house at Hasting-on-Hudson to finance the trip, the Sangers left for Europe in October 1913. She returned to New York in late December, leaving Bill behind to paint.[40]

Bill's letters to his wife from Paris provide an intimate account of their debate over woman's rights and proper role. He offered his services for the new journal she was planning but refused to believe that pursuit of her cause justified ending their relationship and insisted that, as the mother of his three children, she belonged to him. Her attitude toward him, he argued, had been distorted by her friends in "this *so* called *Labor Revolutionary Movement* in New York'" which was nothing but "sexuality under cover of Revolution" and "a Saturnalia of Sexualism—Deceit-fraud and Jesuitism let loose." She replied that she wanted to stand alone and to establish herself as a professional reformer, free to pursue her cause wherever it took her. She claimed the right to have relationships with those men with whom she developed a sense of spiritual kinship through mutual interest. Sexual intercourse was simply one possible result of spiritual communion. Bill repeated his determination to "stand on the old ground—they call me conservative but if Revolution means promiscuity—they can call me a conservative and make the most of it." In France, he wrote, the anarchist movement had a serious intellectual tone, was "clean" and "dignified."

> Do you realize why I hate New York. And why I loathe even the thought of going back. Why these papier Mâché Revolutionaries . . . have branded me an 'institutional' husband holding you in marital subjection with three children! Forsooth this must be broken if this family is too damn happy to suit us. Why—the family is passing—their mother must be freed!
> I know there are a few that would be glad to be 'institu-

tionalized' with a marriage certificate—if they were given the chance—But I'm not a lover—I'm a 'husband' to them! The coming months *you are to prove whether I am the one or the other or both or neither.*[41]

Margaret had already decided that Bill would be neither lover nor husband. He returned to New York in the fall of 1914 and made a career as a moderately successful painter. After much bitterness on his part, she finally obtained a divorce in 1920.

In the future, her relationships with men would be based on common interests and attraction. She had resolved that her life would be defined by the needs of her cause and not by the demands of any man. She had many lovers but realized that as a sexual reformer she could not afford to be labeled promiscuous. Her affairs usually ended without rancor. Often an abiding tenderness and mutual respect remained for years. Her public career provided a justification for personal freedom in an age when women were not supposed to enjoy untrammeled lives of their own. But the private life also provided an inspiration for the public career. Sanger had learned that the joys of flesh and of spirit were one; women in control of themselves held the key to a more abundant life, and she meant to spread the good news to all of her sisters. In 1936, Mabel Dodge Luhan recalled Sanger's influence:

I really got something from her, something new and releasing and basic. Nina and I, I remember, had a wonderful talk with her one evening—just the three of us at dinner—when she told us all about the possibilities in the body for "sex expression"; and as she sat there, serene and quiet, and unfolded the mysteries of physical love, it seemed to us we had never known it before as a sacred and at the same time a scientific reality.[42]

Sanger returned from Europe in early 1914 armed with French pessaries, formulas for suppositories and douches, and new determination to defy the Comstock laws. Her first task, she believed, was to raise the consciousness of working women so that they would support her demand for free dissemination of birth control information. In March 1914 she published the first issue of *The Woman Rebel*, with the old anarchist slogan "No God, No Masters!" tacked to the mast. Subscribers recruited through labor union lists and notices in radical journals heard in eight issues of the degradation of labor through overproduction of children. The *Rebel* bitterly denounced "the diseased, perverted, hypocritical ghouls of American civilization," "the Baptist Church and its allies, those 'Christian Associations,' that are subsidized by the Rockefellers and other criminals in order to kill the spirit of the workers of America." Readers were exhorted to remember Ludlow, the Colorado strike against Standard Oil during which thirteen members of strikers' families were killed by state militia. "Remember the men and women and children who were sacrified in order that John D. Rockefeller, Jr. might continue his noble career of charity and philanthropy as a supporter of the Christian faith."[43]

Max Eastman, editor of *The Masses*, found Sanger's "overconscious extremism" irritating and complained that "the Woman Rebel seems to give a little more strength to the business of shocking the Bourgeoisie than the Bourgeoisie are really worth." Emma Goldman, however, approved the *Rebel*'s tone; the journal sold splendidly at anarchist lectures, "as the subject you are treating is really the main thing people are interested in. Not one of my lectures brings out such a crowd as the one on the birth strike. . . ."[44]

The *Rebel* devoted most of its space to calls for autonomy for women. Sanger believed that a great revolution was building in women's expectations about themselves. This awakening had found expression in renewed demands for the vote. But suffrage, Sanger argued, was a superficial reform and had little appeal to the working woman. More advanced women believed in changes "more psychological" in effect. They wanted "the right to work! the right to ignore fashions, the right to keep her [sic] own name, and such poor longings of a bourgeois class suffering for loss of vitality." Sanger knew many cloak makers, scrubwomen, domestics, and shop workers, "who would gladly change places with those women who wanted the right to work." Successful professional women like Katharine B. Davis, New York City's commissioner of corrections, treated radical women just as harshly as male officials. Women social workers tried to teach working-class women "a slave morality" of courtesy, punctuality, loyalty, honesty, duty, "ask no questions but obey when you are told." This kind of philanthropy sought to make "these girls a tame, life-less, spiritless mass without personality or life—and as Nietzsche says, a guilty-grunting domestic animal." Sanger wanted to provide a counterpropaganda, to teach the working woman "only to sell her labor to the boss—not her morality— It's none of his business if she's courteous, loyal, honest, du-tiful, obedient." Just as the working woman had to "fight for this right to retain her own morality and psychology—so must she fight for the right to own and control her own body . . . to do with it as she desires—and it's no one's business what those desires may be." [45]

While denouncing the "slave morality" of the middle class, Sanger expected liberated women to adhere to a demanding code of conduct. Self-rule "naturally involves a high standard of idealism as well as knowledge of the prevention of disease and conception. It is none of Society's business what a woman shall do with her body unless she should inflict upon Society the consequences of her acts, like venereal disease or off-spring—then Society is concerned and it is its right to be con-cerned." [46] Her essential demand was that women be allowed to become free moral individuals, self-directed in both work and their relationships with others. Most of the do-gooders she despised intended no less. During the 1920s, Katharine B. Davis, as director of the Rockefeller-funded Bureau of Social Hygiene, played an important part in enlightened efforts to make information on venereal disease and contraception avail-able to working women. In 1914, however, Sanger saw only hypocrisy in both institutionalized reform and accepted stan-dards of sexual conduct. Her demand for birth control was a first step in a revolt against the paternalistic feminine models imposed by a petrified social code. She insisted that the energy released as women learned to develop their special sensibil-ities and powers would remake society. Just how was not clear. For the moment hatred of the existing order made its transformation seem inevitable. [47]

Postal authorities declared the first issue of *The Woman Rebel* unmailable even though no specific contraceptive advice had been given. By mailing the journal in small batches all over the city, Sanger evaded the Post Office censorship. Subscriptions increased rapidly, letters came in from feminists all over the world, and she prepared *Family Limitation*, a pamphlet providing detailed contraceptive information. The federal government indicted Sanger for violation of the postal code after the August issue of *Rebel* carried an article on assassination that "was vague, inane, and innocuous, and had no bearing on my policy except to taunt the Government to take action." Facing a possible forty-five years in prison on nine counts of violating the federal law against mailing obscene material, she found a radical printer willing to take a "Sing Sing job" and had 10,000 copies of *Family Limitation* printed, bundled, and prepared for release. When the judge refused to postpone her trial, she left for Europe in October 1914, leaving the children with Bill, who had just returned from France. She wired her friends from aboard ship to release *Family Limitation*.[48]

When Sanger returned to the United States in 1916, her case had been widely publicized, and the government refused to prosecute. But by then she had decided to open a birth control clinic. The guardians of public morality were to have no rest.

CHAPTER 7 **European Models**

$\mathbf{M}$ARGARET SANGER'S year of exile in Europe marked a turning point in her career. She found new models of reform, gained valuable friends and contributors—both financial and intellectual—met a perfect lover and spiritual counselor, and at last found a contraceptive device in which women could place complete confidence.

On arrival in London she wrote to Dr. Charles Vickery Drysdale (1874–1961), who was running the nearly moribund Malthusian League from his suburban home. The nephew of Dr. George Drysdale (1824–1904; author of *The Elements of Social Science*, the "textbook" of neo-Malthusianism) and the son of Dr. Charles Robert Drysdale (1829–1907) and Dr. Alice Vickery (1844–1929), both presidents of the league, C. V. Drysdale represented an established tradition of freethinking utilitarianism begun by Jeremy Bentham and Francis Place (1771–1854).[1]

Place, primarily concerned with awakening the working classes to their own interest, had been disappointed by his failure to persuade labor leaders that overlarge families were a cause of poverty, but he had made a convert of Robert Dale Owen, who later started a number of American physicians on careers as sex reformers. Other Place converts included John Stuart Mill, arrested at seventeen for distributing birth control pamphlets, and Richard Carlile (1790–1843), the first in a line of radical agitators in the atheistic, republican, neo-

Malthusian tradition. Although the neo-Malthusians got tremendous publicity during the prosecution and trial of Charles Bradlaugh and Annie Besant (1877–1878) for republishing Knowlton's *Fruits of Philosophy*, by the early twentieth century those who continued to discuss poverty in the formulas of the old political economy were left isolated by the emergence of an effective trade union movement that showed how living standards could be improved through organization, and by the success of the competing ideologies of Fabian and Marxian socialism.[2]

Neo-Malthusianism was a doctrine left over from the world of nineteenth century liberalism, able to command respect in the twentieth century only as the economics of growth developed by the heir of classical economics, John Maynard Keynes, proved inadequate in a world of expanding population and shrinking resources. In 1914 the great days of Marxist and Keynesian economics lay ahead, and those who insisted that poverty and population growth were inextricably connected found few listeners.[3]

C. V. Drysdale provided Margaret Sanger with an enthusiastic welcome badly needed by a "lonely soul." Drysdale's mother, Alice Vickery, one of the first women to practice medicine in Britain and, at seventy, still a hard worker in the suffrage movement, found the American a room next to her ivy-covered home in Hampstead Gardens, and spent hours with her talking over the history of the woman's movement, old free-speech and family-limitation fights, and the future of reform. Through Dr. Vickery, Sanger was invited to lecture at Fabian Hall and gained supporters among leading British intellectuals. In addition to tangible aid, she found a new style of reform aimed at educating social leaders rather than appealing to the silent masses. She still believed in "direct action," but her accent changed. She had found a genteel activism that suited her.[4]

One of Sanger's new friends saw to it that she received an invitation to tea from Havelock Ellis (1859–1939), author of the encyclopaedic *Studies in the Psychology of Sex* (1897–1910) and the world's leading prophet of sexual enlightenment. Ellis was a great naturalist in the "English amateur" tradition—a collector of case histories and careful classifier, who was criticized by Freud for his unwillingness to generalize from the masses of data he collected. Ellis, in turn, found the Viennese Jew's dogmatism grating and advised a young friend contemplating psychoanalytic training to follow Freud's example rather than his theory, and make up his own system. More artist than rationalist, Ellis believed fetishism to be "the supreme triumph of human idealism," and showed in his studies that sexual values were a function of culture—different in other places and other times. Moreover, by showing the broad range of deviations common to Western cultures, he demonstrated the inadequacy of accepted definitions of normality.[5]

Ellis' delight in the infinite variety of human sexual expression provided a startling contrast to the Victorian and Freudian view that sexual drives were dangerous and required careful discipline. Why, he asked, should "people be afraid of rousing passions which, after all, are the great driving forces of human life?" In a "sane natural order, all the impulses are centered in the fulfillment of needs and not in their denial." Rather than an ethical imperative, abstinence was an aesthetic exercise, part of the "art of love" which involved the cultivation of desires through a discreet blend of license and abstinence. Sexual expression should be governed by "the gracious equilibrium of Nature. And the force, we see, which naturally holds this balance even is the biological fact that the act of sexual union is the satisfaction of the erotic needs, not of one person, but of two persons."[6]

Ellis questioned almost every tenet of Victorian sexual morality and anticipated many of the findings documented since by behavioral scientists, including infant sexuality, universal masturbation in both sexes, the androgynous nature of sexual response, the myth of female asexuality, and the psychological sources of male impotence and female frigidity. Ellis, in contrast to Freud, provided a view of sexuality congenial to feminism. Penis envy was not very important in his view; indeed, "The sexual impulse is not, as some have imagined, the sole root of the most massive human emotions, the most brilliant human aptitudes—of sympathy, of art, of religion. In the complex human organism, where all the parts are so many fibred and so closely interwoven, no great manifestation can be reduced to a single source." While sexual drives were "the

91

deepest and most volcanic of human impulses," they "can, to a large extent, be transmuted into a new force capable of the strangest and most varied use." The mystic Ellis believed there were no sexual imperatives; even the profoundest love did not require overt coital expression.[7]

Ellis' views on sex reflected a personal quest for self-understanding. His father had been a sea captain seldom home, and even then only a guest in his wife's house. His childhood was dominated by a pietistic mother, none of whose four daughters ever married, and whose only son had great difficulty in combining love with sexual response. Extremely shy, he was troubled in adolescence by wet dreams, then viewed as a debilitating disease in medical texts, and resolved at sixteen to make sex research his life's work. His mother's religious values were transmuted into a remarkable devotion to plain living, high thinking, and the independent pursuit of truth. Although Ellis had many passionate friendships with women, premature ejaculation prevented satisfactory coitus until he was over sixty, in his relationship with Françoise Delisle, his second wife.

He was not, however, sexually inactive. When Ellis was twelve, visiting a fair with his mother, she asked him to keep watch while she urinated, standing. Thereafter, Ellis enjoyed "a slight strain of urolagnia," sexual excitement in viewing a woman urinating. He claimed urolagnia "never developed into a real perversion nor ever became a dominant interest," but "my vision of this function became in some degree attached to my feeling of tenderness toward women—I was surprised how often women responded to it sympathetically."[8] In what Ellis described as "my finest piece of poetic prose," "A Revelation," a description published in 1924 of his relationship with an American poetess, he hinted at his method of lovemaking:

> . . . it was only by intimate contact that one might know or divine the scent and the taste of the mysterious salts and essences that distilled from the guarded places of her form and helped to suggest the firm underlying structure beneath a shape that at first seemed so ethereal, befitting large appetites and a great thirst for water or for wine. . . .[9]

Ellis confided in his autobiography, "I have never been the victim of any definite morbid impulse, phobia, or obsession, but the mother liquid out of which such things crystallise is forever flowing in my veins."[10] Françoise Delisle, with whom he eventually fulfilled all the Freudian imperatives of normal coitus, described how Ellis introduced her to cunnilingus and brought her sexual satisfaction for the first time, although she had already been married twice and had borne two sons.

> But presently it was time to go. I said so, and proceeded to his bedroom . . . to put on my hat and coat. . . . But he had recently declared that he would 'have to look after me better in future!' So he followed me to minister to my needs . . . and did this in so unexpected a fashion as to reduce me to utter bashfulness, but delicious bashfulness, . . . as I stood in front of him and he, on his knees, let me caress the glorious head fully accessible to my hand. . . . Henceforth we were more than friends, not withstanding the bashfulness . . . that day he lent me *Sex in Relation to Society.*

The first time they "were naked in each other's arms," she

> expected the marital act I had so far known, but now with a man I truly loved. There was therefore, a slight dread when this did not happen. . . . This 'travail' of my soul proved the birth of my new being: Woman at last, woman in soul. On that bed, in broad daylight, his hands and his kisses, never jerking me with fear, tenderly brought me to this delight.[11]

In 1953, Vincent Brome, a biographer of H. G. Wells, wrote to Margaret Sanger asking about her relationship with Ellis. Was he impotent? Sanger pointed out that she was "still out of the grave," the president of the new International Planned Parenthood Federation, and passionately hated by Communists and Catholics; any admission of intimacy with Ellis would have results "most unfavorable to the cause with which my name is linked." As to Ellis' sexual prowess, she wrote, "in 1914 to 1920 when I first knew him, he was alive, alert to all physical impulses and delights, as his relationship with two other women testified." She did not see how premature ejaculation could be equated with impotence, since "then about 65 percent of the American men could be called sexually impotent." Ellis had told her of this problem, "one which made him feel that he could not be a satisfactory lover," but she and Françoise Delisle agreed

> That there are various means of receiving physical satisfaction . . .
> the important thing to make the union perfect or satisfactory is not
> alone the physical method, but the reverence and the spiritual
> one-ness created through the physical contact. This was a subject
> . . . Havelock and I often discussed. . . . [12]

From their first meeting in December 1914, Margaret Sanger and Havelock Ellis found a complete compatibility. To the homesick refugee from Comstockery he seemed "a veritable God," while Ellis, living in "retirement and loneliness" while his wife toured America telling of the joys of detached marriage, never formed a friendship so quickly. Within weeks she was his "delicious and gorgeous" passion. "I still love all that I have loved, and even if I loved another I should still love you." When she forgot her purse in his apartment he wrote: "I fear that that money bag . . . is not safe as it ought to be—I've no objection to women leaving *liquid* gold behind." [13]

Ellis' wife, a diabetic, suffered a physical and nervous breakdown on her American tour, after he innocently wrote her of his good fortune in finding a new friend. Edith Ellis died shortly after her return to England. A large portion of Ellis' autobiography is devoted to justifying his relationship with his first wife. He could never quite escape a sense of guilt over her death, and commented, ". . . beautiful as my new friend [Margaret Sanger] was to me and continues to be to this day, I have sometimes been tempted to wish that I had not met her." [14]

For Margaret Sanger there were no regrets. Under Ellis' guidance she developed a more cautious and prudent propaganda, couched in the language of social science but with even greater emotional appeal. Ellis provided a model of the ideal man and an interpretation of human sexuality in which woman's equality and right to self-determination were recognized.

Sanger believed that her ideas about releasing womankind from biological slavery could not be translated into practical action until a completely effective birth control method was found. Neo-Malthusian propaganda attributed the low infant and maternal mortality rates in Holland to the ready availability of contraceptive services. Dr. Aletta Jacobs (1854–1929), Holland's first woman physician and its representative to the Women's Peace Conference being organized at the Hague by Jane Addams, had opened a contraceptive clinic for the poor in Amsterdam in 1882 and had introduced an improved spring-loaded pessary that was completely effective when properly fitted. In 1915 there were about fifty midwives or other "practitioners" who fitted pessaries.[15]

Despite C. V. Drysdale's letter of introduction, Dr. Jacobs refused to see Margaret Sanger, pointing to her lack of professional credentials. Dr. Johannes Rutgers (1851–1924), secretary of the Malthusian League, let Sanger attend the regular classes for midwives he gave, and she learned to fit pessaries.[16]

Sanger claimed in her autobiography that her visit to Holland taught her that birth control would have to be a medical service. Thus, making contraception available to everyone was no longer simply "a free speech fight." In *Family Limitation,* however, written before her exile, she recommended the pessary as the best method. "Any nurse or doctor will teach one how to adjust it; then women can teach each other."[17] She did find a better pessary in Holland and was probably impressed with the importance of trained personnel in effective fitting.

Her shift of strategy as a reformer, however, from the woman rebel model she got from Emma Goldman to the nurse-mother lobbying among social and professional elites, did not result from any technological imperative. Rather, the image she projected began to change under the influence of Ellis and the Drysdales. On her return to the United States the people who supported her cause were the "bourgeois do-gooders" so despised by her old comrades. Radicals, in turn, preoccupied by the war and persecuted for their opposition to it, offered little help. Worse, she thought, they lived in a world of myths. Bill Haywood wrote her from Leavenworth that the revolution was coming, despite appearances to the contrary.

> You remember what I said at the subway station one evening about "it coming." Margaret all my dreams are coming true. My work is being fulfilled. Millions of workers are seeing the light. Russia, Poland, Germany, France, Great Britain, Australia, South America, we have lived to see the breaking of the glorious Red

Dawn. . . . The world revolution is born, the change is here. We will of course not live to see it in its perfection. But it is good to have been living at this period.[18]

Sanger opposed the war and saw no better world coming from the carnage. She realized, however, that effectiveness as a reformer depended on limiting herself to one issue. As she explained to a friend in 1917:

The other pioneers have all made the same mistake; they have not concentrated on the one object to the exclusion of everything else. Their work was important, but their sacrifice was in vain. I am determined to bide my time, consolidate my forces, continue my studies, my lectures, my letters to the countless women who are writing me every week, . . . until this madness is ended and one can think and work with the hope that something may be accomplished.[19]

CHAPTER 8   **Competition for Leadership**

WHEN Margaret Sanger returned to the United States in October 1915, "Birth Control" blared out from the cover of the *Pictorial Review* at the first newsstand she passed.[1] While she was away an *agent provocateur* from the New York Society for the Suppression of Vice had tricked William Sanger into giving him a copy of *Family Limitation*. Her first reaction was anger at Bill; perhaps he was trying to martyr himself to win her back. Anthony Comstock hoped Bill would tell his wife's hiding place in order to escape prison. Instead, the entrapment made martyrs of both Sangers, drew the active support of wealthy women, and helped create a circus atmosphere in which over twenty sympathizers were arrested for distributing birth control literature. Comstock died of a chill caught at the trial. Bill got thirty days.[2]

The Sangers' youngest child, Peggy, died of pneumonia in November. Public sympathy made the federal attorney hesitant to prosecute Mrs. Sanger on the old *Family Limitation* charge. She made headlines by repeatedly demanding a trial. After Elsie Clews Parsons, the Columbia anthropologist, suggested that "twenty-five women who had practiced birth control should stand up in court . . . and plead guilty before the law," and a distinguished group of British intellectuals wired the anglophile President Wilson that "such work as that of

97

Mrs. Sanger receives appreciation and circulation in every civilized country except the United States of America," the pro-
secutor realized that the legal soundness of his case was irrelevant and dropped the charges, despite Sanger's refusal in court
to promise not to break the law again.[3]

Despite her public visibility, Sanger found that others interested in the cause expected her to forfeit leadership to them.
Although plans for a birth control league had been announced
in *The Woman Rebel*, the first National Birth Control League
had been formed during Sanger's exile by a group of liberal
New York women who wanted nothing to do with anarchists
and hoped to appeal to a large public by campaigning to repeal
obnoxious laws rather than by breaking them.[4]

The leader of this group, Mary Ware Dennett (1872–1947),
came from old New England stock, had married a Harvard
man, and worked with her architect husband as an interior
decorator. She became active in the suffrage movement, obtained a divorce and custody of their three children in 1913,
and served from 1910 to 1914 as an executive secretary of the
National Woman Suffrage Association. A worker in many
good causes, in 1916 Dennett was field secretary for the American Union against Militarism and campaigned for Woodrow
Wilson's reelection. After the United States entered the war,
she resigned as executive secretary of the Women's Section of
the Democratic National Committee to become a leader of the
antiwar movement in New York and an organizer in the campaign of Morris Hillquit, the Socialist candidate for mayor.[5]

The National Birth Control League, formed in March 1915,
accomplished little during its first year of existence under Dennett's leadership except to recruit members with the help of
the *Woman Rebel* subscription list. On her return, Sanger approached the new group to find out how much support she
could expect. Dennett told her that her group did not approve
of her tactics, and the two women began a competition for
leadership of the birth control movement that lasted for ten
years.[6]

Sanger interpreted the rescinding of the federal charges
against her and the letters of support pouring in from all over
the country as vindication for her strategy of flamboyant defiance. She circulated a letter asking for donations to continue

distribution of *Family Limitation*, announced plans to establish birth control clinics where "All married women or women old enough to be married will be admitted free and without question," and set off on a whirlwind tour—delivering the same speech 119 times, fighting rousing battles with Roman Catholics in St. Louis and Akron, and going to jail in Portland for distributing *Family Limitation*.[7]

The 1916 tour kept Sanger and birth control in the headlines, but the newspapers were exploiting a serious public need. Everywhere Sanger was besieged by people of all classes. Profoundly disturbed by her daughter's death, she needed to lose herself in her cause, but still longed sometimes, she later remembered,

> to avoid people for a few hours. . . . It was not to avoid Mothers. It was just weary, sleepless, humdrum of meeting people in crowds—I loved meeting the mothers—but the people I was meeting were Society Club women and Social Workers . . . Everywhere always asking about *morals*, the Yellow Peril—the nonsense of confusing contraception with abortion, over and over and over again—and always *behind* these questions was the desire to know *what* was the safest method.

The people that she wanted to reach were often afraid to approach her in public. Some came to her hotel, "working couples—kind good husbands wanting to know how 'the wife' could get 'safe' information—Sometimes it was as early as seven on the way to work—They came unannounced, just knocked at the door and expected to be welcome and they always were."[8]

Sanger believed that the way to help working people was to establish birth control clinics and to defy the law openly. Dennett, however, argued that the time had come when legislators would be willing to remove contraception from the obscenity laws. While Sanger was grabbing headlines, Dennett organized a lobby in Albany against the New York state law prohibiting the provision of contraceptive information.[9]

The failure of the National Birth Control League's 1917 effort to change the New York law revealed a pattern of resistance that was to continue until 1965 in New York and 1971 in the national legislature. Dennett assumed that what legislators practiced in private they would endorse in public. She offended some congressmen in 1924 by pointing out that the 225 congressional families averaged 2.7 children each. One hundred sixty-six Congressmen had three or fewer children, the largest number were in the one- and two-child categories. Approached privately, many legislators admitted that family limitation was a good thing, but most of them were quick to add, "I can't afford to touch it."[10]

Dennett noted that congressmen, like most citizens, wanted information on birth control but did not want to make themselves "conspicuous in getting it." ". . . the sticking point with them was that they would have to be conspicuous in regard to it, if they sponsored the bill or voted it out of committee." "The levity, the stupidity, and the irrelevance" of the responses of legislators to sincere efforts at lobbying infuriated serious women. As Sanger complained in 1921, "we did expect something more among men elected to public office than the embarrassed giggle of the adolescent, the cynical indecency of the gangster, in the consideration of a serious sexual and social problem." [11]

Legislators offered the same excuses for inaction again and again, and attempts to explain why objections to change in the law were invalid failed to move them. They warned that no one would have children if they could be avoided; there would be a terrible decline in moral standards; birth control information was already available to those who really wanted it; the rich already had too few children and the ignorant poor were beyond help; finally, Roman Catholics were hostile and organized. [12]

In 1917 and 1918, Dennett lobbied without success in Albany. After a state legislator pointed out that the New York law followed the federal example, she decided that the only sensible tactic would be to seek repeal of the relevant portion of the Comstock Act rather than lobbying separately in each state. In 1919, Dennett formed a new organization, the Voluntary Parenthood League, and began work in Washington. A federal bill was introduced in 1923 and 1924, but never got out of committee. [13]

Meanwhile, a group led by Sanger lobbied in New York in 1921, 1923, 1924, and 1925 for a "doctors only" bill that simply recognized the right of physicians to give contraceptive information. None of these bills got out of committee. Despite the failure of the "doctors only" bill in New York, many of Dennett's contributors were convinced that the Sanger bill was the only one with any chance of success. In 1925, Dennett quit the Voluntary Parenthood League. Her salary was in arrears, but the real reason was lack of support for her "free speech" bill among her supporters. After Dennett's resignation, the Voluntary Parenthood League existed only on paper, and Sanger gained unchallenged leadership of the birth control movement. Dennett poured out her chagrin against irrational laws and opportunistic reformers in *Birth Control Laws* (1926) and won new fame in 1929 as the author of a sex education pamphlet that ran afoul of Comstockery.[14]

Dennett attached great importance to a clean repeal of the laws against contraception. Anything less was dishonest. She did not see how a "radical" like Sanger could campaign for "class and special-privilege legislation" establishing a "medical monopoly" in contraception. "[W]ould it not be best," she asked, "to have the laws simply provide an open field, and let the dignified authoritative scientists compete with the quacks and the spurious folk with faith that eventually the best would win, very much as the increased public knowledge of general hygiene is steadily putting quackery into the background."[15]

Sanger was willing to compromise on the kind of legislation that she supported because she realized that she needed all the medical help she could get. Only by making concessions to the self-conscious professionalism of doctors could she recruit the trained personnel needed if a national system of birth control clinics was to be established. *Family Limitation* went through ten printings between 1914 and 1925. Self-help methods were described, but the most effective female method, the vaginal diaphragm, required skilled fitting. In the United States the idea of using paramedical personnel to deliver secondary services was an anathema to organized medicine. Physicians demanded that "the quacks and spurious folks," as well as any other competitors, be put out of business. The price of medical acceptance of contraception was formal recognition of a medical monopoly on the new service. Besides, nothing could bring greater prestige to contraception than to have it associated with the triumphant magic of medical science. Sanger's bill not only provided a rebuttal to the claim that birth control undermined morals, it offered a necessary concession to medical egos. For most people birth control might remain a matter of self-help, but Sanger's approach mitigated the hostility of organized medicine, associated contraception with science, and made it possible for sympathetic doctors to cooperate by reducing the grounds for censure by colleagues.

Sanger's differences with Dennett, however, went beyond the kind of legislation needed. She had little faith in legislation. Contraception was not removed from the Comstock Act's prohibitions until 1971, after four years of effort by Representative James H. Scheuer of New York, who became involved when a customs officer made one of his constituents throw her diaphragm into the harbor before entering the country. Despite dozens of efforts, no bill to amend the law in New York got out of committee until 1965, when the intervention of Mayor Robert Wagner made possible the passage of an innocuous bill, which still prohibited the display of contraceptives in drug stores and their sale to minors.[16]

The legislative process could be useful, Sanger believed, in publicizing her cause and educating the public. She found the committee system of legislation much better suited to public debate than to passing laws. Birth control bills did not get out of committee because legislators, by disappearing when a quorum was needed and by other parliamentary devices, used the committee system as a means of escaping the necessity of publicly declaring themselves for or against birth control with their votes.[17] Although this behavior angered Sanger, she realized that favorable legislative action would not precede great changes in public opinion. As she explained in 1919, changes in law follow changes in "expressed general sentiment."[18] Only agitation, education, and organization would make favorable legislation possible.

Agitation through violation of the law was the key to the public which would ultimately make the other tactics workable. We hold the law as rather a sacred thing, and the only way that you can awaken people to the question that was before us, was to challenge that thing which all of us hold sacred. That arouses attention, and when this is done, then we come to plan the means of giving the message and educating. So the process goes, agitate, educate, organize, and legislate.[19]

Breaking the law also provided access to the courts, another public forum, but more important, a forum in which the political power of Roman Catholics would be minimized. It was through the courts that Sanger eventually established the right of physicians to receive contraceptive devices through the mails.[20]

Sanger bested Dennett in the competition for leadership of the birth control movement in part because she was better at capturing the public imagination, a master of the dramatic, and a skillful exploiter of the media and of uncommonly silly laws. But Sanger also had a more realistic understanding of the reform process. Dennett's faith that legislators would remove hypocritical laws was naive. A diary kept by Sanger's lobbyists during their 1926 congressional campaign reveals the barriers faced by women reformers.[21] They interviewed every senator and many congressmen. Senator Albert A. Cummins of Iowa had cosponsored Dennett's bill in the previous session, but he frankly admitted that he would not reintroduce the bill because, he explained, "it was difficult to get men to consider the subject seriously—that it still seemed a joke." Secretary of Labor James J. Davis was very friendly and believed in birth control, but said that he "could not actively work for us, as it would embarrass the President. Telegrams would come from all the Roman Catholics in the country asking to have him removed from office . . . but he felt the subject of great value to the nation." Senator Lynn J. Frazier of North Dakota at first seemed willing to introduce a bill, then said,

> . . . that he had been consulting with politicians who were interested in his political work and that the advice had been to him not to introduce the bill, that it would hurt his political career . . . in so many words [he said] there was no political gain in the introduction and sponsorship of it, but the prospect of a great loss.

In an effort to change Senator Frazier's mind, the women lobbyists approached his friend, Senator George Norris. The notes on the interview are worth quoting at length:

We had a long talk to the effect that he thought it would be a great mistake for Senator Frazier to introduce the bill, because he is not regular [a party-line Republican], and would do more harm than good to the subject. I argued this point with him, to the effect that we could not get Senators who had wide political influence to be interested in its introduction and where they had Catholic constituents it was impossible to get them to consider it. Said he did not believe we would ever get it passed through the Senate. For instance [he said]: "I approached Senator Copeland [Royal S. Copeland of New York, an M.D.] to find out how he stood on the subject of Birth Control, without letting him know my opinion. I was surprised to find him say: 'Well, there are two sides of the question and they are controversial. I am not sure, as a physician, whether it is advisable.' But when I told him I was in favor of it, he spoke entirely different—so you see, that even those in the Senate who are in favor of it in their hearts haven't the courage or do not care to publicly support Birth Control."

Senator Norris confided that the hearing on Dennett's bill (Cummins-Vaille Bill) had been the laughingstock of the cloak-room for several days. Dennett was assured of the support of several senators who confessed to their colleagues that they were absolutely opposed but simply enjoyed humoring her.

Although the birth control lobbyists got some respectful hearings and rational responses to their arguments, ridiculous responses were also frequent and pointed to the fact that legislative campaigns were more useful for publicity and to educate the public than for changing the law. Senator W. H. McMaster of South Dakota said, "You cannot cheat Nature. I do not think it should be left to the whim of woman to decide whether she shall have children or not." Senator James E. Watson of Indiana declared "that he believed that everyone who was born was born because of an accident and not because they were wanted. He felt that if the law was amended . . . it would permit the women to have more lap-dogs and encourage the idle to be still more idle."

Faced with this pervasive resistance to reform, Sanger concluded that the only solution was constant agitation by all available means until birth control became an everyday topic that could be rationally discussed in public forums. When G. Stanley Hall (1844–1924), psychologist and author of the pioneering study of adolescence, the man who as president of Clark University brought Freud to America in 1909, was asked to join the Massachusetts Birth Control League in 1916, his pained reply spoke for a whole generation for whom sex was a problem.

> I regret to say that I cannot give the use of my name in connection with your work. If you want to know why, I will tell you frankly that I have borne my share of *odium sexicum* for almost a generation of men. Some fifteen years ago I wrote a book on adolescence advocating what I believed was true and right, and for that have been pilloried severely and ostracized by some of my friends. The same was true because I went into the sex instruction movement with Morrow [Prince Albert Morrow, M.D., leader of the social hygiene movement]. I have done my bit in this movement and now I am retiring and am going to have a rest from this trouble for the remainder of my life.[22]

Margaret Sanger understood that reform would only come after birth control became a daily topic of conversation, removed by commonness from the context of nastiness and fear in which G. Stanley Hall's generation perceived it. Public attention, access to judicial and legislative forums, and changes in the law through judicial decisions all were fruits of "direct action." More important, however, by breaking the law Sanger was able to provide thousands of women with contraceptive services without waiting for legislative action.

CHAPTER 9 **Providing Clinics**

ON October 16, 1916, Margaret Sanger opened the first center for contraceptive instruction in the United States. The "clinic," in the Brownsville section of Brooklyn, was advertised by leaflets in Yiddish, Italian, and English and by defiant press releases. For a fee of ten cents, Sanger and her sister, Ethel Byrne, showed applicants how to use pessaries, condoms, and other contraceptives. A police spy testified that Sanger told her, "the best method of birth control was the covering for the womb. 'There are many womb supporters on the market, costing from seventy-five cents to ten dollars, but I would recommend a pessary called the Mizpah as strongest and cleanest, which costs one dollar and a half to two dollars in any drug store.' She said: 'A doctor or midwife may fit this for you, or if you bring it to me, why, I shall adjust it myself.' "[1]

Sanger apparently fitted some of the 488 women who applied for help in the ten days the clinic remained open. An examination table was confiscated by police. She claimed that she had tried to find a woman doctor to work in her clinic but none dared. In her nationwide tour, however, she had made it clear that the Dutch contraceptive advice centers were staffed by nurses, and the "American Trained Nurse is the best equipped and most capable in the world." The Mizpah pessary was a cervical cap, not as effective as the spring-type vaginal pessary used in Holland, but the latter was not available in the United States. When police raided the clinic they

106

found a two-dollar bill on display which Sanger boasted she received from "a woman spy" for a pessary.[2]

Sanger and her sister had clearly broken Section 1142 of the state penal code, which made it a misdemeanor to give away or sell any information on contraception. Their interpreter and receptionist, Fannia Mindell, arrested under the same ordinance for selling Sanger's pamphlet, "What Every Girl Should Know," which contained no contraceptive advice, had her conviction overturned on appeal by the state appellate court.[3] Sanger argued in her appeal that Section 1142 was unconstitutional because it compelled women to run an unnecessary risk of death in childbirth against their will. Pointing to the correlation between high fertility and poverty, disease, infant mortality, and low intelligence, she argued that the law did not promote the health, welfare, or morals of the community.[4] On first appeal the judge responded to this sociological evidence by emphatically denying that "a woman has the right to copulate with a feeling of security that there will be no resulting conception."[5] On final appeal Judge Frederick Crane noted the social arguments for birth control but rejected the questions they raised as "matters for the legislature and not for the Courts." Crane did feel the need, however, to justify Section 1142, passed in 1873, by noting that in 1881 the legislature added Section 1145 exempting doctors from the prohibition on contraceptive information. This exemption, "the VD clause," was commonly understood to provide tacit justification for the prescription and sale of condoms, as much to protect men in intercourse with prostitutes as to prevent conception. Crane argued, however, that the statute under which Sanger had been arrested was reasonable because there was an exemption for physicians to prescribe contraceptives for the "cure and prevention of disease." In *Webster's International Dictionary,* Crane found a satisfactorily vague definition of disease, "an alteration in the state of the body, or of some of its organs, interrupting or disturbing the performance of vital functions, and causing or threatening pain and sickness, illness, sickness; disorder."[6] In an effort to show the reasonableness of a nineteenth century statute defining contraception as obscenity, Crane established the right of physicians to prescribe contraception, an idea unacceptable to Anthony Comstock.

Sanger and Byrne both spent thirty days in jail, but their challenge to the law had forced its clarification and a more liberal treatment of contraception than the nineteenth century legislature probably intended.[7] Their martyrdom provided fabulous publicity. Ethel Byrne, copying the tactics of the British suffragettes, went on several strikes in prison, and refused for a time to eat, drink, work, or wash, but finally settled on a hunger strike. Because the warden would not let Sanger see her sister, she was able to tell the press that Ethel was dying in a coma, while officials vainly argued she was in better health than when she entered. Sanger, in turn, heroically resisted fingerprinting, which would mean she was a common obscene criminal, and, upon her release, marched off with a crowd of friends singing the *Internationale* to the Plaza Hotel where a "coming out" luncheon was held in her honor.[8]

The United States entered World War I shortly after Sanger's release from prison. Her appeal was not decided until 1918, and it was another five years before she could open a birth control clinic with a physician in charge. In the interval she increased her support by founding the *Birth Control Review* and the American Birth Control League, made a movie that was banned, wrote two best sellers, toured the Far East, and married a millionaire.[9]

Sanger hoped during her imprisonment that other women would follow her example and open birth control information centers. Although lecture dates multiplied, no new clinics appeared. As Sanger realized, "There was no use upbraiding, accusing, or censuring women for not doing what I hoped they might do. The fact was that they did not feel this need as I did, and it was now my job to make them *see* and *feel* it by greater agitation and wider education."[10]

Sanger reconciled herself to the long campaign recommended by her British friends and began to cultivate the favor of "the women of wealth and intelligence," who had shown increasing interest in her cause since the arrest of William Sanger. Mrs. Amos Pinchot and her sister, Mrs. John Sargeant Cram, wife of the public service commissioner, had helped to pay for Bill's defense. Pinchot also paid the fine of Fannia Mindell, the receptionist at Brownsville, and took Sanger to Albany to protest the treatment of her sister before the governor, who listened politely and promised an investigation.[11]

Ethel Byrne resented one club woman who told of "her pride! in knowing the Birth Control sisters! And I thought when I looked at her all done up in her thousand dollars worth of elegance, you should worry: Ain't it a fact."[12] But Sanger accepted and cultivated the support of women like Juliet Rublee and Frances Ackermann, both heiresses, because they were financial angels and loyal workers. Moreover, they allowed Sanger a freedom denied in most reform organizations. As Dorothy Brush later explained, organizational meetings were few and informal, "Margaret was rather like a lion tamer. She kept us each on our boxes until she needed us—then we jumped and jumped fast. Weeks might go by without a word from her. Then perhaps a telephone call and I had to be down at 17 West 16th Street in an hour."[13]

Sanger's friendships with women were seldom relations of equals. She had a great ego and inevitably clashed with other strong-willed women. Nevertheless, "This small committee of personal friends, who loved Margaret (and also excitement and lack of routine) was distinctly successful."[14] The loyalty she inspired allowed Sanger to launch projects without seeking approval beforehand. Her will to dominate finally split the American Birth Control League in 1927. For a decade, however, she led the birth control movement without any serious objections from her financial backers.

Sanger's first clash over money for the cause was with Frederick Blossom, a social worker she met on her 1916 tour. Blossom worked for Cleveland's Associated Charities and got Sanger an invitation to speak at the National Social Workers Congress in Indianapolis. Her speech in Indianapolis led to other speaking engagements and helped make the 1916 tour a success. Blossom, endowed with a wealthy wife, next volunteered to move to New York and help set up an office where the thousands of letters asking for help could be answered and a foundation laid for a national organization. By February 1917, Sanger was able to begin publishing the *Birth Control Review*. Blossom had established an efficient office and a New York Birth Control League, and the future seemed bright for the movement, until he was divorced by his wife, decided he did not need Sanger anymore, and ran off with office furniture, subscription lists, and money that Sanger had raised. Sanger went to the police. Blossom appealed to the Socialists and got a resolution from them denouncing Sanger for turning the law on a comrade. Sanger had had little to do with New York socialism for several years, but the Blossom affair marked her final break with radicals. Juliet Rublee and Frances Ackermann organized the New York Women's Publishing Company to support the *Review*, and in the future its deficits were made up by special contributions from club women.[15]

By 1921, Sanger was ready to establish a national organization that could provide institutional backing for birth control clinics. Having secured letters from interested academicians and medical men testifying to the need for a national conference on birth control, she organized the American Birth Control League from the augmented staff of the *Birth Control Review* and brought a group of notables to New York for a three-day conference, timed to coincide with the convention of the American Public Health Association.[16]

The main event of the National Birth Control Conference was to be an address by Harold Cox, former member of Parliament and editor of the *Edinburgh Review*, an old friend from Sanger's stay with Dr. Alice Vickery. When Sanger and Cox arrived at Town Hall, where he was to conclude the conference with a speech entitled "Birth Control, Is It Moral?" the entrance to the auditorium had been closed by police, who were trying to remove the audience. A near riot ensued, ending with police removing Sanger from the stage and arresting her.[17]

Investigation revealed that the closing of the meeting was arranged by Monsignor Joseph P. Dineen, secretary to Archbishop Patrick J. Hayes, without the knowledge or authorization of any municipal official higher than police precinct captain. Sanger had finally found a worthy successor to Anthony Comstock as chief symbol of the forces of bigotry and repression. Her statements to the press denouncing the Roman Catholic hierarchy as a threat to civil liberty ended in the spectacle of an archbishop debating with a laywoman in the press the question of whether small or large families produced the most geniuses.

In the 1920s the debate over birth control became a focus for ethnic antagonisms that often obscured the relevant issues. At Town Hall, Sanger had been lifted onto the stage by Lothrop Stoddard, the nativist sociologist, and her Irish ancestry made all the more infuriating her mocking of the church's position that women should

> continue to bear children misshapen, deformed, hideous to the eyes, in the hope that Heaven may be filled! It's a monstrous doctrine, abhorrent to every civilized instinct in us. The only comfort I have is to know that the Catholic women themselves have grown out and beyond this medieval doctrine.[18]

Beneath the bombast lay two competing definitions of woman's place in the modern world. Sanger stood for the small family system prevalent among the middle classes, equality for women in the family and in society, and the pursuit of personal satisfaction as a right. The church considered her views antinatalist, reaffirmed that the married woman's place was in the home, her duty was to bear many children, and social duty should always overrule the hedonistic impulses of the individual. Both views appealed to the needs of middle-class Americans who were searching for higher standards of living and greater personal freedom but clung to the ideal of the stable family as a fixed standard in a world of change. The final acceptance of contraception would come only in the form of "family planning," an ambiguous term that conveyed no psychological animus against large families. In the 1920s, however, Sanger profited from both the distaste of native-born Protestants for the high fertility of the foreign born and from the crude attempts of Catholic spokesmen to protect the old family system by suppressing contraceptive practice. Most of all she appealed to the determination of a growing majority of middle-class Americans to have small families without foregoing sex.

The closing of the Town Hall meeting had a boomerang effect.

> The idea of birth control was advertised, dramatized, given column after column of free and favorable publicity. Only a small section of the public had been aware of the first American Birth Control Conference. . . . The clumsy and illegal tactics of our religious opponents broadcast to the whole country what we were doing. Even the most conservative American newspapers were placed in the trying position of defending birth control advocates or endorsing a violation of the principle of freedom of speech.

The day was fast approaching when a birth control clinic could remain open. As Sanger later boasted, "It was no longer my lone fight. It was now a battle of a republic against the machinations of the hierarchy of the Roman Catholic Church."[19] It was the kind of fight Michael Higgins relished.

Town Hall had linked birth control with civil liberty. In 1922, Sanger toured Japan lecturing at the invitation of a group of liberal journalists who also sponsored lecture tours by Bertrand Russell and Albert Einstein. The refusal of the Japanese government to grant her a visa, an obstacle she overcame with the help of Japanese delegates from the Washington Peace Conference whom she befriended on ship, dramatized her mission as an envoy of modern culture opposed by the forces of nationalism and aggression.[20]

The tour of the Far East ended in London, where Sanger attended the Fifth International Neo-Malthusian and Birth Control Conference. There she heard of the birth control clinic opened in March 1921 by Marie Stopes (1880–1958), the University of Manchester paleobotanist turned philosopher of marriage, who had no knowledge of contraception until she was introduced to Margaret Sanger in 1915. Stopes had gone on to write a best-selling sex advice book, *Married Love* (1918), and had toured the United States under the auspices of Mary Ware Dennett's Voluntary Parenthood League. Dennett never missed a chance to point to Stopes as the sort of professional-scientific woman the birth control cause needed, in contrast to the sensation-mongering Margaret Sanger. It must have galled Sanger to see Stopes, whose scientific career was over and who was second to no one in ego or flair for self-advertisement, establish the first birth control clinic in Great Britain, a venture made possible by her new millionaire husband, Humphrey Vernon Roe, an aircraft manufacturer.[21]

Providing Clinics

Sanger promptly followed Stopes' example by marrying J. Noah Slee (1861–1943) in September 1922. Slee was the manufacturer of Three-in-One Oil, a staunch member of the conservative Union Club, and the happily divorced father of three grown children, until he met an elegant redhead who arrived from a lecture to spend the night at a friend's home just as Slee was leaving. Slee refused to believe that the lovely creature was the infamous Margaret Sanger and began following her about, trying to be helpful. After he promised to accept separate apartments, respect her autonomy, and help with the cause, Sanger said yes to the dapper executive, who built her a mansion on the Hudson, kept all their bargains, and convinced his bride that "Domesticity," at least in the form of detached marriage, "had its charms after all." [22]

In 1923 the *Birth Control Review* had a budget of $24,565; the American Birth Control League spent $30,000 and had more than 18,000 dues-paying members, and Sanger had more invitations to lecture than she could accept at $100 a throw. The time had come to see if agitation, education, and organization had proceeded far enough to support clinical services. Freed from the need to support herself by lecturing, confident after the Town Hall victory, and goaded by Marie Stopes' success with her clinic run by midwives, Sanger set out to find a doctor with a New York license willing to risk license and jail for the cause. [23]

No gynecologist wanted to work for Margaret Sanger. Friends told of a young woman from New York working for the Division of Child Hygiene of the Georgia State Board of Health and willing to take a chance to get back to civilization. Dorothy Bocker had an A.M. in Physical Education from Columbia, an M.D. from Long Island College Hospital (1919), had been an Instructor in Physical Education at Columbia Teachers College, and had gone from New York to Lewiston, Idaho, to Columbus, Ohio, to Milledgeville, Georgia, in search of professional opportunity. If Sanger could guarantee a salary of $5,000 a year, she was willing to learn something about birth control.

The American Birth Control League, as a membership corporation, could not operate a medical dispensary. Officers of the ABCL hesitated to support Sanger in a venture that might

113

put her back in jail. Clinton Chance, another British friend and prospering Birmingham manufacturer, had promised in 1920 to fund a clinic and now provided a thousand pounds of seed money. Sanger wrote Dr. Bocker, "You may not wish to take on this work, in view of the fact that the League would not be behind you, but personally I think if you and I take the responsibility of opening this clinic without another soul, we would get on much better than bothering with a committee of either lay people or doctors." The clinic would have to be run as Dr. Bocker's private practice, but an office would be provided across the hall from the ABCL. Sanger could not assure Dr. Bocker "a peaceful, harmonious, or uneventful year," but "for one doctor to stand up and assert her right under this legal opinion [Crane decision of 1918], would give tremendous impetus and encouragement to thousands of other doctors throughout the country. . . ." Dr. Bocker might go to jail or lose her license, but, Sanger confided, "If this does happen, I believe you will get such a good boost of publicity, that we can put you on the platform lecturing throughout the country for the next two years." If the clinic remained open, its records would prove that safe, effective contraceptive practice was possible.[24]

The Birth Control Clinical Research Bureau opened on January 2, 1923. During the first year Dr. Bocker provided contraceptive advice to 1,208 women, mostly referred from the ABCL office across the hall. Spring-type vaginal diaphragms were obtained for the clinic by J. Noah Slee, who had the devices shipped from Germany to his warehouse in Montreal and smuggled into the United States in "Three-in-One" cartons. Slee, who never took breaking the law lightly, resorted to smuggling only after the collector of customs assured him "there was no possible way of bringing them in lawfully." Available contraceptive jellies proved overpriced and unreliable, so Slee began manufacturing tubes of lactic acid jelly at his Rahway, New Jersey, plant, while trying to find a reliable drug firm to take over the business.[25]

The search only ended in 1925 when Slee financed the founding of the Holland Rantos Company by Herbert R. Simonds. An engineer and plastics manufacturer, Simonds had been an ardent admirer of Margaret Sanger since, as an army captain during World War I, he had escaped the monotony of waiting to be shipped overseas by taking the pacifist Comstock fighter dancing "almost every evening." Although he believed the business would be "against the law" and "fully expected to be arrested," Simonds began manufacturing diaphragms.[26] Once Holland Rantos showed that contraceptives could be profitably manufactured and ethically retailed through the medical profession, Julius Schmid and other established pharmaceutical houses entered the business. The availability of reliable contraceptives in the United States by the late 1920s was made possible by J. Noah Slee and Herbert Simonds, two staunch capitalists who sought the favor of Margaret Sanger more than profit.

Dr. Bocker's report of the Research Bureau's first year of activity drew considerable criticism.[27] Bocker had tried thirteen different contraceptive regimens, with the result that she had no more than a hundred patients in any one series. No systematic follow-up of clients had been attempted. If a woman failed to return to the clinic, she was counted a "success" while no attempt was made to compare "failures" by months of exposure to pregnancy. Despite limitations of time, money, and supplies Bocker had actually begun the tedious process of collecting hard data, but it was obvious to Sanger that a physician of greater ability was required if the clinic was going to gain acceptance from the leaders of the medical profession. When Bocker was told that her contract would not be renewed for a third year, she got a measure of revenge by taking the case records with her, forcing Sanger to begin from scratch the tedious process of building a clinical record.[28]

Bocker had, however, tentatively established the high effectiveness of the spring-type vaginal diaphragm when used with a spermicidal jelly. During the next three years Dr. Hannah Stone (1893–1941), who volunteered her services as Bocker's replacement, gathered an impressive series of more than 1,100 cases, which included systematic follow-up by a social worker. Her findings, published in 1928, with a preface by Dr. Robert L. Dickinson, at last provided documentary evidence that safe and effective contraceptive means existed. Organized medicine refused to notice. Stone was forced to give up her connection with Lying-In Hospital because of her work at the Sanger clinic, and for years membership in the New York County Medical Society was capriciously denied her. Nevertheless, increasing numbers of individual practitioners learned contraceptive technique through the Clinical Research Bureau. When Sanger brought the Sixth International Birth Control Conference to New York in 1925, over a thousand physicians sought admittance to the session on contraceptive technique, making a larger hall and two sessions necessary.[29]

To exploit this interest among doctors, Sanger promised Slee that she would "retire with him to the Garden of Paradise," if he would provide $10,000 in salary and expenses for Dr. James F. Cooper (1880–1931), whom she had recruited to lecture on contraceptive practice among physicians unable to come to New York for instruction.[30] Despite her promise, Slee had to wait a long time for the undivided attention of his wife, but Dr. Cooper got the job done.

In 1913, Cooper had left a job as instructor in the Boston University Medical School to become a medical missionary in China for the Board of Foreign Missions of the Congregational Church. After World War I he returned to Massachusetts, where obstetrical practice in Boston's slums persuaded him that the United States provided as rich a field as the Far East for a medical missionary. Beginning in 1925, he spoke before hundreds of county medical societies and compiled a list of several thousand physicians to whom patients could be referred by the American Birth Control League for competent contraceptive advice.[31]

It cost $6,000 to run the Clinical Research Bureau in 1921. Patient fees provided $500. By 1930 the clinic cost $35,000 and fees provided $10,000. The average patient cost the clinic $6.50, yet $5.00 was the highest fee charged. Patients who could afford to pay standard fees were referred to private practitioners, usually from among the staff of women doctors who worked part-time at the clinic. The more successful the clinic, the greater its potential deficit.[32]

At times the constant necessity of raising money for the clinic irritated Sanger. She often declared she hoped to put it on a self-supporting basis. Always the ultimate goal was to have government take over the burden. But she went on from year to year, finding support and increasing the number of women accepted. Slee helped more than once; in 1925 the Rockefeller-funded Bureau of Social Hygiene provided $10,000; in 1930, $5,000.[33]

The Bureau of Social Hygiene increasingly put pressure on Sanger to recruit a committee of eminent physicians to advise the clinic staff, and she tried over and over again, despite the high cost of medical labor of any kind. But her first concern was to provide contraceptive services, not an experimental medical facility. Faced with a $17,000 deficit in 1931, Sanger pleaded with an executive of the Rockefeller Foundation for $5,000. "It will give me breathing time to carry on to get the rest." John D. Rockefeller, Jr. gave her the money, probably against his better judgment, since it was foundation policy to avoid situations where institutions came to count on support for normal budgetary needs on a continuing basis.[34]

Money spent on the Clinical Research Bureau was, however, seed money in a sense. In 1930, 300 physicians learned contraceptive technique at the clinic. There were 4,733 new patients and 12,487 visits from old ones. Their histories provided the most extensive data on the practice of contraception in existence. In 1924, Margaret Sanger had staged the Midwestern States Birth Control Conference in Chicago to help Hull House's Dr. Rachelle Yarros launch the second birth control clinic in the United States. The Clinical Research Bureau's example, experience, and case histories provided the inspiration and justification for more than 300 birth control clinics in the United States in 1938.[35]

In 1930 the Julius Rosenwald Fund provided $5,000 to match the $5,000 Sanger raised to establish a clinic in Harlem. The gratitude of Harlem residents for this attention in the depth of the Great Depression is striking. W. E. B. DuBois presided at the opening of the Harlem clinic, and the only negative reaction in the black community came from Negro physicians. The president of the North Harlem Medical Society complained that the clinic gave treatment to patients who could have paid for it.[36]

Physicians were opposed on principle to the delivery of any kind of medical care by special clinics. It smelled like socialized medicine. In addition, Sanger's clinics operated without a dispensary license. In 1922, Sanger first applied to the State Board of Charities for a license. Never one to be intimidated by small laws, Sanger went ahead anyway when the license was refused. Another application was made in 1925, this time to incorporate the clinic under an outstanding board of directors which included Adolf Meyer and Raymond Pearl from Johns Hopkins, Robert L. Dickinson, past president of the American Gynecological Society, and William A. Pusey, past president of the American Medical Association. Again the license was refused. Sanger continued to operate her clinic with a staff of women general practitioners, all of whom were licensed in New York, but none of whom were eminent specialists.[37]

Although several distinguished gynecologists joined the clinic's advisory council after 1930, men of that caliber also objected to the fact that Margaret Sanger dictated policy at the clinic. Her direction meant that the phrase "for the cure and prevention of disease" was interpreted by the standards of a feminist rather than by those of middle-aged gentlemen. Several hundred women were refused every year because they were unmarried, pregnant, or simply the healthy mothers of less than three children. Nevertheless, the emphasis at the clinic was on helping women who wanted to avoid pregnancy for whatever reason rather than on saving the desperately ill.

By 1933, Sanger was even ready to see if something could be done for "overdues," women who came to the clinic after having missed a menstrual period. These women were usually pregnant. Dr. Stone had established the policy that staff members should refuse to examine overdue applicants. "If a woman after having been examined at the Clinic should be pregnant and decide to have an abortion, and should there be something wrong with the abortion, they may link up this case with the Clinic." The staff believed that decoys seeking abortions were occasionally sent by Roman Catholics or the police in an effort to close the clinic. Sanger was concerned, however, because in birth control clinics all over the country "overdues" were being turned away without any counseling. She hoped to use the Clinical Research Bureau to try to establish another precedent. "I have come to the conclusion," Sanger wrote to Dr. Stone, "that I want to make a special study of all overdue cases applying to us either in person or over the telephone, and I would like to set aside the noon hour—from 12 o'clock to 2 o'clock each day beginning tomorrow, . . . for these special cases." The physician in charge of this project should be chosen for "her contact with hospitals or doctors who may, in therapeutic cases, give proper attention to those coming under that term." A series of 1,000 cases, showing economic, psychological, and medical justification for abortion, would make a more humane policy toward these women possible in clinics all over the country.[38]

The law did not catch up with Margaret Sanger's vision until 1973, when the Supreme Court decided that during the first three months of pregnancy the question of abortion should be a matter of concern for the pregnant woman and her physician, rather than legislators, but at least one healthy, single woman was given a pregnancy test and referred to a sympathetic physician by the clinic, despite the risk involved.[39]

Physicians resented the business lost to the Clinical Research Bureau, the precedent set by the delivery of medical services through a system of subsidized practice, the technical illegality of the services, and the dictation of medical policy by a laywoman, propagandist, and biting critic of organized medicine. Nevertheless, in 1929 influential members of the New York Academy of Medicine found their professional interest threatened by Sanger's latest clash with the law and helped save the Clinical Research Bureau from the last police attempt at direct suppression.

On April 15, 1929, the police raided the Clinical Research Bureau and arrested Dr. Stone, another physician, and three nurses on the charge of violating Section 1142, the statute prohibiting the giving of contraceptive information. The arrests were carried out with unnecessary brutality. Policemen tried to force their way into rooms where patients were on the examining table, drawers and file cabinets were dumped into trash baskets and hauled away, innocuous items like physicians' gloves and medicine droppers were seized. Seven complete histories were taken, along with 150 index cards containing names and addresses of patients with incomplete diagnoses. The latter were never returned and were used to intimidate some patients.[40]

Three weeks before the raid a policewoman had received advice at the clinic under an assumed name. In court expert testimony established that she was suffering from several pathological conditions of the uterus and was entitled to help under the strictest definition of the law; the case was dismissed.

The seizure of medical records was denounced by a resolution of the New York Academy of Medicine. Probably more important in insuring that attempts to suppress the clinic would cease was the revelation that the raid originated at the precinct level when Catholic social workers on the Lower East Side sought clerical advice on the handling of Catholic mothers who wished to go to the clinic. The precinct magistrate claimed he had signed the clinic search warrant automatically with a number of others on his desk, and the chief of police ended by apologizing for the affair after receiving a letter of protest from the president of the Academy of Medicine.[41]

The 150 incomplete histories were apparently taken in an effort to find the names of Catholic women, some of whom came to the clinic begging that their names be kept out of the newspapers after receiving anonymous phone calls threatening to expose them if they continued to go to the clinic.[42]

Two Roman Catholic attempts to suppress Margaret Sanger's activities had backfired. The Town Hall raid made Sanger a martyr to civil liberty; the clinic raid forced physicians to come to her aid in order to protect the right of their own patients to privacy. In fact neither episode had much to do with the future of free speech or medical ethics in America, but the Clinical Research Bureau was an accepted part of the landscape after 1929. Ironically, the issue of a dispensary license was never raised during the 1929 trial.[43]

With or without dispensary licenses, birth control clinics were doing a booming business by the early 1930s. The federal prohibition on the importation of contraceptive devices and the illegality of sending them through the mails remained irritating nuisances. In 1930, at a conference on contraceptive technique she organized in Zurich, Sanger had been shown an experimental pessary designed by a Japanese physician. Hoping to test the device at the Clinical Research Bureau, she had ordered several from Tokyo, but these were seized and destroyed by United States Customs.[44]

During the clinic raid Morris Ernst (1888–1976), a lawyer fast making a reputation as a defender in civil liberty and obscenity cases, had donated his services. For years Sanger had been collecting instances of contraceptive devices and literature confiscated by customs which were intended for physicians. Now Ernst began following all such cases and in the early 1930s Sanger's National Committee on Federal Legislation for Birth Control was participating in sixteen court actions, most involving the section of the tariff act banning contraceptives.[45]

The seizure of the Japanese pessaries provided precisely the kind of opportunity that Ernst had been looking for. Once again Hannah Stone proved herself a perfect martyr. One hundred twenty Japanese pessaries were ordered sent to Dr. Stone for potential use in her private practice. To avoid any chance of their getting through because of bureaucratic incompetence, customs officials were informed of the shipment.

In *United States* v. *One Package,* Judge Augustus Hand solved the problem of making a nineteenth century obscenity law reasonable in the 1930s by ruling that although the language of the Comstock Act was uncompromising, if Congress had had available in 1873 the clinical data on the dangers of pregnancy and the usefulness of contraceptive practice available in 1936, birth control would not have been classified as obscenity. As Morris Ernst observed, "The law process is a simple one, it is a matter of educating judges to the mores of the day." Judge Hand's decision opened the mails to contraceptive materials intended for physicians. The right of individual citizens to bring such devices into the country for personal use was not established until 1971. Nevertheless, *One Package* represented the long-sought qualification of the 1873 legislative classification of birth control as obscenity.[46]

For a decade after the *One Package* victory Sanger was a less important figure in the effort to spread contraceptive practice. She reemerged after World War II to play key roles in the establishment of the International Planned Parenthood Federation and the development of the anovulant pill. She was fifty-

seven in 1937, glad finally to be able to devote herself to
J. Noah Slee in his last years and to pursue her interest in
painting.[47] Her semiretirement also reflected a change in the
direction of the birth control movement. During the middle
1930s the birth rate fell below the replacement level for the first
time in American history.[48] Irresistible pressure existed to
change the emphasis of the movement, a shift reflected in the
change in title of the national organization from Birth Control
Federation of America to Planned Parenthood Federation of
America in 1942.

Sanger despised the term Planned Parenthood, and it is
ironic that the 1972 stamp commemorating her work bore that
title. She wrote to a friend in 1942, "it irks my very soul and all
that is Irish in me to acquiesce to the appeasement group that
is so prevalent in our beloved organization. We will get no further because of the title; I assure you of that. Our progress up
to date had been because the Birth Control movement was
built on a strong foundation of truth, justice, right, and good
common sense." She did not believe in "balanced" campaigns
intended to encourage the middle classes to have more children. Nor did she believe in disguising the fact that large
numbers of people should not have children—the ill, the indigent, and in general anyone who could not provide twenty
years of support and loving nurture to a child, as well as epileptics, diabetics, the feebleminded, and anyone else who
might give a child a load of botched genes. There was no question of nature versus nurture, heredity versus environment in
her mind. She knew an incompetent parent when she saw one.
Coercion was not a realistic answer, but unceasing efforts to
spread contraceptive practice so that every birth would represent a conscious decision was a duty. Despite declining birth
rates, despite World War II, despite the need for national
unity, in 1942, as always, the time had come "to strike while
the iron is hot. By this I mean that the present administration
in Washington is friendly, not only to us but is definitely out
to give the 'under-dog' knowledge and opportunity to better
himself, and Birth Control does just that."[49]

Despite Sanger's belief that birth control helped the "under-
dog," her critics argued that her activities mainly benefited the
middle-class women who supported the movement financially

and by volunteering their time in clinics and in campaigns to change repressive laws. They claimed that the Sadie Sachses of America lacked the motivation or ability to seek help in birth control clinics. Sanger's supporters were helping themselves by making it easier to obtain birth control services, but they also wanted to share their new sense of personal control with as many women as possible. Although wealthy women largely financed the movement, less fortunate women also participated in it. As Francis Vreeland, a Ph.D. candidate from the University of Michigan who studied the American Birth Control League's records, pointed out in 1929:

> Women of the working-class have participated actively in the birth control movement, but their efforts have been of a different kind from those of the upper-middle class women. They do not have the habituation to secondary groups, the money, or the leisure to express their social discontent and social wishes through organizations . . . the main response of women of the poorer class . . . was by letter to the main agitators, usually looking for help.

No one, Vreeland wrote, who had read these letters could doubt their authenticity or fail to be moved by the "pathetic tales of poverty and suffering they told."[50] Sanger published a selection of these letters in *Motherhood in Bondage* (1928). The American Birth Control League needed a staff of three to seven workers in the 1920s to handle Sanger's correspondence. At first her pamphlet on contraceptive technique, *Family Limitation*, was sent to these women, later a list of sympathetic doctors was compiled for referral. These letters profoundly affected those working with Sanger and created an especially vivid awareness of the need for a national system of birth control clinics.[51] By 1940 hundreds of thousands of working-class women had participated in the birth control movement by seeking contraceptive advice. Viewed in terms of those helped rather than those who remained untouched, Sanger's crusade had been a enormous success.

The sex histories gathered by Alfred Kinsey and his associates during the late 1930s and 1940s reveal that Sanger's work led to dramatic changes in contraceptive practice among the middle classes[52] (see Table 1). Of Kinsey's married white female subjects born before 1899, only 12 percent claimed never to have practiced contraception. Clearly many middle-class women were practicing birth control before Sanger began the establishment of a network of birth control clinics. The main result of the birth control movement at the behavioral level among Kinsey's subjects was not the initiation of contraceptive practice, but the substitution of the vaginal diaphragm for douching and withdrawal. The Kinsey group recorded four degrees of familiarity with each birth control method discussed in a sex history—ranging from "never this method," to "little use," to "some use," to "much use." Only those who reported "much use" of a method are represented in Table 1. Neither rhythm nor jelly and suppositories are included because a very small number of women reported "much use" of these methods.[53]

Table 1
Kinsey's Married White Women

	−1899	1900–09	1910–19	1920–29
Sample = 2,328	323	560	867	578
Never Practiced Contraception	12% (40)	7% (37)	8% (65)	5% (31)
Diaphragm	24% (77)	42%(237)	53%(455)	57%(327)
Douche	24% (76)	15% (85)	8% (66)	6% (35)
Withdrawal	23% (72)	15% (85)	7% (61)	7% (41)
Condom	36%(116)	37%(206)	34%(296)	37%(215)

Of the 323 women born before 1899, 24 percent reported "much use" of the diaphragm, but 24 percent relied heavily on douching and 23 percent on withdrawal. Among the women in the next three cohorts, "much use" of the diaphragm greatly increased, while douching and withdrawal lost their popularity. Since Sanger was responsible for the popularization of the diaphragm in the United States and was the key figure in the establishment of the birth control clinics where the great majority of physicians learned to use this method during the 1920s and 1930s, she should be credited as the person most responsible for the switch among Kinsey's subjects from "much use" of douching and withdrawal to greater use of the diaphragm.

Although Sanger wanted to place contraception under the

control of women, the increased availability of the diaphragm did not lessen the popularity of the condom. Thirty-six percent of Kinsey's female subjects born between 1920 and 1929 were still relying heavily on it. The condom's persistence in comparison to douching and withdrawal probably reflected its high effectiveness. Also, condoms could be more easily and cheaply obtained than diaphragms, since one did not have to go to a doctor to be fitted. American soldiers abroad during World War I were encouraged to use them, and there were dramatic improvements in their quality during the 1930s.[54]

Sanger hoped that better contraception would lead to fewer induced abortions, although she believed that women should be able to end unwanted pregnancies. Women born between 1900 and 1909 reported more induced abortions (29 percent had at least one) than those born before 1899.[55] This difference might reflect the possibility that the older women in Kinsey's sample were recruited more heavily from religious groups than other voluntary associations.[56] The rise in induced abortion could be interpreted, however, as a reflection of a greater unwillingness to maintain unwanted pregnancies among women during the 1920s and 1930s. Possibly these women were learning that effective contraception was possible and were therefore less passive in the face of "accidents" or contraceptive failure. Only 17 percent of those born between 1910 and 1919 reported induced abortions. This decline reflected the relative youth of these women, who were between the ages of 30 and 39 when they were interviewed, but they might also have been more effective contraceptors and thus would have experienced fewer unwanted pregnancies.

Kinsey's subjects were not representative of American women. His sample was disproportionately drawn from urban, well-educated, Protestant groups. These women averaged only 1.09 live births. This low figure partly reflects the age of these subjects, only one-fifth of whom had reached the end of their child-bearing period, but a comparative sample of 1945 urban white females had an average of 1.33 live births. Thus, Kinsey's sample was biased toward infertility in comparison with women of similar socioeconomic status.[57] The women in Kinsey's sample who attended college switched to the diaphragm sooner than those who had not attended college (compare Tables 2 and 3). Noncollege women in every age group were less frequent and less sophisticated contraceptors than the college women. Their contraceptive practice was probably closer to that of the majority of American women, but like the college-educated women, they were a disproportionately urban, well-educated, Protestant group.

Table 2
Kinsey's College-Educated,* Married, White Women

	−1899	1900–09	1910–19	1920–29
Sample= 1,597	210	422	563	402
Never Practiced Contraception	10%(21)	5% (19)	4% (20)	3% (13)
Diaphragm	31%(64)	51%(216)	61%(345)	64%(259)
Douche	21%(45)	13% (55)	4% (24)	4% (16)
Withdrawal	21%(45)	14% (57)	6% (31)	6% (23)
Condom	41%(85)	38%(159)	33%(187)	36%(146)

*College-educated means that these women attended college, not that they graduated.

Table 3
Kinsey's High School or Less,† Married, White Women

	−1899	1900–09	1910–19	1920–29
Sample= 731	113	138	304	176
Never Practiced Contraception	17%(19)	13%(18)	15% (45)	10%(18)
Diaphragm	12%(13)	21%(29)	36%(110)	39%(68)
Douche	27%(31)	22%(30)	14% (42)	11%(19)
Withdrawal	40%(45)	20%(28)	10% (30)	10%(18)
Condom	27%(31)	34%(47)	36%(109)	39%(69)

†These women never attended college.

Although Kinsey's subjects were not representative of the whole population, they were drawn from the same social groups that supported Sanger. This phenomenon is illustrated by the "oral history" of Emily H. Mudd, one of a series of interviews with women active in the birth control movement sponsored by The Schlesinger Library.[58] Mudd, who would become one of the key figures in the development of marriage counseling in the United States, first met Sanger in the early

1920s. She was working as an unpaid research assistant to her husband in the Rockefeller Institute. After the birth of her first child, she wanted contraceptive advice and explained in her oral history how she got help at the Clinical Research Bureau.

> Well, of course, through Margaret Sanger we knew of the clinic which she had started, and after the baby was born, I went down to the clinic. Hannah Stone was working then. We called her the Madonna of the Clinic. . . .

When asked why she did not go to her obstetrician for contraceptive advice, Mudd replied:

> It's funny . . . I don't remember . . . I guess he seemed to be such a kind of establishment, reserved person, and I had heard about Margaret Sanger. I just thought that she would know more than any obstetrician, and that I would go to her clinic.[59]

Mudd moved to Philadelphia when her husband left the Rockefeller Institute for a position in the University of Pennsylvania. She was unhappy to learn:

> that the laws in Pennsylvania were extremely rigid about any kind of availability of contraceptive materials or advice and that there was no clinic in the whole state . . . which offered any woman, rich or poor, any contraceptive information. Feeling deeply grateful to Dr. Hannah Stone for my personal advice and knowing what Margaret Sanger had done, we felt that it was just terrible not to have anything available in Pennsylvania.[60]

Mudd began working to change the birth control situation in the state. With the help of two feminist friends, who donated $1,000 each, Pennsylvania's first birth control clinic was opened in West Philadelphia. Mudd served as receptionist.

> At that time I was pregnant with my second child, and I found two laws that intrigued me. . . . One said that two people couldn't ride abreast on bicycles down Chestnut street. . . . And the other said that a pregnant woman could not be incarcerated.[61]

Mudd went on to found the Marriage Council of Philadelphia, which played a role in the development of marriage counseling in the United States analogous to that played by Sanger's Clinical Research Bureau in contraception. She obtained a Ph.D. in sociology and became the third woman promoted to full professor in the Medical School of the University of Pennsylvania. In 1944 she was Alfred Kinsey's key contact in Philadelphia and supplied him with the introductions that helped him to recruit a large number of his subjects.[62]

Sanger's clinic gave Mudd help at a crucial stage in her life, and she in turn helped other women to obtain reliable birth control services. By the 1930s the efforts of Sanger, Mudd, and dozens of other concerned women had made it possible for the highly motivated woman, whatever her socioeconomic status, to obtain contraceptive services. Sanger and her supporters were acutely aware of the limitations of the birth control clinic and of the diaphragm. While thousands of poor women were helped, millions remained out of the reach of the mostly urban clinics and lacked the courage or motivation to seek help. Sanger raised money for contraceptive research and supported experiments in the mass distribution of spermicidal jellies, condoms, and other contraceptives that did not require medical prescription, but birth control for every American would have to wait for fundamental breakthroughs in contraceptive technology, huge improvements in the level of health care provided for the poor, and a decline in the pervasive pronatalism of American culture.[63]

CHAPTER 10 **Woman and the New Race**

IN a hospital bed interview in May 1965, when asked to name the most important influence on her career, Margaret Sanger replied, "It was my father more than any other person, who influenced me through his teachings and his vital belief in truth, freedom, right."[1] It was no fluke that *the* strident voice calling for controlled population growth in the midst of the Great Depression was the daughter of an Irish freethinker whose fighting faith rested on the revelations of Robert Ingersoll and Henry George.

Margaret Sanger combined a feminist vision with the prophetic style of her father's heroes, and their moral animus against the swarming concentration of mass society. Ingersoll had exclaimed:

> Why have the reformers failed? . . . I will tell them why. . . . Ignorance, poverty and vice are populating the world. The gutter is a nursery. People unable even to support themselves fill the tenements, the huts and hovels with children. . . . The babe is not welcome, because it is a burden. . . . The real question is, can we prevent the ignorant, the poor, the vicious from filling the world with children? . . . To accomplish this there is but one way. Science must make woman the owner, the mistress of herself. Science, the only possible savior of mankind, must put it in the power of woman to decide for herself whether she will or will not become a mother.[2]

While Ingersoll offered the religion of science as the solution to the world's disorder, Henry George proclaimed the single tax

129

on unearned wealth as the key to unleashing the initiative of everyman and the restoration of a manageable, decentralized natural order.[3] Margaret Sanger too had a clear idea of where to begin the world's transformation. She believed that women in control of themselves would remake the world by restricting the production of children, thereby revaluing human life cheapened by plentitude. Evolution had given women, as the breeders of the race, great powers of endurance. If women gained control of their fertility, vast energy formerly consumed in mothering would be freed for the work of social reformation. Sanger demanded absolute equality for women, but she also claimed special powers for them. In short, she was a feminist who wanted equal opportunity for her sex and believed that with it they could be more than equal.

Other reformers found Sanger's belief in the revolutionary potential of birth control naive, but much of her success depended on her ability to concentrate her energy on a single goal: to give every woman the opportunity to control her fertility. She never equivocated in her crusade, although she changed tactics and rationalizations with an adeptness that bedeviled opponents and competitors. The genuine inconsistencies in Sanger's published statements and correspondence lend themselves to misinterpretation. Her two autobiographies were campaign documents. *Birth Control Review* under her editorship printed articles by authors representing a wide ideological spectrum—the main criterion for acceptance was to add prestige to the cause. Her one ideological loyalty was to Havelock Ellis, an idealist who remained in the Fellowship of the New Life long after the Fabians had abandoned the commitment to "the cultivation of a perfect character in each and all" through the "subordination of material things to spiritual."[4]

Sanger was an activist committed to social change through available practical means, but she never believed that environmental change alone would improve the world. A religious conversion was required to awaken women to full human potential and to develop what Charlotte Perkins Gilman called "an active sense of social motherhood." "The business of the female," Gilman declared, "is not only the reproduction but the improvement of the species."[5]

William O'Neill has argued that Sanger was the prophet of a new form of domesticity, rendered more palatable by divorce reform and birth control, and finally exposed by Betty Friedan in *The Feminine Mystique* (1963).[6] Another historian has declared her an exponent of evolutionary naturalism and has given her a prominent place in the American eugenics movement.[7] She was neither an apologist for marriage nor a eugenicist, but her relationship to both feminism and the eugenics movement was complex. While she shared values with other feminists and with eugenicists, she always maintained her distance, insisting that birth control was the essential first step in any rational plan for freeing woman or breeding a better race. She took help wherever she could get it, but the demands of her cause came first, and cooperation did not reach beyond borrowing additional justifications for spreading contraceptive practice.

Sanger considered herself *the* woman's rights activist of the twentieth century. Her criticism of the limited vision of other feminists was often shrill. Most women of advanced view, however, would have agreed with Crystal Eastman:

> Whether we are the followers of Alice Paul or Ruth Law, or Ellen Key, or Olive Schreiner, we must all be followers of Margaret Sanger. Feminists are not nuns. That should be established. We want to love and be loved, and most of us want children, one or two at least. But we want our children to be deliberately, eagerly called into being, when we are at our best, not crowded upon us in times of poverty and weakness. We want this precious sex knowledge not just for ourselves, the conscious feminist; we want it for all the millions of unconscious feminists that swarm the earth,— we want it for all women.[8]

Some feminists, recognizing the cathartic effect of freer sexual expression, found Sanger's heroic posture congenial. Harriet Stanton Blatch wrote Sanger that she liked the aspiring tone of *Woman and the New Race*. "Especially did I appreciate your placing in the hands of the mother of the race control of her life giving principle. If women would listen and act they would be as gods not only knowing good and evil but creating good at will."[9]

There was, however, a certain uneasiness among many women reformers in dealing with sex. Charlotte Perkins Gilman endorsed birth control, but for her it was simply another part of a Spartan regimen, one of woman's higher duties to the race. She made clear her contempt for the "slackers" who refused to have any children, those "men and women to whom marriage is merely legalized indulgence," deplored the rise of "a degree of sex indulgence without parallel in nature," and believed the "wholly safe and normal method" of family limitation was "to develop a race less sex crazy than at present, and capable of rational continence when it is necessary." Nevertheless, until an ethical consciousness compatible with the higher continence could be realized, the middle-class woman's chance for personal development, relief for the overburdened poor, and international peace depended on controlled fertility, so it was better to accept birth control than "to keep on in blind overproduction." [10]

Other women leaders simply rejected birth control as unnecessary. For them it was possible to banish sex. Carrie Chapman Catt explained that she stood for continence "not to prevent conception but in the interest of common decency." ". . . a million years of male control over the sustenance of women has made them sex slaves, which has produced two results: an over sexualizing of women and an over sexualizing of men. No animal is so uncontrolled as in the mass of men. Now, merely to make indulgence safe doesn't do enough." [11]

A telling commentary was provided by Vida Scudder in 1952, then professor emeritus at Wellesley after a long and rich career as a social reformer and teacher. She did not want to be a sponsor of the International Conference on Planned Parenthood. She was old and tired, but "it is also because I decline to endorse or sponsor anything in which I am not interested; and I am an old spinster who has never followed the Movement concerning Parenthood with any intelligence or concern." "P.S. I don't want to sponsor anything concerning which I should never say my prayers." [12]

Characteristically, Sanger exploded at this sincere admission of indifference. "It is sad to have your letter . . . sad because your education has been deplorably neglected by *me*. Now that I look back over the years a bit, I realize that Wellesley is one of the few colleges that did not invite me to give an address, or speak my views to faculty or students—Alas! Otherwise you might have included in your prayers those forgotten women whose bodies are human incubators from puberty to grave." Sanger ended, however, with a warm apology of sorts. "I love you. As all who have known you, or of you, do."[13]

In the mid-thirties Sanger expressed disgust toward women who failed to seize the opportunities for self-development for which her generation had fought. "The American woman, in my estimation," she complained to a former British suffragist, "is sound asleep. Suffrage was won too easily and too early in this country. A harder fight and a longer one would have put more iron in her tissues, and she would have had a vision and perhaps a goal which she lacks today." Great expectations had been aroused by the prospect of women serving in Congress, but few sought office, and "As soon as a woman gets into politics, she becomes abject, spineless and aims only to be agreeable. . . . She scarcely ever takes a stand on broad economic issues aside from what the Party leader tells her to stand for. I am thoroughly disgusted with her, and hope with all my heart that she learns the lessons of defeat before she continues to hypnotize herself that she is free."[14]

When Carrie Catt wrote in 1940 to announce the organization of a Woman's Centennial Congress to celebrate the advance of women since 1840, Sanger wondered "how much advance women really have made, considering the dictator countries—Japan, Italy and Germany, have thrust their women back into the misery and breeding pen, while women of France and England and China are spending all their efforts in taking care of the men at the battle front." On December 8, 1920, twenty-one years to the day prior to America's declaration of war on Japan, Sanger had predicted that Japan's unchecked population growth would force expansion and conflict with the United States. Now she saw her nightmare being realized. "As long as women respond and obey the edicts of the militarists and hierarchy and spawn . . . for nation or church, there will be wars, ignorance, poverty. In fact, if you look back over the past hundred years there is actually very little fundamental improvement except for a handful of women who have been able thru Birth Control to achieve their independence and to pursue their professions or develop their innate talents."[15] So much for celebrating one hundred years of woman's progress. Sanger was soon in the field again, organizing the International Planned Parenthood Federation, descending with Katharine Dexter McCormick on scientists to see how much longer they would have to wait for a birth control pill, exhorting womankind to do better.

There was, however, a genuine ambivalence in Sanger's attitude toward reform. She both passionately believed that women would help themselves if given a chance and recoiled in disgust from those who could not or would not rise to her standard. The kind of strategy she emphasized usually depended on her audience. In 1923 she wrote to Professor James Field at the University of Chicago, "I have come to realize that the more ignorant classes, with whom we are chiefly concerned, are so liable to misunderstand any written instruction, that the Cause of Birth Control would be harmed rather than helped, by spreading unauthoritative literature." She was trying to win the professor's support for federal legislation giving "doctors only" the right to send birth control information and devices through the mail. At the same time she was publishing *Family Limitation* and mailing it to *anyone* who asked. As late as 1928 she ordered 10,000 more copies of *Family Limitation*. [16] The "ignorant classes" might be "harmed rather than helped, by spreading unauthoritative literature," but there was no danger in their reading *Family Limitation*, it was written by an expert!

Sanger's relationship with the eugenics movement reflected a similar disingenuousness. Eugenicists from the beginning damned birth control for its dysgenic effect. The best people were already limiting their families too much. The worst were beyond help. Besides, eugenics was a respectable scientific reform; association with birth control propagandists would damage the movement. Charles B. Davenport, founder of the Eugenics Record Office and director of the Station for Experimental Evolution at Cold Spring Harbor; Harry L. Laughlin, director of the Eugenics Record Office and Expert Eugenics Agent for the House Committee on Immigration and Naturalization; and Paul Popenoe, secretary of California's Human Betterment Foundation—all refused to associate themselves with either attempts to set up clinical studies of contraception or efforts to change birth control laws. In explaining their positions, Popenoe and Davenport specifically referred to their abhorrence of Margaret Sanger. Laughlin wrote Sanger that he would shun birth control until efforts were made to encourage "a higher birth rate among persons best endowed by nature with fine mental, physical, and moral qualities. . . ." and sent her a copy of his new book *Eugenical Sterilization* (1926).[17]

Though craving the respectability and institutional support the eugenicists enjoyed, Sanger refused to endorse any schemes for "positive" eugenics. When a major contributor to the birth control movement suggested a campaign to encourage college graduates to have more children, she was unequivocal in her rejection of "that strange argument." In 1925, Edward East, the Harvard biologist and member of the Clinical Research Bureau's advisory council, persuaded her not to publish an editorial in *Birth Control Review* attacking eugenicists for failing to support birth control because, he argued, she needed them, and they, in time, would need her. "No matter what you say," East warned, "Birth Control is only a part of a eugenical program. It is a secondary aspect of a larger whole, but it is the key. The mere fact that so many eugenicists have not been able to think straight does not make the abstract subject itself any less valued."[18]

Professor Davenport's laboratory at Cold Spring Harbor, Long Island, enjoyed the sponsorship of the Carnegie Institution, had ample funding by Mrs. E. H. Harriman, and was a model of acceptance and respectability among well-intentioned laymen.[19] Davenport and Laughlin were invited to give their views at the Sanger-sponsored Sixth International Neo-Malthusian and Birth Control Conference in 1926. Sanger got a measure of revenge in her autobiography by noting that eugenicists were simply following in the footsteps of the notorious Moses Harman, publisher of a nineteenth century freethought journal called *The American Journal of Eugenics*, and by mocking Davenport:

Protoplasm was the substance then supposed to carry on hereditary traits—genes and chromosomes were a later discovery. Professor Davenport used to lift his eyes reverently and, with his hands upraised as though in supplication, quiver emotionally as he breathed, "Protoplasm, We want more protoplasm."[20]

The eugenicists, she noted, talked about more children for the fit, but none of them seemed willing to breed large broods. "They wanted upper-class women to have more children because they were more intelligent, have better health, more time to care for their children, and better means to support them. These qualities, however, resulted from their ability to limit their families." [21] The eugenicists failed to "recognize the difficulties presented by the idea of 'fit' and 'unfit.' Who is to decide this question?" She was all for discouraging births in all doubtful cases, but "among the writings of the representative Eugenicists one cannot ignore the distinct middle-class bias that prevails." Eugenicists from Galton on had a limited appreciation of the contribution made to culture by individuals "pathologically abnormal," including Rousseau, Dostoevsky, Chopin, Poe, and Nietzsche. Most of the laws they proposed were unenforceable and reflected an excessive emphasis on heredity, ignoring the correlation between high fertility and bad environment, as well as with low intelligence. In Sanger's view the decline in the birth rate was a good thing. The solution to the problem of differential fertility between classes was to make available to all the same knowledge and opportunities the middle class enjoyed. After that evangelical endeavor was completed would be the time to talk about sterilization. [22]

Under the influence of Frederick Osborn the old leadership of the American Eugenics Society was replaced in the 1930s by men who stressed heredity less and environment more. Osborn was anxious to cooperate with birth controllers in spreading contraception among the poor. But he too insisted that there be more emphasis on the "positive" aspects of contraception. Osborn wanted birth control to be replaced by family planning and encouragement of large families for those who could afford them. Physicians also were much more comfortable with the family planning idea, and it had the advantage of mitigating the hostility of Roman Catholics. With the advice of Kenneth Rose, a public relations consultant and fund raiser with the John Price Jones Corporation, "birth control" was replaced by "family planning" in the title of the national organization, and affiliated clinics were encouraged to take seriously an elaborate set of medical indications for contraception.[23]

Sanger was appalled by the Planned Parenthood Federation's new policies. A fund-raising pamphlet written at the John Price Jones Corporation was especially galling. She wrote to an officer of the federation, ". . . that statement of John Price Jones about raising the reproductive rates of the 'mentally and physically sound' . . . was such cheap twaddle that I could not stand it and I could not believe that you . . . 'read and approved'. . . ." Even worse was the stricter definition of eligibility for contraceptive advice. "If the Roman Catholic Church had sent that sheet out to weaken our force I should have understood it. The objective of the Federation should be to expand and strengthen the minds of all those associated with the movement. The health indications should be wider each year than they have been before. . . . That would be leadership, and if this sort of reactionary policy continues to take hold of the movement many people will withdraw entirely from the Federation."[24]

The new leaders of the birth control movement found it next to impossible to raise money without Sanger's name, but they insisted that the changes in emphasis they brought were necessary if organized medicine, professional social workers, and government were to increase their part in the spread of contraception. It would be another twenty years before the growth of world population would provide new social justification for Sanger's vision.

In her two major works, *Woman and the New Race* (1920) and *The Pivot of Civilization* (1922), and in her major speeches, Sanger returned repeatedly to a few themes that reflected her primary concerns and values. As she explained in 1965, she always gave the same speech.[25] She believed that more and better sex was a positive good in any community. She practiced what she preached, and Havelock Ellis provided her with a comprehensive interpretation of human sexuality. In her view the practice of continence was impossible for normal people. Only by accepting their sexual needs could men and women develop a healthy attitude toward one another and toward their children. Custom and ignorance united in the suppression of normal sexual expression and resulted in "the monotonous misery of millions who do not die early nor end violently, but who are, nevertheless, devoid of the joys of natural love life." The key to a better life for women was to substitute for sexual repression "the greatest possible expression and fulfillment of their desires upon the highest possible plane." The end of marriage was not procreation but spiritual communion, one expression of which might be voluntary parenthood.[26]

She believed that no woman could compete in a profession who could not control her fertility. But social order also depended on the use of contraception by women of all classes. The main source of disorder in industrial society, she argued, was the excessive fertility which prevented women from providing their children with the nurture they needed. Contraception gave women the opportunity to improve society by making every child a wanted and valued citizen. Birth control was "the pivot of civilization" because it provided the individual with the means to "adapt himself to and even to control the forces of environment and heredity." It provided a "new instrument of self-expression and self-realization" and "the possibility of new and greater freedom." Controlling one's fertility was for her a metaphor for individual initiative and responsibility, respect not only for oneself but for future generations as well.[27]

Sanger failed to recognize the complexity of the sources of social dependency. The attitudes of the poor toward themselves would not be changed simply by access to birth control services. They needed social justice, higher wages, concrete reasons for believing that they could control their lives and dramatically improve their condition. She pandered too much to the social biases of some of her wealthy supporters who were not interested in social reform but in lower tax rates. No one was more disturbed by or worked harder to publicize the conditions that breed the high infant mortality rate in the United States in comparison to other industrial nations, but she failed to broaden her criticism of the inequities of the American health care system into an attack on the distribution of income in the United States.[28]

She drew back from radical criticism of American capitalism, in part because she realized that association with radicalism would limit her access to the social elites who controlled American society, but also because she, like advocates of other causes, truly believed in the revolutionary potential of her reform, "free motherhood." She never wavered in her belief that the vast majority of women wanted fewer children and would control their fertility if given a chance. Moreover, a better future required better human beings, the kind of citizens who could only come from willing parents, in a society which could afford the investment required to make every child a whole, self-directed, moral individual. No society, she believed, could afford to make these things the right of every child unless birth rates were controlled. She failed to consider the possibility that evil might continue to exist in a society of sexually well-adjusted adults and of children blessed with health and love. But in her new society women could compete on equal footing with men. Margaret Sanger needed no better world.

PART III

ROBERT L. DICKINSON AND THE COMMITTEE ON MATERNAL HEALTH

CHAPTER 11   The
              Medical Man
              as Sex
              Researcher

AFTER the *One Package* decision
(1936), the further progress of the birth control movement depended on the acceptance of contraception by organized medicine and its incorporation into public health programs. Sanger
had forced changes in the law, had seen to it that reliable contraceptives were available, and provided the clinical data to
prove that birth control worked. Organized medicine, however, could never accept demands from a laywoman. Medical
endorsement of contraception depended on a different kind of
lobbying, necessarily by interested physicians. This crucial
role in the professional forum was to be played by Robert
Latou Dickinson (1861–1950), Sanger's most astute critic,
sometime rival, and finally, comrade-in-arms.

Dickinson's efforts to organize medical sex research revealed
the deep antagonism of his profession toward sexual reform
and the barriers that even a distinguished gynecologist faced
in attempting to study contraception. The most dramatic medical reform of the twentieth century, the improvement of medical education accelerated by the Flexner Report (1910), had an
ambiguous relationship to the broad involvement of physi-

cians with social issues. Suppression of quackery required public support for licensing laws, and high standards of medical education depended on the control of public hospitals by medical schools, as well as financial support by private philanthropists and state legislatures. This dependence on the community's good will meant that organized medicine could not afford to challenge established standards of sexual morality or to engage in controversial activities. Among the costs of medical reform were increasing exclusion of women, Negroes, and anyone who could not afford the cost of rigorous, full-time education.[1]

While medical leaders were intent upon establishing the authority of their profession as a scientific discipline, they generally shared the concern of social conservatives over the low birth rate among the middle classes and the dissatisfaction of young women with traditional female roles. They had no strong motive for a positive attitude toward birth control. A future editor of the *American Journal of Obstetrics and Gynecology* explained in 1917 that birth control was associated with the "unrestrained harangue of the reformer, usually a lay person with little conception of the medical aspects involved," with "radical socialists," "anarchists," "the spirit of license," and "seditious libel on the medical profession."[2]

Morris Fishbein, editor of the *Journal of the American Medical Association* and the leading evangelist of professionalism of the 1920s, provided an example of the use of the rhetoric of scientific professionalism to avoid a disagreeable problem in his *Medical Follies.* In the shrill tone characteristic of his attacks on all heresy from faith healing to the Sheppard-Towner Act (which provided federal subsidies for state programs to improve infant and maternal health), Fishbein unequivocally asserted that there existed no "method of birth control that is physiologically, psychologically and biologically sound in both principle and practice."[3] Fishbein's criticism of the "ardent economists, biologists, sociologists and philosophers who favor birth control" was part of a larger concern with the defense of a profession just coming into its own after years of struggle with quackery and with public indifference to the needs of the ethical practitioner.[4] Yet his categorical rejection of contraception was logically, if not emotionally, inconsistent with the brand of medicine which he wanted to defend.

One of the most objectionable traits of quack systems of medicine was the oversimplification of complex issues, the a priori rejection of empirical treatment and the exaggeration of the effectiveness of crude therapeutics. Fishbein stood for a sane positivism based on both science and common sense. On the issue of contraception, however, he contradicted his own belief that "The great fallacy of all the 'systems' of disease and their healing lies in that 'all or nothing' policy. When that policy runs counter to demonstrable fact the result is invariably disaster." Arguing for "positive treatment" that included some risk where warranted, Fishbein concluded, "Granted that there are instances in which the wrong use of drugs may have hastened death, there unquestionably are many more instances in which the lack of medicament—the failure to apply the remedies of science—has resulted in anguish to the sufferer and in the spread of disease." [5]

Fishbein emphasized the "lack of any sure device for birth control." The efficiency of the known methods ranged from "ten per cent to somewhere about ninety per cent; none of them is perfect. Moreover some of them may produce irritation of the tissues and grave consequences, including cancer. Little need be said of their psychological effects." Refusing to distinguish between methods or to recognize that medicine might have a responsibility to try to improve what was available, Fishbein saw sterilization by X-ray or the development of a spermatoxin as possible future sources of relief, and concluded that in 1925 there was nothing that could be done for the patient who sought birth control advice except to advise continence. The majority of physicians, like the editor of their journal, were willing to wait for the development of some tidy form of contraception and displayed a therapeutic nihilism toward the topic that had been slowly banished from the rest of medicine by a new positivism based on basic research. [6]

Fishbein's hostility to contraception had little to do with professionalism in the best sense. As James F. Cooper pointed out in *Technique of Contraception*, there was a "great deal of thoughtless talk about 'no one hundred per cent method.' "

It is fair then, to ask, have we any one hundred per cent methods in medicine, or surgery, or serum, or vaccine therapy? . . . The only ethical attitude a physician can take is to guarantee nothing. He can only promise to do his best.

This being true, how clearly absurd it is to single out one department of medical practice, namely contraception, for criticism on the ground that it is not one hundred per cent perfect and for that reason to regard it with indifference! If all physicians had adopted the same general attitude toward every other branch of medicine and surgery, their profession long since would have discontinued its activities.

As a matter of fact, there are very few fields indeed in the practice of medicine where such uniformly good results can be obtained as in contraception. It is a fact that the method recommended . . . in this book [vaginal diaphragm with spermicidal jelly] is safe, simple, and when properly followed, *almost uniformly reliable.* [7]

Some medical leaders were involved in controversial issues, however, by the realization that many of the diseases they were finally beginning to understand were reflections of social disorder and could only be controlled if the social environment were changed. Doctors led campaigns against venereal disease, tuberculosis, and hookworm because their new expertise made clear the frequency and tragic results of these plagues. Advances in medical science gave them confidence that something could be done, while personal experience showed that disease was often "an index of socioeconomic conditions." Tuberculosis was "a disease of civilization" produced by tenements and sweat shops, while hookworm spread because southerners defecated on the ground their shoeless children trod instead of in latrines. [8]

Voluntary associations like Prince Morrow's American Society for Sanitary and Moral Prophylaxis (founded 1905) and the National Tuberculosis Association (founded 1904) were organized or supported by individual physicians. While Fishbein used the rhetoric of professionalism to shun social responsibility, ambitious efforts by doctors to change social habits and values were a striking feature of the Progressive Era (1905–17), the period of intensive search for social norms and forms of organization compatible with an industrial, urban civilization. The men who led these public health campaigns

146

were upper-middle-class citizens who had always considered it their duty to preserve existing values and to admonish those who were not measuring up. Now, however, they found themselves trying to change public prejudices against victims of tuberculosis and syphilis, or leading evangelical campaigns for more sanitary privies. An abundance of self-confidence, optimism, and public spirit were necessary in order to brave public ridicule, loss of social position, and the indifference of the masses to force recognition of problems the general public preferred to ignore.[9]

Robert Dickinson, the most important medical advocate of contraception, was drawn into a reform career by the combination of professional experience and sense of social duty that compelled other medical crusaders in the first decades of the twentieth century. As one of Brooklyn's busiest gynecologists, he could not avoid the questions raised by the contrast between what conventional wisdom dictated as normal and what he saw as a practitioner. In one of his earliest case histories he wrote, "Pregnant, have not asked particulars. I would never have believed it of this girl. My mother often praised her. . . ."[10] His response to the tragedies resulting from venereal disease, illegitimacy, illegal abortions, and marriages wrecked by sexual incompatibility was a search for values consistent with the facts he daily confronted.[11]

Lean and of middling height, Dickinson's trademarks were a neat Vandyke and a directed exuberance in work and play. A walker, cycler, and sailor, he blended the ethical idealism of his New England ancestors with a knack for committee politics rare even in the upper-middle-class achievers among whom he worked. He impressed a co-worker as "one of the few people she had observed who had apparently grown through affirmation without having to overcome instinctive negation."[12] A gifted artist, he revealed in the mild impressionism of numerous pen and ink drawings an eye for detail and delight in the order he found in nature.

Dickinson was always committed to the maintenance of stable families in a changing world. His years of struggle to win medical support for sex research, contraception, and marriage counseling were inspired by a positive vision of a richer existence for millions through better sexual adjustment. Believing

147

marriage should be the ultimate in human relationships, he saw it as more than a union for procreation. Most important was the process of growth and self-discovery gained through the sharing of intimate experience with another human being.[13]

A liberal Episcopalian, one of Dickinson's functions as a reformer was to bear Christian witness that sex was a force to be accepted and enjoyed. In 1908, when separating sex from procreation was still regarded by many as unnatural, Dickinson began lobbying among fellow physicians for recognition of the value of sexual expression as an end in itself. Birth control was not a simple solution to the world's ills, but it was an essential first step in sexual adjustment.

Dickinson's interest in services like contraception and marriage counseling reflected the experience of a practicing gynecologist, but his dedication to enlarging the physician's role as spiritual adviser also sprang from his personal situation as a doctor trained in a medical tradition antedating the Flexner Report and the rise of modern medicine. The ideal of the doctor as marriage counselor was his response to changes in the profession that seemed to be taking the human element out of medicine. His "second career" as a sex researcher and medical reformer, beginning in 1920, was in effect an extension of his first career as a busy practitioner and clinical teacher who was a stranger to the laboratory and found time to write only through driving self-discipline.

Dickinson was the eldest of three children born into a prosperous clan of successful entrepreneurs and professional men. His father owned a Brooklyn hat factory along with his partner, William E. Doubleday, the father of the publisher. While his early childhood was exceptional only in the richness of experience offered by life among the brownstones of Brooklyn Heights and summers spent on an uncle's Connecticut farm, Dickinson recalled that a canoeing accident when he was ten provided him with inspiration for a career in medicine. He and his father had built a canoe of boards. "The stem was of galvanized iron, with the top bent over sharply so that the point was sharp as a knife." He was standing waist-deep in water when an eddy swung the canoe into him, leaving an eight-inch laceration in the abdomen. [14]

The local doctor was crippled with arthritis, so a carpenter was summoned and put in the stitches under the country surgeon's direction. The carpenter "missed some things, so that now I'm a little lopsided." Dickinson was in bed eight weeks; the wound suppurated and sand oozed out with the pus. When the carpenter took the stitches out,

> he just cut and pulled them and they dragged at every cut. My mother leaning over, held my head behind her arm. She wore those long complicated earrings, and when I gasped I got a whole mouthful of earrings. So for the rest of the time I was too busy spitting out earrings to pay attention to the stitches being pulled out.

But, "That man I adored so, that doctor,—Strong—that's what I wanted to be." [15]

Fifty years later Dickinson was nauseated by a pair of earrings which reminded him of his mother's. He was never able to pitch a ball very well because of the injury, but he did develop skill as a rider, swimmer, and sailor, and at eighty-five could still do a flip across two canoes into New Hampshire's Squam Lake. The scar, that was "literally from one side to another—skin drawn in and puckered all the way across his stomach," symbolized a surgeon's lifelong aversion to human suffering. [16]

When Robert was twelve, his father took the family to Europe for a vacation that lasted four years. The Dickinsons returned to the United States in the summer of 1876 and resettled for good on Clinton Street in Brooklyn Heights. Robert entered Brooklyn Polytechnic Institute. The curriculum stressed a classical liberal arts regimen, so the two years there were the equivalent of the last years of high school. After graduation from Brooklyn Polytechnic in 1879, he turned down a job as an artist with a lithographic firm and entered the medical school of Long Island College Hospital. Admittance to medical school did not then require a college degree. Of the forty-four graduates in 1875 of Long Island College Hospital, only two were college graduates, and one of those was a foreigner. [17]

Long Island College Hospital was a natural choice for a family establishing roots in Brooklyn. The city took pride in its new medical school and the spirit of constructive innovation reflected in the importation of the European school-hospital idea. Still, the institution's claim to being the first to inaugurate the hospital-college system of medical instruction in the United States rested on rather formal distinctions. The Johns Hopkins ideal of a university-teaching hospital base for research was neither attainable nor sought. Long Island College Hospital simply combined under one roof a proprietary medical school and private hospital. The school's facilities were no scandal by the standards of the time, but Long Island College Hospital received a "B," or second-class rating, in the Flexner Report.[18]

The school's charter authorized the granting of degrees to "candidates twenty-one years or older, who passed three years of tutorship under a reputable physician, and completed two courses at LICH." The degree served as a license to practice. The two courses were repetitive series of lectures, each lasting no more than five months. During Dickinson's first year, pathology was made a separate course. In 1882, the year he graduated, compulsory attendance at autopsies was established. Adequate laboratory facilities for training in histology, physiology, bacteriology, and pathology were not acquired until 1882.[19] These innovations reflected well on a school that had to compete with its neighbors across the East River for paying customers and could not afford to market an education more demanding or expensive than the traffic would bear. Long Island College Hospital's limitations reflected the general state of medical education in the United States before fabulous gifts from the new rich and advances in basic science made possible the rise of modern medicine and the high standards demanded by the Flexner Report.

There were, however, some distinguished physicians teaching part-time at the school, including Austin Flint, Samuel G. Armour, and Alexander J. C. Skene (1837–1900). Skene had a decisive influence on Dickinson. A Scot who came to the United States in 1857 and gave up an appointment as an assistant to Austin Flint to serve in the Union army, Skene was known for his magnificent physique, full beard, and capacity for hard work. He encouraged his students to consider specialization in gynecology before most physicians were willing to recognize it as a special field of practice. In 1880 he published an article describing the paraurethral ducts in women, then a frequent and unrecognized source of infection. Based almost entirely on clinical observations, the description of these "glands" gained him the distinction of having his name connected with a part of the human body.[20]

Skene's eminence among Brooklyn physicians did not rest on research, for which he had little time, but on his skill as a practitioner of the art of medicine. He constantly improved techniques and tools at a time when many instruments were still "invented" by resourceful healers. An excellent lecturer who stressed visual aids and clinical demonstration, Skene noticed a young man who did not seem to be paying attention during one of his performances. On demand, Dickinson showed the professor the sketches he was making of the demonstration. Very much impressed, Skene later asked the student to do the illustration in a textbook he was planning. The two men became close friends and Long Island College Hospital's most famous alumni.[21]

Dickinson finished his course work in 1881, but had to wait until the next year to graduate owing to the age requirement. The year was spent as Skene's assistant and plans were begun for *Treatise on Diseases of Women* (1888), which went through three editions and seven printings, and dominated the American textbook market in gynecology for a decade. The *Treatise* was remarkable for both the quality and quantity of its illustrations, 161 of which were Dickinson originals.[22]

Dickinson finished first in his class, but a career in research was not a feasible alternative to general practice in 1882. Like his mentor Skene, he plunged into the business of healing. As a young practitioner Dickinson witnessed the transformation of "Manhattan's dormitory" into a great industrial center crowded by factories and slums. An appointment as one of Brooklyn's first civil service ambulance surgeons helped provide patients for the new physician, and in 1885 he scored highest in the competition for examiner in the police and fire departments. Proud of these jobs, he later ran for coroner several times without success.[23]

A few years earlier these positions might have been beneath

the notice of a patrician from that "citadel of gentility," Brooklyn Heights. As Brooklyn experienced the growing pains characteristic of American cities, the social elite securely lodged in the Heights managed to ignore the problems posed by urbanization, leaving municipal government to political bosses who could make it pay. In time, stinking streets and rising taxes for nonexisting services aroused Brooklyn's best. Reformers got a bill through the state legislature which gave the mayor the power to appoint his department heads and hold them directly responsible for their performance. "The Brooklyn idea" made good city government possible. Later events proved that the new system under an incompetent or corrupt mayor could be worse than the old tangle of divided responsibility. Fortunately, the new system went into effect on January 1, 1882, the first day of Seth Low's mayoralty. The founder of Brooklyn's Bureau of Charities brought an evangelical zeal to city affairs and drew national attention to an experiment in good government. For four years "the people of Brooklyn were never permitted to forget that they were sharing in a novel and thrilling adventure in self-government."[24]

Dickinson shared Low's "vigorous village pride" that found expression in municipal service made desirable by the willingness of young professionals to seek social order through institutional means. Civic pride, extra income, and exposure to working-class ways helped make a great adventure out of a potentially boring job. As late as 1894, after he had developed a specialist's practice, Dickinson noted "nearly $200 due from Civil Service" and relished the human contacts with Brooklyn's democracy provided by the job.[25] Later when he needed data on male sex anatomy, he had his own records from several thousand municipal service physicals as a base.

Membership in one of Brooklyn's best families, good hands, and the contacts provided by work with Skene assured Dickinson of a clientele. He established an office in the basement of the family home among the brownstone and brick townhouses of Clinton Street. The process of professional growth began with general practice shading into obstetrics and gynecology. In 1886, Long Island College Hospital hired him as a lecturer in obstetrics. He had worked in other departments after graduation and remained a teacher at the hospital until retirement. He was also active on the staffs of Kings County, Methodist Episcopal, and Brooklyn hospitals, holding important clinical positions in all three.[26]

Dickinson received immense satisfaction in playing the role of healer. He thrived on human contact and often stressed the importance of drawing upon psychological and spiritual resources in treatment. Two of his favorite anecdotes described Skene and Abraham Jacobi, his most respected exemplars, pulling rich, elderly ladies through grave illnesses by therapeutic hand holding. "Glory to God" often punctuated his conversation in his later years. His religion shared much with the nature celebration of John Burroughs. One son-in-law remembered that, "Walking through the woods he would suddenly stop and exclaim 'Glory to God!' and point up to the tracery made by interlaced branches overhead, at the pattern of birch-leaves against the sky, or at the stripped patch of sunlight coming through the boughs and falling on the ground." Still, God's creation sometimes needed tidying up. Dickinson was a compulsive pruner of bushes, an inducer as an obstetrician, and a cautious supporter of euthanasia. He had little patience with those who viewed contraception or sterilization as violations of nature. The natural order was good. It could be and should be improved by human agents.[27]

Neither Darwin nor exposure to the political corruption and social disorder of South Brooklyn put a dent in the ethical idealism and faith in the basic soundness of society which was part of Dickinson's social heritage. He differed with his bride-to-be over her conduct of a Bible class.

Do you not feel as if you were shirking in skipping the evolution question when studying Genesis? . . . How can it weaken the effect of these early books to show them as tradition—tribal legends? Do you believe with Geikie in an age of primitive goodness—or in moral evolution as the last step after the physical evolution is complete? God working by definite laws and slow processes is as great—nay, greater—than by sudden and strange changes in the order He hath seemed to set.

He believed that the character of Christ was also misinterpreted.

. . . the adjectives "meek, lowly, humble" . . . are more frequently used with the name of Christ than those which must come first . . . the weakness is not our aspiration, but the quiet, voluntary subjection and self-control, carried to a habit. The manliness of Christ is farthest carried herein—that he is perfectly patient.[28]

The Savior seemed most real when placed in a contemporary setting. In a vision of December 19, 1889, Christ appeared to Dickinson as the most perfect of several young men living together in good fellowship on Clinton Street and pursuing various careers, "but with this in common—each had a good earnest streak in him." Jesus

didn't need to work more than just to get a living. All his time otherwise being busied with other people. A man every inch, well built, fine of face, with a marvelous voice wherein all his character showed, quiet of manner, hearty in his sympathy, of the same age as the other fellows, but stronger and purer, for he lived up to his good resolutions.

Capable of a hearty laugh at a good joke, Christ was a warm friend, who

didn't stick at little things. He worked easily and didn't get tired and slept and ate well. He could see through our motives pretty clearly, and it never seemed to make much difference where you were, you felt he got at your bottom reason. In talking over personal purity he said he knew what a fellow's temptations are and could help other men.[29]

Dickinson wrote these statements to justify character and calling to a pert and headstrong young Packer Institute graduate with whom he had fallen in love. Sarah Truslow demanded an account and justification. She also felt that perhaps they could better serve God as foreign missionaries. In analyzing his profession for Sarah, Dickinson explained that medicine provided an excellent opportunity for Christian witness.

Equipping men to save human lives and bodily suffering, and doing it better every year—caring for the sick poor in hospital and other ways—these seem his [Dickinson's] worthy work. Are they his best? Or is it in the opportunity this work brings in the way of a betrayed girl, or weak man, [brought] back to the only Strength and Highness. One man or woman saved from reckless wickedness is worth all the science. Could this be oftener done by setting himself to less honored positions?

When it became clear that most denominations were more interested in recruiting clergymen than doctors, the lovers decided that their place was in Brooklyn, showing by example that "happy and simple, comfortable and tasteful homes are possible without large outlay."[30]

After their marriage in 1890, Sarah's need to do good was realized in the founding of the Brooklyn branch of the Young Women's Christian Association, as a charter member of the Brooklyn Auxiliary of the New York Committee of Fourteen, which exposed commercialized vice and the white slave traffic, in the founding of the Travelers Aid Society, to guide the Sister Carries of New York in their first perilous months in an urban environment, and in the writing of *Problems of Life* (1900) and *Fellowship Prayers* (1918) for the YWCA.[31]

Dickinson combined doing good and doing well in a growing practice which drew heavily from the best society but always included many who could not pay, especially domestic servants, who provided subjects for some early research. In his early practice Dickinson delivered his share of babies in the notorious tenements of South Brooklyn, but he was less affected by confrontation with the plight of the city's wretched than those like Henry George, Jane Addams, and Charles Beard whose lives were changed by the discovery of the desperate situation of the urban poor. He did not have a traumatic encounter like Margaret Sanger's with the problem of self-induced abortion in the tenements of the Lower East Side. He participated as a Republican ward captain in attempts to clean up Brooklyn government, and as a vestryman of Holy Trinity Episcopal Church, he supported liberal pastors who sought to build the institutional church demanded by social gospelers. But his personal efforts to help the poor were confined to a heavy load of charity cases.[32]

Dickinson's professional interests found expression in a steady stream of articles. Until his retirement from active practice more of his publications concerned surgical technique than any other subject—descriptions of new instruments, discussions of when to repair an injury and when to leave it alone, how to stitch a wound, when to cauterize. Most of his ideas, like Skene's, represented minor improvements swallowed up in the general progress of the profession. Initial excitement in 1892 over "Dickinson's sign," the appearance during the first two to eight weeks of pregnancy of a transverse fold in the body of the uterus, died when he reported that further observation revealed this same furrow in the unimpregnated uterus.[33]

His passion for order and efficiency is revealed in articles on the improvement of office procedures and the application of the principles of efficiency engineering to hospital administration and the more efficient division of labor within the "health factory." He was active on local and national boards that sought a standard medical nomenclature and was a busy campaigner for uniform and complete hospital records. In recognition of this work he was made a colonel in the Surgeon General's Office during World War I and helped to plan the mobilization of the medical profession.[34]

From the beginning of his career, Dickinson's intense interest in female anatomy and sexuality led to a series of remarkable studies that found their way into print along with his much more numerous but soon forgotten contributions to surgery and clinic management. The records he made of female sex anatomy in its diverse normal and pathological forms were unique in their accuracy. He recorded his observations in minute detail and then carefully compared and classified the specimens. The illustrations in many of his articles were so fine as to seem almost out of place in a medical journal, and the number and quality of his sexual anatomies show the naturalist's most endearing fault, the tendency in time to value the subject of study for itself. Providing a series stretching over forty years of practice, these records were a medical natural history and the essential source on which he drew in founding American medical sex research.

His records began to take their permanent form in 1893. Five-by-six cards were substituted for ledger books, rubber stamps were devised which printed anatomical outlines on which pathological structures could be sketched, and "color stenography" in the form of crayon tints added detail and contrast. Eventually, photography saved some painstaking sketching. A fake flower pot pedestal installed at a strategic angle to the examining table was "actually a tall hollow box with a camera built in at floor-level, and a hinged lid, with a mirror on the under side. It stood loaded with a photograhic plate, and the shutter-spring set to expose a negative . . . when a switch was pressed."[35] This daring innovation was made when many gynecologists avoided local examination of the unmarried and prescribed marriage for the ills of virgins "in the usually vain hope of curing his patient without the infliction of a local examination." "Many [young women] would rather suffer a lifetime than subject themselves to such harsh and, to their understanding, disgraceful treatment."[36] In contrast, Dickinson was examining and recording, while correctly pointing out that hymens stretch enough to allow local treatment of the uterus, and that presence of the structure was no sure sign of virginity anyway. It made sense, he felt, to see that every woman was in good health before marriage. When left to nature, minor pathology often developed into debilitating illness through both physical deterioration and psychological stress. Through premarital examination many "subclinical" but potentially dangerous conditions could be eradicated. Happier marriages, healthier children, and less psychosomatic disease would result, he argued, if the profession would see its duty and substitute "preventive gynecology" for makeshift patching.

Dickinson's lasting contributions to his specialty were made possible by his willingness to discuss sex with his patients and to base treatment not upon an abstract code of proprieties but upon the needs revealed by pelvic examination. The secret of his success as a sex counselor is illustrated by a patient's letter written in the last year of his life.

> I don't know by what magic RLDism you broke my inability to take care of my particular problem. . . . *Before,* I'd gotten it entangled with all the inter-personal highly emotive values I have always connected with a love relation, but putting it in purely physiological terms . . . gave it a whole different semantic meaning, and one I can happily accept. Isn't it amazing how important just plain words are? And how changing them around can make such tremendous differences to people? I'm so grateful to you, because with all the will power in the world I couldn't buck physiology by any rational means I could muster and it was a crippling thing to go through.[37]

Dickinson was more effective as a spiritual adviser because he had a firm awareness of the functional basis of much sexual maladjustment. Simple willingness to handle female sex organs when some specialists still avoided the most routine local examination and the ability to talk about sex in counseling his patients made him a prophet of reason protected from charges of prurience in his interests by the fact that he made them a legitimate part of his craft. By the late 1920s, Dickinson had 5,200 heavily illustrated case histories, some running to twenty pages, and 1,200 detailed sex histories.[38] This material and an awareness of its meaning emerged gradually as experience won out in bits and pieces over conditioned social attitudes.

The fourth article Dickinson published, "Studies of the Levator Ani Muscle" (1889), described an experiment to find out if reported instances of the vagina gripping the penis during coitus could be confirmed by measurement of pressure exerted by contraction of the levator ani. Dickinson found that "contraction which is so readily appreciated by the finger" could be "graphically shown." A wax phallus was greased and inserted into the relaxed vagina of the subjects, domestic servants, who were asked to contract the muscle firmly. This experiment showed in wax impressions that the uninjured levator ani was capable of powerful gripping pressure, confirming "Sims' prediction concerning a vaginal constrictor that presses the glans penis firmly against the os uteri." The rubbing of semen against the os, rather than a sucking action by the uterus, appeared to be the usual means by which sperm reached the mucus of the cervix.[39]

The great debate over corsets also drew Dickinson's attention. Characteristically, he found that most writers on the subject had no empirical evidence. "To obtain clear perception of the action of the corset" Dickinson measured the pressure exerted by the corset with a manometer, recorded vital capacity of subjects laced and unlaced, and made tracings of the feminine figure with the corset on and off. He showed that thoracic breathing patterns, so common among women as to lead some doctors to consider them normal and different from those of men, were pathological conditions caused by excessively tight corsets. The hourglass figure celebrated in Lejeune's Eve was

nothing but an example of "trunk atrophy of the model transformed literally and constantly to art."[40] By 1890, however,
Dickinson felt that "anti-corset talk was waste of breath in my
experience . . . my duty in this direction lay in furthering ladies' gymnasiums to strike at the root of the evil."[41]

If one could not always beat fashion, the new fad of cycling
might encourage society ladies to get desperately needed fresh
air and exercise. Some feared that straddling a bicycle was
harmful. An enthusiastic rider himself, Dickinson set out to
provide authoritative information to dispel the "grave objection" that "wheeling" might "beget or foster the habit of masturbation." While he conceded that "under certain conditions" the bicycle saddle could stimulate "this horrible habit,"
this would be an extreme case and all danger could be avoided
by teaching proper posture.[42]

Dickinson's studies of "Saddles and Postures for Women on
the Wheel" provided the definitive discussion of proper seat
and posture in cycling, with three pages of photos of a skele-
ton, nude model, and clothed model, showing correct and in-
correct perches on the bicycle. He concluded with a characteristic demand that the profession do its duty.

> The practical outcome of this paper is that we physicians ought to
> have personal knowledge of this means of exercise, and that it is
> our duty to instruct prospective wheelwomen, in order that each
> rider be carefully trained by competent instructors as to right pos-
> ture, right methods of pedaling, correct height of saddle, correct
> position of saddle, and, finally [the patient] should be told that she
> must insist—in learning or in buying a wheel—on such trial as
> will enable her to judge what saddle suits her.[43]

Whether initially drawn to the topic by the cycling controversy or by the need in his practice to account for the "presence and meaning of certain alterations about the vulva,"
Dickinson established himself as the American authority on
female masturbation with "Hypertrophies of the Labia Minora
and Their Significance" (1902). The article might have been
titled, "Masturbation: Its Frequency and Effects." Dickinson
argued that enlargement of the labia minor, the corrugated
folds associated with that condition, and frequent accompanying hypertrophy about the meatus, were not normal but "en-

tirely artificial and pathologic" conditions, *"clearcut evidences of traction, pressure,* or *friction."* [44]

"Frank speech" was necessary. "Four of the notable recent American text-books on gynecology depict what they call the type of the normal virgin vulva in illustrations which show typically abnormal forms, all excellent examples of the deformities which will be described." Drawing on 427 cases, Dickinson sketched and explained the symptoms of autoeroticism, noting frequent appearance among all social classes and age groups. While he was not yet ready to accept self-stimulation as a normal or desirable practice, he unequivocally asserted that it was common and should be recognized and treated, not hysterically denounced. The habit by itself produced no serious pathological conditions. Indeed, "the effect of self-massage of the pelvic floor on delivery is beneficial" for most women. Nor was a lack of purity in mind necessarily correlated with self-relief.

> Let it be clearly understood that in a very large proportion of the instances of masturbation in women the matter is a physical rather than a sexual one. By this is meant that sensual images and desires are infinitely less often consciously associated with the practice in women than in men. Among refined and delicate women, the pent-up sex hunger may take this outlet without recognition of the real meaning of the impulse. Among emotional or emotionally religious women the tendency is strong.

Although he later saw masturbation as a normal part of sexual adjustment, in 1903, Dickinson cautiously agreed with Havelock Ellis that "masturbation, when practiced in excess before the age of puberty, has led . . . to an aversion for normal coitus in later life . . . owing to the physical sexual feeling having been trained into a foreign channel." [45]

Two years later Howard Kelly of Johns Hopkins innocently described hypertrophy of the lips of the meatus as the result of normal heterosexual intercourse. Dickinson, "as a disciple of Skene," was quick to correct Kelly. Kelly responded cheerfully to the criticism, and Dickinson provided the section on masturbation for Kelly's *Medical Gynecology* (1908). [46]

Dickinson approached the study of sex as a Christian gentleman and an orthodox physician rather than as a radical social critic. The correctness of his social and professional attitudes guaranteed a tolerant reception for his unorthodox work. He was one of the three founders of the American Gynecological Club, a society dedicated to "the general advancement of obstetrics, gynecology, and abdominal surgery" through clinical travel. The fellows of the club toured hospitals in America and Europe comparing techniques. Limited to fifty members who could afford extended travel, the fellows of the AGC were the elite of their line. They sometimes took their wives along, and considerable social activity was fitted into a busy itinerary. Dickinson cherished these professional holidays and described one European trip when wife and daughter accompanied him as "the most happy time" he could recall. A diary kept during travels in 1912 provided a running commentary on personalities and places. Notes on improvements to be made dominated. In his descriptions of individuals, the main theme was admiration for professional peers, pride in the doctor's life style, and satisfaction in belonging to this group. Laymen were judged by their attitude toward the medical profession.[47]

Always conscious of the feelings of the colleagues with whom he proudly identified himself, Dickinson often adopted an apologetic tone in bringing a controversial topic to their attention. He began a 1907 talk on "Marital Maladjustment" by explaining that a "stubborn conviction that certain things have got to be said, even at some risk," compelled him to "take up certain important neglected factors in the chronic nervous trouble of women."[48] His approach to sexual counseling reflected his belief that the physician was responsible for the moral as well as the physical welfare of his patients. Experience as a physician, he explained to a meeting of the Associated Physicians of Long Island, had convinced him that "no single cause of mental strain in married women is as widespread as sex fears and maladjustments." He believed court records would show "that in most divorces the initial source of friction lies in a real or fancied physical incompatibility." These facts were evidence that physicians, "the proper agency for oversight," were failing in their duty. Although sex counseling as a matter of routine "bristles with difficulties and misunderstandings and aversions and false constructions and temptations to evil-mindedness," the physician who was "clean of mind and happy in his marriage" was the only person with the knowledge and objectivity to "save his people from their ignorance." As his contribution to this evangelical endeavor, he outlined the techniques he had developed in his own practice. "What I teach is based, every clause of it, on the wreck of some marriage or some mind." [49]

One problem was that "Good people possess no language or terminology either for their feelings or their anatomy." Yet plain talk was necessary and effective. "Our high function as confessors and advisers of the saintly half of the race, and the imperative need, at times, of one step within the Holy of Holies is impossible without intimate speech, gentle, reverent, direct." The first crucial need was for instruction before marriage. Usually this required that the physician take the initiative by seeking permission from the bride's parents to give basic instruction a day or two before the wedding. Her fiancé was called in separately to be advised. The main burden of these talks was to make clear that "This ultimate surrender and intimacy is not alone necessary for the perpetuation of the race, but is one of the exalted expressions of love between husband and wife." Mutual satisfaction was a necessity. "It is all wrong if just 'submitted to,' or 'a duty.' " Although it might take months, "harmony must come, or a reason [be] found. Otherwise, you see, a constantly recurring cause of friction exists. This always increases in time, however considerate the husband is. . . ." In most cases, "patience and desire and the use of vaseline will overcome all difficulty." [50]

Dickinson gave instruction in contraception as part of normal premarital advice. Six months should pass before leaving coitus open to conception. Always, children should be planned and spaced. Not only was regulation of pregnancy "right and wise," "abstinence [from sexual intercourse] is not good for either husband or wife." He could not understand why men who prescribed alcohol and morphine should "balk at imparting . . . knowledge of the means of preventing conception because . . . of fears that it furnished information giving safety to sexual immorality or immunity to the selfish." If conditioning in home and community ideals did not succeed, then ignorance and fear would not. Worse, withholding this information undermined the basic institution of society, stable family life.[51]

His friends at Long Island College Hospital joked that in ten minutes he could bring any conversation around to birth control.[52] He believed, however, that sexual adjustment was the key to happy marriage. Birth control made that adjustment easier; many times it was the only thing that made it possible. His own wife had been freed from childbearing after three pregnancies and their marriage was blissful. No hypocrite, he concluded that what was good for him was good for anyone who could learn from experience. During his long struggle to have contraception added to the normal repertoire of medical services, he often posed rhetorical questions about the effectiveness and safety of contraception. But his own mind was made up twenty years before the Committee on Maternal Health was founded in 1923. Clinical studies were necessary to win over colleagues and perfect techniques. A diplomat's strategy rather than personal doubt was behind his constant theme that clinical research was needed because no one knew anything about contraception. If the profession did not do its duty and make scientific studies, then some "Sanger group" would fill the void.[53]

Considerable anxiety existed among the "uterologists" (Dickinson's improvement on "obstetrician-gynecologist") during the first two decades of the twentieth century over the future of their specialty. Abdominal surgeons seemed to be taking over more and more of the operations they had pioneered. It was difficult to support a practice on obstetric fees alone, and the first-rate had to compete with midwives and general practitioners. J. Whitridge Williams, the head of obstetrics at Johns Hopkins, did not make many fellows of the American Gynecological Society feel better when he demanded that they take up basic research for which by education and economic interest they had little enthusiasm. Williams would lend his support to Dickinson's program of education in contraception during the 1920s and 1930s. In 1914, however, he was more concerned with the more fundamental deficiency in American medicine symbolized by the fact that when he graduated from the University of Maryland in 1888 with the obstetric prize, he had witnessed only two deliveries, and had had little opportunity to obtain the basic insights he would seek at Hopkins in William Welch's laboratory.[54]

Elected president of the American Gynecological Society in 1914, Williams delivered a scathing reproach to his colleagues. In reviewing articles published in the society's *Transactions*, he failed to find a single fundamental contribution to obstetrics. The society was a provincial club, rather than a national association of scientific men dedicated to "free exchange of thought between competent experts with a view to broadening their field of vision and increasing the general store of knowledge." Lack of the research habit was revealed by "an entire absence of reference to the biochemical aspects of pregnancy." The fellows of the American Gynecological Society had ignored the advances in biological science that represented the future of medicine.

The society did, however, represent the best of the American profession, and its failings were not due to individual inadequacies but to the lack of "university ideals" in American medical schools. While economic necessity excused the ordinary doctor from "patient scientific work," more "should be expected from those who have important hospital connections or hold teaching posts." They failed in their duty if technical virtuosity took the place of serious attempts "to extend the limits of knowledge."[55]

Williams' speech was propaganda for the Johns Hopkins ideal, but it must have been filled with pathos for Dickinson. His whole situation had consigned him to a career in the old medicine for which Williams had contempt. For an ordinary man a life of healing needed no defense. For Dickinson, Williams' call for "broadly trained scientific men who are prepared to give full time to their duties" had bite. If he could not make a fundamental contribution to the new science, he could do his part in raising up a generation of physicians who would "be interested in and devote themselves to the study of the problems connected with the entire sexual life of women." The doctor as marriage counselor would be heard from.

Throughout his career Dickinson demanded that medical men cast their nets wider and take personal responsibility for advising patients about sexual adjustment, contraception, and other matters for which most felt they had neither time nor competence. These pleas for enlargement of the healer's role, while in some aspects part of the new emphasis on preventive medicine, sometimes ran against the growing utilization of more basic science in diagnosis and treatment. The best of the younger men were increasingly committed to continuing education and research that put a premium on their time and diminished their ability to concern themselves with the ordinary cares of patients. The new professional who emerged in the early twentieth century was more concerned with the basic mechanisms of disease than with increasing the priestly role. Dickinson boasted that he always kept the perspective of the family doctor. Younger men often had an awareness of medicine's social dimension, but they were willing to leave to specialists in psychiatry or marriage counseling the therapeutic hand holding that compensated for serious voids in the old practitioner's knowledge of physiology and pathology.

Dickinson had gained eminence as a surgeon. But the further perfection of technique was a dead end. He had an aptitude for research, energy, and intellectual curiosity that demanded a serious outlet, but no training in basic science. He had devoted his life to "the study of womankind," and like all great naturalists, he knew what could be discovered by the naked eye about his subject. Williams wanted to revitalize the specialty through basic research. Dickinson made a new career for himself by living his own recommendation in his 1920 presidential address to the American Gynecological Society to take an "interest in sociological problems" falling within the uterologist's domain. He already had data in his own records to answer the rhetorical questions he posed. "Is there a simple method of preventing propagation among women who are idiots, epileptic, hopelessly insane or incurably criminal?" What about clinical evidence on the "distasteful" but burning issue of contraception? "What, indeed, is normal sex life?" [56]

He had an excellent practice in Brooklyn, had served on many professional and civic committees, spent much time writing, had taken more than his share of charity cases, and still managed to do well financially. His two daughters were grown and would be away to China as missionaries. Relieved of financial responsibility for them, secure in the knowledge they would be safe from scurrilous abuse resulting from his active role in reform, he could depend on an income of several thousand dollars a year from investments and do good by imitating those "teachers and students of the modest life" who

> by their scientific product, put us to shame. In our land the doctor must be a failure who has not car and clothes as good and house and habits of the class of his best patients. Sessions for pure science must be housed in palatial hotels. . . . A whole house for a doctor with offices busy for one work-hour in four is the custom in most of our towns. This is a formula which any business would condemn. Little wonder that the pace is such there is scant time for study or clinical travel. The younger men cannot voice the protest. It is for us of the senior group to voice and act out a protest. . . .[57]

He abandoned the office-home in Brooklyn for a small apartment in Manhattan and took buses or subways instead of taxicabs. Full-time sex research replaced routine office gynecology.

CHAPTER 12

Clinical Studies

Cry cry what shall I cry?
The first thing to do is to form the
committees:
The consultative councils, the
standing committees,
select committees and sub-
committees.
One secretary will do for several
committees.

T. S. Eliot
"Difficulties of a Statesman"

NO ONE could outtalk Robert Dickinson, and no one could ignore him. "There's nothing like a gray Van Dyke and crow's feet to each temple . . . to get you past the people who are hired to keep you out."[1] Willing or not, the medical profession was going to be informed on contraception. As Margaret Sanger learned from bitter experience, getting some things done required support from the rich and the competent. The best society was Dickinson's natural milieu.

Dickinson's election as president of the American Gynecological Society had been engineered with an eye toward the title's value when he was no longer practicing and had assumed the role of reformer. It seemed to him that opportunities for constructive change were being ignored by his peers, while Emma Goldman and Margaret Sanger were giving birth control a bad name through their irresponsible behavior. In 1916 he told a group of Chicago physicians, "we as a profession should take hold of this matter [contraception] and not let it go to the radicals, and not let it receive harm by being pushed in any undignified or improper manner." When

167

Margaret Sanger approached him asking for his support, he politely refused.[2]

Still, it was hard to stay ahead of Mrs. Sanger. In 1922 rumor had it that she was about to open another birth control clinic, this time with some obscure woman doctor in charge. If investigation of contraception was going to receive the careful direction it needed, Dickinson would have to get a clinical investigation under way. Most important, however, Sanger's successes provided him with the excuse he needed for action. By March 1923, Dickinson had secured financial backing from several society ladies, the most important of whom was Gertrude Minturn Pinchot (Mrs. Amos Pinchot). He then recruited physicians to create the Committee on Maternal Health to sponsor medical investigation of contraception, sterility, abortion, and related issues.[3]

The first step in gathering information on contraception was to establish an office of record where data could be collected from those hospitals allowing contraceptive advice to be given. Dickinson hoped for sponsorship from some medical organization in order to facilitate hospital cooperation, to certify the legitimacy of the investigation to the profession, and to protect the researchers from the caprice of the police and the antivice crusaders. Lura Beam, who was coauthor with Dickinson of two monographs based on his case histories, remembered that during the committee's early years there was constant fear that their publications might be declared unmailable or that intervention by John Sumner, Anthony Comstock's heir on the New York Society for the Suppression of Vice, might scare off support.[4]

Dickinson began his quest for institutional backing at the March meeting of the New York Obstetrical Society. He used discussion of a paper by George W. Kosmak (1873–1954), "The Broader Aspects of the Birth Control Propaganda," as a platform for proposing the creation of a committee to study contraception, failing to mention that he had already established one. An old friend of Dickinson's from clinical travel days, Kosmak was also an old foe of birth control, editor of the crucial *American Journal of Obstetrics and Gynecology*, and a practicing Catholic.[5]

Dickinson revealed his knack for professional politics by

turning Kosmak's denunciation of birth controllers ("the so-ciologists, society leaders, uplifters, reformers, and radical thinkers of every type, with a few doctors") into an endorse-ment of a committee to study contraception. Having admitted the need for the study, Kosmak had to serve on the committee conducting it, and despite repeated efforts to resign, his name remained on the letterhead of the Committee on Maternal Health. Dickinson was determined that the committee would be representative of medical opinion, and it was. But the need to justify all actions to Kosmak and other more cautious col-leagues was a constant source of tension and frustration, over-come only by Dickinson's irrepressible single-minded cheer-fulness in pursing his goals.

That Kosmak and Dickinson were able to cooperate in an in-vestigation of birth control was a credit to both men. In per-sonality and professional opinion they were diametrically op-posed. A man "devoted to the machinery of life," Kosmak loved to call the *American Journal of Obstetrics and Gynecology* the "Gray Journal," and his influence was always on the side of caution.[6] Dickinson had a surgeon's temperament and was an "inducer" who always sought to minimize pain. Kosmak, primarily an obstetrician and medical editor, thought high maternal death rates were caused by unnatural attempts to speed up deliveries.[7]

From 1917 until his death in 1954, Kosmak repeatedly stressed his fear that American women were shirking their duty to bear the four children apiece that he believed popula-tion maintenance required. Indeed, birth control propaganda had "instilled in the minds of the public an actual growing fear of pregnancy which [it] may take years to overcome."[8] While Dickinson thought abstinence in normal married people pathological, Kosmak argued, "No one has yet conclusively demonstrated that sexual abstinence, partial or complete, is fatal or even dangerous to health."[9] Most people who could qualify for contraception on medical grounds were in such bad shape they should not have sex anyway.[10]

Kosmak cooperated with Dickinson, however, in order to keep contraception under strict medical control. Kosmak wanted contraception taught in medical schools so that no woman with serious medical indications would be denied ad-

vice by a private practitioner.[11] In this way charges of neg-
ligence could be refuted and the justification for clinics
backed by lay groups preempted. But most important, along
with techniques, medical students would learn proper attitudes toward contraception. In 1939, Kosmak explained to the
New York Times that birth control had got out of hand because
it did not remain strictly under the control of private practitioners. The schools gave

> insufficient attention to the teaching and practice of birth control
> measures when they were definitely indicated. Most of the stimu-
> lus for what has been done in a scientific way has come from lay
> groups whose sense of direction and application has not as a rule
> been satisfactorily guided. For this state of affairs . . . physicians
> must assume the blame.[12]

Kosmak wanted to investigate birth control in order to condemn it; he wanted medical control of the dissemination of
birth control information and supplies because that was infi-
nitely better than its free dissemination in any form.

Dickinson, well aware of the attitudes of colleagues like Kosmak, used the strategy in 1923 of shaming them into action. It
certainly was frustrating, he told the fellows of the New York
Obstetrical Society, to watch "the confounded lay groups that
butt into our business and find out something we need to
know." While gynecologists sat still, the National Research
Council had created its Committee for Research in Problems of
Sex; Katharine Davis of the Bureau of Social Hygiene had sent
a questionnaire to 1,000 college women and found that 74 percent of them practiced birth control. While scientists, social
scientists, and the Sanger people were investigating these
matters, the gynecologists were abdicating their right "to decide physical harm or harmlessness" in this practice.[13]

Tired of foot-dragging, Dickinson made it clear that the real
objects of contempt should not be those who were responding
to a felt need in the community in the absence of authoritative
medical information, but the obscurantists in the profession.
"Dr. Kosmak cannot see the necessity for an office [of record
for analysis of clinical case histories]. Well, there has got to be
some kind of secretarial office; there has got to be some kind of
loose organization to start the experiment. . . ." If the profes-

sion refused to act, then it had failed to employ its only means to "avoid the very things which Dr. Kosmak objects to." [14]

A committee of five was appointed to study Dickinson's proposal that the New York Obstetrical Society sponsor a study of the effectiveness and safety of birth control methods. The committee voted four to one (Dickinson dissenting) that such a study was not one of the functions of the society. [15]

Dickinson decided to risk going ahead without the New York Obstetrical Society's support. He hired a nurse to help establish relations with hospital officials, established an office of record in his apartment, and announced the founding of the Committee on Maternal Health. Next, he made a survey of the literature and found "a library of argument" based on "acceptable reports" covering the "histories of thirty-four patients." [16] Since the Dutch, English, and German literature on the clinical use of contraceptive pessaries was inadequate, he paid Dr. Gertrude Sturges to survey the methods used in foreign clinics. Like Margaret Sanger, he had to go to Europe for a technique that was controlled by the woman and proven in clinical trial.

Faced with the *fait accompli* of the Committee on Maternal Health's existence, the New York Obstetrical Society voted to send out a questionnaire to the membership. A majority of those who answered were in favor of the society's cooperating with a medical investigation of contraception. This questionnaire was important because Dickinson found hospital cooperation impossible to get until this modest official approval was secured. While half of the respondents thought economic indications deserved consideration, there was almost unanimous opposition to "special clinics for contraceptive instruction," "teaching [of contraception] by nursing organizations . . . , or release of information to the general public." [17] These objections were important because the Committee on Maternal Health was eventually forced to depend on Sanger's Clinical Research Bureau for case histories in significant number.

Dickinson hoped to supply materials for three methods to cooperating hospital clinics for trial: the condom, lactic acid jelly, and the Mensinga spring-type diaphragm. Unfortunately, the diaphragms, although "extensively used in Holland and England," were "not yet obtainable here." [18] The twenty-four patients being treated under the committee's supervision by May 1924 did not like the spermicidal jelly that was the only female method the committee could provide. "Since this is the case it appears that the work will remain more or less at a standstill until the pessary is made available for use." [19]

Dickinson ordered spring-type diaphragms from Germany in January 1924, but the first of many instances of "nonsense at the border" occurred. Customs officials intercepted 600 of the 1,000 devices and sent them back to Germany, despite a supposed understanding with the chief appraiser at the customs house. The 400 diaphragms that got through were of the smallest and largest sizes, suitable for only about 20 percent of the potential patients. [20]

The question repeatedly asked James F. Cooper, medical director of the American Birth Control League, in his nationwide lectures to medical groups was, "Where can we obtain diaphragms?" A few druggists smuggled pessaries, but their prices were too high for the semicharity trade of the birth control clinics. [21] Committed to absolute propriety and legality, the Committee on Maternal Health was powerless to prove that this method was safe and effective unless it could circumvent the law. Finally, in 1926, an agreement was reached with the American Birth Control League to buy diaphragms from them at fifty cents apiece. [22] Still, until the Holland Rantos Company began to manufacture European-quality diaphragms in 1928, good contraceptive supplies were hard to obtain.

Patients for study proved as hard to obtain as diaphragms. Dickinson had assumed that hospital clinics would provide an efficient means of gathering case histories. He set up a rigid set of rules and procedures that he hoped would establish the legality of the investigation and guarantee cooperation. Only patients would be accepted who qualified under the New York state law "which permits a physician to prescribe contraceptives to cure or prevent disease." Patients were referred to a hospital clinic only "over the signature of one or more physicians of recognized standing." This requirement caused physicians in hospital departments that were being paid to refer patients to the committee to send their patients to the Sanger clinic. As one physician explained to the committee, "however positive he might be that a certain patient would be in very grave danger if she conceived, yet he doubted whether he would be willing to put his name to a recommendation for contraceptive advice to be handed the patient, for fear of the use that might be put to such a paper." The committee dropped this requirement, but at the same time voted not to give slips of printed instructions to patients; "it might be copied or lost or otherwise convey information where it should not be available." If a patient were in mortal danger and could get a doctor "of recognized standing" to explain why in writing, then she would be referred to the outpatient department of a cooperating hospital for treatment. The hospital in turn kept the CMH informed on the case and furnished case histories of any patients seeking advice who came directly to them.[23]

Dickinson began with a belief that any reasonable goal could be gained by working only through proper channels and dealing only with the best people. He assured his colleagues who had consented to serve on his committee that their work was distinct from and more important than "the extensive work in contraception done by the 5th Avenue clinic of Mrs. Sanger" that was so much in the news.[24]

Fitting diaphragms was just difficult enough to require special training and a willingness to devote time to work for which no professional prestige would result. These techniques were not taught in medical schools. Either faulty fitting or carelessness on the part of the patient could lead to pregnancies, demands for abortion, and trouble with the law. With no glamour and some risk attached to the work, it was much easier to send a patient to a special clinic like Sanger's where doctors specialized in contraceptive technique. Usually women, these doctors were held in contempt by men "of recognized standing."

Dickinson made a determined effort to work through the outpatient departments of the hospitals. Despite small returns for money and time invested, the committee persisted in the project; given their original assumptions there was no acceptable alternative. After eight months, nine patients had been referred to the committee, three of them already pregnant.

Hospital officials either refused to cooperate or stalled. The committee paid $300 to the heads of six outpatient departments "in conspicuous hospitals in order to obtain a proper collection of records." Later the committee paid $3 per record. These "honorariums" were ineffective. One doctor "received $25 a month or a total of $125" and turned in six cases.[25] The assumption that hospital outpatient clinics would be a more efficient means of delivering contraceptive advice than special birth control clinics proved false. Fifteen hundred dollars to five hospitals brought twenty-three patients. There were a few exceptions. By December 1925, Mount Sinai had sent twenty-five case histories and "the clinic chief refuses honorarium."[26]

In late 1925, Dr. Gertrude Sturges, who had made a survey of European clinics for the committee, was hired as executive secretary. "An old clinic hand," Sturges had worked for both the Association of Out Patient Clinics and the Association of Tuberculosis Clinics. The original office of the committee had been Dickinson's apartment. Dr. Sturges established an office "among other social organizations" in the Penn Terminal Building, freeing Dickinson to write.[27] She began a new hospital offensive but reported that the renewed effort was futile. Three years' effort had yielded 124 incomplete case histories. The main reasons for the disappointing result were:

1. We really refuse patients who present only economic indications.
2. Physicians and agencies are not informed of our service. . . .
3. Physicians . . . are to a greater or lesser extent already quietly giving advice in their own Out Patient Departments.
4. Unsuccessful efforts have previously been made to use our clinics.
5. There is great inconvenience in securing admission to Out Patient Departments whereas admission to an independent clinic (e.g., American Birth Control League) is convenient and simple.[28]

Dickinson could do little to remedy this situation. The issue of indications was nonnegotiable with conservative members of the committee. His suggestion that the committee have its name inserted in the "Directory of Social Agencies" that appeared in each issue of *Survey* was voted down in 1925.[29] Finally an item in *Medical Week* was allowed, despite "the fact that Mr. Worthington [legal counsel] has given his opinion that the insertion of such a notice might make *Medical Week* unmailable." Dr. Sturges distributed 1,500 "circulars of information" in dozens of interviews and visits to metropolitan-area hospitals, but Sturges resigned in late 1926.[30] Dickinson's interest in the project had been waning for some time. By October 1927 there were 335 case histories, all incomplete. The commitee's minutes noted that while its clinical data did not compare "with the American Birth Control League work, where there are 1200–1500 cases a year, it is better than nothing."[31]

Better than nothing was never good enough for Dickinson. He was inevitably drawn to the one available source of data, the Clinical Research Bureau opened by Margaret Sanger and Dr. Dorothy Bocker in January 1923 and necessarily maintained as Bocker's private practice. In January 1924 committee members made surprise inspections of the Sanger clinic, which had been in operation for one year, had given advice to 1,208 patients, and had a supply of diaphragms.[32] Bocker had no professional standing beyond a license to practice and was referred to with contempt in Committee on Maternal Health meetings—until Dickinson found out she was a 1919 graduate of his alma mater, Long Island College Hospital, and competent enough to fit a diaphragm.[33]

During the next six years, Dickinson found more and more in common with the people at the Clinical Research Bureau. After several unsuccessful attempts to completely disassociate the clinic from all lay influence and to place it under the control of distinguished medical men, Dickinson joined the advisory board of the clinic in 1930. This entente with the birth controllers ran counter to the wishes of most members of the Committee on Maternal Health. Dickinson's unsuccessful attempt to take the Clinical Research Bureau "out of the American Birth Control League" and place it "under responsible medical supervision" revealed the serious limitations imposed by law and professional propriety on medical investigation of contraception and showed why that "promiscuous" and "self advertising" woman succeeded where her social betters failed.

The Clinical Research Bureau's main departures from medical ethics were in advertising and in dispensing free treatment. Most of the women treated at the Sanger clinic would never have gone to a private practitioner for fear of refusal. Louise Bryant, successor to Sturges as Executive Secretary of the CMH, explained the real sin of the Sanger clinic in a candid letter to a friend. ". . . you can't imagine how fearful the medical profession is of any suggestion of economics or sociology— it instantly conjures up for them 'State Medicine,' 'medical socialism' and what not." [34]

Margaret Sanger's attitude toward the medical profession became increasingly conciliatory as she realized the complexity of the problems involved in making birth control available to every woman. Some of her advisers stressed the prestige that medical recognition of her clinic would bring. She feared, nonetheless, that turning her clinic over to a group of eminent medical men would mean that many women would be refused for lack of sufficient medical indications to satisfy a law she thought unjust and a denial of human rights.

Nurses sent secretly by the Committee on Maternal Health to inspect the Sanger clinic reported, "Dr. Bocker gives information only to physicians concerning her methods or procedures. Social workers or nurses who want to learn the methods usually get this from their patients after their attendance at the clinic." When a woman wrote to Sanger for help, she received a letter asking for the name of her physician. The physician was then offered the services of the clinic. There was no deliberate effort to come between a doctor and his client. [35]

Sanger, in response to criticism of Bocker's first clinical report, approached Dickinson about providing first-class medical supervision for her clinic. [36] He jumped at the opportunity. The Bureau of Social Hygiene (Rockefeller money through Katharine B. Davis) made a $10,000 grant for the creation of the Maternity Research Council to run the clinic. Sanger was temporarily willing to accept direction from medical men chosen by Dickinson, but the scheme failed because Dickinson could not overcome both legal barriers and the limitations imposed on his action as a member of the Commitee on Maternal Health. When he finally did associate himself with the "real birth controllers" in 1930, it was as an individual, and not as an officer of the committee. [37]

176

Dickinson promised Sanger that he would obtain the coveted dispensary license for her clinic and began campaigning among committee members for permission to negotiate a take-over. The members of the committee showed a complete lack of enthusiasm for the take-over of the Sanger clinic. At the same meeting in which Dickinson put forth his plans for the creation of the Maternity Research Council, his colleagues voted not to send a delegate to the international conference on birth control being sponsored in New York by Sanger. Dickinson attended anyway and actively participated.[38]

An executive committee controlled the Committee on Maternal Health. All initiative was taken by the executive committee, and no one could act for the CMH without its approval. As secretary and the most interested and energetic member of the executive committee, Dickinson managed CMH policy. He initiated most programs. The other members served as a litmus test by which he could try his ideas to see how they would have to be altered to gain acceptance by the profession at large. Usually Dickinson was willing to compromise to get committee backing. Failing this, he would go ahead with his original plan anyway, having learned how to present his idea in a better light from the reaction of his colleagues.[39] By making the creation of the Maternity Research Council a question of taking the Sanger clinic "out of the hands of the propaganda groups," Dickinson forced acquiescence to his plan. But in guaranteeing the absolute legality of the new clinic, he set a requirement that he could not meet and provided conservative members with a means of vetoing a project they disliked.

Dickinson's first step in the negotiations with Sanger was to get the New York Academy of Medicine to appoint a three-man committee, consisting of Harold C. Bailey, George Kosmak, and himself, to investigate the Clinical Research Bureau. Their findings were predictable since the clinic had already been inspected several times by Dickinson, Kosmak, and other CMH members. Dickinson thought that, "In a few instances advice concerning contraception had been given without evident disqualification for child bearing; in some others advice appeared to be given on insufficient evidence of examination." Bailey did not like the "propaganda" posters pointing out that birth control was cheaper and safer than abortion.[40] Kosmak wanted to close the place down as a "violation of the law" and "a public menace."[41]

Sanger seemed willing to meet all criticism. Despite some initial disagreement over who had to be fired and whether the *Birth Control Review* could be displayed at the clinic,[42] by November 1925 the plans for the Maternity Research Council had been endorsed by Michael M. Davis of the Rockefeller-funded Committee on Dispensary Development, eleven distinguished sponsors had been recruited, and only a dispensary license from the State Board of Charities was lacking.[43]

There were three standard requirements for the granting of a license, Dickinson later explained, "proof of need, proof of character of the incorporators, and sufficiency of funds." The Board of Charities never questioned the fact that these were met. The board, however, developed a fourth requirement, "novel in such procedures. It demanded waivers of objection from certain religious groups. These had sent no representatives to speak at either hearing. On inquiry such waivers were found to be available from churches other than the Roman Catholic." This placed the Catholic hierarchy of New York "in the position of making a categorical statement or letting inaction serve the same purpose." "In a period covering seven months letters forwarded to the proper authorities in the Catholic Church concerning a waiver have received no answer." Dickinson's frustration was vented in a talk he gave in England in 1926. "One is reminded of clerical declarations against vaccination and chloroform, but hardly recalls that a church went so far in its crusade as to attempt to blockade a state licensed inquiry affecting every fertile married couple."[44] His history was muddled, but the anger was real and legitimate.

The three members of the Board of Charities served without pay. Whether real tampering or simple caution dictated their policy was not known. They found the grant of a license to the proposed Maternity Research Council "inexpedient from the stand point of public policy." The members of the Board of Charities were not consistently unfriendly, however. In late 1926, Michael Davis spoke with two of them, was convinced that a license was hopeless, but thought "that the Board will

really welcome the idea of the Maternity Research Council pro-
ceeding without a license." Davis pointed out:

> . . . there are about 125 of the 350 odd clinics in New York which
> are not licensed. Among these the prenatal and well baby clinics
> are most nearly analogous to ours. The theory on which these
> clinics continue unlicensed is that they do not give medical treat-
> ment in the ordinary sense of the word, but that their activities are
> practically limited to examination and advice.

Dickinson attempted to get permission from the committee to
go ahead with the Maternity Research Council without a license, as Sanger had done, but the executive council of the
committee refused to sanction any clinic without a license.
Last-minute attempts to find a hospital to sponsor the clinic in
its own plant failed.[45]

The action of the State Board of Charities prevented the
model clinical investigation in which Dickinson had invested
so much emotional capital. The next time Dickinson wanted to
take over Margaret Sanger's clinic (1929), he still could not
guarantee a license, and she was not willing to make another
attempt. There was no enthusiasm for the project on the Committee on Maternal Health anyway.[46]

At least one member of the committee agreed with Sanger's
decision not to give up her clinic. Before Gertrude Sturges
resigned as executive secretary in late 1926, after months of
frustration in trying to get important medical men to cooperate
in a clinical investigation of contraception, she addressed a
memorandum to the executive committee that showed some
sympathy for Sanger's fears about the fate of her clinic under
complete medical control.

> The Executive Secretary proposed that the Committee consider in
> the fall efforts to secure records in other states where the law does
> not limit intake of patients. It is her considered opinion that even
> if a State Board License could be secured for the Maternity Re-
> search Council, it might not be wise to assume this responsibility.
> She had been repeatedly informed of patients treated there who
> are apparently healthy. If the MRC assumes responsibility for this
> clinic they could not of course give advice except "to cure or pre-
> vent disease." Such a policy would probably inconvenience
> various agencies and individuals who are using the clinic to secure
> information on economic indications, etc.[47]

After Hannah Stone became medical director in 1925, the Clinical Research Bureau provided good case records for study. Dickinson was instrumental in getting these records published in a representative journal. Under strict medical control there is little reason to believe the Maternity Research Council could have found many more women in mortal danger than the CMH did in its years of frustrated effort to secure records from hospital clinics.[48]

Dickinson and Sanger were often at odds, but the longer they knew one another the closer they became. When she came under fire for her flamboyance from the more conservative professional leadership of the American Birth Control League in the late 1930s, he was quick to her defense. He reminded the new leaders,

> Mrs. Sanger is the symbol, the international figure, possessed of ability to beget enthusiasm for this work beyond anyone else whatever. . . . She has a way of delivering the goods which makes our other groups appear somewhat as though mechanisms of organization, conformities, . . . and fear of the medical guild were their main concern.[49]

Dickinson and Sanger were able to cooperate in the end because they shared one animus given expression by Dickinson in 1926. He wrote in one of his memorandums to himself:

> There can be only one real discouragement for those who urge that certain world questions must be answered, and that is to discover real indifference. Concerning birth control there is indifference. . . . This indifference is not met except among two classes. Where woman is exploited as mere breeder and legitimized mistress or where the ascetic teaching prevails of marriage for procreation only [;] there the question is treated as settled.[50]

CHAPTER 13 **Publisher and Clearing House**

DICKINSON was determined to make contraception a recognized and valued medical service. Bitter experience taught that the medical profession was unwilling to sponsor a clinical investigation of the subject. By 1929 the lay birth controllers in cooperation with individual doctors were collecting case histories in more than seventy medically supervised clinics.[1] These clinics, responding to Dickinson's advice and criticism, improved general examinations, follow-up procedures, and records. Data was available to prove that many women could be taught to control their fertility without danger to their health or morals. Next to a breakthrough in basic science, the primary need became collation and publication of the facts in forms acceptable to the profession. Dickinson realized his committee's main role was no longer to pioneer clinical research but "To furnish every doctor knowledge and courage that he may give to every patient information and comfort concerning the contraceptive best suited for her proven need. . . ."[2]

The Committee on Maternal Health became a clearing house for information on human fertility and sponsored a series of definitive monographs that served as handbooks for doctors and as justification for shifts in opinion for which most medical men were ready. They could only change their minds, however, in response to "scientific" evidence rather than propagandistic demands. Dickinson was more successful in the role of professor to the guild than as an organizer of basic research. He was the mediator through whom organized medicine made its peace with the birth control movement. By persuading colleagues that they could live with birth control, he made the inevitable less traumatic and did his profession a great service by helping it to deal with change and to make change an opportunity to strengthen its position.

When Gertrude Sturges resigned her paid position as the CMH's executive secretary in late 1926, she was replaced by Louise Stevens Bryant (1895–1956; Ph.D., 1914, University of Pennsylvania, Medical Science), an editor and statistician.[3] The next eight years were the committee's most productive. Dickinson and Bryant provided different but compatible sensibilities and skills and got things done.

Bryant came to the CMH after four years as editor for the Committee of Dispensary Development, created by the United Hospital Fund and the New York Academy of Medicine to study soaring hospital costs and the delivery of care to the two-thirds of New York families whose incomes provided no surplus to meet the cost of serious illness. Her first job after graduation from Smith in 1908 was with the Russell Sage Foundation, where she established herself as an expert on school reform. She moved on to Lightmer Witmer's clinic for disturbed children at the University of Pennsylvania and got a thorough training in clinical psychology and the Ph.D. In 1914 she became chief of the Women's Division of the Criminal Department of the Municipal Court of Philadelphia. Her job was to provide the court with the relevant data in domestic relations cases as part of a then daring attempt to apply the social sciences to the problems of juvenile delinquency and illegitimacy. During the war she compiled statistics in the Chief of Staff's Office, then turned down a job in VD control because she wanted "nothing related to pathological psychology or to criminology, because eight years of it was enough." Educational and publications secretary of the Girl Scouts was a long way from the Philadelphia municipal court. Four years was enough, and in 1923, Bryant joined the Committee of Dispensary Development.

Bryant was forty-two in 1927, a pioneer woman professional. When Dickinson interviewed her for the Committee on Maternal Health, he noted, "a scholar, not a money-raiser." There were tensions and risks in sex research but an aura of detachment and gentility was maintained in the committee's new offices Bryant chose in the Academy of Medicine at Fifth Avenue and 103rd Street. The academy provided the priceless resources of "the right psychological background" and an excellent library.

Bryant became a money-raiser, taught the committee's authors to count, conciliated medical egos, and provided creative editing during the eight years when the committee published *Control of Conception* (1931), a handbook on contraceptive technique that set a standard of excellence for other works in the field,[4] and a number of other influential works, including the first study of normal sex life based on physical examination as well as interviews,[5] a pioneering study of the sexual adjustment of the single woman,[6] a badly needed atlas of human sexual anatomy,[7] a survey of the organization and clientele of medically supervised birth control clinics,[8] a history of contraception that was the only scholarly monograph on the topic for thirty years,[9] the first monograph on the physics and chemistry of contraception,[10] and a cluster of articles and books on topics like sterility and abortion that literally defined a new field of social biology.[11]

Bryant left the committee in 1935, her health seriously affected by the tensions resulting from a Dickinson-sponsored proposal to put two homosexuals on the CMH payroll and make a study of patterns of sexual inversion. Sexology in the open was not Dr. Bryant's idea of medical science.[12] By 1936, however, Dickinson's committee had answered in print the questions he raised in his 1920 address as president of the American Gynecological Society and had laid the basis for the official acceptance of contraception by the AMA through influential publications and personal lobbying by committee members.

Dickinson's 1924 article "Conception: A Medical Review of the Situation" marked the beginning of *informed*, open discussion of contraception as clinical technique in the leading journals. Besides providing clear information to hundreds of doctors who always wanted to know about birth control but were hesitant, this article, read before the American Gynecological Society and mailed to 3,000 physicians in defiance of the Comstock Act, really established the subject as one "susceptible of handling as clean science, with dignity, decency and directness." [13] After 1924 Dickinson published a steady stream of pieces that kept contraception before the profession as a medical issue. Sometimes an article like "Average Sex Life of American Women" was "the only feasible way" to get discussion of birth control into the *Journal of the AMA*, but it still got there. [14] When an article based on one case claiming injury to the bladder from diaphragms was printed in the *Journal of the AMA*, Dickinson was quick to show that in the future such unfounded claims would not go unchallenged. [15]

By the late twenties the committee's reputation as a source of advice on sex subjects and publications was attracting many requests for help from doctors, journalists, and would-be sexologists. Bryant had to constantly reassert her position that she had limited time to spend on evaluating unsolicited manuscripts and that the committee had to keep its activities within the bounds of medical science and maternal health. [16]

The committee had originally planned to subsidize basic research, and a number of grants were made, but the committee lacked both the personnel to supervise such projects and the money required to back research from which no immediate results could be demonstrated to donors. [17] The National Research Council Committee on Research in Problems of Sex (founded 1921) was already doing an excellent job of stimulating work in sexual physiology. [18]

In November 1928 the Committee on Maternal Health voted "to divert all resources to publication" and to broaden its audience to include "non-medical scientific and professional societies, not only as a means of raising money but in response to the increasing demand by lay groups for help." In 1930, "National" was added to the committee's title and thereafter its main function was the publication of monographs on relevant topics, along with lobbying among medical groups for birth control and for increased recognition of the importance of sex research. [19]

Dickinson felt that *"contraception alone* will carry with less difficulty if bracketed with sterility when it comes to enlisting professional interest."[20] Birth control should be treated as part of a broad program of preventive medicine in which education for motherhood, cure of sterility, and general sexual adjustment were equally important. One member of the committee took offense when Gertrude Sturges mentioned population control as the committee's main concern.

> As I understand it, we do not undertake to touch the problem of population through birth control . . . the objects . . . of the CMH may be summed up as follows: 1. To conserve maternal health 2. To prevent the transmission of disease 3. To stop the propagation of defective and substandard types in general.[21]

George Kosmak attempted to resign when Dickinson named study of contraception as the committee's main interest in the preface to *Control of Conception* and bitterly opposed the reissue of Charles Knowlton's *Fruits of Philosophy*. Haven Emerson "disliked very much" the committee's placing manuscripts with the same publisher that sold William Robinson's *Fewer and Better Babies.*[22]

Dickinson, Sanger, and Stone viewed the birth control clinic as part of a broad program to improve the quality of life. In Stone's view, "The birth control clinic of the future will serve as a bureau of information and advice concerning many problems of parenthood, fertility, sterility, marital relations and so on. In such a center . . . the emphasis will be placed not merely upon family limitation, but upon family regulation in the interests of the parents, the offspring, and the race."[23] Dickinson saw the birth control clinic as a means of bringing medical services to thousands of women who would never receive medical attention through any other means. "Women come for spacing of children or general health protection and then the pelvic examination which is required . . . uncovers a surprising amount of disorder, sometimes unsuspected. On this score alone the birth control clinic has already justified itself as a factor in preventive medicine."[24]

Dickinson gave untiring support to Sophia Kleegman, Robert Laidlaw, and other pioneers in marriage counseling. He wrote introductions and provided illustrations for works ranging from a new edition of Mary Ware Dennett's pamphlet for adolescents, *The Sex Side of Life,* to Ford and Beach's scholarly *Patterns of Sexual Behavior.*[25] His support got books into print and denial of his endorsement kept them out. As the most influential person in American sexology before Kinsey, he received and answered hundreds of letters from colleagues asking his opinion on novel problems that came up in their practice, ranging from whether a dog could impregnate a woman to the best technique for treatment of frigidity.

The Dickinson-Belskie sculptures, depicting the cycle of conception, fetal growth, and birth, were viewed by more than 2 million people at the 1939 World's Fair in what was probably the most successful single effort at sex education ever staged.[26] First and last, birth control was simply part of an effort to help people to a richer existence through better understanding of themselves. Reform was joyous exposition.

> In the days when the New York World's Fair was being built, Dr. Dickinson often carried his sculptures out to Flushing Meadows on the BMT subway. He would sit in the corner of the subway car and then with a pixie-like gleam in his eyes, slowly unwrap the birth model. Soon his blasé neighbors in the car would take notice. Some would begin to ask questions. Then a crowd would collect and he would begin a public lecture on human reproduction.[27]

Dickinson continued to devote much time to the changing of medical opinion on birth control. It was a necessary first step in sexual adjustment.

> In all marriages whatever, except a marriage where both partners are ascetic, sterile or impotent, birth control and the mechanism of love loom large as techniques of happiness. Honoring all honorable acts of love means teaching them. Herein Nature is no better guide than in other works of art. No act of life is without a technique of training.[28]

In 1925 he got the AMA's Section on Obstetrics, Gynecology, and Abdominal Surgery to pass a resolution recommending "the alteration of existing laws wherever necessary, so that physicians may legally give contraceptive information to their patients in the regular course of their practice." This resolution was ignored by the House of Delegates in 1926 and 1927 despite active lobbying by Dickinson.[29] The AMA continued to avoid the issue until 1935 when the booming business in "feminine hygiene," supported by unscrupulous advertising that flourished in the absence of any medically recognized standards for discriminating between methods and products, forced the formation of a committee to investigate the situation. Initial optimism on Dickinson's part turned to chagrin when the committee, which included George Kosmak, was "unable to find evidence that existing laws, federal or state, have interfered with any medical advice which a physician has felt called upon to furnish his patients"; went out of its way to attack lay organizations concerned with the problem along with "the support of such agencies by members of the medical profession"; and denied that any safe and effective methods existed.[30] All of these conclusions were diametrically opposed to Dickinson's carefully worded and heavily documented position in *Control of Conception*. The committee was instructed to continue its investigation.

When Carl Davis, chairman of the committee, showed up at the American Gynecological Society meeting in Atlantic City, Dickinson was ready for him and loaded for bear. Dickinson and Frederick Holden spent three days with Davis, E. D. Plass, another member of the AMA committee, and Kosmak, refuting point by point the committee's report. Dickinson emerged from these sessions with a request "to study the report in detail and make to the Committee suggestions on further steps thought desirable by the group or groups" that he and Holden represented. They cheerfully complied. Before the next meeting of the committee in February 1937, the Committee on Maternal Health supplied "a voluminous amount of data" "bearing on clinical prescription and success of contraception in this country."[31]

The CMH also received a request for "material bearing on the 'safe period' " from another member of the AMA committee, John Rock.[32] Rock was then a devout Catholic and his views were far from those he later eloquently expressed in *The Time Has Come* (1963). But he was on good terms with the members of the CMH and felt an obligation to listen with respect to their views. Rock's attitude was in part the result of an astute bit of lobbying.

Beginning in the early 1930s, the CMH sponsored a series of

187

Round Table Discussions, luncheons or dinners to which distinguished guests were invited, expenses paid, to share their views on some topic in the area of human fertility. The topic chosen for December 4, 1936, was "Should the Newly Married Practice Contraception." Dr. Raymond Squier chaired the meeting. He had invited John Rock as special guest of honor because "Dr. Rock's point of view had been presented to him recently and had aroused his interest as an approach deserving consideration by physicians whose functions in contraception had not yet been delineated."[33]

Rock was glad to present his position because he "objected to the emphasis on *contra*-ception" and wanted "a more positive approach to fertility." There was only one valid reason for birth control, definite medical contraindications to pregnancy. But such situations should not arise, for "those with medical contraindications should not get married." The purpose of sex was reproduction. Marriage existed to provide support for woman so that she could fulfill her nature. "Nature intended motherhood to be woman's career, and her proper career, she should start right away. . . . Anything which diverts her from her prime purpose is socially wrong." Economic arguments about the burden of children were "9 / 10s subterfuge and distortion of value. . . . Cases come to mind of wives supporting their husbands' scholastic activities; far better to let the man take off a year so that she can have her baby, and then go back to his educational work." Last, sex could not "be made an end in itself without dire consequences," yet that was the result of most decisions to postpone pregnancy in early marriage.[34]

Kosmak praised Rock's views and gave his opinion that "the unfortunate part of the birth control propaganda is that the young people are being led to believe that children are a pathological occurrence. . . . Whenever a young wife fails in her contraceptive practice one thanks God that she did." Still, Kosmak blamed physicians for this dire situation. Contraception should be taught in medical schools. Doctors had to take a more active part in shaping attitudes toward birth control than merely doubting its wisdom out loud.[35]

In earlier Round Table seminars on contraception some sarcasm crept into discussions of Catholic doctrine on birth control. When told of support for rhythm at the 1934 AMA convention, Dickinson wanted to know, "Did they give out jelly with the calendar?" Bon mots were exchanged as frustrations found an outlet:

> Mr. Cautley: Have you heard that small men in big towns and big men in small towns have opposed birth control because of not having more obstetrical practice.
> Dr. Cary: That is not limited to small men or small towns!
> Dr. Gamble: Miss Topping had heard that it was not necessarily the obstetrical angle, but the fractures, measles, etc. to go with it.

Still, the attitude toward the legitimate opposition was conciliatory. Randolph Cautley pointed out,

> The general opposition . . . from the beginning has been an opposition to any divorce between sexual intercourse and procreation, and once you admit separating the two, the whole case is broken down immediately. No fine distinction is valid. The whole attitude of opposition rests on some Christian concept of the uncleanliness of sex. Any departure from it is a complete departure. Anyone who emphasizes the safe period is playing a very clever game in favor of birth control in medical practice.[36]

When Dr. Rock came to call, all was sweetness and light. His views were cordially received and criticism was modest. Frederick Osborn, "as a student of population," pointed out that birth control was "an accomplished fact which will not disappear, but which will spread." Regine Stix argued that her studies with Raymond Pearl showed that contraception had "very little to do with the . . . advice of physicians," and medical influence in this area waited on a better informed profession. Dr. Mayer observed that Rock's "view was, of course, not a biological one but a philosophical one." He "failed to mention that his view makes of the physician a deus ex machina controlling the masses through enforced ignorance. Decisions should not be based upon ignorance, but upon knowledge." Sophia Kleegman made it clear that there was "no evidence that the early use of contraception leads to a diminution in desire for children," or to functional inability to have them when medically supervised. Finally,

> Dr. Dickinson pointed out that the National Committee on Maternal Health 13 years ago stressed the positive side of birth control.

When the first child comes too soon, the second may come never. Early marriage and shorter period of engagement are necessary; yet they are impracticable unless contraception may be employed. Anyone who thinks young people do not want children is wrong.[37]

The AMA's committee on contraception issued a second report at the 1937 convention that seemed hardly compatible with its 1936 report in view of the fact that there were no wholesale changes in its membership. An AMA-sponsored study of techniques and standards was recommended, along with the promotion of instruction in medical schools. Significantly, criticism of the lay-backed organizations in the field and of their medical allies was omitted. Finally, the committee declared contraceptive advice should be given by the physician "largely on the judgment and wishes of individual patients."[38]

This reversal of opinion was the fruition of the campaign begun in 1923 and anticipated by Dickinson in 1908. The CMH's program of education for the medical profession had finally paid off. The victory proved hollow.

The internal crisis that resulted in the resignation of Louise Bryant in 1935 symbolized the realization of an original purpose, the testing and justification of contraceptive methods available since the nineteenth century. The evidence was complete several years before the AMA accepted Dickinson's position. Information on technique and supplies was readily available to the practitioner who wanted to use it. Several hundred clinics offered effective methods to those referred by doctors and to those who were able to seek help, whether their reasons were medical or not.

Yet by 1935 the Committee on Maternal Health had defined a new issue and begun to direct its program toward a new audience. The emphasis fell on reaching those not reached by professional journals or the existing clinics. Millions of women had no family doctor and would never see the inside of a clinic. Methods were needed which could be sold to the indigent masses, the underprivileged who seemed incapable of learning "the birth control habit" required if the diaphragm was to be effective.

Robert Dickinson continued to write on "Household Contraceptives," "Contraception with Intra-uterine Silk Cord," and "Sterilization without Unsexing." But his crucial contribution to the control of fertility had been made. At eighty-nine Dickinson battled cancer with characteristic courage and wit. Several hours before he went to the operating room for the removal of his prostate and testicles in an attempt to retard the spead of cancer, he wrote to Robert Laidlaw:

> I am in the happy frame of mind of being on the verge of positive action. . . . I went to a good night's sleep saying and wake saying "Glory to God." And with not a little amusement that I who have thought it not altogether dull witted to have characterized those monastic minds which framed the [sex] dogmas . . . as not "non-compos mentis" but "non-compos testis"—that I should come to castration.[39]

Dickinson died in November 1950 of complications following his operation. While a central theme of his medical career had been a search for values compatible with human needs in an affluent society, his views toward sexual expression changed considerably over time. The man who had been disturbed by his discovery of widespread autoeroticism among women in the 1890s had become by the 1930s the proponent of self-stimulation with the electric vibrator as a means of overcoming frigidity.[40]

In 1950, facing the possible end of his life, Dickinson outlined his hopes and convictions in his letter to Laidlaw. He had retained his belief that social behavior had to be taught; it could not be left to chance. "You know how I have argued that instruction in sex behavior and all its phases should be subject to the same processes and principles as other preparations for living and for vocation. You recall my outcry that for every life work there was examination for fitness save for the most important of all, marriage." If marriage was to be preserved and improved, allowance had to be made for profound changes in sexual conduct. The "three terrors" of detection, conception, and infection that had inhibited the sexual expression of previous generations would no longer be effective due to increased privacy, better birth control methods, and penicillin. Empirical study showed masturbation and homosexual contacts to be common. It was clear that adolescents had sexual drives as strong as those of adults. "Now that we can . . . regulate the consequences of sex union, it is up to us [physician marriage counselors] to draw up a new program of sex behavior if we are honest and of reasonable courage." New conditions made "change of the conceptions of morality inevitable." Social order depended on new codes of conduct in line with the truths established by investigation.[41]

Dickinson did not live to see transvestite singers become the idols of adolescents, movie starlets boast of conceiving children out of wedlock, or radical feminists question the value of the conjugal family. At times his hopes that every facet of social behavior could be wisely managed, if only the best men would concern themselves, bordered on the quixotic. The same broad social changes that weakened sexual inhibitions also made the supervision of sexual expression by social elites impossible. Services like contraception, abortion, and treatment for venereal disease would be most effective when provided to everyone without any moral sanctions beyond those dictated by the immediate medical problem at hand.

Nevertheless, the tradition of sex research that Dickinson helped to establish was an empirical one. Like Havelock Ellis, whom he admired, and Alfred Kinsey, to whom he looked as the sex researcher of the future, Dickinson ignored Freud.[42] His method was that of the collector. Dickinson believed that the unvarnished facts had to be obtained before effective social prescriptions could be written. He stood midway between Ellis, whose data were drawn wholly fom literary sources and an extensive personal correspondence, and Kinsey, who relied completely on extremely sophisticated interviews conducted only by himself or his carefully trained staff. Ellis, always the artist, often combined aesthetic judgments with his reporting. Dickinson's case studies provided a unique combination of physical data with insight into personality, but his purpose was the definition of mechanisms of adjustment with the end of happy marriage always in view. Kinsey, through concerted effort, banished the evangelical note. No long case histories were included in his work. His subjects were all melted into statistical measures. He did his best to hide his own values. Kinsey established sex research as an empirical discipline, but in 1941 he wrote Dickinson, "It was your own work which turned my attention to the purposes of research in this field some ten or twelve years ago although circumstances were not propitious for starting the work until three years ago."[43] Although Dickinson did not live to see the end of "The Age of Hush and Pretend," he had initiated the process of preparing his profession to deal with the sexual needs of modern America.

PART IV

THE PROSPECT

OF

DEPOPULATION

CHAPTER 14   **Birth Control in American Social Science: 1870–1940**

SOCIAL scientists have debated the meaning of population trends since the late nineteenth century, when universities began to include statistics in their curricula. By the 1970s, America had gone through a century of population crises in the literature of social science. While concern about the social implications of vital statistics has been a constant, the nature of the population problem perceived by demographers has changed radically over time. After World War II a series of best sellers announced that time was running out for mankind unless population growth could be curbed and fundamental changes made in attitudes toward nature. Although population growth posed real threats to human well-being, the new population crisis provided a focus for diverse complaints about the quality of life in industrial civilization, many of which were first voiced in the nineteenth century.[1]

After the first United States Census in 1790, President Washington and Secretary of State Jefferson were disappointed that fewer than 4 million had been counted and feared that this figure might provide ammunition for European critics of American climate and institutions. During the middle decades of the nineteenth century, nationalistic population forecasters, eager to justify their country's mission to fill a continent with good republicans, exaggerated the rate of growth. Beginning in the 1870s, however, population watchers began to emphasize the importance of the sources of growth in contrast to an earlier generation's glorification of sheer size.[2]

Francis Amasa Walker (1840–97), the director of the Ninth Census (1870), noted the tendency of previous census takers to maximize their figures, but emphasized his commitment to an objective social survey. The reforms that Walker instituted as director of the census resulted in a more accurate count, with the unpopular result that the rate of population growth was shown to be declining. American politicians were loath to spend tax money on better social planning. A census that did not show things getting bigger and better forever was not worth the investment.[3]

Criticism of the census for uncovering disagreeable facts infuriated Walker. Rational business and political decisions depended on the empirical data that only a national fact-finding agency could provide. A Civil War hero, disciplinarian, and president of the Massachusetts Institute of Technology, Walker aggressively defended education in useful skills against classicist critics. He hoped that better social surveys and quantitative techniques would give the investigator the power to discover statistically "the laws which govern the action of social and economic forces." Like Lester Ward, Walker wanted a strong central government led by a scientific elite, and, as president of the American Economic Association and the American Statistical Association, he sought to replace the rigid political economy of antebellum moralists with an analytical social science based upon empirical fact.[4]

Walker's commitment to reporting unvarnished facts weakened, however, as he became disturbed by the pattern which the numbers revealed. Some social groups had more children than others. Specifically, the birth rate among native-born white women was falling, and immigrants were replacing their shrinking contribution to national population growth. Initially Walker viewed the declining fertility of American women as an inevitable result of economic development. Mocking the wishful prediction of James DeBow, the director of the Seventh Census, that the population of the United States would exceed 100 million in 1900, he pointed out that DeBow, in assuming uninhibited geometric growth, ignored the tendency of birth rates to decline in a developing society through changes in "social habits." Indeed, he argued, the rate of population growth would have declined much earlier if the high fertility of immigrants had not bolstered the figures. He mistakenly thought that the fall in native fertility began in the 1840s but noted that it might have been expected earlier. The change came "when the people of the United States began to leave agricultural for manufacturing pursuits; to turn from the country to the town; to live in up-and-down houses, and to follow closely the fashions of foreign life." He scoffed at predictions that the United States would have a population of 330 million in 1950. For one thing, he doubted "the capacity of the American people to adapt themselves to the use of dogs, cats, and mice, as food, upon such short notice." In short, American population growth could not continue indefinitely, and declines in the rate of growth were to be expected as Americans sought a higher standard of living in an industrial civilization.[5]

Walker's increasing fear that "beaten men from beaten races" would supplant his own "Anglo-Saxon stock" changed him from a social scientist into an advocate of more Anglo-Saxon babies. By the 1890s, when the new immigration from Southern and Eastern Europe was approaching more than half a million a year, he was no longer interested in debunking the inflated expectations of hopeful nationalists. He blamed the low birth rate among native Americans on their hesitancy to bring children into a world polluted by wretched immigrants. The foreigners, he explained, had "shocked" the native born into infertility.

> Throughout the northeastern and northern middle States, into which . . . the newcomers poured in such numbers, the standards of decency, had been singularly high. Life, even at its hardest, had always had its luxuries; the babe had been a thing of beauty, to be delicately nurtured and proudly exhibited; the growing child had been decently dressed, at least for school and church; the house had been kept in order, at whatever cost, the gate hung, the shutters in place, while the front yard had been made to bloom with

simple flowers; the village church, the public schoolhouse, had been the best which the community, with great exertions and sacrifices, could erect and maintain. Then came the foreigner, making his way into the little village, bringing—small blame to him!—not only a vastly lower standard of living, but too often an actual present incapacity even to understand the refinements of life and thought in the community in which he sought a home. Our people had to look upon houses that were mere shells for human habitation, the gates unhung, the shutters flapping or falling, green pools in the yard, babes and young children rolling about half naked or worse, neglected, dirty, unkempt. Was there not in this a sentimental reason strong enough to give a shock to the principle of population?

In Walker's view, immigrants not only demoralized potential American parents, they introduced labor unrest and class consciousness into the American Eden.

. . . there was, besides, an economic reason for a check to the native increase. The American shrank from the industrial competition thus thrust upon him. He was unwilling himself to engage in the lowest kind of day-labor with these new elements of the population; he was even more unwilling to bring sons and daughters into the world to enter into that competition. For the first time in our history, the people of the free States became divided into classes. Those classes were native and foreigners.[6]

Faced with the immigrant threat to Anglo-Saxon fertility, Walker stood for "Muscular Christianity" and candid recognition

that population growth has been an important force in, if not the direct cause of, the growth of the principle of nationality among us; . . . quantity has . . . in no unimportant degree, determined and helped to constitute quality.

No other race, he assured his readers, could have built the American republic.[7]

Walker's attempt to blame immigrants for all the ills of a society in transition sprang from his fear of an emerging mass society, symbolized for him by the increasing visibility of foreigners.[8] His perception of a relationship between immigration and the decline in native fertility was not, however, simply a nativist delusion. Immigrant labor played an important part in the growth of the American economy and therefore contributed to the social mobility of native Americans. Insofar as the pursuit of higher standards of living led to smaller families, an indirect relationship did exist between immigration and family limitation among the middle classes.[9] Still, Walker's wholly negative assessment of the part played by newcomers contradicted the analytical approach to social problems that he had originally championed. Forgetting that correlation does not prove causation, ignoring his own early observation that "the principle of population" changes in a developing society, and ignorant of the fact that the decline of fertility had begun by 1800, he found the "shock principle" congenial because it placed all the blame for the disorder of industrializing America on the immigrant. Through the "shock principle" the proud patrician father of five could show that the declining influence of his class was not due to lack of vigor or high ideals but to regard for posterity. In a world in which the health of men and nations was still measured in children, the demographer had to do more than count. He had to justify his graphs in nationalistic terms. Walker had squared the facts with the Anglo-Saxon myth that many of his peers found indispensable in a world of eroding certainties.

As a solution to the problem of the differential fertility of the native and foreign born, Walker proposed a $100 tax on every immigrant entering the country. His criticism of immigrants provided ammunition for the founders of the Immigration Restriction League and for defenders of labor like the populist sociologist Edward A. Ross, who believed that immigrant competition undermined the wage-bargaining position of American workingmen. In 1901, Ross translated Walker's "shock principle" into "race suicide," the idea that a higher race quietly eliminates itself rather than compete with a lesser breed. Theodore Roosevelt, in turn, used the term "race suicide" in his exhortations to the middle classes to abandon the self-seeking frugality of the small family and to do their part in the cradle competition between nations. In a State of the Union message to Congress and other writings Roosevelt declared that America's future as a world power was being undermined by the pursuit of the soft life symbolized by barren marriages. Between 1905 and 1909 more than thirty-five articles appeared in popular magazines discussing the infertility of native Americans. Fear of the foreigner's fertility found expression in the racist rhetoric of the Immigration Restriction League and in the excesses of the eugenics movement, but pleas for more children had little effect on the social habits of Americans reaching for higher standards of living. After passage of the Immigration Restriction Act (Johnson-Reed Act) of 1924, the fertility of American women continued to decline, falling briefly below the replacement level by 1936.[10]

While fertility continued to decline in the United States despite the end of free immigration and the economic optimism of the 1920s, birth rates in most of Western Europe also fell. England, France, Germany, and Sweden all had birth rates below the replacement level and faced the prospect of declining numbers if the retreat from parenthood could not be reversed. In England fear of depopulation inspired a series of monographs that attempted to delineate the causes and effects of "the twilight of parenthood," but no specifically pronatalist legislation was enacted. France developed a national system of family allowances supported by taxes upon employers; France also increased efforts to suppress abortion and contraceptive practice. The Swedish response to the problem was unique in that social legislation was enacted to encourage parenthood but no attempt was made to suppress contraceptive practice. Pronatalist legislation, whether enlightened or repressive, did not have any appreciable effects on fertility in the Western democracies, but in Germany marriage and birth rates rose dramatically after 1933. While the unwillingness of the fertile to assume the burdens of parenthood seemed to symbolize the decadence of free societies, National Socialist policies, including marriage loans, family allowances, and the suppression of birth control clinics, were credited by German writers for the "spiritual rebirth" of a nation where birth rates prior to 1933 had been lower than in any other European nation, with the exception of Austria.[11]

Americans shared the concern of Europeans over the economic and political consequences of dwindling numbers. Immigration could no longer be blamed for low fertility of native Americans, but the question of the future ethnic composition of the population remained unresolved. Fertility varied with

Birth Control in American Social Science: 1870–1940

religious, class, and ethnic differences. Beyond the nativist stereotypes concern remained high over the consequences of an increasing percentage of the population being provided by the socially deprived, whether they were native Americans in economically depressed rural areas or "hyphenated Americans" crowded into urban slums. Between the world wars population study in the United States was dominated by concern over the interrelated phenomena of declining fertility moving toward a stable or decreasing population and the differential fertility between classes and ethnic groups.

A permanent Census Bureau had been established in 1902, giving demography a recognized role in the federal government. The Census Bureau, however, was primarily a data-gathering agency and lacked the resources to analyze all the information it collected. Concern among social scientists and philanthropists over dysgenic population trends and the rising specter of depopulation led to the institutionalization of population study in the United States in the two decades following World War I, represented by the founding of the Scripps Foundation for Research in Population Problems (1922), the Research Division of the Milbank Memorial Fund (1928), the Population Association of America (1931), and the Office of Population Research at Princeton (1936).[12]

Edward Scripps, the newspaper entrepreneur, established the Scripps Foundation for Population Research because of his interest in the population problems of the Far East. The foundation supported the early studies of Warren Thompson and Pascal Whelpton, who were the coauthors of influential monographs on population problems which predicted a stationary or declining population after a peak of about 150 million in 1970. Having learned something of the perils of future reading from harsh experience, Whelpton later devoted himself to the refinement of mathematical models for predicting population growth.[13]

The Milbank Memorial Fund's sponsorship of population studies began when an influential trustee, Thomas Cochran of the Morgan Bank, declared himself unwilling to continue voting grants for the fund's work in public health unless the fund also investigated the effect of its work on the quality of the population. When Frank Notestein (born 1902), a future presi-

203

dent of the Population Council and one of the influentials in population studies in the twentieth century, came to work at the fund's newly established Division of Research in 1928, his first assignment was the analysis of unused data from the 1910 census on the relationship of social class to fertility. Notestein's study, published in 1930, provided the first extensive investigation of differential fertility and was followed by a series of similar articles written by the Milbank staff.[14]

In 1931, Margaret Sanger obtained $600 from the Milbank Fund for the founding meeting of the Population Association of America. It was originally expected that Sanger would be voted some honorary office in the new organization, but Frederick Osborn "persuaded the meeting . . . that the fortunes of the field would be advanced if the new Association were to guard its scientific nature and keep free from attachment to the birth control movement."[15] Ironically, Henry Pratt Fairchild, the New York University sociologist, author of *The Melting-Pot Mistake* (1926) and the leading academic racist of the 1930s, was chosen as the association's first president. Fairchild's work has now been discredited, but his popularity rested on his ability to exploit widely felt fears about the threat of biological deterioration.[16] He was not identified with loose talk about freeing women from the burden of childbearing. His selection as president of the Population Association symbolized the widespread concern that demographic study not be associated with the declining birth rate among the middle classes. Rather, demographers were anxious to make clear their awareness of the possible harmful effects of contraceptive practice on trends in differential fertility.

Mere mention of contraception sent chills up academic spines. When the Population Association of America and the United States National Resources Committee cooperated in forming the blue-ribbon Committee on Population Problems, the event seemed to imply a larger role for population studies in the formation of governmental policy. Clyde Kiser of the Milbank Fund contributed a chapter entitled "Social Conditions Affecting Birth Rates" to the committee's 1938 report. Kiser's manuscript gave several paragraphs to possible biological causes of declining fertility, but he went on to argue that biological factors were relatively unimportant compared to contraceptive practice. Edwin B. Wilson of Harvard's School of Public Health, chairman of the Committee on Population Problems and editor of its report, was afraid to publish Kiser's article and deleted all reference to contraception without Kiser's permission, thereby radically altering the meaning of the text. Frank Notestein later reminisced, "The interesting thing about it is that, so far as I know, there was no political pressure. The Chairman of the Committee, a highly respected and responsible professor of statistics, made the cut on his own to avoid expected trouble and did not tell either the author or his colleagues about his ruthless bit of censorship." [17]

Frederick Osborn helped to end episodes like the Wilson censorship by providing a proper academic setting for population research through the establishment of the Office of Population Research in Princeton's Woodrow Wilson School of Public and International Affairs. Osborn's father and Alfred Milbank were both trustees of Princeton. The younger Osborn persuaded Milbank that a good school of public administration should have someone working on the world's population problems, and in 1936 the fund made a five-year grant to the university that provided Frank Notestein with the title of lecturer, complete with research assistant and an annual postgraduate fellowship. [18]

The institutional backing for population studies led to extensive empirical investigations aimed at defining the causes of the declining birth rate. Walker's scapegoat theory was no longer acceptable. Hard facts replaced invidious distinctions between native and foreign born. Massive immigration had ceased, and children of the foreign born tended to adopt the small family system of middle-class America. Social scientists found, however, that the indigent and unskilled had more children than skilled workers or the college educated. The scientists equated socioeconomic status with the ability to provide children with adequate nurture and fretted about the possible consequences of differential fertility. [19]

Investigators differed over the question of precisely why the poor had more children. Raymond Pearl, the Johns Hopkins geneticist who specialized in devising mathematical formulas to account for biological phenomena, believed that fertility trends were a function of changing biological capacity. Human fecundity changed, he argued, in response to population density and this change could be predicted by statistical measures. Pearl's biological determinism was an updated version of the old claim that easy living sapped human vitality.[20]

Pearl's graphs showing the relationship of declines in fertility to broad changes in social environment had the advantage of being esoteric, and they did away with the need to measure the effects of psychological attitudes or to discuss the sticky topic of birth control. A rather pompous academician, he was nevertheless a first-rate scientist. Under the sponsorship of the Milbank Fund, he dutifully began an investigation into the extent and effectiveness of contraceptive practice, interviewing several thousand hospital maternity patients.[21] In 1934, Pearl reported his results to a Milbank Fund symposium. Clearly, "the existing fertility differentials" did not rest "upon deeply rooted, innate biological differences. Instead, the responsibility for them appears to rest primarily, overwhelmingly, and directly upon that body of doctrine and practice popularly called birth control." Pearl ended his presentation with a dramatic flourish: "Gentlemen, you realize that this evidence destroys the basis of my life's work."[22]

Milbank Fund–supported studies by Frank Notestein and Regine K. Stix of the fertility of birth control clinic clients in both urban and rural areas uniformly reinforced a voluntary rather than biological interpretation of declining fertility.[23] Differential fertility was a function of differing attitudes toward birth control, and ultimately toward sex, children, and woman's place in society. These findings marked "a critical change during the twentieth century in the approach to research in demography . . . the shift from excessive emphasis on biological factors . . . to a more mature investigation of processes determined by the interaction of biological, social, and cultural factors."[24]

Neither cultural despair brought on by swarms of foreigners nor physical deterioration stemming from city life caused the declining birth rate, but voluntary decisions made within the family. Birth control was biological dynamite, fraught with potential for good or evil. Population watchers divided between those who viewed the prospect of the end of population growth with alarm and urged vigorous pronatalist policies and those who were comfortable with the concept of a stable population and pointed to differential fertility between classes as the main danger. The pronatalists generally shunned birth control. Those who accepted lower birth rates as inevitable saw the spread of contraception to all classes as an essential part of any population policy.

Louis Dublin, statistician for the Metropolitan Life Insurance Company and a leader in many public health campaigns, criticized the birth control movement for contributing to dysgenic population trends. His great contribution to demography was a formula for taking the age distribution of a population into account in determining the rate of growth. Previous estimates of natural increase based on the difference between the birth rate and the death rate provided inflated population forecasts because they failed to take account of the large number of persons at ages of peak fertility in a young population and of the inherent decline in the birth rate as an unusually large number of young marrieds moved into less fertile middle age. In his 1924 presidential address to the American Statistical Association, he warned

> against the current unwarranted optimism as to the country's demographic future. . . . If we computed the true rate of natural increase, we should see that what maintained our high birth rate was not our inherently high reproductive capacity but rather the fact that the surviving descendants of a more highly reproductive generation were now swelling the ranks of middle life and participating in parenthood.

This lent a spurious appearance of vigorous growth to an otherwise meagerly reproducing population. A continuation of the decline in the birth rate would soon produce a stationary or declining population.[25]

Dublin, a Lithuanian Jew, blamed the birth control movement for reinforcing the selfish propensity of the middle classes to limit family size. In a stationary population "the real danger" lay "in the change in our internal composition," the weakening of "the social organization by increasing the proportion of defective and dependent stock. For it is always the least desirable parents who are the last to curtail their fecundity." He believed the birth controllers should "help arouse a public sentiment in favor of parenthood among the rank and file of normal people."[26]

In contrast, Norman Himes, the Colgate sociologist and historian of contraception, argued that the decline in fertility reflected a "vital revolution," a change in modern industrial society from a high rate of conception offset by fetal wastage through abortion and infant mortality to a biological economy in which fewer children were conceived but more lived. Himes was concerned, however, because the "vital revolution" was not reaching the lower third of the population. Those less able to provide for children continued at a high rate of increase, and their children, although scarred by their environment, survived because of crude improvements in public health and standards of living. Himes believed it was impossible to induce the middle classes to return to higher fertility patterns and saw the "democratization" of contraceptive practice as the ultimate solution to the problem of differential fertility. Outmoded laws and habits of mind inhibited the spread of birth control, however, prolonging dysgenic population trends.[27]

In preaching the gospel of birth control, Himes frequently claimed that the intelligence of the American people was declining. Eugenicists generally accepted Himes' analysis of population trends, but they divided over the possibility of correcting the situation through the spread of contraceptive practice. The founders of the American eugenics movement, Charles B. Davenport, Harry Laughlin, and Paul Popenoe, were hostile toward birth control and hoped the spread of eugenic ideals would inspire increased baby production among the fit. By the early 1930s, however, the old leaders had been replaced, and Frederick Osborn was actively working to establish a common ground through emphasis on "planned parenthood," or democratization of contraceptive practice for the indigent and encouragement of parenthood among the fit.[28]

More egalitarian social analysts viewed the declining birth rate as a primary cause of the economic depression. In 1938, Harvard's Alvin H. Hansen devoted his presidential address to the American Economic Association to his doctrine of "secular stagnation." Hansen argued that the decline of population growth was a large factor in the stagnation of the American economy. In the past rapid family formation had provided a heavy demand for new housing and household furnishings, precisely the kind of consumer goods that increased capital formation. A stationary population meant inadequate demand and a low rate of capital investment. John Maynard Keynes was both a birth controller and a eugenicist, and Hansen believed that technological innovation, rather than population growth, would have to play the key role in stimulation of capital investment in the future, but in the new economic theory the low birth rate posed a threat to economic growth that no one was certain could be overcome.[29]

While liberal economists sought to discover means by which the free market could be saved, Gunnar Myrdal, the Swedish sociologist, perceived the socialist's opportunity in capitalism's plight. In 1938 the Carnegie Institution of New York brought Myrdal to the United States to study the race problem, an investment that led to the classic study *An American Dilemma* (1944), but when he delivered the Godkin lectures at Harvard, he chose to discuss population policy rather than race. Myrdal saw the prospect of depopulation as the ultimate indictment of the capitalist system. Birth control, operating in the social environment created by capitalism, had become "a truly serious peril," threatening the survival of Western society. Those who refused to be alarmed by the decline of the large family system were apologists for a sick society.[30]

Rather than a cause for despair, however, the population problem provided a compelling justification for fundamental social reforms. The solution was not suppression of birth control information and enforced biological slavery but "vast distributional reforms in the interest of families with children." Only a state-supported system of family services from medical care to day nurseries could provide the incentives required to reinstate the four-child family norm and save the race. Thus, the threat of depopulation provided a radical opportunity to seize the initiative from conservatives. The priestess of the hearth of conservative mythology could now be replaced by the socialist ideal of woman as worker and mother, supported in both endeavors by an egalitarian society.[31]

On the eve of World War II, conservatives, liberals, and socialists were united on the need for more children. When the National Resources Committee published its 1938 report, *The Problems of a Changing Population,* need for fertility control was not one of the problems mentioned. In 1940 a bill was introduced into Congress to provide family allowances as a means of raising birth rates.[32] War saved a sick economy, and Margaret Sanger, by then in retirement, was one of a very few who questioned the need for more people. The course of the American birth control movement in the late 1930s and the 1940s can only be understood, however, in the context of a society that doubted its virility, a world in which Malthus was still a prophet without honor.[33]

CHAPTER 15   **Birth Control Stalled**

BLAMED for projected declines in the quality and quantity of the population, birth controllers fought an uphill battle in the late 1930s and the 1940s. In May 1937, in an effort to take advantage of the acceptance of contraception by the American Medical Association in January, the National Committee on Maternal Health called together a group of interested demographers, doctors, and educators to discuss criticism of birth control. Heated debate over "The Eugenic Effect of Contraception—The Significance of the Decline in the Birth Rate" revealed deep antagonism between eugenicist and feminist, social scientist and physician. The participants shared concern, however, over the prospect of an end to population growth and the possibility of public reaction leading to crude attempts to suppress contraceptive practice.[1]

Opinion varied as to why the middle classes were failing to replace themselves. Haven Emerson, professor of public health at Columbia, took a moralistic position.

What we have got to do . . . is to teach the hazards of universal liberty in the application of biological dynamite. It is a fine thing to have as the ambition of any society that all facts belong to all people . . . but facts which are capable of such destructive effect upon the individual family and household cannot be thoughtlessly let loose without accompanying that information with precautions and with advice to use it with restraint. . . . Enthusiasts in the determination that all their fellows shall know all the biological information they can use, have got the front page. . . . There is quite as

211

much obligation on doctors, nurses, social workers, etc., to urge people to save their own sanity by having children instead of to save their own club membership and automobiles by not having children.[2]

Emerson was rebutted by the journalist Dorothy Dunbar Bromley, who observed, "I think it is ridiculous for you men to sit here and say the things you have said tonight about a woman's duty to have children. Many of us have found other interests and compensations very absorbing."[3]

Frederick Osborn and Dr. Joseph Folsom argued that better housing, education, cooperative day care centers, subsidized medical care, and other public investments easing the burden of parenthood were the only acceptable means of raising the birth rate. They believed that young people wanted more children but hesitated because of fear of economic hardship.[4] As usual, the vaguest suggestion that government should play a bigger role in providing medical care aroused immediate antagonism. George Kosmak fervently advocated more babies but denounced any incentives to higher fertility that involved socialized medicine. Kosmak declared:

> Economists and sociologists look at the big side of the thing, but we, as doctors, must continue to look at the individuals, and I hope there will always remain these individual contacts. I, for one, don't care to live to the time when mass treatment of the sick is going to be developed as it is in these mass insurance schemes.[5]

Kosmak's outburst touched on a frequent complaint against birth control—it was not being delivered to the people who needed it most, the indigent. The need to spread contraceptive practice to the lower classes might be used as an excuse for socialized medicine.

The social scientists were unanimous on the dysgenic effect of the uneven spread of contraception. As Frank Notestein explained:

> I can't see a time ever when birth control shouldn't be foisted on some parts of our population. We face the terrible defect that the lower economic groups are our population reservoir. It seems to me to be carrying things to a vicious degree when one part [underdeveloped rural areas] is supplying the population to other geographical parts. I think the birth control group should become in-

terested in spreading its service to the groups where it is specifically needed.[6]

Frederick Osborn, sensitized by the blunders of earlier eugenicists to the need to avoid invidious ethnic or racial comparisons, was quick to distinguish his position from those who blamed particular ethnic groups or classes for social disorder. "The eugenist is not worried so much about differential fertility between classes as he is about differential fertility within the classes." Public health nurses observed that

> . . . any nurse who was worth her salt and knew her district knew darn well which families in that district ought to have fewer children and which families ought to have more children. . . . The question I want light on is how the spread of contraception can be carried on in such a way that it will give opportunities for contraceptive practice to those families who shouldn't have children without indoctrinating too much those families who should have more children?[7]

Osborn thought differences between individuals were more important than differences between groups. The effects of heredity and environment were too closely interrelated to be measured separately. Too often, however, the people who should not have children were the ones who lacked both motivation to practice contraception and access to medical care. As Osborn and Frank Lorimer explained in 1934,

> Those situations in which excessive fertility tends to destroy economic balance, to spread family traditions rooted in ignorance, or to have dysgenic effects are situations in which individuals find themselves unable to control their own destiny, baffled, and led to despair or indifference. . . .[8]

In order to silence some of their critics, birth controllers would have to reach the millions of Americans who had no doctors, lacked the courage, will, or motive to visit a birth control clinic, or were far away from the city-based clinics. Reaching those people seemed to require a vast expansion of medical care. Organized medicine stood militantly opposed to anything that smelled of socialism, and the American Medical Association successfully played on the interests of other groups committed to the maintenance of the free enterprise system to forestall the rational reorganization of medical care. With birth control newly established as a medical monopoly, the prospects for the spread of contraception seemed limited.[9]

Even if they could reach the impoverished, birth controllers had no effective methods for the poorly motivated. The diaphragm and jelly regimen, while close to 100 percent effective among women who accepted it, was nevertheless rejected after brief trial by about 60 percent of the women who came to birth control clinics. Analysis of case records showed that clinic patients were recruited from women who were already using folk methods (withdrawal, douche, condom) with considerable success. These women often returned to the folk methods after instruction in the use of the diaphragm. Those who rejected the clinic method used other methods more effectively after the clinic experience. Nevertheless, for two-thirds of clinic patients the clinic visit merely reinforced habits gained from nonmedical sources.[10]

Robert Dickinson wondered whether "publicity of our actual paucity of knowledge will help or hinder" the birth control movement. The harsh truth was that even if governments decided to offer birth control "to millions of families on relief, or to the swarming populations of . . . Oriental countries, medical science would be in doubt what to advise for most of these people." Diaphragms seemed "practically out of the question for the impoverished, for those of low intelligence, and for the millions out of the reach of skilled instruction." While all birth controllers agreed on the need for more clinics, many believed that major progress would have to wait for breakthroughs in basic science that would provide methods requiring less motivation or skill from the user.[11]

Mary McCarthy, in *The Group*, her evocative portrait of Vassar women from the class of 1933, provided a fictional but realistic description of the diaphragm's inherent drawbacks. In a genital-shy culture, even a Vassar woman had problems managing the gadget:

> Dottie did not mind the pelvic examination or the fitting. Her bad moment came when she was learning how to insert the pessary by herself. Though she was usually good with her hands and well co-ordinated, she felt suddenly unnerved by the scrutiny of the doctor and the nurse, so exploratory and impersonal, like the

doctor's rubber glove. As she was trying to fold the pessary, the slippery thing, all covered with jelly, jumped out of her grasp and shot across the room and hit the sterilizer. Dottie could have died. But apparently this was nothing new to the doctor and the nurse. [12]

Some birth control activists were not willing to wait for scientific salvation in the form of tidy contraception. They assumed, largely on faith, that the poor would limit their fertility if given access to the methods successfully used by middle-class Protestants, especially simpler methods. Better jellies, suppositories, powders, and condoms, delivered by any feasible means, would work. The masses were simply waiting for the word. Birth control was not a medical problem after all, but a matter of giving middle-class secrets to the eager poor. Persistence in that kind of endeavor required the faith of a missionary.

In December 1932, Doris Davidson (Registered Nurse, New York) wrote Margaret Sanger asking to be trained in contraceptive technique at the Clinical Research Bureau. A native of Fort Fairfield, Maine, Davidson had come to New York to attend nursing school and had stayed on as superintendent of Kips Bay Day Nursery. She began to doubt the usefulness of her work as year after year more children were brought to her from the same indigent families.

Davidson decided to give up patchwork and dreamed of bringing a traveling birth control clinic to rural Maine. After six months of training at the Harlem clinic, she poured out her thanks and hopes to Sanger.

> I know that without this fundamental training . . . I should never have been equipped to proceed with the future work of starting a traveling clinic, the importance and need of which is constantly and daily in my thoughts. Oh! to reach the women in the tiny villages and in the backwoods!—and how can it be done unless we go to them? It seems to me that it must be done, eventually, all over this country: that someday each State must have its own traveling clinic. . . . I know you will pardon my enthusiasm, but I see this thing so clearly, and what it could mean to future generations. [13]

Grub-staked with a loan from her father, $20 borrowed from Florence Rose (Sanger's personal secretary), and a list of birth control supporters in Maine, Davidson set out for Portland in October 1933. She recruited a sponsoring group of women, each of whom pledged $5 a week to get the work started. The city was "buzzing" about Davidson's presence when she got a request for a conference from a Dr. Gehring, the president-elect of the Maine Medical Society. Gehring told her of his plans to bring up birth control at the next meeting of the society and wondered if Davidson would like to teach contraceptive technique to local doctors.[14] When Davidson wrote back to New York of Gehring's kindly interest, Rose immediately sensed danger and warned Davidson to avoid any mention of teaching doctors about birth control.[15]

Assured of support by women leaders in Portland, Davidson moved on to Bangor, where she found the going much tougher. After several weeks of unsuccessful effort in Bangor, Davidson discovered the source of her chilly reception there. Gehring had written to an influential colleague in Bangor that Davidson was some sort of confidence woman, interested only in making money for herself. Gehring's poison pen led to the collapse of plans for a clinic in Bangor and to a campaign of vilification against Davidson. She was warned that the doctors were " 'hot on my trail' and that they would make it hot for me if they caught me practicing without a doctor's license."[16]

Davidson had volunteered to work for room and board. No doctor had been asked to contribute to her project, which was to be financed by interested women. After the debacle the general secretary of the Bangor Young Women's Christian Association wrote to Rose to express her personal approval of Davidson's character and conduct.

> The opposition arising here, I believe, was almost inevitable . . . and the charge against Miss Davidson, one of convenience only. There had to be something and this happened to have come out. My heart is sore for her because the charge is so utterly untrue and therefore the more hurtful to her. I have tried to make her see that it 'happened to be' this particular handle which they chose. . . . Miss Davidson must pay the price of a spirit beyond her age and time.[17]

Davidson moved on to West Virginia, where she worked as an organizer for the American Birth Control League, a more cautious and wiser birth control missionary, never again advertising any desire to teach birth control except under a doctor's supervision. Her plan of delivering birth control through paramedical personnel was soon adopted, however, by other birth controllers, who, being millionaires, were more successful.

CHAPTER 16   # The Parents' Information Bureau

I N her eagerness to win allies for
birth control, Margaret Sanger often minimized ideological
differences and ignored bureaucratic or professional proprieties. Critics claimed that Doris Davidson and other well-
meaning idealists not only failed but usually hurt the chances
for permanent progress. To a feminist activist like Sanger,
however, continual effort through every available means was a
moral imperative. The distribution of simple contraceptives to
women who could not be reached by clinics was perfectly consistent with her overall strategy of autonomy for all women.

Delivery of birth control through nurses and social workers
could also be defended on wholly utilitarian grounds. In 1930,
Alvin R. Kaufman (born 1885), a Canadian manufacturer who
was being drawn into the cause by the problems of business
survival during the depression, sent a company doctor to the
Sanger clinic for training. A harshly practical man, Kaufman
shared little of Doris Davidson's idealism, but he too concluded that birth control was too important to be left to
doctors.[1]

Kaufman owned the Life-Buoy trademark and also manufactured rubber boots and raincoats, but contraceptive devices
were not part of his stock-in-trade. His demand for labor was
seasonal, and, when layoffs were increased by depression

218

markets, he received complaints "that I was discharging the employees who needed their income most and retaining those in better circumstances." Kaufman sent a company nurse to investigate and learned that he had indeed laid off the workers with the largest families and the worst living conditions. Alarmed by the discovery that the least skilled workers had more children than his more valuable employees, Kaufman concluded that he would go broke if he kept personnel on the basis of the number of mouths to be fed. Both unable and unwilling to support his unneeded help, he

> decided to suggest birth control to the parents of large needy families although I did not know at the time what the reception would be. I soon learned that the suggestion was gratefully received, and I was then faced with the necessity of furnishing the parents of such families with the desired birth control information and supplies.[2]

Having discovered the philanthropic style that suited him, Kaufman was soon spending $75,000 a year on "spreading the gospel of birth control to needy people." As he explained to H. L. Mencken, the future of civilization was at stake.

> . . . we must choose between birth control and revolution. We are raising too large a percentage of the dependent class and I do not blame them if they steal and fight before they starve. I fear that their opportunity will not be so long deferred as some day the Governments are going to lack the cash and perhaps also the patience to keep so many people on relief. Many of these people are not willing to work but I do not criticize them harshly for their lack of ambition when they are the offspring of people no better than themselves.[3]

Kaufman's crude view of the sources of social dependency and his simple-minded solution to the problems of economic dislocation are less important than his criticism of the clinic-doctor-diaphragm regimen. Kaufman began by setting up a clinic in Toronto and later opened another in Windsor, but he found that "about 50% of the patients cannot be fitted with a pessary for various reasons, some of which apparently are no credit to obstetricians." Less than half of the women referred to a doctor for examination kept their appointment. Moreover, Kaufman found "the greatest need and the most pathetic home conditions in the outlying districts, where doctors frequently are not available at all and more frequently do not know how to fit pessaries anyway and do not care." A large percentage of the needy simply lacked "the clothes, initiative, courage, and freedom to go to a clinic." Finally Kaufman "gave up in disgust" and decided that "if we wish to contact patients by the thousands we cannot do it with a pessary."[4]

Physicians working in birth control clinics generally insisted on prescribing the diaphragm because of the device's high effectiveness. It seemed unethical, if not immoral, to give other methods that were simpler or cheaper but less effective. The diaphragm regimen became a dogma among some birth controllers who insisted that all classes of patients receive the same treatment. Robert Dickinson had long argued, without much success, for a more flexible approach. Less effective methods were paradoxically more effective if patients would use them consistently. Depositing contraceptive jelly in the vagina with a long glass nozzle appeared to be more acceptable to some women, especially the less well educated ones, than inserting a diaphragm. The method was easier to learn, did not require examination, and was therefore much less expensive.[5]

Kaufman, lacking the concern of the physician and the feminist over the consequences of contraceptive failure for individual women, and guided by the businessman's instinct for economy, began experimenting with contraceptive jelly as an alternative to the pessary. He paid nurses and social workers to canvas the women in poor neighborhoods, offering to mail a free contraceptive kit (jelly, applicator, condoms, and an illustrated booklet describing proper technique) to any woman who would sign a form acknowledging her desire to receive the material. To process the orders Kaufman established the Parents' Information Bureau near his Kitchener, Ontario, plant and in seven years mailed more than 60,000 birth control packages.

Kaufman's recruiters explained all of the available methods to potential clients. About 10 percent chose the diaphragm and were referred to clinics or to cooperating doctors, who were supplied with diaphragms by Kaufman. Kaufman found that the door-to-door method cost him $2.30 a patient, less than half of his clinic cost. He kept the Toronto clinic open for "educational reasons" but tried to persuade birth controllers in the United States to invest more in simple methods. Clinical tests showed that the best contraceptive jellies prevented 80 percent of expected pregnancies. Kaufman believed the jelly was almost 100 percent effective among careful women who had fewer than three children and were thus less likely to be suffering from pathological uterine conditions. Interviews of clients by company nurses indicated "that the variation in efficiency of different kinds of contraceptives is not half as important as the caliber of the patients we contact." In short, the pessary was prohibitively expensive and psychologically unacceptable to many of the indigent. Anything was better than nothing.

> I claim that with the lower types of people there will be more failures with the pessary than with Jelly and Nozzle because shiftless people cannot be bothered inserting the pessary, and apparently find Jelly and Nozzle less trouble. A test of the two methods with intelligent people will no doubt be in favor of the pessary, but I claim just the opposite result with careless people who are the ones who need birth control most. I believe I can prevent at least twice as many babies per dollar in the unfortunate classes by spreading the use of Jelly, Nozzle, and Condom.[6]

The resources of private philanthropists would have been exhausted by the costs of providing even the simplest methods to all of the poor. Kaufman saw his Parents' Information Bureau as a model that he hoped would be adopted by public health authorities. Canadian officials believed their limited funds should be spent on other services of a less controversial nature, but Kaufman did win wide publicity for his methods and established their legality in court.

In the autumn of 1936, one of Kaufman's visiting nurses was arrested in Eastview, Ottawa. As Kaufman explained to Margaret Sanger, the province had:

> a large percentage of Catholics with the result that a large percentage of the needy mothers visited by the nurses were Catholic. The priests apparently became considerably incensed and have complained at various times to the Chief of Police. The result was that the nurse was watched and was finally met by a policeman when she left a Catholic home.[7]

Canadian law prohibited the giving of contraceptive information, but there was a clause excepting those who could demonstrate that "the public good was served" by their actions. After a trial marked by frequent biblical quotations and dramatic testimony from suffering mothers, the magistrate declared Kaufman a public benefactor.[8]

Most of the American physicians and social workers active in birth control were motivated by a desire to provide better health care for the poor. Kaufman's crude measures of success had limited appeal to those who saw the birth control clinic as part of a broad program of preventive medicine, including marriage counseling. By the mid-thirties, however, it was obvious that while birth control clinics were doing valuable work in terms of individuals helped, even dozens of clinics in every state could not guarantee the spread of contraceptive practice among the poorest third of the population.

Three strategies were available to birth controllers—support of research that might lead to a fundamental breakthrough in contraceptive technology; campaigns for better public health that included more birth control clinics and better sex education; crash programs to spread simple, cheap methods by the most expedient means. Robert Dickinson and Margaret Sanger supported all three of these strategies. Research was expensive and required patience. Better public health was even more expensive and logically led to subsidized health care for millions of Americans. For those primarily concerned with curbing the growing costs of social welfare programs and making the philanthropic dollar go further, birth control for the indigent seemed a good buy, if the cost could be kept low.

From the late 1930s the old goals of autonomy for women, family stability, and better infant and maternal health were less important motives for aggressive innovation among birth controllers than before, because all that could be done by private sources to promote these causes, short of major scientific advances or a social revolution, was being done. Initiative fell to those who were willing to pursue the goal of fewer babies for the poor at the lowest possible cost. A. R. Kaufman's birth control activities were minimal compared to those of Clarence J. Gamble, who did not have to spend any of his time running a business but shared Kaufman's desire to get the widest control of births with the limited resources available.

PART V

BIRTH CONTROL ENTREPRENEUR: THE PHILANTHROPIC PATHFINDING OF CLARENCE J. GAMBLE

CHAPTER 17   **A Recruit for Birth Control**

WHEN Margaret Sanger asked Robert Dickinson for his public support in 1916, he turned her down. His career as a physician came first, and he believed that association with Sanger would end his influence among other medical leaders. Dickinson, in turn, had great difficulty in recruiting younger men for contraceptive research. In October 1925, Clarence James Gamble (1894–1966), an assistant professor of pharmacology in the medical school of the University of Pennsylvania, and heir to the Ivory soap fortune, wrote his mother about an interview with Dickinson. Dickinson had explained that first-class scientists neglected contraceptive research because of the belief that birth control was illegal or associated with immorality. Most young medical men could not afford association with a controversial issue, but Dickinson hoped that Gamble, thanks to his independent wealth, would be able to help him with his work and take it over when he could no longer continue.[1] Just as medicine took precedence over birth control for Dickinson in 1916, Gamble was committed in 1925 to a career in basic science, a calling for which he was uniquely qualified by academic achievement and independent wealth. After his original ambition was frustrated, however, he expressed his need to do good through the birth control movement, which became "the Great Cause" providing purpose and justification for a man who never worked for a living but, nevertheless, had to work.

In succession, Sanger, Dickinson, and Gamble provided the innovative leadership in the birth control movement between the two world wars. Gamble concentrated his efforts on a search for alternatives to the doctor-diaphram-special-clinic regimen. The majority of indigent Americans had no private physicians and would never see the inside of a birth control clinic. If the goal of making every birth in America the result of a conscious decision on the part of responsible parents was to be approached, then some simple, cheap contraceptive that could be distributed without the aid of highly trained personnel seemed essential. From the late 1920s until his death in 1966, Gamble devoted a large part of his considerable wealth, energy, and intelligence to a search for better contraceptives. He participated in almost every important experiment in population control, and he initiated, organized, or financed a considerable number of them.

Gamble's efforts to promote contraceptive research were constantly hampered, however, by conflict with the professional leadership of organizations from the American Birth Control·League to the International Planned Parenthood Federation and the Population Council. These conflicts in part reflected the dilemma of any wealthy social activist in a democratic society, where the power provided by money must be justified. The rich are expected to make gifts that are controlled by experts whose right to deal with social problems rests solely on professional credentials. Thus, the contributions of the wealthy to reform must be "laundered" or legitimized by vesting power in the hands of theoretically disinterested social engineers. The Rockefellers developed great skill in sharing the power of their money with others. John D. Rockefeller, Jr., subsidized activities of both Margaret Sanger and Robert Dickinson, but his contributions were channeled through organizations like the Bureau of Social Hygiene, where Katharine B. Davis and other experts made specific policy decisions. Gamble had less money than John D. Rockefeller, Jr., and he resented paying salaries to policy makers whom he felt had less knowledge of population problems than himself. Thus, the prejudice against the rich posed a cruel dilemma.

His credentials as an expert could never be separated in the minds of others from his financial power.

His disagreements with other population controllers also grew out of conflicts of value. His birth control activities began in 1929, and his reform style reflected a context of declining birth rates and economic depression. Sanger fought for autonomy for women; Dickinson sought to preserve stable families. For Gamble birth control was a reform that went beyond the palliatives of New Dealers and struck at a fundamental source of social disorder, differential fertility between classes. His mission was to make the world safe for his kind of people, the frugal, hard-working, and prosperous leaders of American society. The tradition of hard work and social service that he inherited was a great asset, but his inability to appreciate the values and aspirations of those from other cultures limited his credibility as a philanthropist and his effectiveness as an engineer of social change. Nevertheless, his career provides a case study in the problems inherent in any attempt to change social habits without resort to large-scale social reorganization.

Gamble was born in Cincinnati, Ohio, on January 18, 1894, a third son and the last of four children. His father, David Berry Gamble, was one of the last Gambles to play an important role in the operation of the Proctor and Gamble Corporation (founded 1837), the producer of Ivory soap and steady dividends for stockholders as indoor plumbing and hot water became staples of American life. The Gambles had traditionally provided the technical genius in the Cincinnati-based business, and the Procters were the marketing experts. David Gamble's sons went to Princeton and found careers outside the family corporation, but Clarence inherited his father's attachment to family life, Scotch-Irish thrift, aptitude for bookkeeping, mechanical ability, and love of gadgets.[2]

Mary Huggins Gamble was the daughter of a Presbyterian minister and the stepdaughter of a University of Michigan theologian. According to family lore, she was an ardent Republican as a girl and did not want to play with children who were Democrats! She went through life with a firm sense of what was right and remembered a year at Smith College as one of her happiest, but married David Gamble after five years of courtship and thorough investigation of his character. The newlyweds became pillars of Cincinnati society, taking care that their children were not spoiled by wealth and had respect for hard work.[3]

The Gambles believed in Christian stewardship and made large and usually anonymous contributions to the Presbyterian Church, Occidental College, the Young Men's Christian Association, and Christian missions to China, and they built a rest home in Pasadena for retired missionaries and "Y" secretaries. When Clarence received his first million dollars at twenty-one, his parents were confident that they had molded him in their own image and attached only one condition to the gift, that he contribute at least one-tenth of his income to the church and other benevolences.

Clarence Gamble's estate grew to about $50 million by the time of his death. He managed his own investments and did his own income tax, yet devoted a great deal of energy to spending from 10 to 30 percent of his income for the improvement of the world. His brother Sidney continued the family tradition of Christian action as a leader of the Presbyterian Board of Foreign Missions. Clarence, however, sent organizers into cities and villages in America, Asia, Europe, and Africa to try to spread a habit rather than a religion. The good news they brought was that even the lowliest human beings could control their fertility, and thus gain the mastery over nature essential to economic advancement and social improvement.

A last child, precocious and willful, Gamble's self-possession reflected the confidence of his parents in their values, his own ability to excel academically with little effort, especially in physical sciences and mechanical studies, and the independence provided by money. When he entered Princeton as a sophomore in the fall of 1911, he was two years younger than his classmates. He banged out a steady stream of letters to his parents on his Underwood portable, keeping both carbons and count of the words he typed, and reporting on his unsuccessful efforts to win a place as flutist in the Triangle orchestra or as circulation manager for the *Tiger*. He graduated magna cum laude and Phi Beta Kappa, first in a class of 102 L.B.'s.

David Gamble was helping to finance the California Commission on Immigrants and Housing, a privately funded state agency providing legal assistance to immigrants, and Clarence went to work for the commission after graduation, unaware that his father was paying his salary. The commission folded from lack of public support, but he had already decided to go back to Princeton for graduate study in preparation for a medical career, an ambition inspired by the example of a San Francisco physician, an old friend whose family had partly adopted the young man from Princeton.

After an academic year in the life sciences, Gamble entered Harvard Medical School, finished second in his class (1920), and won one of the most coveted internships at Massachusetts General Hospital under Richard Cabot, the father of medical social work and one of the great internists of the era. Gamble had decided, however, that his best chance for human service lay in a research career. He explained to his father that his inheritance would make it possible for him to define his own research interests and to hire whatever assistance he needed in contrast to less fortunate scientists who had to consider costs and possibilities for institutional support in defining their research goals.[4]

After graduation from Harvard, Gamble planned to seek an apprenticeship in methods of medical research with Alfred N. Richards, director of the Department of Pharmacology at the University of Pennsylvania. Gamble's academic record and ability to support himself made arrangement of an appointment as an instructor in Richards' department easy, and, having completed his internship, he was scheduled to report to Richards in September 1922.[5] He did not get to Philadelphia until April 1923, however, and was lucky to make it at all. Plans to fly home in his new airplane ended in a July crash that killed the pilot and left Gamble with a concussion and fractures in his collarbone, left arm, and left leg. He could not walk in September, but he was well enough to be shipped home from the hospital. He suffered from insomnia, had trouble making decisions, and was not able to resume normal activities until March. Despite his enormous energy he had never been robust and had suffered from recurrent respiratory infections during college and medical school. He also needed unusual amounts of sleep. A fellow intern remembered that while Gamble worked intensely on projects that interested him, he was careless with ordinary work and often disappeared from the hospital because of exhaustion. After his accident Gamble's "energy deficit" grew worse.

Patient sustained concentration is essential to scientific research. After his delayed arrival at the University of Pennsylvania in April 1923, Gamble's work was continually interrupted by long vacations. He blamed physical disability, but fellow workers sometimes felt that his financial independence allowed him to take his work less seriously than others. His problem was more complex than he or his critics realized. Science offered a means of establishing an identity and sense of worth independent of inherited wealth or privilege. While he excelled as a student, he apparently lacked an aptitude for biological research. Having planned his life around the ideal of the physician-scientist relieving suffering and advancing knowledge, he found the everyday tedium of science intolerable. Thus, his "energy deficit" no doubt had some physiological basis, but it also represented an identity crisis, an inability to find a rewarding means of expression for his idealism and talent.

His first assignment in Richards' laboratory was to help devise a method of measuring the amount of blood flowing through a dog's kidney, but a summer vacation and his father's death kept him away from Philadelphia until October 1923, and the project was reassigned to other researchers. He spent much of the next two years traveling and dealing with family business. Finally, in May 1925, he began a three-year collaboration with Isaac Starr, another young Harvard M.D. The researchers devised improved methods of measuring cardiac output and published three papers, but Starr began to resent Gamble's frequent absences, claiming he could accomplish as much without Gamble's help.[6]

In July 1927, Richards, who was expected to referee disputes between his researchers, wrote Gamble that he feared that it was the glamour of research rather than the research itself that interested him. Gamble asked for another chance, however, and accepted Richards' suggestion that he undergo psychiatric evaluation at a private mental hospital. Having received a clean bill of health, he searched without success in 1928–29 for a research project of his own.

Gamble approached Richards about full-time teaching. Richards told him bluntly that he did not believe he was suited for teaching. Richards remembered that in preparing a lecture on an experimental drug he had been content to read a minimum of the relevant literature. He could stay as a researcher, as long as he paid all of his own expenses. He lingered on at the University of Pennsylvania until 1937, when he moved his family to Milton, Massachusetts, close to his wife's family and far away from memories of frustrated ambition. Between 1934 and 1938 his name appeared on six papers on heart physiology published by Richards' department, but his name was first on none of them. Meanwhile, he had found a new focus for his life in the birth control movement.

Birth control captured Gamble in bits and pieces. In preparation for marriage he had read all of the available literature on contraception, and his interview with Robert Dickinson in 1925 was probably inspired by a desire to make sure he had the best information (his wife was eight months pregnant with their first child at the time). Things were not going well on the research front, and he later remembered a discussion with several medical students in his crowded laboratory. Somehow the limitations of birth control methods came up, and one of the students joked that if he could not find anything better than the diaphragm in all that clutter, then pharmacology was not worth much.

His involvement in trying to get other people to practice birth control began through his friendship with Stuart Mudd, a University of Pennsylvania microbiologist and leader of the Pennsylvania Birth Control Federation, one of the more active state organizations affiliated with the American Birth Control League. Mudd and Gamble had become close friends in 1915 when they were both taking premedical courses at Princeton. Later they were fraternity brothers at Harvard.[7]

At Princeton, Mudd was greatly impressed by Professor Edwin Grant Conklin, an embryologist. The reigning philosopher in the biology department, Conklin was a popular mediator in "the war between science and religion." Both a Methodist lay minister and a distinguished zoologist, he devoted much time to assuring an uneasy public that evolution through natural selection was part of God's sublime design.[8] Conklin shared with Lester Ward and other reform-minded Darwinists the belief that the time had come for man to assume control over his evolution. An outspoken eugenicist, he argued that modern medicine saved the weak and left an increasing load of harmful genes to future generations. Caught up in the Mendelian enthusiasm of a generation of biologists who believed they at last had an explanation for the riddle of heredity, Conklin combined a biological millenarianism with fear of social catstrophe:

> . . . the development of our inherited nature has not kept pace with the development of our moral civilization. . . . Social heredity has outrun germinal heredity and the intellectual, social and moral responsibilities of our times are too great for many men. Civilization is a strenuous affair, with impulses and compulsions which are difficult for the primitive man to fulfill, and many of us are hereditary primitive men. . . . The great growth of alcoholism, depravity, and insanity is an ever increasing protest and menace of weak men against high civilization. We are approaching the time when one or the other must be reduced and the march of civilization stayed, or a better race of men, with greater hereditary abilities must be bred.[9]

The breeding of more good citizens depended on the discouragement of parenthood for those suffering from hereditary disease. The feebleminded and habitual criminals would have to be segregated and sterilized. "Negative" eugenic measures should be supplemented, Conklin argued, by a "positive" program including education in the laws of heredity and encouragement of early marriage among those of sound mind and body.

Advances in genetics soon made it clear that intelligence and other socially desirable traits were not transmitted in tidy Mendelian ratios but resulted from complex interactions between sets of genes and the environments surrounding them, both inside and outside the body. The problem of separating the effects of inherited potential from social environment remained insoluble. Breeding for good citizenship would have to wait for more advances in genetics. Conklin's ideal of human improvement was used by others to justify vicious ethnic and racial discrimination, culminating in the nightmare of Nazi science. The ideal that man might improve himself through genetic engineering was preserved, however, by a series of iconoclastic biologists like the Nobel laureate Herman J. Muller, and finally regained intellectual respectability in the 1960s following the rise of molecular biology and the cracking of the genetic code.[10]

Conklin left Mudd with an enduring interest in improving human quality. Since the most important part of the eugenics program was the encouragement of more children for the fit, Conklin sternly disapproved of feminism and birth control, although he accepted coeducation because it brought together the best young people and led to early marriage. Mudd, however, heard Margaret Sanger lecture during his last year at Harvard and was profoundly impressed by her argument that the spread of contraception provided the most realistic hope for assuring every child a good heritage. Whatever the relative importance of nurture and nature in the molding of character, wanted children were more likely to lead productive lives.[11] Mudd's wife Emily met Margaret Sanger and Hannah Stone while she was working with him in the Rockefeller Institute, and when they moved to Pennsylvania, the Mudds were appalled to learn that no birth control services were available. They organized the Committee for Maternal Health Betterment, which opened a birth control clinic in 1929. Gamble became interested in the clinic when he was asked to determine which of the contraceptive jellies would be most effective. In time he became a one-man foundation for testing and distribution of contraceptives, but his interest focused on finding the best jelly, suppository, foam powder, or condoms only after experience as a founder and funder of clinics convinced him that something cheaper and simpler than the diaphragm was needed.

In the five years following the opening of the first Philadelphia clinic, eight other birth control services were established. By 1933 the budget for the nine clinics was $10,832, with $3,200 coming from patient fees and the rest contributed by a small group of philanthropists including Gamble. The need for more clinics was vast, but each new clinic meant a larger deficit.

Money would have to be raised from a reluctant public at a time when the depression had already exhausted the resources of community charity.[12]

As a physician and scientist with both money and free time, Gamble was an ideal member for a voluntary health organization. In the fall of 1933, he was elected president of the Pennsylvania Birth Control Federation. Under his leadership the organization's fund-raising literature stressed the limits of private charitable sources, yet denounced the increasing resort by New Dealers to public relief.[13] One of the Birth Control Federation's pamphlets explained that the "New Relief" was a radical departure from traditional American welfare administration because "it is mass relief, in contrast to individualized case work treatment." Clients were not treated as maladjusted individuals that had to be rehabilitated. Rather, the need for public support for millions was accepted without any clear end in sight. Since the fertility of relief recipients was much higher than average, there seemed to be danger of a permanent and growing class of social parasites.[14] The Pennsylvania Birth Control Federation argued that it was wiser to give money to birth control clinics to prevent the production of relief babies than to the Community Chest to care for them. Birth control provided a means of going beyond mere amelioration, a positive step toward reducing the numbers of the indigent.[15]

Birth control, however, was not simply a negative program singling out those on relief for special treatment. The Pennsylvania birth controllers sought to establish as a social ethic the concept that

> human life is too fine and too sacred a thing to be brought into the world except by the voluntary act of responsible persons. To do else is to do violence to that belief in the eternal worth of the human personality which is the basis of the highest values of human life.[16]

The propaganda distributed by the Pennsylvania Birth Control Federation made much of the right of every child to be wanted but ignored the possibility that those on relief might want more children. It assumed that no one dependent on charity had a right to have a child. The virtuous poor would surely accept the opportunity to emulate their social betters and control their fertility. Indeed, society must demand as much in self-defense.

Gamble shared Conklin's belief that differential fertility between classes posed a serious threat to the future of civilization. He assumed that the visible elect represented by the middle classes or "good stock" should have more children and those of "poor stock" fewer and took great pride in his own five planned children, never feeling any contradiction between his own high fertility and his crusading for birth control.

Despite his disdain for the welfare state, Gamble was committed to spending at least 10 percent of his income on good causes. He preferred to keep his monetary contributions secret but insisted on active direction of the spending of his money. Robert Dickinson's Committee on Maternal Health and Margaret Sanger's Birth Control Clinical Research Bureau were ideal organizations through which to spend his tithe. They provided institutional sanctions and tax shelters, but more importantly, they made him an officer so that he could participate in the good works he was paying for. [17]

Gamble sought out Dickinson in 1929 to propose a cooperative project. He wanted to establish a birth control clinic in Cincinnati under Committee on Maternal Health auspices as a memorial to his recently deceased mother. [18] The founding of the Cincinnati clinic marked the beginning of Gamble's full-scale commitment to birth control, and his decision to invest in Cincinnati was made easier by the enthusiasm of a remarkable woman doctor for the project.

After his mother's funeral Gamble discussed birth control with her physician and friend, the venerable Elizabeth Campbell (1862–1945). [19] Dr. Campbell had been struggling to make Cincinnati a healthier place for over thirty years. The eldest child of a genteel but impoverished family, she had made the transition from art teacher to physician at the age of thirty-three despite her father's opposition and the necessity of going all the way to the University of Michigan to find a first-rate school that admitted women. "Dr. Elizabeth's" dignity, self-possession, and competence won her a following among Cincinnati's wealthy women. She refused to join suffrage organizations or the Medical Women's Club, preferring to work in causes where both sexes labored toward a better world, and took pride in acceptance by the male physicians of Cincinnati as a colleague rather than a "she doctor."

Dr. Campbell's four-month internship at the Prison Hospital for Women at Framingham, Massachusetts (1895), where many of the patients were prostitutes and venereal diseases frequent, left her with a resolution to do something to provide better medical treatment for the poor, including sex education. After establishing practice in Cincinnati, she organized a Visiting Nurses Association to bring a modicum of health care to the neglected needy. Next she enlisted Cincinnati in the social hygiene movement. Following the lead of her friend, Dr. Rachelle Yarros of Hull House, Campbell gave dozens of sex education lectures to women's clubs. Recruitment and training of lay speakers was an important part of her program. Clarence Gamble's mother shared Dr. Campbell's interest in "education for parenthood." In 1913 she told a Parent-Teacher Association meeting that the nation's mothers had the power and responsibility to eliminate the menace of prositution and venereal disease through enlightenment at home. If boys learned respect for women at home, they would not fall prey to commercial vice when they left it.[20]

Club women all over the United States were listening to similar talks. Cincinnati's Noonday Club, a literary society lead by Dr. Campbell's sister, even had Robert Dickinson come to talk about birth control on the eve of World War I. During the war Dr. Campbell and Dr. Yarros were recruited along with male physicians to lecture soldiers on the dangers of venereal infection. After the war Dr. Elizabeth included high school classes among her audiences.

> Members of the P.T.A. were always on hand to care for the occasional girl who fainted on hearing sex discussed for the first time in open meeting, although meetings were always limited to members of the same sex. By 1921, there were sex education classes in nineteen public schools.[21]

The establishment of a birth control clinic was a logical extension of Campbell's efforts to provide better health care and self-knowledge to women both rich and poor. Yarros had already established a number of clinics in Chicago, and when Clarence offered Campbell $5,000 to start a birth control clinic in

236

Cincinnati, she accepted it, and Mary Gamble's memory was honored by a permanent organization that in 1971 was operating six clinics from its headquarters next to the Campbell home.

In Cincinnati, Gamble's first concern had been to find out if a clinic could be organized. Once it became clear that there was sufficient support in the community for the project, then he began cutting back his financial aid, hoping that local people would take up the slack. In 1930, Gamble reduced his contribution to the Cincinnati Maternal Health Clinic to $2,500. Despite fear of the antagonism that might be aroused by a local money-raising campaign, the Cincinnati clinic was successfully weaned.[22]

Next Gamble hired Dr. Christine Sears to organize a clinic in Columbus. This time, however, he made it clear that he was providing seed money or what he liked to call "risk capital." His purpose was to demonstrate that a clinic could be started and to show its value. The clinic's future would depend on the support of local leaders. Gamble explained to Dr. Sears that his initial goal was not to provide services to the poor but to convince the charitably minded in Columbus that a birth control clinic was an efficient way to spend their money.[23] As in Cincinnati, the Columbus birth controllers at first feared to risk the publicity involved in fund raising, but, having been led into the project with outside money, they were able to continue on their own after Gamble withdrew. Gamble was succeeding in his program to educate social leaders in the value of birth control.

Gamble believed he could make his money go even further if he hired social workers as organizers instead of doctors. His first traveling missionary was Elsie Wulkop, a friend from intern days. Wulkop had studied social work at Simmons College and was superintendent of a summer camp for underprivileged children. Gamble had financed several of her projects, including the reorganization of social service records at Massachusetts General Hospital under the direction of Richard Cabot. Robert Dickinson was willing to have Wulkop on the Committee on Maternal Health payroll if the clinics she established kept good records for study, and, in November 1930, Wulkop began interviewing key individuals at Detroit's

Harper Hospital, where the presence on the staff of one of Gamble's classmates from Harvard Medical School, to whom he had lent tuition, assured a friendly hearing. Opposition from some hospital doctors was overcome by a two-year grant of $3,500; $900 was enough to start a clinic at Woman's Hospital. Over a five-year period, Wulkop spent her winters organizing clinics in sixteen cities in the Midwest.[24]

Things did not always go smoothly. In Lansing, Michigan, Wulkop found that there were no public health clinics of any kind. Local physicians had succeeded in closing the city's only free clinic on the ground that it threatened their incomes. Wulkop reported that social agencies were forced to pay for private office visits. She thought that it would be impossible to establish a birth control clinic in a city of 90,000 where there were no general health clinics at all even for life and death problems.[25] Finally, in 1934, a Gamble grant helped establish a birth control clinic in Lansing, but for three years local doctors were subsidized by the city's unwilling social agencies.

Wulkop's activities were not only seen as a threat to the doctors' incomes. As an employee of the Committee on Maternal Health, she was linked to the International Bolshevik Conspiracy. The minutes of the committee reported:

> One amusing difficulty cropped up in one state, where a book called "The Red Net Work" appears to be a sort of bible. The names of some of our directors and contributors appeared in this book, as supporters of Communism and radicalism. The local doctors and the women chosen to head the lay committee had to receive letters signed by Dr. Holden [Frederick Holden, head of obstetrics at Bellevue Hospital] assuring them that the National Committee on Maternal Health was not financed from Moscow, and Dr. Holden called on the lay representative chosen to head up the local committee, who was in New York for two days, and explained to her the work of the Committee.[26]

CHAPTER 18   **Policing the Marketplace**

WHILE Elsie Wulkop was win-
ning the Midwest for birth control, Gamble, inspired by correspondence with A. R. Kaufman and the high cost of doing business with doctors, began searching for contraceptives that
would allow him to reach the indigent without aid of clinics or
of organized medicine.[1] In the 1930s an estimated 13 million
fertile married couples in the United States faced the question
every night of whether to risk creating a new life. The great
majority of married people limited their fertility, but marriage
without children was still a disreputable state. Family limitation was justifiable as a means of improving the quality of family life—just as work for women gained acceptance as a tempo-
rary aid in family finance. The ambiguous attitude toward
contraception—one did it but did not talk about it—meant that
birth control was a matter of self-help for most people.[2]

Birth control was a $250 million a year business, "slightly
bigger than the barbershop business and very slightly smaller
than the jewelry business," a business without any rational
public regulation. In the mid-1920s, Margaret Sanger had to
recruit friends to manufacture contraceptives. The fact that a
few ethical businessmen entered the trade did not prevent the
exploitation of the market by charlatans. In 1937, Americans
spent $38 million on condoms and over $200 million on "feminine hygiene." According to the law contraceptives could only
be sold with a medical prescription. Thus, condoms were "for

the prevention of disease" and tons of douche powder passed over the counter in the name of internal cleanliness, despite agreement by medical authorities that the genital tract was self-cleaning and douching might cause disease.[3]

The clandestine nature of the contraceptive industry allowed manufacturers and retailers to charge exorbitant prices. A gross of condoms that cost the manufacturer $4.80 and the druggist $6 retailed for $24, a markup of 400 percent. Because testing condoms almost doubled the cost of manufacture, many defective articles were sold. Advertisements claiming a product was "sure, safe, and dependable" for "feminine hygiene" were interpreted by the public to mean "sure, safe and dependable" for contraception. The result was an enormous amount of money spent on useless, marginally effective, or harmful products.

A *Ladies' Home Journal* poll showed 79 percent of American women "believe in birth control." They also considered four children the ideal. The most important reason for favoring birth control was "family income." Thus, in the midst of the depression the desire of Americans to maintain a decent standard of living was being used to cheat them out of millions of dollars.[4]

In 1937 the Consumers Union, whose *Consumer Reports* provided objective information on a wide range of products, issued a "Report on Contraceptives" to subscribers who signed an application saying that they were married and had been advised by a physician to use contraceptives. The tenuous nature of the acceptance of contraception as a subject for free public discussion was reflected in the 1941 decision by the Post Office Department to bar the report from the mails. The Consumers Union brought its case to court, pointing out that the pamphlet had been approved by the medical advisory committee of the Planned Parenthood Federation and was sold only to married adults. The Post Office Department's action was upheld in United States District Court in January 1944, but the decision was reversed by the Court of Appeals in September. Nevertheless, authoritative information was suppressed for three years while misleading advertisements continued to circulate through the mails. Attorneys for the Planned Parenthood Federation declined an invitation to participate in the case because the federation's interest was "in the medical aspects of contraception, that is, in making it available through physicians, hospitals and public health services, . . . the right of laymen to disseminate information on the subject would require careful consideration." While a reluctant medical profession gradually conceded that physicians ought to sell contraceptive advice to those bold enough to demand it, consumers were denied information on the services and products available.[5]

The Planned Parenthood Federation was ignoring the needs of the vast majority of Americans in its refusal to support lay education in contraception. Diaphragms accounted for less than a million dollars a year in contraceptive sales, 0.5 percent of the trade.[6] Many Americans tried to reconcile their desire to control their fertility with the pronatalist values of American culture through resort to products for "feminine hygiene," but the conflict of values was overcome at an appalling cost. And the poor, laggards in the pursuit of the good life, simply let nature take its course.

A central goal of the birth control movement had been to win medical acceptance of contraception. Under medical supervision the public would presumably get reliable, safe advice and public morality would be protected since the young, unmarried, and healthy would not be able to protect themselves from unwanted pregnancy except through abstinence. Clarence Gamble had never practiced medicine for a living. For him medical monopoly on birth control increased cost. While most physicians denounced the clandestine trade in contraceptives as quackery, he took heart from the obvious desire of the masses to do something for themselves and set out to help them by establishing standards by which contraceptives could be judged.

In 1934 he established a research program through the National Committee on Maternal Health directed toward "the discovery of better, cheaper and more generally available contraceptives for the underprivileged masses." The "Standards Program" provided for the development of methods for testing the effectiveness of the products on the market. Evaluation of these substances would make possible a "white list" of reliable brands and show exactly what chemical properties were desirable in a contraceptive. Finally, the most promising materials would be tested in field trials.[7]

The Standards Program would help the medical profession by exposing the "feminine hygiene" quacks and by providing a list of brands that doctors could prescribe with confidence, but the ultimate purpose was to make birth control so easy that people could doctor themselves effectively.

Birth controllers in America and Great Britain had recognized the need for systematic rating of commercial contraceptives in the 1920s, when the opening of clinics necessarily entailed the provision of reliable products. The Committee on Maternal Health administered a three-year (1929–32) grant of $10,000 provided by the Rockefeller-funded Bureau of Social Hygiene to F. A. E. Crew's Institute of Animal Genetics, at the University of Edinburgh, for the study of spermicides. The project culminated in the publication of Cecil Voge's *The Physics and Chemistry of Contraception*. Voge tested proprietary compounds as well as the contraceptive potential of common substances (soaps, vinegar, alum, lemon juice) and showed that some chemicals assumed to be spermicidals were not.[8]

Meanwhile, the Birth Control Investigation Committee (founded 1927), a British group formed by activists of the clinic movement to promote contraceptive research, began financing work on chemical contraception by John R. Baker at Oxford. Baker concentrated his work on the spermicidal value of pure chemicals in contrast to Voge's interest in common substances. Baker's research led to the development of Volpar, a spermicide of phenylmercuric acetate that became a mainstay of British birth control clinics during the diaphragm and/or jelly days of contraception.[9]

The Committee on Maternal Health used the University of Edinburgh because of the difficulty of placing such research in American universities. Upon recommendation of Professor Crew, Voge's support was not continued after the publication of his monograph. Crew feared that Voge's future as a research chemist was endangered by his enthusiasm for birth control. "After all, there are only a certain number of substances and phenomena which he can possibly examine, and it would appear that Baker and Voge between them have completed the list."[10] Baker was forced to leave the Department of Zoology at

Oxford when the director discovered the purpose of his experiments, but he was allowed to relocate in the Department of Pathology. For Baker, contraceptive research in the 1920s was "permanently symbolized in his recollection of assembling his apparatus and reagents on a handcart and trundling this from department to department." [11] Voge fulfilled the worst fears of his colleagues when he went into business as a consulting industrial chemist, but Baker stayed in academic chemistry, aided in 1938 by a $1,000 grant from the Committee on Maternal Health. [12]

To many scientists chemical contraception seemed a dead end. One medical editor observed, "Caustic self-analysis leads to only one honest conclusion: candid physicians are ashamed of these messy makeshifts. . . . there is a sense of relative inadequacy, . . . nourished by the contemplation of these disreputable paraphernalia." "The messy little gadgets, the pastes and creams and jellies" were simply an embarrassment to "the scientific mind." [13]

First-class investigators like Earl Engle and Howard Taylor, Jr., both members of the Committee on Maternal Health and colleagues on the Columbia Medical School faculty, believed real progress would have to wait for fundamental advances in knowledge of human sexual physiology. They opposed further experimentation by the NCMH with simple methods. As Engle bluntly exclaimed, "We don't give a damn about contraception. We want a study of basic factors in human reproduction." [14]

In contrast, Robert Dickinson argued that the committee should maintain an interest in delivery of contraceptive services, serving as a liaison between the scientific establishment and the birth control movement. In 1934 generous grants from the Bureau of Social Hygiene to support the committee's publishing program were exhausted. An impressive list of monographs testified that the money had been well spent, but the function of publisher and clearing house had been largely fulfilled. The Voge project was ending. Louise Bryant was quitting over Dickinson's proposal to study homosexuality. It looked as if the committee was in danger of running out of projects that could attract funds. There was talk of closing up shop. At this crucial juncture Clarence Gamble offered to finance further studies of simple methods. With Dickinson's support Gamble's proposal was accepted, and for six years his projects represented the bulk of the committee's expenditures.[15]

Gamble began his "attack on the present state of chaos in commercial contraceptive products" by hiring Randolph Cautley, a management consultant, to do a study of the industry. Much of the information Cautley gathered was incorporated into the 1938 edition of Dickinson's *Control of Conception* and an excellent article in *Fortune* on "The Accident of Birth." All advertisements submitted to the *American Journal of Obstetrics and Gynecology* were referred to Cautley for approval, and for the first time manufacturers were asked to substantiate their claims.[16]

In June 1935 the Oregon legislature passed a law giving the state board of pharmacy authority to set standards for contraceptives sold in the state. The Committee on Maternal Health supported this legislation by supplying a list of approved products. In October the committee provided a report on condoms to the New York City department of health, but no action was taken to regulate the trade.[17]

Intervention by the federal government made lobbying at the municipal level less important. Since condoms with holes in them prevented neither disease nor conception, the surgeon general's campaign against syphilis provided an opportunity for involving federal agencies in the effort to improve contraceptives. After consultation with the NCMH, the Food and Drug Administration began to apply the Federal Trade Commission Act's false advertising clauses to the contraceptive industry. In 1938–39, seventy-five shipments of condoms were destroyed after testing revealed defects. Suddenly it became profitable to test condoms, and a permanent improvement in the quality of prophylactics on the market resulted.[18]

Efforts to control the feminine hygiene racket were less successful. Peddlers of useless powders and appliances were fined and forced to change their advertising in a series of Federal Trade Commission actions, but the lack of a clear means of establishing the usefulness of a product made suppression of the industry difficult. Also, birth controllers had ambiguous attitudes toward the industry. Gamble wanted to see the completely useless or dangerous concoctions forced off the market, but he knew that douching did reduce fertility and was opposed to complete suppression of "lay advertising as it had value in bringing to the attention of the public that there was such a thing as Birth Control." [19]

Gamble even considered hiring a writer to plant stories in the pulp magazines for women in which the heroine would be saved by birth control.

> It would seem to me that the material could be made quite adequately pornographic [to capture and maintain the reader's interest], in fact it would be just the type of material desired. For example, in a current number of 'Modern Romances' the hero, because of fear of childbirth, insists on his wife's avoiding children. He follows one failure of self-control with an abortion. . . . It would seem to me that the editor who chose this would be glad of birth control as a variant solution. [20]

While trying to exploit the successful techniques of the popular press, Gamble moved quietly to provide authoritative information to the profession. To continue the work begun by Voge and Baker, he established a Robert L. Dickinson Research Fellowship in Chemistry at New York University in December 1935. The fellowship was held by Leo Shedlovsky, a recent Ph.D., who began measuring the physical and chemical properties of the more than forty contraceptive jellies on the market. Reprints of Shedlovsky's articles were mailed to 1,500 physicians holding teaching positions. [21]

Advertising Shedlovsky's work was part of a lobbying campaign to get the AMA's Council on Pharmacy and Chemistry to issue the same kind of reports on contraceptives that were already provided for other drugs. The 1937 report that recognized contraception as a legitimate service also recommended an investigation of commercial contraceptives, but no action followed. Finally in 1939, thanks to the skillful lobbying of Stuart Mudd, a committee on contraceptives was organized with Gamble as chairman. The first of the committee's reports, "Use of Roentgen Rays for Contraception," was of no value, but it was followed by better articles on condoms, jellies, and

245

intrauterine devices, and they paved the way for a 1943 article under Dickinson's signature that defined standards for contraceptive products and listed the commercial brands that met those standards. This article marked the first time that standards for contraceptives were adopted by an official medical body.[22]

Chapter 19 **Experiments in Population Control: Logan County, West Virginia, and the North Carolina Public Health Department**

Logan

The Standards Program of the National Committee on Maternal Health provided the factual basis for federal regulation and AMA reports. These activities were merely by-products of Gamble's central concern, the mass delivery of contraceptives. After Randolph Cautley completed his survey of the birth control business in early 1936, he was replaced on the NCMH payroll by Gilbert Beebe, a Columbia Ph.D. candidate in statistics. Gamble and Beebe began publishing statistical studies of the effectiveness of simple methods, beginning with data drawn from the obstetrics department of a single urban hospital and ending with attempts to lower birth rates in rural coun-

247

ties through door-to-door distribution of contraceptive jelly.[1]

Encouraged by improvements in commercial contraceptive jellies and experiments in Philadelphia that showed a low failure rate with jelly alone (15 pregnancies per 100 years of exposure), Gamble began planning a large-scale test of the effectiveness and acceptability of contraceptive jelly. Opportunities for experimentation with urban populations were limited because the established clinics were using the already proven diaphragm. Large-scale use of a less effective method could only be justified where nothing else could be provided. The mountaineers of West Virginia—poor, numerous, and too isolated for normal clinical service—provided an ideal population for experiment.[2]

The depressed areas of the Appalachians were "a fine place for men and dogs, but hell on women and cows," an area of eroded, low-yield farms and company towns clustered around coal mines that offered underemployment to the surplus population produced by the farms. One woman doctor in the region wrote to Margaret Sanger of the plight of "these poor women of the hills" whose lives were used up in bearing children in an already overpopulated region.

> At twenty-five years of age they look forty and at forty they look sixty if they survive. They marry so young and bear children so frequently that they get no opportunity to rebuild their bodies and consequently marriage and child bearing is nothing but a dreadful burden instead of joyful relationship.

A Red Cross worker in Florida wrote:

> . . . I feel as if I shall never complain about anything for by comparison [with rural poor women] I am a luxurious, lazy, healthy, wealthy, 'right smart' individual, who should thank her lucky stars hourly that she had the good fortune to be born elsewhere, but for the Grace of God I too could have been bitten by mosquitoes, redbugs, fleas, gnats, etc. the past forty years, lived on corn bread and pork and had at least 18 children![3]

Since 1933, Gamble had been trying to begin birth control work in West Virginia through contacts with social workers in the region. After Doris Davidson was forced to abandon her effort to bring contraceptive services to rural Maine, her plight was brought to Gamble's attention. He persuaded Davidson to return to Maine, where, with the advantage of outside money, she organized a clinic in her home town of Fort Fairfield, as well as in Caribou and Presque Isle. Next Gamble provided a donation that made it possible for the American Birth Control League to hire Davidson as a traveling organizer. Her first assignment was Logan, West Virginia, where the American Friends Service Committee, a Philadelphia-based Quaker philanthropy, had established a public health service. Gamble had learned that the director of the Logan program sympathized with the birth control movement, and Davidson organized a birth control clinic in cooperation with the Friends program, setting the stage for a more ambitious project.[4]

Between June 1936 and August 1939, the most extensive and sophisticated field trial of a chemical contraceptive (lactic acid jelly used alone) ever completed in the United States took place in Logan County. Gilbert Beebe got a Columbia doctoral dissertation out of the project, and Gamble had the satisfaction of seeing the American Friends Service Committee, the American Birth Control League, the National Committee on Maternal Health, and the Milbank Memorial Fund unite in sponsorship of his investigation.[5]

Gamble initiated the Logan experiment by offering to pay for distribution of jelly by the nurse attached to the Friends project. The field secretary for the Friends feared that if their nurse in Logan took part in the work she would "come to be known as a contraceptionist exclusively" and her general effectiveness would be hampered, so Gamble found an R.N. in Philadelphia willing to move to Logan and devote full time to birth control.[6]

The American Birth Control League usually opposed deviation from the doctor-diaphragm regimen, but a visit by the league's medical director to the area resulted in approval of Gamble's experiment. He explained to Gamble:

> I have become convinced of the need for a contraceptive technique which could be placed in the hands of rural women by the district nurse or relief worker, without examination by a physician. Many of these women . . . have never been examined by a physician at anytime and the use of a vaginal occlusive diaphragm presents not only the disadvantage of having to be fitted by a

physician, but the fact as well that the prevalence of marked cystocele and rectocele [displacements of the uterus and the bladder], relaxation of the perineum and the entire vaginal canal, make the satisfactory use of this method impossible.[7]

The sexual anatomies of the mountain women reflected the result of childbearing without medical attention. Another observer might have used these conditions as justification for socialized medicine. For Gamble they provided an opportunity to experiment with doctorless birth control. Even giving away contraceptive jelly was further than most physicians were willing to go, and it took considerable work on Gamble's part to gain the consent of the medical interests involved.

The National Committee on Maternal Health had voted in 1935 to leave routine delivery of contraceptive services to other organizations, but Gamble needed the prestige the committee commanded for his project and wrote a protocol they would accept.

> The idea behind the work is not particularly to study a given contraceptive agent, but rather to determine whether by use of a simple means the population increase can be modified. It is felt that there is great need of some such biological, rather than the conventional economic or sociological, approach to certain complex and important issues which now beset society, both in America and in many other parts of the world.[8]

Through the NCMH a grant from the Milbank Memorial Fund was obtained for the analysis of the case records of the project, and Ortho Pharmaceutical Corporation supplied jelly at cost.

The last obstacle was approval by the Logan Medical Society. County medical societies usually objected to free medical service, but, following a visit by Raymond Squier, executive secretary of the NCMH, tacit acceptance was secured in March 1936, when the local doctors approved the distribution of jelly by a nurse "in homes where there is illness preventing the mother from attending a clinic." Gamble rejoiced, "Further liberation of the nurse will follow gradually. Logan, I am sure will furnish a valuable precedent for the entire country."[9]

By June the nurse had begun door-to-door recruiting of women for the project. Over a three-year period 1,345 indigent women agreed to try the contraceptive jelly. These women represented about half of the fertility of Logan County. The birth rate fell by 41 percent among the accepters, demonstrating that the population growth of a rural county could be significantly reduced through the delivery by paramedical personnel of the simplest and cheapest method available.[10]

Gamble considered the project an unqualified success. Beebe found another meaning in Logan, however, and, having published his doctoral thesis as an NCMH monograph, he quit Gamble to join the Milbank staff.

In Logan County the indigent were offered an inferior method on the assumption that it was easier to use than the diaphragm and would therefore be used more consistently. A theoretically less effective method might be more effective in actual practice. Only about one-third of the women reached agreed to use the jelly. At the last interview about 60 percent of the accepters had stopped using the jelly. Lack of confidence in the method was the most frequent reason for dropping out. Thus, the jelly had proved less acceptable and less effective in Logan County than the diaphragm and jelly regimen in other experiments, including one among the rural poor.[11]

The dissatisfaction with the jelly did not result from a lack of desire on the part of accepters to limit their fertility. Most were interested in other methods, but only jelly was provided. Beebe concluded that the diaphragm did not require more effort or intelligence than jelly alone. The researchers had been led into a false belief in the greater acceptability of chemical methods because that theory "harmonizes nicely with the dearth of funds available for contraceptive service."[12]

The only valid distinction between "simple" and "complex" methods was whether the method required the special skills of a physician. The average cost per patient of Logan experiment was $5.90. Beebe estimated that by integrating contraceptive service into preexisting public health programs the cost could be held between $2 and $3 per patient year. In 1938, West Virginia spent $1.25 a year on public health per rural family. To propose large-scale contraceptive programs in problem areas of high fertility was to ignore the desperate need for the most basic services like inoculations and emergency surgery. Birth control could not serve as a cheap substitute for social justice. As an integral part of greatly expanded public programs it could play an important role in the improvement of the condition of the poor.[13]

North Carolina

In late 1936 the American Birth Control League transferred Doris Davidson to North Carolina, where she found Dr. George M. Cooper, the assistant director of the State Board of Health, "a perfect lamb" and began laying plans for a clinic in Raleigh. Gamble had been interested in North Carolina since 1934, when he had been asked to contribute to a church relief fund and had countered with a proposal to make a contribution for contraceptives to be given to the poor along with the food and clothing. In early 1937, however, an opportunity arose to exploit Dr. Cooper's good will and get birth control into the state public health program.[14]

Elsie Wulkop was organizing distribution of contraceptive foam powder on the densely populated island of Boca Grande, off the Florida Everglades. Dr. Lydia de Vilbiss of Miami had reported considerable success with contraceptive foam powder, applied to a damp sponge and inserted in the vagina. Gamble was anxious to give the method an extended trial. The actual distribution of the foam powder on Boca Grande was being done by Frances Pratt, R.N., a native of North Carolina and old friend of Dr. Cooper. The Florida project was nearing completion, but there were several months left in Pratt's agreement with Gamble, and she often talked of going back to North Carolina, so he asked Wulkop to drop in on Dr. Cooper on her way back to Boston to see if he was interested in having a foam powder project in his state.[15]

Dr. Cooper presided over the Maternal and Infant Hygiene Program in a state where 66 of every 1,000 infants died in their first year compared to 40 in Connecticut and a national average of 54. Every year the State Board of Health received "literally hundreds" of letters from indigent and diseased women pleading for contraceptive advice. Cooper had been instrumental in the passage by the North Carolina Conference for Social Service of a procontraception resolution (1933) and in the organization of a Maternal Health League (1935), but more pressing medical problems and hesitancy to ask the state legislature for family planning funds prevented further action.[16]

When Wulkop interviewed Copper, ". . . he said something to the effect that 'if I only had the money I'd add contraception to our work in North Carolina.' "[17] If Gamble was interested in giving away money, he had come to the right man. North Carolina had been the first state to establish full-time county health officers and much of the extension of public health work in the state was financed by outside money—the Rockefeller Foundation, United States Public Health Service, and Children's Bureau. The Social Security Act of 1936 provided funds for greatly expanded maternity services. Outside money had been used to gradually overcome the opposition of county health departments to "domination" from Raleigh by enabling the state to offer special services like dental examinations or immunizations in exchange for meeting state standards.[18]

Cooper would be glad to accept Gamble's money—provided Gamble gave enough to maintain a program for a full year, gave Cooper complete control over the project, and agreed to a policy of no publicity and no connection with any "propaganda" organization. Gamble responded with $4,500 for the first year. When one member of the State Board of Health objected to the project, Cooper was able to tell the board that he had received the check that morning and had never turned down a contribution. The project was approved.[19]

Cooper used the time-tested formula of announcing to county health officers that another free service was available, after discreetly starting pilot projects in a few counties to assure himself the service would be accepted. When help was requested, Frances Pratt arrived with supplies and advice. Foam powder was recommended, but local units were allowed to decide on the method.

Within four years 61 of the state's 81 public health units had added birth control to their list of services. Foam powder was prescribed 72 percent of the time, diaphragm and jelly 27 percent, and condoms in a few cases. Cooper proudly noted that 70 percent of the state's indigent lived within the area covered by the cooperating clinics, yet only one letter of criticism had been received, despite unexpected publicity in *Reader's Digest*, *Life*, and state newspapers. Success in North Carolina reflected the wisdom of avoiding "fanfare, ballyhoo, or overaggressiveness. . . . There had been no hurry. Approval by local practitioners has been insisted upon by the State Health Department before inauguration of the program."[20]

The inauguration of a statewide program in North Carolina was an important breakthrough for birth controllers. North Carolina was the first state to incorporate contraception into its public health program. Aided by Gamble money and lobbying, six other southern states—South Carolina, Alabama, Florida, Georgia, Mississippi, and Virginia—followed North Carolina's lead and officially recognized contraception as part of their public health effort. Cooper threatened to allow the North Carolina program to lapse when Gamble stopped paying for it in 1941, but birth control was included in the regular budgets of the county health units and remained a permanent part of the state health program.[21]

In 1942 the United States Public Health Service ruled that funds allocated for local health services might be used for family planning by the states. In 1963, however, only fifteen state health departments offered family planning services. In some states fear of Catholic opposition and political pressure inhibited action. In the Northeast especially it was prudent to leave birth control for the poor in the hands of the voluntary health organizations that had already established several hundred birth control clinics. North Carolina was especially fortunate in the mutual trust that had been established between state public health officers and the private medical establishment. In contrast, county medical societies in Tennessee successfully opposed a birth control program "largely on the ground that child spacing as a part of public health is another step toward socialized medicine and that such procedures will take away from the private physician legitimate health services and the resultant income." Some public health administrators simply believed that birth control had not yet proved itself on a cost-benefit basis and that they could buy more public health for their dollar by investing in less controversial services of demonstrated value.[22]

Even the effectiveness of the North Carolina model was questionable. Cooper's claim in 1941 that "70 percent of the underprivileged mothers of the state may now receive instruction and supplies to aid them in spacing their children" was misleading. Gamble had hoped to see a program covering the whole indigent population of the state. The number of women who actually received advice—262 in 1937; 3,233 in 1940; 2,454 in 1945; 4,291 in 1950—remained a small percentage of the eligible women in the state, 4 percent in 1940. Moreover, the effectiveness of the advice given in the county clinics was never empirically demonstrated.[23]

Cooper's medically oriented strategy of "working quietly" with "no hurry" gained nominal acceptance by local officials, but no intensive effort to recruit patients for the program followed. Indeed, the great value of the foam powder technique was that "materials can be distributed and adequate instructions given without requiring a large investment of a physician's time." Doctors were not interested enough to make the program a significant experiment in population control, partly because of contempt for the patients.

> On one occasion a health officer didn't think his county needed contraception. He was asked to check his vital statistics. When he discovered that the Negroes were accounting for 85 percent of the births, he quickly changed his mind.[24]

Other physicians felt that "any efforts made along this line among the indigent and ignorant class of the population, particularly the negroes, will be useless."[25]

Other health officers pointed out that a large family was still considered an asset in rural North Carolina. Given the state of public health, birth control was a luxury. As one report explained, after brief instruction patients often received no further attention.

> The follow-up has been definitely inadequate and no apology is offered for the present lack of statistical material because the program has been carried out in local health departments having only about fifty-cents per capita for all activities of a balanced public health program.[26]

Birth control for everyone in North Carolina would have to wait for a decline in poverty and racism or a method that required little of physician or patient. Gamble was disappointed that good records on the effectiveness of foam powder never materialized. They probably would have been discouraging, since by 1959 foam powder had been quietly dropped from the program.[27] Undaunted, Gamble continued his search for a method that was foolproof, but he found himself increasingly isolated from other birth controllers.

CHAPTER 20   **Conflict and Isolation**

Cᴸᴬᴿᴱᴺᴄᴱ GAMBLE wanted to be known as a working philanthropist and not just as a rich man. He believed he had ideas and experience, as well as money, to contribute to the cause. Anxious to give of himself, he hated "gold digging" and frequently demanded greater efficiency from the professional staffs of the organizations he supported.[1] He won a reputation as tightfisted with nickel tips and by always traveling economy class, but he was also capable of secret acts of real generosity. When the wife of a part-time employee died after a long illness, Gamble sent him a check for $700 without explanation, and over the years he helped many fellow laborers at crucial times, while maintaining his position that birth control was a cause, not a career, with pay to match.[2]

The public show of economy was based in part on the rules of Christian benevolence as laid down by Gamble's parents and in part on the fact that, by comparison with the Rockefellers or the Fords, Gamble's wealth was modest and could never begin to pay for all the promising projects in birth control that he wanted to initiate. Nevertheless, the fundamental source of Gamble's frugality was fear that others might love his money more than him. He was jealous of his wealth.[3] His one inflexible requirement as a donor was that he be allowed to participate actively in the planning and execution of the projects he sponsored.

Unlike Margaret Sanger, Gamble preferred a low public profile, but his sense of personal involvement, the burning need to be part of the action, brought him into conflict with those who were trying to make the birth control movement just another voluntary health organization like the National Tuberculosis Association or the American Cancer Society. Sanger and Gamble, separated by background and motive, ended up on the sidelines for the same reason—they were not team players. They wanted to win too much.

Gamble's troubles with the American Birth Control League began in 1935 when, while still serving as president of the Pennsylvania Birth Control Federation, he decided to educate the club women of America to the value of birth control. Gamble hired Boston-bred Phyllis Page, the wife of a University of Pennsylvania librarian, to organize the project, then wrote the executive secretary of the American Birth Control League, Marguerite Benson, offering to pay the costs of printing and postage for sending out "an American Birth Control League 'Outline for Group Study' to women's organizations throughout the country." He did not tell Benson that the outline was already being written. Benson received Gamble's proposal politely, but no action followed for five months, while a stream of Gamble letters poured into the national office suggesting that action be taken on his proposal.[4]

Frequently in the years to come Gamble would bombard officials of birth control organizations with suggestions, requests, inquiries, and demands. Preoccupied with the ordinary business of institution building, they had less time and energy than he had, and eventually would run out of patience. Benson had other things on her mind besides the club women proposal and found writing a letter a week to that man in Philadelphia trying, even if he was a member of the board of directors. Finally, she rejected the proposal.

> . . . women of that type are not in any sense a good source of funds, and . . . mere mailing of printed matter on a large scale would be a waste of time and postage. . . . In fact, I believe you are inclined greatly to overemphasize the value of the printed word and of correspondence.

In Benson's view the initiative for national educational projects should have come from the professional staff in New York.

A review of her Pennsylvania file showed that there was plenty of state business with which Gamble might occupy himself more profitably. The clinic at Wilkes-Barre had "ceased functioning"; six other Pennsylvania clinics had not yet met ABCL certification standards. "During 1935 we received 239 mothers' letters from an organized state boasting 24 clinics, it would seem that publicity and meetings and an increase in your staff might find fertile fields in that state."[5]

Gamble never forgave Benson for her "masterpiece of tactlessness" and distributed his Women's Club Study Outline in Pennsylvania, Massachusetts, Michigan, and Connecticut. Phyllis Page proved to be an effective organizer, and Gamble decided to keep her working for the cause. With the help of Gamble's contacts with William J. Hutchins, president of Berea College in central Kentucky and the father of the president of the University of Chicago, Page organized a clinic in the Berea College hospital that provided a base for a large-scale contraceptive jelly experiment analogous to the Logan project.[6]

The ABCL already had organizers working in the area, and Benson objected to a member of the league's board of directors hiring a private field worker instead of cooperating with the New York office. Confusion would result among potential supporters. Gamble's action implied criticism of the league. If he wanted proselytizing done, why not make a donation to enable the league to hire more qualified field workers?

Gamble believed that his ability to work through personal contacts and provide on-the-spot financing was largely responsible for Page's success in Berea, where the league had previously failed to organize a clinic. When an opportunity arose to exploit Page's talents in Puerto Rico, he did not hesitate to act, despite league objections.[7]

A birth control program established in May 1935 by the Puerto Rico Emergency Relief Administration was being discontinued because of complaints by Catholic officials in the United States.[8] When he heard of the termination of the Puerto Rican program, Gamble sent Phyllis Page to Washington to interview Dr. Ernest Gruening, the future senator from Alaska, then administrator of the Puerto Rican Reconstruction Administration. Dr. Gruening recommended the organization of private sponsorship for clinics. Gamble proposed to send Page to the island as a representative of the ABCL and provided Dr. José Belaval, a distinguished obstetrician who had been the key figure in the island's birth control movement, with $200 a month to reestablish a clinic at the Presbyterian Hospital in San Juan. The executive committee of the ABCL balked at Gamble's initiative, refusing to accept Page as their representative.[9] Page caught the boat for Puerto Rico, pursued by a letter from the league to Belaval pointing out that she did not represent them. Belaval was glad to have Page anyway. Within a month the *Asociacion Pro Salud Maternal e Infantil de Puerto Rico* had been organized on the model of the Mountain Maternal Health League which Page had helped to start in Kentucky.

Eventually a network of twenty-three privately sponsored clinics was organized. In 1937 the new maternal health association successfully pushed through the insular legislature a law enabling physicians to provide contraceptive services, and this victory was followed by a test case in federal court that established the compatibility of the Puerto Rican statute with federal legislation. In 1939 contraceptive services were included in the Insular Health Department Program.

While the Puerto Ricans were announcing the opening of their first nine clinics in March 1937, Gamble continued to embarrass the American Birth Control League by personally exploiting opportunities. In late February, Elsie Wulkop had engineered the North Carolina triumph, while Doris Davidson, the ABCL representative, had made only slight progress. Dr. Cooper went out of his way to stress the complete disassociation of his program from any "propaganda organization," thereby rubbing salt in wounded New York egos. Davidson, who maintained a warm correspondence with Gamble, had in a sense set up Wulkop's visit to Dr. Cooper by writing Gamble of the favorable situation in North Carolina, and in 1938 the league fired her, but Gamble found her another birth control job in California.[10]

In May 1936, following the activities of Phyllis Page in Kentucky, Marguerite Benson had a resolution passed by the ABCL's board of directors that she hoped would force Gamble to work through the New York office. Although a member of the board, Gamble did not attend the meeting.[11] Gamble ignored several suggestions that he might like to resign from the board and persisted in his maddening habit of initiating a project, offering to "share" it with the ABCL, and then going ahead anyway if they would not cooperate on his terms.[12]

By early 1937, Gamble's personal staff of field workers rivaled the league's. During the winter of 1936–37, Margaret Sanger was in the process of dismantling her National Committee on Federal Legislation for Birth Control, following the *One Package* decision in November. Gamble hired two lobbyists from the committee staff as field workers, arranging to have them paid through donations to Sanger's Clinical Research Bureau. Edna Rankin McKinnon, an attorney and the sister of the first woman member of Congress, began work in her home state of Montana, and Hazel Moore, a veteran of the women's suffrage movement and a former Red Cross relief administrator, began organizing Virginia. Thus, Gamble had four field workers, two on the National Committee on Maternal Health payroll (Phyllis Page and Elsie Wulkop), and two on the Clinical Research Bureau payroll.[13]

The American Birth Control League was, of course, also trying to establish more clinics but was even more concerned with maintaining a uniform standard of practice. The contrast between the league's idea of field work and Gamble's was reflected in a series of letters from Hazel Moore describing her problems in escorting a gynecologist from New York through Virginia birth control clinics. Dr. Dorothy Fogel represented an effort by the league and the Sanger clinic to cooperate by providing a roving birth control expert to advise clinic staffs all over the country. Dr. Fogel, Moore complained, seemed to feel "that she is to be merely a Sherlock Holmes with regard to clinics," issuing reprimands when New York standards were not met and engaging in very little public relations work. One of their first stops was the Stafford County Court House, where the cooperating public health nurse had made a special effort to have patients and a local doctor on hand so that Fogel could demonstrate contraceptive technique. When Fogel learned that only foam powder was being used, she refused to see the patients and lectured "the old country doctor who had never seen a diaphragm and who had been especially anxious to have the foam powder used."

It was good to have the country doctor educated in diaphragms but he was so confused it was pathetic. The nurse gives out the foam powder in the homes—and the clinic is merely the fact that she is in her office at the court house on Saturday mornings—the doctors (only three in the county) are invited to come in any Saturday morning and send in patients that day—but the rest of the time the powder is given out in the homes as the nurse visits them. All of this disturbed Dr. Fogel of course and if I had not been there I think she would have ruined everything. [14]

To Gamble, something, even a public health nurse distributing foam powder with the permission of local doctors, was better than nothing. The league felt that real progress depended on physicians taking over the work and refused to sanction anything less. Fogel was pleased with a clinic that had only thirty-two patients in a year but met New York standards. She disapproved of the setup in another town where the nurses had been taught to fit diaphragms.

The City Health doctor who has pioneered in the work can't get the doctors to help him and cannot do it himself. He feels the nurses are more expert at it then [sic] many physicians and he cannot get the physicians to help him, so for years his nurses have been doing the work. That may be all wrong in the eyes of other doctors—but it did not help to bluntly tell him it should not be done. [15]

Gamble finally forced a showdown with the league office when he committed the ultimate sin of asking the Clinical Research Bureau to sponsor one of his field worker recruits after the ABCL refused to accept her quickly enough.

While Elsie Wulkop was organizing the Boca Grande project, she met a nurse on the staff of the Florida State Board of Health who seemed ideal to carry on the work in Florida. Joyce Ely had been engaged for several years in training the midwives who still delivered most of the black babies in Florida, and she was willing to try her hand at organizing birth control clinics.

Gamble wrote to the ABCL office, asking if they would "care to have Miss Ely, working under my supervision, be their representative in Florida? This can be arranged without cost to the League. It is, of course, unfortunate that the distance is too great for the Board to meet Miss Ely. However, both my wife and I feel that she is suitable. Miss Wulkop speaks of her as a real find. . . ." While waiting for the league to make up its mind, Gamble hired Ely, who began her "education in the Birth Control field" under Wulkop's direction.

Having been burned before by refusing Gamble offers, the league office made a series of noncommittal replies to Gamble's stream of letters and phone calls asking for immediate appointment of Ely as a league representative. The New York office asked Gamble to wait until Allison P. Moore, chairman of the board of directors, who was traveling to Florida anyway, could interview Ely. Gamble initially agreed to wait for Moore to arrive, but when a key physician in Tampa told Ely that he would prefer to work "under the auspices of Margaret Sanger's organization," Gamble telegraphed the Birth Control Clinical Research Bureau to ask if Sanger would sponsor Ely and got a prompt acceptance. The stormy climax to the episode was described by Mrs. Gamble in one of her family newsletters:

> Mrs. Moore has continued in the meantime with her plans to go to Florida and is interviewing Miss Wulkop and Miss Ely today. I hope they have spirits of ammonia handy when they tell her that the request of the leading Tampa doctor was that the work be under the auspices of Mrs. Sanger.
> I don't think I shall dare let Clarence go to New York—at least without a special escort to taste his food after the manner of those dining with the Medici's. [16]

When Allison Moore did interview Joyce Ely, she was "very much upset" over Ely's request that the league "stay out of Florida." [17]

Benson and Moore tried to have Gamble censured at the next meeting of the board of directors but only got a mandate to haul him in for a hearing. [18] According to Benson, the ABCL had invested $4,000 in organizational work in North Carolina which was wasted by Gamble's intervention. He thought she was exaggerating, and the New York office eventually listed North Carolina among its successes. [19]

Gamble got out a defense letter to members of the board, citing Benson's failure to act on his proposals when he asked for cooperation and hinting that without his initiative nothing would ever get done.[20] Gamble "won" at the board meeting in that no action was taken beyond restatement of the policy that members of the board should work through the league.

Gamble's defiance of Benson and Moore only underlined the essential weakness of the birth control movement. The ABCL and Sanger's Clinical Research Bureau were still competing for local affiliates, while neither had a method that inspired the confidence of public health officials. Most league partisans wanted to see the birth control movement absorbed into the voluntary health organization establishment, confined to the safe role of clinical promotion of the doctor-diaphragm regimen, and disassociated from any vestiges of feminism, irregular medical practice, or neo-Malthusianism. As Gamble explained in a memorandum to his field workers following the board meeting:

> Scattered through the morning were discussions of methods which were to be permitted. The present ruling of the Medical Board of the League . . . is that the League can not back any procedure in which the client does not have a complete examination by a physician. . . .
> Behind the whole discussion is the thought that I am cheering for methods which tend to remove birth control from the hands and budget of the physician and the fear that my activities may furnish a precedent whereby persons or organizations other than the League may be allowed to organize clinics. Probably, it is more fundamentally anti-Sanger than anti-Gamble.[21]

Gamble was able to do as he pleased because he could choose between the American Birth Control League, the Clinical Research Bureau, and the National Committee on Maternal Health when he needed institutional backing. The divisions in the movement had long hampered the ABCL's fund-raising, but Sanger, who raised $150,000 from 1932 to 1936 for her campaign to change the federal birth control laws, refused to return to the league as "a mediocre organization functionary" and was content to bide her time.[22]

The *One Package* decision exempting medical contraception from the federal obscenity laws had brought Sanger's legislative campaign to an end and removed one major source of tension with the league, which had maintained that no changes in the law were necessary. The AMA acceptance of contraception

264

followed the *One Package* decision, and the time seemed right for "an assault by statesmanship" to get birth control into both federal and state health programs. General recognition of the unique opportunity offered by the recent breakthroughs led to the formation of a Birth Control Council of America in June 1937, with representatives from all factions, to try to create a strong national organization through merger of the league and the Clinical Research Bureau.[23]

An outside mediator, D. Kenneth Rose of the John Price Jones fund-raising and public relations agency, was called in and reported that a successful national fund-raising campaign would be impossible without Sanger's name. Rose also believed that complete public acceptance of the movement depended on a new image. The movement's propaganda had been directed too much toward women. Rose wanted a man to head the new national organization, and he wanted to replace "birth control" with "family planning." As he explained, family planning suggested child spacing rather than avoidance of children, while birth control was "still a 'fighting' word," was still confused with abortion, and "tends to limit support to women." The need for a new approach "is clear when we face the fact that most pivotal groups upon which advancement of birth control is dependent are controlled by men, such as, Federal and State legislatures, hospital boards, public health boards, etc."[24]

The first few meetings of the coordinating committee degenerated into squabbling over who started the *Birth Control Review*, but Gamble's activities and fiscal necessity brought the ABCL's executives back to the bargaining table, and Sanger, drawn by the prospect of finally capturing the government for birth control, reluctantly consented to the merging of the ABCL and the Clinical Research Bureau into the Birth Control Federation of America (January 1939), with Rose as acting director. Finally, in April 1941, Rose engineered a membership referendum on a second name change, and the Birth Control Federation of America became the Planned Parenthood Federation of America (January 1942).[25] The question was: Could Madison Avenue sell family planning to big government?

Clarence Gamble was optimistic about the new leadership in New York. Marguerite Benson was demoted to director of the Regional Organization Department of the federation, and Allison Moore soon resigned from the board of directors. The federation let Joyce Ely go, but Edna McKinnon and Hazel Moore were hired as field representatives, and Gamble was allowed to continue to pay the salary of Frances Pratt, the nurse working with the North Carolina Board of Health.[26]

When Hazel Moore discovered that officials in the Farm Security Administration were willing to have contraceptive advice supplied to their clients, Rose and Gamble traveled to Washington together and an arrangement was made whereby the federation provided two nurses trained in contraceptive technique to work with the FSA field staff in the South and the far West. A federation nurse (salary provided by Gamble) began instructing the FSA county agents in the South in April 1938.[27]

The federation nurse reported complete cooperation from the FSA personnel, and by March 1939, 350 FSA county workers had been "equipped to distribute contraceptives." The program broke down, however, because of the difficulty of getting the foam powder into retail outlets in the rural areas. Even in Miami one client was told by a druggist that she could not get foam powder without a prescription. The federation's budget of $2,000 for demonstration kits was exhausted in Alabama alone, even though that money only represented thirteen cents per family in the state's Farm Security program.[28]

Agency officials in Washington were adamant in their stipulation that their cooperation not be publicized, and they were not willing to have contraceptives appear in official accounts. The Birth Control Federation, with a budget of about $50,000 for all of its field work, simply could not begin to reach the rural masses, even with the cooperation of federal agencies. Direct government funding was a necessity.[29]

Title Five of the Social Security Act of 1935 provided more than $5.5 million a year for state maternal and child health programs. This money was administered by the United States Children's Bureau. Before the merger of the ABCL and the Clinical Research Bureau, Hazel Moore had written Gamble advising that a campaign be launched to have some of the bureau funds spent on contraceptive services.[30]

It seemed that the Children's Bureau might take a positive

stand on contraception when invitations were arranged for representatives of the Clinical Research Bureau and the medical council of the ABCL to attend the Conference on Better Care for Mothers and Babies sponsored by the Children's Bureau in July 1938. But Hannah Stone, although a fully accredited delegate, was refused permission to speak "on the ground that some of the groups represented would not have participated had they known that the birth control issue was to be considered." Eric Matsner, the ABCL's medical director, introduced a resolution "That all obstetrical services and maternal health clinics be equipped to give contraceptive instruction to mothers for the purpose of child spacing," but this was transformed in committee into "Preconceptional and premarital care will help to safeguard the mother from possible later disaster."[31]

Another possible source of funds was the Venereal Disease Control Act of 1939, administered by the United States Public Health Service. The service had been quietly referring inquiries about contraceptive advice to ABCL clinics, in contrast to the Children's Bureau's policy of silence. One of D. Kenneth Rose's first initiatives as director of the federation was to interview officials of the service, and in October 1941 he obtained a statement from the surgeon general that applications from states for child-spacing programs would be given "the same consideration as would be given to other proposals in connection with the health program of the state."[32]

Most of the relevant applications for funds would need the approval of the Children's Bureau as well as the surgeon general, but Rose believed the surgeon general's action would put pressure on Katharine Lenroot, director of the Children's Bureau. "My guess is that she feels she is getting behind the eight-ball and may, by some miracle, want to play ball."[33]

Lenroot, a career bureaucrat, was not so easily intimidated. For years officials of the Children's Bureau, which was a division of the Department of Labor, had been trying to maintain their autonomy in the face of efforts to merge the bureau with the United States Public Health Service. Rose, ignorant of this rivalry, doomed any plan for winning the cooperation of the Children's Bureau when he enlisted the aid of the Public Health Service. Through Eleanor Roosevelt, a long-time supporter of Margaret Sanger, Rose was able to arrange a White House conference with Lenroot and representatives from other concerned agencies. Lenroot was not impressed. Bitterly recalling how the maternal health programs established by the Sheppard-Towner Act of 1921 had been allowed to lapse in the late 1920s, she doubted that the good will of Mrs. Roosevelt could be translated into congressional support and "expressed the fear that inclusion of birth control would jeopardize her other programs of maternal and child welfare."[34]

Lenroot finally agreed to release Social Security Act funds for family planning after the need for women workers in war industries made it impolitic to refuse. Few requests came from state public health officers for family planning funds. Birth control was not a high priority item in the midst of the war effort. In 1941 the president of the Birth Control Federation suggested that it might be advisable to "curtail the Federation's program for the duration of the war." In 1963 only thirteen states offered tax-supported family planning programs, and it was 1967 before the Children's Bureau began to make specific grants to encourage the inclusion of contraceptive services in local health programs. The bureau's activism *followed* a dramatic rise in the demand for such funds at the state level and the passage of the Child Health Act of 1967, which required that 6 percent of grants for maternal and child care be used for family planning.[35]

While Kenneth Rose failed to win a place for family planning in the federal health establishment, he did bring a new order to the Planned Parenthood Federation's affairs. During the late 1930s the ABCL had a yearly budget of about $125,000, with never more than $2,000 coming from state or local affiliates. Rose worked hard to integrate the fund-raising effort at all levels. Before he left in 1948 approximately 37 percent of the federation's budget of about $175,000 came from sources outside of New York, with a total of $713,993 being raised for planned parenthood by all of the participating committees. The federation had become a national organization, "rather than a New York City endeavor." The federation set standards of practice for clinics all over the country, issued authoritative policy statements, and got a respectful hearing in high professional circles and from administrators in Washington.[36]

268

Nevertheless, the federation's growth fell far short of the expectations Rose had raised when he engineered the merger. In 1950 the federation had only $168,000 to spend and had become just another voluntary health service organization, with little influence on policy makers. Changes in name and leadership had failed to bring the goal of "Every Child a Wanted Child" any closer than it had been in 1940. The obstacles posed by fear of depopulation and immorality, the lack of acceptable methods, and the low level of medical care provided for the poor were too great.

After 1942 the scale of Clarence Gamble's birth control activities was greatly reduced. A familiar struggle had begun in March 1939, as Rose tried to channel Gamble's efforts in the same way as Benson had done. Rose ordered employees of the federation to limit their fraternization with board members (a slap at Gamble's continuing personal correspondence with Edna McKinnon and other old employees), had Gamble dropped from the Regional Organization Committee in whose work Gamble had invested so much of himself, and had the federation's executive committee pass a new resolution forbidding board members from discussing possible contributions with local organizations until Rose had approved of the proposal. Unlike Benson, Rose was able to enforce his rules, and by late 1942 Gamble ceased to take an active part in federation affairs.[37]

Gamble's freedom to use the National Committee on Maternal Health was also being threatened. In June 1939, the Rockefeller Foundation gave the committee $12,000 for research in aspects of human fertility that were not being covered by an excellent National Research Council program in endocrinology which the Rockefellers had been funding since 1922. The NCMH sponsored promising research in sperm morphology, spermatoxins, and other studies of sex cells at Yale, Cornell, Johns Hopkins, and the University of Pennsylvania, as well as some small projects in endocrinology under the direction of George Corner at the University of Rochester School of Medicine.[38]

In the past the uncertain nature of committee financing had given contributors a strong influence on committee policy and led to some decisions that in retrospect appear unfortunate.

When Nicholas Eastman, a gynecologist at Johns Hopkins, wanted to change "the direction of his work from sperma-toxins to hormonal means for avoiding pregnancy," Earl Engle decided "the hormonal field is not very promising" and re-fused to sanction the change because the drug company which provided Eastman's funds was interested in spermatoxins and might withdraw the grant. Clarence Gamble had been able to do as he pleased because he was a donor as well as an inves-tigator in a field where there were few of either. The new in-fusion of Rockefeller money strengthened the hand of those who wanted to leave the testing of contraceptives to other or-ganizations.[39]

In June 1940, Kenneth Rose worked out an agreement with the NCMH by which the Birth Control Federation would be responsible for all laboratory and field trials of contraceptives, except where some special technical problem was involved. The federation was to raise $25,000 a year to support the com-mittee, and, in early 1941, Robert Dickinson's dream of hiring a vigorous young medical researcher to head the committee came true when Clair E. Folsome, an assistant professor in the University of Michigan School of Medicine, became executive secretary of the NCMH. Folsome immediately began fulfilling the agreement with Rose by pointing out to Gamble that both the statistical analysis of case records being carried on by Gil-bert Beebe and Leo Shedlovsky's chemical testing of commer-cial contraceptives at New York University fell within the Birth Control Federation's sphere of interest, whereas "the function of our Committee is to consistently direct our activities toward the new unexplored fields in the realm of human reproduction as a whole unit rather than as a small part dealing only with control of conception." Beebe and Shedlovsky had found that working for Gamble did not provide much room for develop-ment as statistician or chemist—both were criticized for at-tempting to bring more theory to their work than the relatively straightforward problems involved would support—and they left the committee payroll in 1941.[40]

When Gamble asked for committee endorsement in May 1942 of a "List of Acceptable Contraceptive Jellies and Creams" to be published in the *Journal of the AMA*, Folsome refused to consider the project, citing large plans being worked out with the Birth Control Federation for extensive *in vivo* testing rather than simple test-tube studies upon which Gamble's list was based. The large plan never materialized, but the Clinical Research Bureau did continue the testing of commercial products on a less systematic basis than Gamble had attempted.[41]

The campaign to force Gamble to work through proper channels was almost complete. But research funds dried up during the war, and Clair Folsome left the committee for a secure and lucrative position as research director with Ortho Pharmaceutical Corporation. Instead of Gamble being forced out of a revitalized research organization, the committee became a paper corporation, leaving Gamble free to continue using it as a sponsor for his projects.

In 1948 an attempt was made to revive the committee through an agreement with the National Research Council by which the Planned Parenthood Federation and the NCMH would raise $220,000 to fund the Committee on Human Reproduction. The Planned Parenthood Federation was to give 4 percent of the proceeds of the Nationwide Planned Parenthood Campaign for research, and the Committee on Maternal Health was to be reorganized as a predominantly lay group to raise money from foundations. Howard Taylor, Jr., became chairman of the Committee on Human Reproduction of the National Research Council, and Frank Notestein, Frederick Osborn, and John D. Rockefeller III were added to the board of directors of the Committee on Maternal Health. Less than $40,000 was raised for research in human reproduction. In 1949 the Planned Parenthood Federation withdrew its support from the project, and the resignations of Osborn, Rockefeller, and Notestein from the NCMH followed.

Big money was not yet available for study of the control of human fertility, but during its short life the Committee on Human Reproduction gave Gregory Pincus of the Worcester Foundation for Experimental Biology $7,500 for study of the fertilization and early development of mammalian eggs and $5,400 to John Rock of the Free Hospital for Women in Brookline, Massachusetts, to evaluate his patient records on the treatment of infertility. Both of these researches involved study of the hormonal control of ovulation. John D. Rockefeller III felt that he benefited from service on the National Commit-

271

tee on Maternal Health. He noted that he had gained a great deal of knowledge from the various meetings with authorities in biological and social research as well as recognition of the need for a multidisciplinary approach to problems in human fertility.[42]

While others dreamed of a million dollars for study of human reproduction, Clarence Gamble continued his lonely search for better contraceptives. To replace Gilbert Beebe he hired Christopher Tietze (born 1908), a refugee from Nazi Austria and a medical statistician in the Johns Hopkins School of Public Health. Tietze's first assignment was evaluation of yet another attempt to bring birth control to the southern Appalachians, this time through house-to-house distribution of condoms by a nurse in Watauga County, North Carolina.[43]

The Gamble-Tietze collaboration was interrupted by Tietze's service as an army doctor, the completion, he wrote Gamble, of "a ten year cycle which began when the democratic government of the City of Vienna was overthrown by force of arms. My chance to hit back has now come." They maintained a lively correspondence, as Tietze speculated about the demographic future of the Far East while stationed in the Philippines.[44]

Tietze tried to interest Gamble in a postwar test of contraception in a Philippine community. Gamble doubted that the project could succeed.

> . . . I'm afraid one needed element is missing—that of a sufficiently inexpensive and reasonably effective method. To be permanently successful any such project would have to be based on material which the Philippinos [sic] could produce almost in their own backyard for, as I understand it, the population is almost on the poverty line—so close to it that expenditure for articles which come from a distance is practically impossible. This rules out diaphragms and anything in metal tubes. If we had some indication that the pulp of a native fruit injected through a section of bamboo with a home-made plunger would be effective, it might be worth trying to over-come the prejudice and lack of education. But until that day comes, I am in doubt as to whether the necessarily prolonged and expensive program which you suggest would be worth while.
>
> . . . Perhaps something could be based on a cervical cap made from half a lime or whittled out of wood.[45]

Gamble's pessimism about the prospects for controlling population growth in the Philippines reflected his experience in the early 1930s, when his brother Sidney, a member of the Presbyterian Board of Foreign Missions, had provided him with a list of Presbyterian medical missionaries in thirty countries. Using the Committee on Maternal Health, Gamble sent contraceptives and literature to missionaries all over the world who indicated they were interested in receiving the material. Shipping costs, prohibitive customs regulations, and the effects of radical changes in climate on the materials made the provision of supplies from the United States impractical, and Gamble abandoned the program. The failure of the missionary project was a factor in Gamble's intense interest in simple methods, and he had worked with Dickinson on a booklet, "Household Contraceptives: Simple and Brief Instructions for their Preparation and Use," which suggested substituting wool tampons soaked in vinegar, alum, or the juice of citric fruits for rubber pessaries and jelly. Also included were recipes for homemade spermicidal jellies.[46]

Tietze rejected Gamble's "cheap backyard method" approach. Experience in the United States indicated that "the acceptability of a contraceptive method is in direct relation to its effectiveness." It was unfair to expect Asians to accept methods rejected by Westerners. The threat of "serious demographic disequilibrium" surely justified investment in the best contraceptives available.

> It seems to me that under government procurement and distribution contraceptive materials could be made cheap enough to be practicable even for the Philippino [sic] farmer. I dont [sic] know what it costs to manufacture diaphragms and jellies, but I do know the shocking difference between what the U.S. Army pays for condoms and what the individual consumer in the States has to shell out.

Intervention by government was essential, however, to complete the demographic transition begun by government through the introduction of Western health technology.

> The occidental peoples have developed their 'modern' civilization of which birth control is a part, in over 150 years, after several centuries of preparatory growth . . . the oriental peoples must go

through the same course of development in a much shorter period. How can we expect them to do so—with a completely different cultural background and with no numerous and prosperous middle class of their own—unless the process is stimulated by governmental leadership.

. . . To me the only possibility of success seems to rest in an integration of contraception into the public health program.[47]

Non-Western nations would take the lead in development of population control programs after the war, while the militant opposition of the Roman Catholic Church prevented official action by Western governments and by the United Nations until the 1960s.[48] But Tietze provided Gamble with a new perspective on population. The problem was not bad stock outbreeding good stock but mankind destroying itself. If they did not quite agree on either the nature of the population problem or the usefulness of simple methods, they did agree that a better method was needed, and fast.

After Tietze returned to the United States, Gamble asked him to collaborate on yet another study of a method available for years—a coil of silk suture inserted in the uterus and left in place for long periods of time, the simplest of what were to become known as intrauterine contraceptive devices (IUD). For centuries Arab camel drivers had been placing small stones in the uteri of their animals to prevent pregnancy during long journeys. In the middle of the nineteenth century, when physicians first began to venture into the vagina as a matter of routine, an amazing variety of pessaries were developed for manipulation of the uterus. Among these were "stem pessaries" that consisted of a tube fitted through the cervical canal into the uterus, with a round plate or button remaining outside the uterus against the cervix. These intrauterine pessaries were originally intended to straighten the uterus, open the cervical canal, and thus assist the movement of spermatozoa up to the fallopian tubes.

While some physicians installed the devices to cure sterility, others were soon hailing them as contraceptives. Their use led to many serious pelvic infections, and the devices became the symbol of the suffering sure to follow attempts to thwart nature's law and society's rule by separating sex from procreation.

274

In 1909 a German gynecologist, Ernst Gräfenberg, began to experiment with a true intrauterine contraceptive device that was placed entirely inside the uterus and thus was less likely to provide a path for infection. At the Seventh International Birth Control Congress in 1930, he reported his startling success with a ring of silk gut and silver wire in a series of over 1,000 patients. Considerable experimentation with "Gräfenberg rings" followed, but intrauterine contraception soon fell into disrepute again. Gräfenberg warned of the need to be sure that no pelvic inflammation was present before inserting the device, but other practitioners were not so cautious. Pelvic infections were still very dangerous before the development of antibiotics, and most ethical practitioners believed the risk of infection from an IUD outweighed reasons for avoiding pregnancy. Excessive menstrual periods and cramps were frequent in the first month after insertion. Nevertheless, a few physicians quietly continued to fit IUDs with considerable success. Among them was Mary Halton, Margaret Sanger's gynecologist.[49]

In 1924, Halton showed Robert Dickinson over 1,000 case histories of stem pessaries she had inserted. Her clients included many actresses and professional women (some said prostitutes also) who were determined not to become pregnant and were willing to endure some discomfort and risk. Later Halton began using a true intrauterine device, a ring of silk suture. Dickinson believed the method had possibilities and several times called for expert investigation. Finally, in 1947, Gamble arranged for Tietze to assist Dickinson in publishing Halton's results.[50]

"Contraception with an Intrauterine Silk Coil" was rejected by the *American Journal of Obstetrics and Gynecology*. The NCMH refused to sponsor the paper. As Tietze explained to Gamble, Earl Engle and Howard Taylor, Jr., agreed that "this was too hot to be cleared except by sending it around [to all members of the executive committee] and they did not want to do that at the present stage of the game." In 1964, Howard Taylor, Jr., would preside over a conference during which the IUD was hailed as "a tremendous contribution to the welfare of individual families, and national communities, with all that this means for the economic prosperity, the political stability, and the freedom of mankind. Indeed, I believe that this simple device can and will change the history of the world."[51]

In 1948, however, Dickinson and Gamble were among an extremely small minority of American physicians detached enough from professional taboos to consider clinical investigation of the IUD. The paper was finally published in *Human Fertility*, the journal of the Margaret Sanger Clinical Research Bureau, with an editorial warning that the silk coil "is not a method that can be used without careful discrimination, if at all."[52]

The Halton records showed one of the lowest pregnancy rates ever achieved by a contraceptive. During 468 years of exposure, four pregnancies occurred, corresponding to a failure rate of 0.9 per 100 years of exposure. Rather than being jubilant, however, Tietze was thinking about giving up work with Gamble and taking a civil service job. He explained:

> Please do not believe that I am trying to cut loose from what some people would regard as an unpopular cause. In my opinion population control is one of the most urgent problems in today's world, and if at all possible I should like to remain on the team. I have always been willing to make some sacrifices for that rare privilege of doing precisely the kind of work I like best . . . but I am sure you will not mind my saying that the informal nature of our partnership and the lack of institutional support sometimes cause me anxiety and concern. I believe that there is a need in this country for one person to devote his full time to the statistical aspects of human reproduction from a biological point of view. I further believe that my medical background and my interest in the subject make me a suitable person for the job. There must be a way of keeping me in the field with a modicum of recognition and stability.[53]

The last straw came when the NCMH sponsored a "Conference on Population Trends and the Family" to which Tietze, who was on the committee payroll as a research associate, was not invited. Tietze wrote Gamble:

> This is exactly what I mean by lack of recognition and institutional support. I later told RLD about it and he said that he too had learned about the conference only via the grapevine. He did some telephoning for me and we got a splendid run-around . . . which ended up with a suggestion . . . that I send my paper on the sex ratio of abortion . . . for possible inclusion in the program.

Tietze did not appear on the conference program. He quit soon after to become an intelligence officer in the State Department.[54]

The Committee on Maternal Health became totally inactive in the 1950s except for Gamble's "Standards Program." At a meeting held in Howard Taylor, Jr.'s home in 1952, Gamble was informed by other members of the committee "that it was their feeling that the time had come to close out the Committee, inasmuch as the Standards program was the only present activity. They at least wondered out loud, several times, as to whether the Standards work wouldn't more logically be part of the program of the Planned Parenthood than of the NCMH."[55]

Despite the misgivings of other members of the corporation, Clarence Gamble continued to use the NCMH for his projects until 1957, when he established a family foundation, the Pathfinder Fund, to finance his work and turned the NCMH over to Christopher Tietze, whose expertise had suddenly become very much in demand.

PART VI

PROPAGANDISTS TURNED TO PROPHETS: BIRTH CONTROL IN A CROWDED WORLD

CHAPTER 21 **The Population Explosion**

$\mathbf{D}$URING the decade after World War II the focus of demographic study in the United States shifted from the declining fertility of the West to a startling increase in world population, an estimated 700 million between 1940 and 1960. Revolutionary advances in public health, particularly the control of famine and epidemic disease, accelerated by the wartime use of DDT to control malaria, made possible the rapid population increase. Declines in mortality that had been spread over a century in Europe and North America were achieved in a few years in the Third World, but birth rates remained high, leaving nations like Ceylon stuck in the middle of the demographic transition from high birth rates to a vital economy of death control balanced by birth control.[1]

Agreement on the meaning of the new demographic trend did not come all at once. Some observers doubted that low death rates could be maintained. French demographers declared unqualified satisfaction with the population explosion. Servants of a nation that had been outbred and outfought by its Prussian neighbors for a century, they remained implacable foes of *le malthusianisme anglo-saxon* until the early 1960s when improved censuses showed that population was increasing even faster than the highest projections had suggested, and mankind's ability to multiply "and have dominion over . . . every living thing that moveth upon the earth" had been unquestionably demonstrated.[2]

American demographers associated with Princeton's Office of Population Research and the Milbank Memorial Fund were the prime movers in an effort to focus the attention of world leaders on the crucial interrelation between the rate of population growth and economic progress. Just as differential fertility between classes and regions exacerbated social problems in the United States, the rapid expansion of population threatened the possibility of engineering rapid economic development in the Third World. Two scholars in Princeton's Office of Population Research demonstrated in an extremely influential analysis of India's prospects for economic development that few poor nations could muster the capital investment needed to maintain per capita income if population growth continued at the high rates that followed the introduction of modern public health technology.[3]

It had proved relatively easy to engineer dramatic decreases in mortality because inexpensive mass procedures could be introduced by small numbers of technicians with little more than passive support from the general public. As Frank Notestein explained in 1947 to a Milbank Round Table on International Approaches to Problems of Underdeveloped Areas:

> Human fertility . . . responds scarcely at all in the initial, and often super-imposed, stages of such changes [in mortality]—changes that too often influence only the externals of life and leave the opportunities, hopes, fears, beliefs, customs, and social organization of the masses of the people relatively untouched. These latter are the factors that control fertility, and since they are unmodified, fertility remains high while mortality declines. . . .
> If gains in production only match those in population growth, "improvement" may result principally in ever larger masses of humanity living close to the margins of existence and vulnerable to every shock in the world economic and political structure. Such "progress" may amount to setting the stage for calamity.[4]

Public health campaigns provided a perfect example of the dangers inherent in failure to develop comprehensive plans of development that took into account the effects of population growth on resources. Nations newly liberated from colonial status wanted to share the prosperity of the West. Failure to develop their economies would lead to more bitter internal divisions and rejection of Western alliances in favor of communist models of development. Thus, political stability depended on rapid economic development and that development in turn could only succeed if the rate of population growth did not eat up the capital needed to finance development.

The problems that haunted Notestein had long concerned John D. Rockefeller III. His father, John D. Rockefeller, Jr., had been the single most important supporter of efforts to deal with the crisis in sexual morality that emerged in the first decade of the twentieth century. Rockefeller money had paid for Christian programs to help young people maintain high standards of conduct through the activities of the Young Men's and Young Women's Christian Associations, efforts to provide havens of community amid the impersonality and amorality of the city. The great Progressive campaign against white slavery and venereal disease followed, with John D. Rockefeller, Jr., personally leading the way as chairman of New York County's famous "white slave grand jury" (1910) and as founder of the Bureau of Social Hygiene (1911), which funded influential studies of commercial vice.[5]

The bureau also provided crucial support for three organizations which represented a complete transition from the Christian evangelism of the early vice-suppression movement to a highly sophisticated program of research, education, and social control. Margaret Sanger often turned to the Bureau of Social Hygiene when her Clinical Research Bureau needed help or to Rockefeller, Jr., for the extra money that would make some conference or special project possible. The publishing program of the Committee on Maternal Health was funded by the Bureau of Social Hygiene. While Sanger pursued her program of direct social service and Dickinson laid the medical basis for modern marriage counseling and sex education, the bureau provided a series of grants to the National Research Council, the working arm of the National Academy of Sciences, for the organization of the Committee for Research in Problems of Sex within the Division of Medical Sciences. The committee (founded 1922) virtually paid for the development in American universities of endocrinology, the study of the body's internal system of hormonal regulation, a necessary first step in the understanding of human sexual physiology. When the Bureau of Social Hygiene was terminated in 1931, many of its activities, including the funding of the Committee for Research in Problems of Sex, were taken over by the Rockefeller Foundation. The committee began supporting large-scale study of human sexual behavior in 1941 through support of the research of the University of Indiana zoologist Alfred Kinsey, research described in *Sexual Behavior in the Human Male* (1948), *Sexual Behavior in the Human Female* (1953), and a series of equally distinguished behavioral studies.[6]

Despite the comprehensive commitment of John D. Rockefeller, Jr., to sexual research and reform, the primary focus of Rockefeller philanthropy had been medical research and education, and the development of public health action programs throughout the world. By the late 1940s, however, some of the officers of the foundation's International Health Division had begun to question their right to engineer rapid declines in mortality without first making sure that the lives saved from malaria or cholera would not be lived amid the misery of economically stagnant, strife-torn societies.

In 1950, Marshall Balfour, regional director in the Far East of the foundation's International Health Division, declared, "the justification of health measures in the face of demographic realities presents a challenge." In the future a more comprehensive kind of technical assistance would have to be provided, aimed at helping local leaders to develop "An overall policy that assures concurrent attention to food production and the social changes which relate to fertility. . . ." Otherwise, "the risk exists that health improvement may outrun other phases of socioeconomic development." The days of unilateral intervention to eradicate plagues were over. Future aid would have to wait for initiative from local leaders for two reasons. The legacy of colonialism had left a deep suspicion of the motives of Westerners, and the new philanthropy would have to aim at social changes so vast that it could only succeed as part of national efforts by whole peoples to improve their condition. In the future American philanthropy abroad would have to be both a more modest and a more comprehensive venture.[7]

John D. Rockefeller III, who shared his father's commitment to social service, had a thorough knowledge of the wide range of researches and action programs that had benefited from

Rockefeller money—including Margaret Sanger's activities, the demographic studies by the Princeton-Milbank group,the research programs of the Committee for Research in Problems of Sex and the National Committee on Maternal Health, and the global public health program of the Rockefeller Foundation. Touring the Far East after World War II, he was disturbed by the lack of coordination between the medical and social science groups supported by the Rockefeller Foundation. He commissioned Frank Notestein and Marshall Balfour to write a report on the situation, but was unable to interest key officers of the foundation in adding fertility control to the foundation's programs. Frank Notestein remembered:

> We published our report and the people at the Foundation were polite about it. A mild staff proposal for a project on Demography and Human Ecology in Ceylon was turned down by the Board on, I am told, the opposition of John Foster Dulles [chairman of the board of directors], and that was that for a good many years as far as family planning was concerned. [8]

John Rockefeller III's initiative fell victim to a combination of forces involving both the internal politics of the foundation and the world's political situation. The foundation was going through a period of questioning and readjustment in which the old public health doctors from the International Health Division were gradually being replaced by agricultural scientists. Warren Weaver, director of the Division of Natural Sciences, was militantly opposed to any new program that might threaten the investment the foundation was making in what was to become the Green Revolution. Proposals to study human fertility might compete with agricultural research. Many scientists believed that advances in agricultural technology would make it possible to feed the world despite the rapid population growth, and more food was a noncontroversial program which would not arouse opposition in the Roman Catholic countries in which the foundation worked. [9]

Also, the foundation was on the verge of becoming sex shy. For years Alan Gregg, director of the Division of Medical Sciences, had been trying to interest his more cautious colleagues in a larger investment in studies of human sexuality. Other officers of the foundation were becoming increasingly alarmed, however, by the implications of Alfred Kinsey's foundation-funded research. When Chester Barnard, president of the foundation, was approached about the possibility of a new program in fertility control, he invited New York's Cardinal Spellman to discuss the idea and learned that the cardinal could not approve of an organization with an interest in birth control. The cardinal's opinion was probably sought in order to provide Barnard with justification for his own dislike for such projects, a feeling shared by his successor Dean Rusk. Kinsey's studies would soon attract the attention of congressional witch-hunters and would be used as a means of questioning the very existence of tax-privileged foundations. During the hysteria of the McCarthy era, sex research and the international Bolshevik conspiracy were linked together; the confusion aided by the exploitation of Kinsey by the national press. The Rockefeller Foundation, vulnerable to political attack, international in outlook, and involved in a wide range of research, was suddenly overextended in a provincial culture. Kinsey's money was cut off in 1954, thereby seeming to vindicate those who had been arguing since the late 1940s that the foundation ought to leave sex alone and concentrate on food.[10]

The foundation's involvement in fertility control would have also risked criticism from foreign governments. There were deep-rooted fears that the rich nations might try to shirk the burden of assisting the development of former colonies by blaming the poverty of the new nations on "overpopulation," thus avoiding responsibility for centuries of exploitation. As the Cold War heated up, communist nations became increasingly hostile toward American efforts to aid economic development in the Third World, and joined with Catholic nations to provide formidable opposition within the United Nations to the inclusion of family planning in technical assistance programs.[11]

The inability of the United Nations to meet the requests made by India, Ceylon, and Pakistan in the 1950s for assistance in developing population programs underlined the growing need for help that could only be provided by a nonofficial organization "able to work closely with foreign governments without the publicity about Americans which so often arouses nationalistic feelings." John D. Rockefeller III foresaw this crucial need, and, despite his failure to win the support of the foundation, he founded the Population Council in November 1952 with his own funds. The governing body included Rockefeller, Frank Notestein, and Frank Boudreau of the Milbank Fund, with Frederick Osborn serving as chief executive officer.[12]

The council began spending half a million dollars a year on population research through its Demographic and Bio-Medical divisions and through grants to universities and other foundations. Conscious of the need to avoid ideological conflicts, the council was "anxious to keep the work . . . in the hands of competent scientists, believing that accurate determination of the facts must precede propaganda rather than the other way around, and that when verifiable information was available it would inevitably be used in the guidance of policy." [13]

Time was on their side. Throughout the 1950s the "verifiable information" poured in, its collection spurred by Population Council grants that brought students from around the world to the United States to study and subsidized the establishment of demographic studies in foreign universities. The "intolerable pessimism" of demographers that had aroused the contempt of agricultural scientists in the early 1950s suddenly became acceptable as study after study showed per capita food production actually declining, in part because of inadequate investment by Western nations in developing economies but mainly because of the acceleration of population growth. Fear of famine gained a growing audience for those like B. R. Sen, the Indian director-general of the Food and Agriculture Organization of the United Nations, who insisted that population control was the only alternative to starvation.[14]

Asian nations pursuing development made repeated requests for assistance in population control to the World Health Organization and other United Nations agencies, thus keeping the issue alive and opening the way to an easing of opposition from Communists, who were anxious to show their willingness to help poor nations develop. By 1965 the control of population growth in the interest of economic development had become a relatively noncontroversial part of economic wisdom, and Lyndon Johnson threw the prestige of the presidency of the United States behind the search for "new ways to use our knowledge to help deal with the explosion in world population and the growing scarcity in world resources." In 1967 the United States Agency for International Development won an appropriation of $35 million for population study and family planning, a commitment that would grow while other foreign aid programs were being slashed. The $50 million earmarked for AID population programs by Congress in 1969 was not much compared to the $16 billion already budgeted for putting a man on the moon, but it was a quantum jump in fertility finance, where the Population Council's annual budget of a few million dollars during the 1950s had seemed an awe-inspiring commitment.[15]

Recognition of need and big spending do not necessarily translate into solutions. Considerable pessimism existed in the late 1960s over the prospects for bringing world population growth under control in time to avoid catastrophe. Many veterans of the fight to win recognition and funding for population programs believed that the world had a chance.[16] This optimism was partly based on encouraging gains in food production as new high-yield grains became available, the payoff in the Rockefeller Foundation's investment in agricultural sciences. The Green Revolution bought time, but the chances for success in population control mainly depended on the foundation for action laid in the two decades after World War II.

The growth of the International Planned Parenthood Federation (founded 1952), "a union of indigenous, national, autonomous" associations, helped to create a climate of public opinion that enabled political leaders to accept external assistance. While privately funded urban clinics and a few experimental programs in rural areas had no influence on national birth rates, they helped to remove the aura of strangeness and suspicion surrounding birth control and provided a focus for the organization of middle-class support for government action.[17] A crucial factor in whole-hearted commitment by political leaders to population control was the availability of contraceptives that they believed would work in their countries.[18] The few thousand dollars raised by Margaret Sanger to organize the International Planned Parenthood Federation and the several million dollars invested by the Population Council in contraceptive research would pay high dividends in the 1970s.

Margaret Sanger from Exile: The Founding of the International Planned Parenthood Federation

$\mathbf{M}$ARGARET SANGER had made two dramatic world tours between the world wars (1922, 1936), forcing her way into Japan despite the opposition of the government, debating sexual morality with Mahatma Gandhi in India, and establishing friendships with Western-oriented liberals. Nothing substantial came of these tours. Sanger's Japanese supporters established a few clinics in the 1920s, but they were suppressed when the militarists came to power. The British rulers of India were indifferent, while Jawaharlal Nehru's Congress Party, although advocating a policy of population control, was not able to do much after it came to power (1947) in a country with a population-doctor ratio above 6,000 to 1.[1] Sanger's visits made a lasting impression, however, on some future leaders. In 1956, Mrs. Vijaya Lakshmi Pandit, Nehru's sister and high commissioner for India, told a meeting of the Family Planning Association of Great Britain of her own excitement when the All-India Women's Conference invited Sanger for a visit in 1936.

> I was working on the Municipal Board of my hometown—the only woman among 40 City Fathers. . . . I remember shocking the City Fathers by proposing a birth control clinic for one of the City's hospitals. I wasn't very old then, and I was labelled a dangerous kind of person, but it is interesting that in spite of opposition—it was a rather provincial town with rather a narrow outlook—still we were able to get a small clinic started. It did not do the work one had hoped it would and it died a natural death five years later, but nevertheless something of the kind was started. It focused attention on the need for birth control.[2]

In 1946, Elise Ottesen-Jensen, Swedish pioneer in sex education and contraception, organized an international conference of prewar leaders of the birth control movement. The Stockholm conference led to the creation of an interim committee to work toward a permanent international organization. Margaret Sanger got the Family Planning Association of Great Britain to sponsor a second conference at Cheltenham in 1948 by promising to raise the necessary money. One of Sanger's friends told Sanger biographer Lawrence Lader, "It would be impossible to define Mrs. Sanger's work in this period. Almost single-handed, she created this conference, and those that followed, out of nothing but will power. She was unyielding, relentless, and egotistical in a way that was something to behold." The Cheltenham conference, "Population and World Resources in Relation to the Family," drew 140 participants from seventeen countries—including Pascal Whelpton and Frank Lorimer, two of the founders of American demography, Sir John Boyd-Orr, director-general of the United Nations' Food and Agriculture Organization, and Lord Horder, the king's physician and president of the Eugenics Society, who presided over the meeting.[3]

As in the past, Sanger's "will power" led to concrete achievement because of her ability to find ready workers and fat purses. Dorothy Brush (1894–1968), an old comrade from the federal legislative campaign, paid for the establishment of an office for the International Planned Parenthood Committee formed at the 1948 conference and became an important worker in the new organization. Brush, one of the most devoted of Sanger's club woman recruits, found personal direction and purpose through association with Sanger. After graduating from Smith (1917), she had married Charles Francis Brush, Jr., son of the man who invented the open-coil dynamo and the first practical electric arc light, one of the original partners in the General Electric Company. As a trial member of the Junior League of Cleveland, Mrs. Brush was required to do a year's voluntary charity work and chose a prenatal clinic run by the city, where most of the clients were women her age. Most of them had three or more children. She had one. Many of her clients wanted to know "the secret you rich girls have" for avoiding pregnancy. Suddenly made self-conscious by discovery of her privileged position, she told them.

> We did have sketchy information provided before we married by our mothers—our husbands could buy condoms to protect us, or if they didn't want to, we might use germicidal douches for ourselves. We knew very well that such measures were not foolproof as we told them.[4]

Fired after a "very fat Catholic nurse . . . reported us to the city government which also at the time was Catholic," the slender society matron, inspired by Sanger's work in New York, devoted herself to establishing a birth control clinic in Cleveland. Her husband and friends were enthusiastic, but

> we found that the older group felt it would be fatal to rush into an actual clinic. It seemed that Emma Goldman, the anarchist, had lectured in Cleveland with birth control among her radical proposals and created a climate among the influential conservative people we needed which militated against such an idea.

After waiting six years for Cleveland to get over Emma Goldman, Charles Brush offered $5,000 to a committee of his wife's friends that had been formed to start a clinic. Before the project could be launched, he died, one week after the death of his six-year-old son. Dorothy Brush moved to New York in an effort to put her life back together, hoping to become a writer, but before she left, she gave $5,000 to the Cleveland Maternal

Health Association to open the long delayed clinic (founded 1928). Charles Brush, Sr., established the Brush Foundation to honor his son's memory and the foundation provided an annual subsidy of about $3,000 for the Cleveland clinic, as well as the salary of a field worker to organize other clinics throughout the state.[5]

Brush hoped to begin a writing career in New York and chose Sanger for her first subject. She ended up working for the cause, as secretary of the National Committee on Federal Legislation for Birth Control and advance organizer for the 1936–37 world tour, and by ghostwriting a chapter on Sanger for a book titled *Adventurous Americans*. After the *One Package* decision, she dropped out of active work, although maintaining warm ties with Sanger.

By 1946, Brush's second marriage had failed. Unhappy with "this damned middle-aged adolescence," she wrote Sanger:

> The Brush Foundation has taken a sudden interest in birth control in the Orient. . . . As general interest in the Orient grows, we might try to act as a clearing house for such information? . . . I'd almost abandoned the idea that I could ever be of service again, but maybe I can. Anyway if I can ever do anything for you, you have only to ask.[6]

Sanger too was ready for a new campaign, and Brush became secretary of the International Planned Parenthood Committee. The Brush Foundation funded the establishment of a London office for the new organization; helped pay for the Bombay conference (1952), during which the International Planned Parenthood Federation was launched, and the Tokyo Conference (1955); and provided an annual $10,000 for the federation's newsletter, translated into five languages, distributed worldwide, and edited by Dorothy Brush. When the Planned Parenthood Federation of America insisted on deducting 15 percent from all contributions raised for the international federation, the Brush Foundation became the tax-privileged vehicle through which direct contributions could be made for international work. Finally, in 1957 the foundation gave $50,000 for expanded field work. By that time, however, the IPPF had grown from a shoestring operation into a true international league with member organizations in eighteen nations and a growing ability to attract funds.[7]

In 1958 the Swedish government gave $366,000 to the government of Ceylon to incorporate family planning into its public health program. The Swedish grant marked the first time a Western nation included birth control in its development assistance budget and this breakthrough resulted from contacts developed between Swedish and Ceylonese birth controllers through the International Planned Parenthood Federation.[8]

CHAPTER 23 **The Failure of Simple Methods The IUD Justified**

THE Population Council and the International Planned Parenthood Federation played key roles in bringing the governments of the world to recognize the value of contraception as part of both economic and public health policy. Nevertheless, the theoretical usefulness of birth control was a moot question without methods that were accessible and acceptable to the masses of the Third World. Birth controllers in the early 1950s faced the disheartening fact that contraceptive technology had not advanced since the perfection of the spring-loaded diaphragm in the 1920s. When Robert Dickinson died in 1950, his effort to attract attention to the contraceptive possibilities of intrauterine devices seemed a failure.[1] Clarence Gamble continued to sponsor a few contraceptive research projects but had been pushed out of a leadership role in the Planned Parenthood Federation of America. His interest in population control then focused on promoting sterilization for the mentally deficient and on encouraging college graduates to have more children.[2] He spent the war years teaching physical diagnosis at Harvard (1942–45), while the regular professors were serving in the armed forces. His interest in birth control was rekindled, however, at the thirty-fifth reunion of his Princeton class, when he dropped in on Frank Notestein at the Office of Population Research and heard about the plight of Japan, where a baby boom was causing daily horror stories of infanticide and abortion amid the rubble of a lost empire. Excited by the prospect of a new problem that needed him, Gamble made contact with Japanese birth controllers and began making small contributions.[3]

Dr. Yoshia Koya (born 1890), director of the National Institute of Public Health, heard about the American philanthropist and wrote asking for help. An artist and novelist of note, Koya had not received his M.D. until he was forty-two, and then specialized in public health so he would not have to see blood. Koya had been among a group of Japanese doctors sent to the United States in 1950 to study modern public health methods, and he had made a special effort to visit the American South, where backward rural conditions were most analogous to those in Japan. In North Carolina, Koya met Dr. George Cooper, who got him interested in a birth control program for rural Japan, but Cooper never mentioned Clarence Gamble.[4]

In 1948 the Japanese Diet, with the concurrence of American public health officials in the occupation government, had legalized abortion in an effort to regulate the trade in "take out babies." Koya was appalled by the waste involved in population control by abortion and tried to interest the government in including contraception in the public health program, but legislators doubted that contraceptives would be accepted by the half of the population still living in rural areas. Koya wanted a field study to test the effect of birth control on a rural population, and he had trained personnel to carry out the program but no money budgeted for research.[5]

Gamble gave Koya $23,500 between 1950 and 1957 for what became known as the Three-Village Study, the most successful contraceptive program organized among a rural population before the availability of improved IUDs and the anovulant pill.[6] Koya set out to show that contraception could be substituted for abortion and that a birth rate analogous to Western nations could be achieved through intensive public education and the ready availability of a choice of contraceptive methods. He selected three typical rural villages for his project—a lowland rice-growing community, a mountain hamlet with a diversified agricultural economy, and a seaside fishing settlement. A physician visited these communities several days a month at first, and a nurse was made available in each village. Koya's staff showed the villagers films on family planning and then offered them a variety of methods, including diaphragm and jelly, jelly alone, condoms, foam tablets, rhythm, and a sponge dipped in 10 percent salt solution. In four years the birth rate fell from 26.6 per thousand to 13.7, compared with 21.5 for all of Japan. Intensification of efforts failed to reduce the birth rate further. Apparently, the villagers were having the number of children they wanted. The low rate, however, represented a population growth rate of only 0.80 percent per year. During the first two years the number of abortions followed the upward trend in the country as a whole, but decreased rapidly thereafter. After seven years, 75 percent of the fertile women and 95 percent of those with four or more children were using contraception.[7]

Most population watchers at the time were concerned over the *rate* of growth, not the total number of births per se. Economic stagnation rather than ecological disaster was the great fear. The reproduction rate achieved in the three villages compared very favorably with developed Western nations. It seemed a great victory for family planning, which became a national policy in Japan in 1956.

Koya, however, often pointed out that his success in the three villages reflected the preexisting desire of the people to control their fertility. Others noted the high literacy rate among the women of the villages, the intense indoctrination campaign Koya conducted, the high level of medical attention provided the villagers, the traditional Japanese respect for authority, and the fact that the birth rate had already begun to decline before the experiment began. The three-village success proved hard to repeat in other cultures.[8]

Gamble failed to learn one lesson from the Japanese villagers that might have saved him a great deal of unpleasantness. At Gamble's insistence Koya included the sponge and salt solution in the experiment. Twenty-two percent of the families tried the method, but almost all of them gave it up quickly.[9]

Yet Gamble persisted in using his money to promote salt-based contraceptives, even when the method became a symbol of the white man's contempt for colored people.

Gamble was fifty-six in 1950, and the burgeoning interest in the Third World seemed to offer a chance to prove the value of his twenty years of experience in organizing birth control services in the United States, an opportunity to show how foolish D. Kenneth Rose and his kind had been in their treatment of him. His hopes for vindication through good works in the international field were dashed, however, by conflict with two equally strong-willed and dedicated women, Dhanvanthi Handoo, Lady Benegal Rama Rau (born 1893), the Brahmin founder of the Family Planning Association of India (founded 1949) and wife of the governor of the Reserve Bank of India, and Helena Wright, gynecologist, feminist, and outspoken advocate of sexual fulfillment for women. As chairman of the International Planned Parenthood Federation and leader of the Indian Ocean Region (Pakistan, India, Ceylon), Lady Rama Rau represented the self-conscious indigenous ruling classes of the developing nations, resentful of foreign interference, yet unsure of their ability to deal with the enormous poverty and backwardness of their people. Dr. Wright, chairman of the IPPF's Medical Advisory Committee, was less interested in population control than in bringing first-class medical care to exploited women everywhere. ". . . forthright, opinionated, dominating. . . . She was enormously sure of herself and of the rightness of her views—and she had an almost hypnotic ability to transmit this feeling of certainty to others. She didn't argue or persuade . . . she simply told . . . what was what." Dr. Wright had begun her medical career in the pioneer British birth control clinics of the 1920s, and in her view every woman had a right to the best contraceptive available. In the 1950s that meant a diaphragm fitted by a doctor, and the offer of anything less was an insult to womankind.[10]

Enter Clarence Gamble, the American missionary, exuding self-confidence, come to save the women of the Indian Ocean Region with the cheapest, simplest contraceptive regimen he could devise, a rag soaked in salt water. He began recruiting Christian missionary doctors in India and Pakistan for a comparative trial of methods after Rama Rau failed to act on his

297

suggestion in 1950 that the time had come to give salt a try. Indian-American relations remained cordial, however, as Gamble donated $1,000 to the Family Planning Association of India for the 1952 Bombay Conference and continued to urge Rama Rau to try simple methods in Indian clinics. At the Bombay conference, Gamble sought out Helena Wright to question her opposition to salt as a spermicide, and was bluntly told that salt was unacceptable because it would dry out the vaginal tissues. Gamble used the conference to recruit more missionary doctors for his salt experiment anyway. Rama Rau, engrossed in the organizational chores of the conference, did not get involved in the conflict.[11]

Gamble brought his eldest son Richard to the conference, and afterwards they toured the region, making small contributions to get clinical trials started and helping to form family planning associations. They returned to the United States encouraged by their achievements. Gamble approached officials of the International Planned Parenthood Federation with a request that he and his son be given some official status that would sanction their work and allow the IPPF to be credited for any accomplishments.[12] Helena Wright vehemently opposed dignifying Gamble's efforts by appointing him a field representative of the IPPF, even though the international federation lacked the money at the time to hire any field workers. As C. P. Blacker, the London psychiatrist, eugenicist, and vice-chairman of the IPPF explained to Sanger:

> The plain fact seems to be that some people are afraid that Dr. Gamble might use the women in undeveloped countries for unauthorized experiments in new methods. . . .

Blacker believed it would be best to ask Gamble to continue working "in a private capacity."[13]

Sanger defended Gamble, explaining why experiments with simple methods had been going on in the United States since the 1930s and pointing out, "He is going to do it anyway, as an individual, and when he does . . . we will have no control over him or the methods that he is using and will not be entitled to a report on the methods" if Gamble's work were not recognized by the IPPF.[14] Gamble's relationship to the federation remained undetermined, as he and his son embarked on a thirteen-nation trip in January 1954, a tour that included a long stay in Rama Rau territory.

The Gambles took two weeks off during the tour, which was being paid for by a tax-privileged donation to the Brush Foundation for the IPPF, to go tiger hunting.[15] They did not get a tiger, but they met Margaret Roots, a Canadian widow of fifty-eight, who had left a job on the staff of the Royal Geographic Society to take an automobile tour of the world. Gamble decided Roots would make an ideal birth control missionary and hired her.[16]

Rama Rau rejected Gamble's suggestion that Roots be appointed an IPPF representative in the Indian Ocean Region, insisting that workers be recruited from among qualified professionals native to the region in which the organizational work was to be carried out.[17] When Gamble sent Roots to Ceylon anyway, things got nasty. Previously Rama Rau had not been hostile to experimentation with Gamble methods, simply indifferent. Now she joined Helena Wright in all-out opposition to Gamble, and rumors of Gamble tiger hunts at IPPF expense were circulated. The end result was a letter from the London office to Sanger, cataloging Gamble sins. He was accused of deceiving local doctors by telling them that the salt solution method had been thoroughly tested at the Margaret Sanger Clinical Research Bureau when, in fact, only salt jelly had been tried by a total of three patients. He allegedly used words like "coolie" and "native" in an offensive way and had discussed contraception in graphic terms at the birthday party of the widow of the assassinated Burmese prime minister, offending not only the widow, but also the president of the Burmese Nurses Association.[18]

Margaret Roots apparently won the affection of everyone in Ceylon and helped to organize a number of clinics, but she was asked to leave by the Family Planning Association after a year's work because of fears that her presence might complicate negotiations going on with the Swedish government for technical assistance. Elise Ottesen-Jensen, the leader of the Swedish birth controllers and a future president of the IPPF, shared Helena Wright's dislike for Gamble.[19]

Gamble continued to hire Westerners and send them out on missionary expeditions, while bombarding the IPPF's London office with requests for recognition, cooperation, and clarification of the status of his employees. In the middle 1950s the federation was still a shoestring operation, providing little more than a newsletter, information on national organizations, policy statements, and sponsorship of conferences that attracted eminent scholars and world attention but were financed by an ad hoc committee consisting of Margaret Sanger, struggling to rally the troops for another offensive from her retirement home in Tucson, Arizona. Help was so desperately needed that no one wanted to alienate Gamble as long as there was a chance that he might aid the federation financially. C. P. Blacker was assigned the arduous task of answering Gamble's inquiries. He repeatedly explained the federation's position that it welcomed contributions by Gamble to projects initiated by national groups but could not sanction his private activities and disapproved of his efforts to use contributions to influence local organizations.[20]

Gamble continued on his private way, but in 1952 he had helped to initiate an experiment in population control that came to symbolize the failure of the simple-methods approach and provided justification for radical innovation in contraceptive technology.

The Khanna Study

The Harvard Medical School did not include contraception in its curriculum during the 1940s, but Gamble stirred things up in 1946 by getting the fourth-year students to petition the dean to accept and distribute the doctor's manual Robert Dickinson had written for the Planned Parenthood Federation of America. The dean was too busy to consider the petition, so Gamble distributed the booklet himself and rented a room off the medical school grounds where he showed a drug-company film on technique.[21]

Despite such subversive activity, Gamble was allowed to have laboratory space in the department of anatomy after his part-time teaching job ended with the war. In 1958 he moved to the School of Public Health, paying for his privileges with grants to the school. In 1962 the Gamble family funded the establishment of a department of demography and human ecology in the School of Public Health, the first such department in the United States, and this led to the establishment of the interdisciplinary Center for Population Studies.[22]

Gamble's contacts with the School of Public Health developed through Professor John E. Gordon (born 1890), an epidemiologist, who became interested about 1949 in the relationship between public health, population growth, and economic development. Gordon believed the same methodology used in the study of the control of communicable diseases could be applied to population problems. Gordon heard about Gamble's interest in birth control, and a fruitful collaboration began.[23]

When Gordon went to India in 1951 as a consultant for the World Health Organization, Gamble paid for extension of his stay while he investigated the possibility of setting up a trial population control program in the rural Punjab State. Gamble money followed to bring John B. Wyon, a young British missionary doctor who was working among Indian villagers, to Boston for a year of training at the School of Public Health. Together Gordon and Wyon, with help from Gamble, planned a study that absorbed much of their time for seventeen years, resulted in three dozen articles and a fat monograph, and attracted a million dollars in foundation and government grants. When Gordon's grant money ran out, Gamble provided him with seven years of office space, secretary, and half-time salary to write *The Khanna Study: Population Problems in the Rural Punjab* (1971), a detailed explanation of why Indian peasants remained indifferent to family limitation despite the best-laid plans of social engineers.[24]

With the cooperation of the Indian government and the Christian Medical College in Ludhiana City, Punjab State, Gordon and Wyon organized the first population control program to include a control as well as a test population. One group of villages was carefully studied, and an intense effort was made to get the people to accept contraceptives. Two control areas were established. In one the people were studied but not offered contraceptives. In the other, the people were not approached at all, but vital records were quietly gathered from village leaders.

A pilot contraceptive program showed that foam tablets were the most acceptable of the methods offered (rhythm, withdrawal, and contraceptive paste or salt solution on a cotton pad were the other alternatives). As a result, foam tablets were pushed by the project staff, which visited every family once a month. Although methodological flaws prevent an exact estimate, less than 20 percent of the fertile villagers agreed to practice contraception. During 1957–59, the annual birth rates of the population exposed to contraception rose slightly, as did that of the group that was studied but not offered contraception. The unstudied group's birth rate dropped from 45.4 to 39.2.[25]

The million dollars had not done much to lower birth rates in the Punjab. Gordon concluded that the villagers had children because they needed their labor and loved children. They had so many because a great number of them died. Perhaps lower infant mortality would lead to lower birth rates. Of course, the project was begun in 1953 in an effort to relieve population pressures created by the fact that birth rates remained high after death rates fell. In short, *The Khanna Study* was a convuluted exercise in disguising the failure of an attempt to lower birth rates with foam tablets in rural India; plenty of theory and no results.

Gamble gave up experimenting with salt as a spermicide in 1956, and observers of the Khanna debacle could only conclude that some drastic improvement in contraceptive technology was essential. After the Khanna experiment:

> The village leaders advanced various reasons for the observed failure. They suggested the people were too shy to go to anyone within their own village for contraceptive supplies. They expressed the view that what was wanted was a long-acting method of contraception, whether an operation, an injection, or a pill. The volunteer study workers, reporting on their experience, concluded that shyness was a factor but that willingness to make a sustained effort was the main limitation.[26]

If population control could not wait for basic changes in the structure of rural societies, then a contraceptive would have to be found that would allow birth control to follow the pattern set by the imposition of death control. Successful public health programs had depended on preventive methods that did not require the daily cooperation of the patient and which were administered on an assembly-line basis by a public health bureaucracy. To population watchers it seemed that birth control would also have to become something that could be imposed through mass procedures by small numbers of technicians. A successful contraceptive would require less motivation and attention to detail from individuals than condoms, diaphragms, or foam tablets.

In 1948 the essential social justification for further development of the IUD was lacking. Only ten years later, fear of famine, revolution, and catastrophe had removed many inhibitions.

For several years after the founding of the Population Council (1952) efforts were concentrated on establishing centers of excellence in demographic and biomedical research. Frederick Osborn feared that the overzealousness of some new converts to the cause of population control might weaken the firm foundation he was trying to build for international cooperation. Hugh Moore, the Dixie cup tycoon, was the epitome of the kind of person Osborn dreaded—brash, self-made, aggressively anticommunist, with enough money to insulate himself from the counsel of others.[27]

In 1957, Margaret Sanger was planning a population conference in Washington in the hope of raising funds for the International Planned Parenthood Federation. Moore had donated the services of Tom O. Griessemer, a lawyer and public relations consultant, to help organize the conference. Griessemer's main selling device was Cold War rhetoric. Osborn felt that the risks of a Washington meeting far outweighed possible gains. Catholics would be stirred to vigorous opposition, but more important, Washington, the capital of the richest nation in the world, was the wrong place for discussion of the population problems of underdeveloped nations. As Osborn explained to Sanger:

The remarkable development in China where the Communist government ... is carrying on a large scale government propaganda in developing birth control clinics; the developments in India, in Japan, and in Egypt (in each of these countries there are government population commissions, the beginnings at least of government sponsored clinics and a full acceptance of the program in all government circles), are things which indicate a change, which would have seemed impossible a few years ago.

As a result it is the United States which is a backward country in respect to the control of population growth, and not the Asian countries ... with the battle so nearly won in those countries it would be a great pity if anything coming out of the United States could be seized by Communist propaganda as evidence that the United States was trying to reduce population growth elsewhere. For instance, Griessemer told me that he hoped the Washington conference would arouse the interest of Congress. It seems to me that congressional interest would most likely be shown by some of the people in Congress who are opposed to foreign aid and who would make speeches to the effect that foreign aid should only be given to countries limiting their population.[28]

Sanger fired Griessemer and reluctantly gave up the idea of a Washington conference.[29] A year later a presidential committee on foreign aid, chaired by General William Draper, made headlines by suggesting that assistance for family planning programs should be made available to foreign governments which requested it as part of American aid for development. President Eisenhower tried to ignore the recommendation, and when a meeting of Catholic bishops denounced the use of public money to "promote artificial birth prevention," Eisenhower declared that he could not "imagine anything more emphatically a subject that is not a proper political or governmental activity or function or responsibility."[30]

While avoiding such controversy, the Population Council had been quietly laying a basis for technical assistance through its research program and educational grants. In 1954, India requested help from the council in organizing its family planning program and Pakistan followed in 1959.[31] The council had reached the point in its development where an office for evaluation of action programs was needed. The council was "squeamish" about handling the work directly, but efforts to establish an office at a local university for statistical study of birth control experiments failed.[32]

304

The Failure of Simple Methods: The IUD Justified

Frederick Osborn had known Christopher Tietze since he had helped the Austrian refugee get a job at Johns Hopkins. Tietze had maintained his interest in evaluating family planning programs while working as an intelligence officer in the State Department, and in 1957, Osborn offered Tietze a job evaluating family planning programs in which the council had an interest. The project needed an institutional sponsor, however, and officials of the council asked Clarence Gamble to allow them to use the National Committee on Maternal Health as a tax-exempt corporate sponsor for Tietze's work. Gamble agreed to turn the NCMH over to a group of directors chosen by the council and began to channel his work through the Pathfinder Fund, a Gamble family foundation formed to serve the old functions of the NCMH. Although there was theoretically no direct connection between the NCMH and the Population Council when Tietze set up shop in January 1958 in the New York Academy of Medicine Building, all of the NCMH's funding now came from the council. As Tietze explained, the NCMH was "the favorite child" or "wholly owned subsidiary" of the Population Council. Finally, in 1967, the NCMH and its staff were absorbed into the Council's Bio-Medical Division.[33]

Tietze's new studies showed that population control programs with conventional methods "were getting nowhere fast." Intensive review of old methods continued, but reported results remained contradictory, probably reflecting differences in motivation between populations.[34] Some members of the Population Council were convinced by the futility of programs based on conventional methods that something better had to be found. Frank Notestein, who succeeded Frederick Osborn as president of the Population Council in 1959, remembers his frustration in knowing that something had to be done to control rapid population growth but lacking the contraceptive means that would enable the council to take decisive action. "I've never been in another situation in my life that made me feel so helpless."[35] It was this sense of urgency which prompted a reevaluation of intrauterine devices.

Alan F. Guttmacher, chief of obstetrics at Mount Sinai Hospital in New York City and a member of the medical advisory committee of the council, had warned against intrauterine devices in his popular marriage manual, but when a member of his department at Mount Sinai approached him in 1958 with an idea for a new kind of IUD, Guttmacher listened.

> Dr. Lazar C. Margulies, who was Berlin trained and who had used an intrauterine device in the late twenties in Berlin came to me with the idea that an intrauterine device could be made of molded plastic and the advantage was that you could stretch it to a linear form . . . and it would resume its original shape.[36]

Margulies had been inspired to give the old method a second look when he heard John Rock, the Harvard gynecologist who had served on the AMA committee on contraception in the 1930s and who was the object of an intense lobbying effort by Robert Dickinson, lecture on the dangers of overpopulation. The substitution of plastic for wire meant that the device could be inserted without dilating the cervix (stretching the mouth of the womb), a painful procedure that required local anesthesia. The molded plastic coil was unwound into a thin rod, the rod slipped into the uterus, and the coil pushed out of the rod into the uterus, where it regained its original shape.

Guttmacher allowed Margulies to try out the device "with some fear and hesitation because I was taught in medical school how dangerous the intrauterine device was." They worked. Patients did not die of pelvic inflammatory disease or develop galloping cancer. At about the same time the *American Journal of Obstetrics and Gynecology*, edited by Howard Taylor, Jr., who was a member of the medical advisory committee of the Population Council, invited an Israeli, Willi Oppenheimer, who had also been trained in Berlin, to report on his long experience with Gräfenberg rings. The article was well received, as was a report by Atsumi Ishihama of Japan in the *Yokohama Medical Journal* describing his experience with a device that had been pioneered in the 1930s by Tenrei Ota, the socialist sponsor of Japan's first eugenic protection act.[37]

In 1962, the Population Council gave Guttmacher a grant "to travel around the world to assess what methods of birth control they should back." He reported that conventional contraceptives were not working and advised the council to invest in development of the IUD.[38] The council invited forty-two clinicians to a conference on intrauterine contraception. Tietze remembered the "conspiratorial air" that surrounded the conference. "It was a very exciting period. . . . we were working with something that had been absolutely rejected by the profession . . . we had a great feeling of urgency to produce a method that worked. It seemed to work. Now we had to establish it. And we had to start from scratch."[39]

The council invested more than $2.5 million in the clinical testing, improvement, and statistical evaluation of the IUD, which proved to be highly effective for the approximately seven out of ten women who could retain one.[40] Tietze, an unusually candid man with the habit of precise expression, recalls the care with which clinicians were recruited and the effort poured into making sure that their records were accurate.

> There was such a feeling of urgency among professional people, not among the masses, but something had to be done. And this was something that you could do to the people rather than something people could do for themselves. So it made it very attractive to the doers.[41]

Armed at last with a method that was inexpensive and required little motivation from the user beyond initial acceptance, family planning programs began to have an effect on birth rates in South Korea, Taiwan, and Pakistan.[42] By 1967 a review article in *Demography* criticized the overoptimism of the Population Council technocrats about the prospects for controlling world population growth. Other social scientists claimed that population control was getting too much of the development dollar and pointed out that population control was no substitute for social justice. Lower birth rates did not guarantee a better society.[43] Whether or not world population growth could be controlled remained an unanswered question. Notestein was acutely aware, however, that technology alone could not curb the population explosion. Basic social reforms were essential in many developing countries, but private American agencies could not force others to do anything. "What can a white capitalist do in a very sensitive world?"[44] Notestein's answer was that he could provide high-quality technical assistance when asked.

By the late 1960s discussion of the population problems of underdeveloped countries had helped to stimulate renewed interest in family planning programs in the United States.[45]

Happily, there was a growing discussion about the social and philosophical issues involved in the management of human reproduction, whereas only a decade before, informed interest had been limited to a few social scientists.[46] The whole nature of the debate, however, as well as the prospects for controlling population growth, had been radically altered by the availability of the plastic intrauterine device, an American gift to the world.

PART VII

THE PILL

"I invented the pill at the request of a woman."
Gregory Pincus, interview in *Candide*, 1966.

"There is no power on this earth that can do more than delay by a trifle the final enfranchisement of women."
Katharine Dexter McCormick, address to 1920 convention of the National American Woman Suffrage Association and First Congress of the League of Women Voters.

CHAPTER 24

The Prospects for Hormonal Sterilization

THE anovulant pill was the first absolutely new contraceptive developed in the twentieth century. For years birth controllers had dreamed of a "physiological" method that would be completely divorced from the act of coitus. The movement had suffered from the lack of a universally acceptable method. Robert Dickinson once observed that even if conflicting values could be reconciled, birth controllers still faced the fact that many women would not use a mechanical contraceptive. An oral contraceptive might solve a number of problems. Those who would not use methods that required sacrifice of pleasure or attention to details might be reached at last. Sexual intercourse without procreation could become a completely spontaneous act requiring no forethought. Passion no longer would be dampened by messy fumbling. A method that saved physicians from the awkward chores of diaphragm fitting while increasing their incomes might end the last vestiges of medical hesitancy to prescribe contraception. The magic of science would make contraception easy and aesthetic for physician and patient alike.

The possibility of using hormones to suppress ovulation had been discussed for at least thirty years when scientists at the Worcester Foundation for Experimental Biology began looking for an effective contraceptive agent in the early 1950s. Hor-

311

monal contraception depended upon precise knowledge of the structure and effects of the sex hormones secreted by the endocrine glands. The development of endocrinology, the study of the body's system of hormonal regulation, had been speeded by the availability of funds for the study of sexual physiology in the 1920s.[1]

The National Research Council added the new Committee for Research in Problems of Sex to its grant-making groups in 1922 owing to the initiative of Earl F. Zinn, a psychologist who had become concerned over the lack of information on sexual behavior. After considerable effort, Zinn gained a personal audience with John D. Rockefeller, Jr., and a job as executive secretary of the proposed Committee for Research in Problems of Sex. Zinn's initial efforts to gain sponsorship for sex research from the National Research Council broke down because officers of the new Division of Anthropology and Psychology felt that their own status was too insecure to risk association with investigations in a controversial and ill-defined field. Fortunately, Dr. Victor C. Vaughan, the director of the Division of Medical Sciences and former dean of the University of Michigan Medical School, had been active in the social hygiene movement and understood the need for better sex education based on empirical research. He welcomed the new committee into the prestigious Division of Medical Science.[2]

In 1923 the Bureau of Social Hygiene provided $25,000 to the committee, "To conduct, stimulate, foster, systematize and coordinate research on sex problems to the end that conclusions now held may be evaluated and our scientific knowledge in this field increased as rapidly as possible." Armed with this broad mandate, committee representatives consulted Robert Dickinson, Havelock Ellis, Sigmund Freud, and other authorities on human sexuality in an effort to find research projects offering insights into human sexual problems. It soon became clear to Robert Yerkes, the psychologist and chairman of the committee, that,

> The well-nigh endless extent and variety of research problems of sex makes imperative an order of preference with respect to materials and methods of work. If we should undertake, as a Committee, the conduct or encouragement of all sorts of studies relative to

312

sex life, our energies and resources would, I fear, be hopelessly scattered and largely wasted.[3]

Among the investigators whose work touched on problems of sex, the biologists were in the best position to offer well-defined plans of research. Specifically, prospects for advancing understanding of the female reproductive cycle had been greatly improved by the development of a simple test. In 1917, C. R. Stockard and George Papanicolaou of Cornell Medical School had shown that exact stages in the reproductive cycle could be determined by microscopic examination of tiny samples of the lining of the uterus, thus making it possible to save for further study many experimental animals that had formerly been sacrificed in hormone research. The uterus continually sheds surface cells, and the cells shed at each stage of the cycle are unique. Rapid delineation of the relationship between changes in the ovary and the uterus followed the development of the Pap test. By 1923 estrogen, the primary hormone secreted within the ovary, had been isolated, and its effect on the uterus demonstrated.[4]

The committee recognized that these exciting developments in hormone research provided a strategic opportunity, a field of sex research that fell securely within the bounds of basic science and yet promised to yield practical results. The committee virtually paid for the development of endocrinology in the United States during the twenty-year period when the female sex hormones were identified and clinicians began to use hormone extracts to treat disease.[5]

The medical use of hormones was limited by their high cost. By 1930, George Corner and Willard Allen of the University of Rochester had demonstrated that the monthly preparation of the uterus to accept the fertilized ovum and the maintenance of pregnancy depended upon progesterone, the hormone of gestation secreted by the ruptured egg sack of the ovary (corpus luteum) and by the placenta. Progesterone had enormous therapeutic potential, but the isolation of a single gram required the processing of a ton of animal organs. The ovaries of 80,000 sows were used to obtain the first fraction of a gram of estrogen. The biologist's understanding of the body's system of hormonal regulation would only make an impact on medicine if hormones could be obtained easily and from inexpensive sources.[6]

While endocrinologists described natural processes, organic chemists were beginning to imitate them in the laboratory. In 1928 the German Adolf Windhaus received the Nobel Prize for working out the chemical structure of cholesterol, the main ingredient of animal bile, and for showing how a number of important substances, including digitalis and vitamin D, were related to cholesterol. All three were steroids, compounds sharing an identical molecular structure of seventeen carbon atoms arranged in four rings. One steroid differs from another mainly by the position and the nature of the side chains attached to the basic molecule. German commercial chemists attempting to develop a process for obtaining estrogen in large quantities turned to Windhaus for help. Adolf Butenandt, one of Windhaus' students, was assigned the task of obtaining pure crystalline estrogen from the urine of pregnant mares, a goal he achieved in 1929 simultaneously with two Americans. Butenandt went on, however, to show that estrogen is a steroid, as all of the other sex hormones proved to be. Butenandt developed techniques for manipulating steroid molecules, and in 1939 he shared the Nobel Prize with Leopold Ruzicka, a Yugoslav chemist working in Switzerland, who in 1936 had changed cholesterol into a synthetic duplicate of the male sex hormone testosterone.[7]

Ruzicka's "first" was matched in 1936 by Russell Marker (born 1902), an organic chemist at Pennsylvania State College, who synthesized estrogen from plant steriods. Marker had abruptly quit the University of Maryland on the verge of receiving the Ph.D. and had later stalked out of the Rockefeller Institute over what his colleagues considered a minor disagreement, but he had developed great skill in devising processes for breaking down the complex molecules of plant steroids and recombining them into new crystalline substances, processes upon which Parke, Davis and Company had secured more than seventy pattents. Marker became convinced that a cheap supply of synthetic hormones could be synthesized from sapogenins, steroid materials abundant in the roots of many plants of the lily family. The richest source of sa-

The Prospects for Hormonal Sterilization

pogenins, Marker discovered, was the wild Mexican yam (*Dioscorea mexicana* or *cabeza de negro*). When Parke, Davis balked at Marker's plans to establish a root gathering and processing operation in Mexico, Marker left Pennsylvania State College in midsemester to set up a makeshift laboratory in Mexico City, and in two months during the summer of 1943, he synthesized four and a half pounds of progesterone, worth $160,000, until word got out that relatively large quantities of sex hormones were obtainable from a small firm in Mexico.[8]

Marker's processes were duplicated and improved upon by other chemists, and a race began among American drug houses to market synthetic hormones. When George Corner, who had been the first to demonstrate the specific effects of progesterone, reviewed the prospects for clinical use of the hormone in 1947, he emphasized its power to maintain pregnancy in cases of deficient ovarian function and its sedative effect on the uterine muscle following childbirth. Continuous administration of progesterone disrupted the sexual cycle and suppressed menstruation, so Corner thought that it might be used to control excessive menstrual bleeding, as well as painful menstruation. Progesterone also suppresses ovulation. Corner did not mention suppression of ovulation, however, as one of the potential uses for his hormone.[9] Other researchers recognized the possibility of using hormones to control fertility. In 1937, Raphael Kurzrok, a Columbia endocrinologist, reported that "The Prospects for Hormonal Sterilization" were good. The administration of large doses of estrogen for treatment of painful menstruation inhibited ovulation in Kurzrok's patients. In studies with mice and rabbits, daily injections of estrogen resulted in retention of ova in the fallopian tubes and their rapid degeneration even if they escaped into the uterus. Kurzok concluded: "The potentialities of hormonal sterilization are tremendous. The problem is important enough to warrant extensive work on the human."[10]

Despite Kurzrok's enthusiasm, the high cost of hormones limited their therapeutic application, and their effects were too general and too little understood to warrant giving them to healthy women simply to control fertility. But their contraceptive potential was recognized. As Harvard's Fuller Albright explained in 1945:

315

Since preventing ovulation prevents pregnancy, one could employ the same principles in birth control as in preventing dysmenorrhea [painful menstruation]. Thus, for example, if an individual took 1 mg. of diethylstilbestrol [a synthetic estrogen] by mouth daily from the first day of her period for the next six weeks, she would not ovulate during this interval.

A hormone regimen would have to be worked out that allowed periodic menstruation, but the medication could be administered

to make the menstrual period come on the least undesirable day. Such manipulation of one's menstrual rhythm is probably not to be advocated indiscriminately, but there is no evidence at the present time to suggest that the individual will not return to her pretherapeutic rhythm on cessation of therapy. [11]

By the 1950s both endocrinology and steroid chemistry had advanced far enough so that a hormonal contraceptive was possible. The initiative for a major effort to develop a physiological contraceptive did not come from scientists or physicians, however, but from laywomen. And the scientist that they chose to realize their hopes for better birth control was a refugee from academic biology.

CHAPTER 25 **A Life in Experimental Biology**

G REGORY GOODWIN PINCUS, the father of the birth control pill, was born in Woodbine, New Jersey, in 1903, the eldest son of a teacher and editor of a farm journal.[1] His family on both sides were Russian Jews, farmers who had emigrated to New Jersey in the nineteenth century. One of his uncles was dean of the agricultural college of Rutgers University, and "Goody" Pincus wanted to be a farmer, but his father disapproved, pointing out "the non-paying character of a farmer's life," so Goody's love of nature found expression in a biology major at Cornell (B.S., 1924), where he edited the *Cornell Literary Review*.[2]

Pincus continued his study of nature at Harvard under the direction of the geneticist William Castle (1867–1962), receiving the M.S. and Sc.D. degrees in 1927 for his study of the inheritance of coat coloring in rats.[3] One of his colleagues has suggested that Pincus' interest in heredity grew from his color blindness and the paradox of correspondingly sharp vision possessed by many color-blind people.[4] Harvard's Bussey Institution for Applied Biology (founded 1908) offered outstanding facilities for the study of genetics. A sprawling collection of greenhouses and barns, siding on the Arnold Arboretum in Forest Hills, ten miles from the bustle of Cambridge, and surrounded by gardens where food was grown for the large numbers of mice, rabbits, and other experimental animals used in breeding experiments, the Bussey Institution provided as close an imitation of life on the farm as could be found in academia.[5]

As a fellow of the National Research Council, Pincus did two years of postdoctoral research at Cambridge University and at the Kaiser Wilhelm Institute. He returned to Harvard in 1930 as an instructor in general physiology. During his last year as a graduate student at Harvard, Pincus began to develop new conceptions of how to study nature. His association with Castle had been rewarding, but by the late 1920s Castle's kind of biology no longer seemed to provide exciting opportunities for ambitious young investigators.

Castle, a leader of the first generation of American geneticists, had undergone the conversion to Mendelianism that shaped the careers of a number of American zoologists during the first five years of the twentieth century. A satisfactory explanation of the mechanism of heredity had been the missing link that threatened the whole structure of Darwinian theory, and the development of the gene concept seemed like "a flood of light," a saving revelation. Beginning in 1903, all of Castle's scientific papers for fifty-eight years dealt with genetics and its relation to evolution and animal breeding. With loving care he pursued the details of Mendelian theory, never voicing any strong desire to find out what genes are made of and showing no interest in bringing the insights of chemistry or physics to bear on the problems of development.[6]

Some experimental biologists distrusted Castle's descriptive methodology and sought to treat living things as "chemical machines" whose behavior could be explained by the laws of physical science. The champion of this mechanistic conception of life was Jacques Loeb (1859–1924). Loeb had startled the scientific world in 1899 by showing that sea urchin eggs could be made to develop into embryos by exposure to solutions containing certain salts in higher concentration than in sea water. Clearly, Loeb proclaimed, the role of sperm cells in development was a simple problem in physical chemistry. Theologians and animal watchers alike would have to interrupt their musings over the mysteries of life and take note that the artificial production and the control of living matter were within the grasp of analytical science.[7]

Although Loeb made his impact on the scientific world before World War I, his greatest popular vogue was in the 1920s, when Paul de Kruif, the debunker of philistine science, made Loeb a symbol of the scientist as lonely searcher, immune to the temptations of the Bitch Goddess Success. De Kruif inspired Sinclair Lewis to create his fictional hero, Martin Arrowsmith, a medical student who is drawn into a research career by the example of a Loeb-like professor. Arrowsmith is saved from corrupting social pressures by his final determination to seek knowledge as an end in itself and to ignore society's demands. Loeb became a hero to a generation of American experimental biologists, who were inspired by the Loebian faith that the secrets of life are amenable to a sound research protocol.[8]

The exponent of the Loebian dogma at Harvard in the 1930s was the physiologist William Crozier (1892–1955). Although his Ph.D. was in zoology (Harvard, 1915), Crozier had long been interested in using the methodology of the physical sciences to study animal behavior, and he returned to Harvard as an associate professor in 1925 to head the newly formed department of general physiology.[9]

Crozier's research was largely an extension of Loeb's work on tropisms (involuntary responses to stimuli) and the use of the Arrhenius equation to describe biological processes. Loeb had worked with relatively simple organisms—caterpillars, sea urchins, tadpoles, fish. Crozier sought to bring the same analytical precision to the study of more complicated creatures, including mammals.

Crozier, at thirty-two the youngest associate professor then at Harvard, attracted an enthusiastic group of young researchers to his growing laboratory, including Gregory Pincus and Hudson Hoagland. He exerted the decisive influence on Pincus' career, collaborating with him in quantitative studies of geotropism and phototropism in rats that formed the basis of six of Pincus' first seven publications, all written together with Crozier in 1926–27.[10]

After Jacques Loeb had demonstrated that some animal behavior formerly attributed to infallible instincts for self-preservation could be explained as tropistic responses that continued even to self-destruction, he had moved on to "an assault upon the crux of biological mysticism, the process of fertilization where so many ingenious theologians through the ages had seen their chance to slip a soul in while nobody was looking." [11] Pincus too moved from experimental manipulation of behavior to attempts to create life and control its development. Loeb had produced fatherless (parthenogenetic) sea urchins in 1889. Pincus began working toward the live birth of a parthenogenetic rabbit in 1929 and claimed success in 1939. By then, however, he was no longer at Harvard, and he had been forced out of a promising career in academic biology.

Pincus had succeeded as an undergraduate at Cornell and as a graduate student at Harvard at a time when Jews had to be better than their competitors in order to win equal consideration. His appointment in 1931 as assistant professor in Crozier's department of general physiology seemed to be the first landmark in an academic success story. While he was in England (1929–30), Pincus had begun to develop an original line of research that might justify a permanent position at Harvard. [12] During the next six years, he established himself as an authority on mammalian sexual physiology, specializing in delicate work with rabbit eggs. [13] His studies of the mechanisms of fertilization and of ovum growth attracted the support of the National Research Council Committee for Research in Problems of Sex and of the Josiah Macy, Jr., Foundation. [14] Pincus had chosen an important research problem, and the value of his contributions was widely recognized. For the academic year 1937–38 he received a leave of absence and a university research grant that allowed him to return to Cambridge University for a year at full salary, but he was also informed that he would not be reappointed at Harvard. [15]

Harvard produces many scholars, but there is room for few on a permanent basis. Pincus believed, however, that he was a better scientist than others who were retained and that his dismissal was "political," motivated by personal jealousies and prejudices. Some sensational publicity lent credibility to the charge that some of his senior colleagues wanted to get rid of a brillant but controversial investigator whose work conjured up

Frankenstein–Brave New World nightmares in the minds of many laymen. Pincus first received national attention in 1934, when he announced that he had achieved *in vitro* (inside.a test tube) fertilization of rabbit eggs.[16] His claims led to a great deal of speculation in the newspapers over the implications of his work. The *New York Times* ran a story on its science page under the headline, "Rabbits Born in Glass: Haldane-Huxley Fantasy Made Real by Harvard Biologists." Pincus had transferred the developing eggs to living hosts, which were sacrificed before the embryos grew to term, so the rabbits were not "Born in Glass" but only conceived in test tubes. Nevertheless, the *Times* pictured Pincus as a sinister character bent on hatching humans in bottles.

> It was J. B. S. Haldane who first drove home to the multitude the beauties of ectogenesis—a process whereby eggs are fertilized in test tubes. Aldous Huxley made much of the possibilities in his "Brave New World."
>
> "One egg, one embryo, one adult—normality," explains the Director of Hatcheries and Conditioning in that lively satire to a class of students. "But a bokanovskified egg (Bokanovsky is the fictional biologist who devised the process) will bud, will proliferate, will divide. From eight to ninety-six buds, and every bud will grow into a perfectly formed embryo, and every embryo into a full-sized adult. Making ninety-six beings grow where only one grew before. Progress."
>
> At Harvard are two Bokanovskys in the persons of Professors Gregory Pincus and E. V. Enzmann [Pincus' collaborator in the *in vitro* fertilization study].[17]

Pincus apparently enjoyed his notoriety. His mentor Crozier wrote him, "Hudson [Hoagland] tells a tale of newspapers and enraged Spiritualists which seems choice!"[18] Despite the hullabaloo, Pincus' work was aimed at the legitimate goal of understanding the developmental process, and it might lead to new tools for doctors in the treatment of spontaneous abortion, menstrual disorders, and the diseases of pregnancy.

Pincus' research depended on the development of techniques for the gathering and the manipulation of large numbers of rabbit ova. He faced tremendous obstacles. The hormones controlling ovulation and development were generally known, but many details of their exact composition and specific effects remained to be worked out. Experimental biologists had to make their hormonal preparations from gland extracts, and even cultures for growing tissues were "homemade," so that it was difficult to control or reproduce experiments because of the lack of uniform experimental drugs. These problems would eventually be mitigated by advances in endocrinology and by the synthesis of hormones, but in the 1930s there were many dead ends waiting for researchers. [19]

Pincus' research goals were large, and some of his colleagues believed that his experiments ranged too far beyond established knowledge. They found that they could not reproduce all of his results. Thus, Pincus' effort to achieve a major breakthrough with mammals, analogous to Loeb's activation of sea urchin eggs in 1899, exposed him to criticism from two sources. First, he aroused the hostility of the religious-minded in and out of science who resented his attempt to reduce the mysteries of conception and birth into mechanistic terms. Second, some experimental biologists, who sympathized with his goals, questioned the wisdom of trying to do too much too soon. The growth of knowledge depended on small steps, carefully planned. Loeb's spectacular successes owed much to his genius for selecting simple organisms for tightly structured experiments. He was also careful to be certain of results before announcing them to the world, especially when they could be interpreted as threats to human values. Pincus, in contrast, designed experiments that were too complex to be carefully controlled or easily reproduced. Public criticism of his experimental technique lay in the future, however. During the 1930s the social implications of his work received more attention than the soundness of his methodology or conclusions.

By 1936, Pincus had shown that rabbit ova could be artificially activated by a number of techniques, including exposure to salt solutions or to changes in temperature. While he did not yet claim a parthenogenetic birth, he had successfully transplanted many developing ova into does (female rabbits), and the ova had grown into embryos before the hosts were sacrificed to check the progress of the experiment. [20] His "immaculate conceptions" made good copy for journalists, some of whom delighted in describing "the Wellsian World Pincus' work had postulated." An article in *Collier's* titled "No Father to Guide Them" subtly combined antifeminism, anti-Semitism, and criticism of the "tricks" that biologists were playing on nature in a vicious bit of reporting that caused a sensation in Cambridge and that probably hurt Pincus' chances for tenure at Harvard. An abundance of curly hair and the dark bags under his eyes gave Pincus an Einsteinish air. *Collier's* took the characteristic gentleness and warmth out of Pincus' appearance by photographing him with a cigarette dangling out of his mouth and with a large white rabbit peering out from his arms like the sacrificial victim so dear to antivivisectionist propaganda.[21]

The photographer's unpleasant image was developed by the reporter J. D. Ratcliff, who explained that Pincus' experiments "fit in with the work of that hugely famous Portuguese Jew [Jacques Loeb]." Pincus' "name might have been borrowed from a cop in a detective novel," but his work had "possibilities more thrilling than anything a detective story writer ever imagined: a world in which woman would be a dominant, self-sufficient entity, able to produce young without the aid of man." Since all parthenogenetic young lacked the male Y-chromosome and would be female, "man's value would shrink. . . . The mythical land of the Amazons would then come to life. A world where woman would be self-sufficient; man's value precisely zero." "Working with his slender, almost feminine hands," Gregory Pincus was threatening to castrate American man, whose virility had already been called into doubt by economic depression and declining birth rates.[22]

For a scientific evaluation of Pincus' work, Ratcliff went to Alexis Carrel, surgeon, mystic, and archenemy of the mechanistic conception of life. The ability of the Rockefeller Institute to house such contrasting spirits as Carrel and Loeb has been cited as an example of the broadly tolerant philosophy of an institution where "capacity for discovery was the only test of acceptance."[23] Carrel pointed out the dangerous tendency of Pincus' work for *Collier's* readers. If babies were made in test tubes:

> It would be the ruin of women. Healthy women develop tremendously after they have had children.

Their nervous systems are much improved—sometimes after one child, more after two, but more yet after three or four. And their looks are improved too. . . .

Unfortunately, modern woman has had to forego many of the exercises that make motherhood natural.

We should direct our research to get back to that point. Artificial production of children would take us ever farther in the other direction and would rob us of the most valuable aids in their development. [24]

The father of two and loyal husband to a woman who ran a tight household and looked to her man to make the family fortune, Gregory Pincus found himself pictured as a sexual revolutionary, some kind of social deviant. Hopes for success and acceptance that had been expressed in eagerness to talk about his work were now threatened. Suddenly he began to tell reporters, "I am not interested in the implications of the work." [25] Sex research posed high risks for untenured professors.

Pincus' chances for survival at Harvard were also hurt by the elimination of the department of general physiology as part of a reorganization of the life sciences division. James Bryant Conant, a chemist and Harvard's new president (1934), believed that "the time for pruning" had arrived at a university where special institutes and new departments had multiplied alongside the growth of knowledge. Both financial necessity and the pursuit of excellence in undergraduate education required that fewer subjects be taught more efficiently. [26] Conant was willing to let some "vested academic interests" die of old age. In 1936 the Bussey Institution was closed and its functions transferred to the new Biological Laboratories in Cambridge. William Castle, who had reached retirement age, was forced to move to the University of California in order to find the animal quarters he needed for his work. [27]

William Crozier had attracted many graduate students for whom he was constantly seeking better facilities. He was contemptuous of the claims of competing branches of biology for a share of the university's limited facilities. [28] For Conant, Crozier must have seemed the epitome of the overspecialized empire builder who threatened to disrupt the university. In 1936 the three departments of the division of biology (general physiology, botany, zoology) were reorganized into a single department of biology. Crozier, tenured and too young to be retired, was, in effect, pensioned off as research professor of general physiology, without formal teaching duties or power in the new department of biology.[29]

When the question of promotion for Pincus came up in the spring of 1937, neither Castle nor Crozier, his two sponsors at Harvard, had any influence in departmental affairs. The division of biology informed him that his contract would not be renewed beyond 1937–38. Pincus and his friends believed that the decision reflected prejudice against him as a student of Crozier and as a self-advertising Jew who published too soon and talked too much.[30]

Pincus moved his family to England in the fall of 1937 for a year of research at Cambridge University on a Harvard research grant, confident that some good biology department in the United States would offer him a position for 1938–39. Despite the best efforts of Castle and Crozier, however, no job offers were forthcoming. Pincus' chagrin over being turned out by Harvard hardened into bitterness as Hitler's power grew and England's security was threatened. The Holocaust was approaching and no one seemed very interested in helping him escape. Crozier assured Pincus that his friends had "worked damn hard to get something for you—harder than you realize," but he could not lend him $300 and advised him to move as far west as possible in the event he had to stay in England.[31]

At this nadir in Pincus' life, two friends helped him to continue his scientific career in the United States—Hudson Hoagland (born 1899), who had gone to Clark University in 1931 and was head of the small biology department there, and Nathaniel Rothschild, the third baron and a fellow investigator of the mechanisms of reproduction at Cambridge University's Strangeways Laboratory. Foundation officers were still willing to support Pincus' research, but his salary had to come from elsewhere and some institution had to provide laboratory space and administer his grants.[32] After the failure of Castle's efforts to gain asylum for Pincus at the University of California, Hoagland had him appointed visiting professor of zoology at Clark, a courtesty appointment without salary or faculty privileges. Lord Rothschild provided $2,500 in salary for two years. The Rothschild money, supplemented by another gift which Hoagland solicited from the New York businessman Henry Ittleson, enabled Pincus to move his family to Worcester, Massachusetts. Rockerfeller and Macy money provided a research budget, and Pincus had found a place to continue his research, even though permanent institutional arrangements remained to be worked out.[33]

In Worcester, Pincus continued to publish studies of ovum activation and growth, moving beyond his early emphasis on the mechanism of fertilization to the study of endocrine factors in embryonic maintenance. In 1939 he was back in the news with an announcement of the live birth of parthenogenetic rabbits.[34] In all, he reported fathering seven parthenogenones (one was born dead). Five of these he claimed to have obtained by treating eggs with hypotonic solutions, then transferring them to does. Two of these hypotonic specimens, however, have since been shown to have resulted from failure to properly vasectomize the buck rabbit used to sexually activate the host female.[35] Pincus also claimed to have fathered one rabbit by the cooling of one fallopian tube of a virgin doe and another one by culturing ova *in vitro*, followed by transfer to a host doe. Hundreds of ova were used in these delicate and expensive experiments, and only a small percentage began to develop when subjected to artificial stimuli, with the chances for further growth rapidly diminishing at every stage of embryonic development. In 1954 one experimental biologist estimated that the chances of an artifically stimulated ova developing into a viable organism were no better than 200 to 1.[36] Thus, confirmation or refutation of Pincus' experiments proved very difficult because of the large number of eggs that would have to be treated in order to obtain a statistically significant result. In 1957, R. A. Beatty, the authority on parthenogenesis, was willing to credit five of Pincus' seven parthenogenones, but in reviewing the claims in 1967, the year Pincus died, Beatty concluded that while it was well established that rabbit ova could be parthenogenetically developed into blastocysts, "Whether they can really survive to birth must now be regarded as open to question, since no confirmation has come during the quarter of a century that has elapsed since the first and only reports of such survival."[37]

The large publicity given to these claims was, perhaps, unfortunate, since the birth of a parthenogenone had more to do with technical virtuosity than with the advance of science. Pincus' work commanded the respect of his colleagues without the "virgin births" which aroused opposition among the pious and eventually became a source of embarrassment among Pincus' defenders. By 1939, however, Pincus had learned how to deal with the press, and a *New York Times* article on "the first fatherless rabbit" ended with a strong endorsement of Pincus' experiments, which were lauded because they would "provide much valuable knowledge that will eventually find clinical application for the birth of healthier human beings, the ultimate purpose of the experiments."[38]

Basic research in sexual physiology was making an impact on clinical treatment of reproductive disease through the growing use of hormone extracts from animal glands to treat spontaneous abortions, crippling pain during menstruation, and involuntary sterility. Some biologists even predicted control of uterine cancer through hormone therapy. The high cost of obtaining hormones from animal sources hampered, however, the clinical application of endocrine research. After 1944, when Russell Marker organized Syntex SA, a small wholesale drug firm, to exploit his discovery that hormones could be synthesized from the roots of the wild Mexican yam, a large barrier was removed to the medical use of hormones. Not only sex hormones, but the steroid secretions of the adrenal gland might also be synthesized, providing therapies for arthritis and the dozens of inflammatory conditions treated with cortisone today. American drug companies began a race to duplicate and to improve upon Marker's processes.[39] Their chemists created dozens of compounds from Marker's basic steroid molecule. Biologists with backgrounds in endocrinology were needed to test these experimental drugs on animals in order to determine their possible therapeutic usefulness. The value of Gregory Pincus' knowledge of the biosynthesis of hormones and of their effects on the mammalian reproductive system, long recognized by foundations supporting scientific research, became apparent to the pharmaceutical industry. Pincus did not want to go commercial, but his situation at Clark was not happy.

In 1931, Hudson Hoagland had taken over a three-man Clark biology department consisting of himself, a systematic botanist, and a zoologist. Both of Hoagland's colleagues were still pursuing Harvard Ph.D.'s. President Wallace Atwood, the author of a popular high school geography textbook, had hoped to strengthen the life sciences by acquiring Hoagland, but Hoagland's ambition quickly outran Atwood's plans. The days of the lone researcher were ending in science. Experimental biologists needed the help of other investigators in the form of junior faculty, graduate students, or visiting scholars in order to conduct experiments that called for a variety of skills from those of surgeon and electrician to chemist and endocrinologist. Hoagland was able to attract co-workers and support them on foundation and industrial research grants.[40] After Pincus arrived, their combined research projects, centering on the role of steroids in the body's neural and hormonal messenger systems, began to resemble a research institute attached to Clark University only by loyalty to a common bookkeeper. By 1943 there were fifteen members in their research group, with only Hoagland drawing a university salary. They had outgrown the basement of the Clark laboratories and had moved into the three-story barn that belonged to Hoagland's rented faculty house on the Clark campus.

Hoagland tried to avoid adding to the financial burdens of a small university struggling through the Great Depression. Wages for laboratory technicians came out of Works Progress Administration funds. A small group of Worcester philanthropists paid for the conversion of the barn into a laboratory. When his work involved human subjects, Hoagland arranged sponsorship by Worcester hospitals so that the university would not be liable to suit. Still, President Atwood insisted that Pincus and other members of the Physiology Laboratory were "not members of the University" and had no faculty privileges. Hoagland complained that these men were "notable scientists with national reputations. . . . At Harvard, Yale . . . the Visiting Professors are accorded the same courtesies as any other faculty members. . . ." Of course it was Hoagland and not Atwood who had invited these visitors to the University. If Atwood felt that a fifteen-man department of general physiology had no place in a university with a faculty of less than sixty members, there was nothing Hoagland could do about it. Despite the improvements, the barn still belonged to the university. Atwood could not fire Hoagland, but he made sure that the transients in the barn did not forget their place.[41]

Crozier had plans to bring Hoagland back to Harvard on a permanent basis before the department of general physiology was abolished. Later Hoagland lost an opportunity to go to Columbia's Neurological Institute because of the objections of physicians to the appointment of a nonclinician. In 1943, Hoagland suffered another disappointment. His studies of the role of adrenal hormones in stress resistance had led to tests for evaluating the suitability of candidates for pilot training, and he was asked to join the Operations Analysis Group of the Air Force. Having obtained a leave of absence from Clark and bade farewell to his friends, Hoagland arrived in Washington ready to go to Europe to study the 8th Air Force's pilot stress problems. He was informed, however, that his commission had been revoked because of a letter he had once written criticizing the Office of the Air Surgeon's failure to fund antifatigue studies. It seemed to Hoagland that administrators of Harvard, Columbia, Clark, and the Air Force were more interested in maintaining the status quo than in advancing knowledge. He accepted a Guggenheim fellowship for 1943 and brooded over the situation at Clark. Hoagland and Pincus joked about escaping from academia and setting up shop in the woods like Martin Arrowsmith.[42]

Pincus and I had both come through some traumatic experiences of rejection—he in being dropped from Harvard as an assistant professor and I in relation to not returning to Harvard and not going to the Columbia Neurological Institute, in both cases after negotiations were far along. In addition, the unkindest cut of all had been my rejection for wartime work as an operations analyst overseas. We were not happy with the "Establishment." It was at this time that we first seriously discussed a plan to set up a research institute completely divorced from control by any university or college. We welcomed the idea of freedom from bickering

329

faculty meetings, futile committees, jealous colleagues and teaching prescribed courses to often indifferent students.[43]

Taking potshots at academia is a favorite pastime of professors, who usually continue to cash their paychecks. Hoagland and Pincus were motivated more by faith in themselves as scientists than by jealousy of the claims of others on university resources. They passionately believed that their kind of research represented both the frontier of knowledge and the best hope for improving the human condition. They proved that their work had been undervalued by giving up affiliation with Clark and by surviving solely on research grants. In time grantsmanship would become a way of life for many scholars, but in 1944 it was an exciting and risky adventure.

Hoagland and Pincus founded the Worcester Foundation for Experimental Biology (WFEB), a nonprofit, tax-privileged Massachusetts corporation, in February 1944, with a distinguished board of directors recruited from among their friends, including local businessmen, a rabbi, and scientists of international reputation. The foundation was essentially a two-man enterprise, however, with Pincus and Hoagland sharing some projects and running others on their own. The institution survived and prospered because of the unique skills of the two partners. During his years as a Worcester resident, Hoagland had cultivated warm ties with the city's social elite. Local philanthropists, who saw the foundation as both a new business and a cultural asset, provided $25,000 to purchase an old mansion that served as a plant during the lean early years. Hoagland cut the grass; Pincus took care of the animals; and a steady stream of bright young investigators on the way up passed through Worcester, drawn by both the funds the directors raised and by the opportunity to devote full time to research in an informal atmosphere where achievement was the sole source of status.[44]

Hoagland had some family money, and at least once helped make the payroll out of his own pocket, but essentially the two partners had to live by their wits on a month-to-month basis. Their success depended on expertise in steroid research, which was booming both as a scientific specialty and as a commercial enterprise. Grants came from traditional sources such as the American Cancer Society, from the federal government, which was beginning to assume the major role as a subsidizer of scientific research, and from the drug industry.

Pincus became a scientific entrepreneur par excellence, serving as liaison between academic scientists and businessmen who needed independent evaluation of new drugs. The most important of his business connections was with G. D. Searle and Company. When he first came to Worcester in 1938, Hoagland was testing an anticonvulsant drug that Searle hoped would find a market in the treatment of epilepsy. Through Hoagland, Searle representatives were introduced to Pincus, whom they hired as a consultant in their effort to capture a part of the potential steroid market.[45] When the Worcester Foundation was founded in 1944, the Searle account provided salaries for five investigators of Ph.D. or M.D. status and for four technical assistants, in addition to Pincus' fee as a consultant. In 1946, Searle paid over $44,000 out of a research budget of less than $160,000.[46]

Of Pincus' early Searle projects, the most important was an attempt to develop a process for the commercial production of cortisone, a secretion of the adrenal cortex. Chemists at Merck and Company had first isolated cortisone from acid bile, and in 1948 physicians at the Mayo Clinic used this steroid to dramatically alleviate the symptoms of rheumatoid arthritis. Suddenly there was hope for thousands of sufferers from crippling disease, if only the pharmaceutical industry could find a cheap source of adrenal steroids. Three firms, Merck, Upjohn, and Searle, had technical staffs with a chance of solving the problem, and they began a race to reap the potential profits and prestige provided by human need.[47]

Researchers at the Worcester Foundation had been studying the biosynthesis of hormones by pumping serum through animal glands and then evaluating the changes produced by these natural hormone factories. Pincus believed that the beef adrenal gland could be used to synthesize cortisone by pumping a serum containing an inexpensive steroid through the organ, whose enzyme system would perform the thirty-two stage process used by the Merck chemists to synthesize cortisone. The experimental perfusion apparatus developed at the WFEB was copied on a massive scale and at great expense in Searle's

Skokie, Illinois, plant. Cortisone was produced in unprecedented amounts from thousands of perfused adrenal glands and distributed to clinicians, but the production costs remained prohibitive.[48]

Meanwhile, a biochemist working for Upjohn hit upon the idea of using microbes to do the work of the adrenal enzymes, in imitation of the fermentation processes used to manufacture penicillin and streptomycin. The plan worked, and Upjohn relieved the world cortisone famine, leaving Searle with a huge tax write-off and some doubts about their investment in Gregory Pincus.

A by-product of Searle's participation in the cortisone race was a strong team of steroid chemists. In October 1951, Pincus asked Albert L. Raymond, Searle's director of research, to consider another program of directed research, this time aimed at developing a contraceptive injection or pill. Earlier that year he had begun testing the contraceptive value of steroids under a small grant from the Planned Parenthood Federation of America ($3,100).[49] The most promising of these hormones was progesterone, which causes the lining of the uterus to thicken, providing a hospitable surface for the implantation of the fertilized ovum. After implantation, the placenta takes over from the ovary the secretion of progesterone, flooding the bloodstream with large amounts of the hormone, thereby signaling other organs that a state of pregnancy exists. In 1937, researchers at the University of Pennsylvania had shown that large injections of progesterone inhibited ovulation in rats, apparently by inducing a state of pseudopregnancy. Pincus first duplicated the experiment of the Pennsylvania researchers in rats, and he had also been able to suppress ovulation in rabbits. He naturally turned to Searle, his principal sponsor, when the research began to yield convincing results.

Albert Raymond was skeptical of Pincus' plan to use the perfusion process to obtain large quantities of progesterone for contraceptive purposes. According to Pincus, Raymond complained:

> You haven't given us a thing to justify the half-million that we invested in you. . . . There is, to be fair, still some chance that . . . the perfusion process will prove useful. But to date your record as a contributor to the commerce of the Searle Company is a lamenta-

ble failure, replete with false leads, poor judgment, and assurances from you that were false. Yet you have the nerve to ask for more for research. You will get more only if a lucky chance gives us something originating from your group which will make us a profit. If I had unlimited funds I would undertake a large program in the steroid field, but I do not have such funds and the record to date does not justify a large program.[50]

Pincus still believed in himself, and he continued the progesterone experiment. By the time that the advance of steroid technology had provided Raymond with synthetic hormones with much greater contraceptive potential than progesterone, Pincus was ready to seize the opportunity. This time he would not fail. And he had a woman to thank for the funds that allowed him to take advantage of the biggest opportunity of his life.

CHAPTER 26   **The Lady Bountiful**

A FEW key individuals played crucial roles in the progress of the American birth control movement. Margaret Sanger, Robert Dickinson, and Clarence Gamble irritated professional administrators by their numerous personal initiatives, but they forced innovations that advanced the cause. In Gamble's case the need for acceptance as an expert on contraception rather than as a source of funds became a major point of contention in the movement, just as Sanger's drive for personal dominance had divided birth controllers in the late 1920s.

Katharine Dexter McCormick (1875–1967) gave "tenacious and conscientious attention" to every detail of the philanthropic projects that she chose to support. Like Clarence Gamble, she found herself at odds with the administrators of the Planned Parenthood Federation. She was fortunate, however, because she discovered in Gregory Pincus an expert in whom she had absolute confidence. Unlike Gamble, she was able to participate vicariously in a great scientific enterprise. Although she had taken an undergraduate degree in biology, McCormick's problem had not been to justify her training in original discovery, but simply to gain the right to a scientific education. Gamble, Harvard M.D. and coauthor of papers on heart physiology, bore the stigmata of failure because he could not be happy as just another M.D. McCormick, whose goal was autonomy for women, had expanded the bounds of

334

woman's social role simply by graduating from the Massachusetts Institute of Technology. Self-respect did not require personal distinction as an expert. McCormick, however, did have a need to do something of great importance for the cause of birth control and the autonomy of women. That need to act grew out of her experience as a wife, heiress, and campaigner for women's rights.

Katharine Dexter was born in 1875, the second and last child of one of Chicago's most successful attorneys.[1] Her great-grandfather had been a leader of Massachusetts Federalists, a United States senator, and secretary of war and of the treasury during the administration of John Adams. Her grandfather moved to Michigan after he graduated from Harvard in 1812, established the town of Dexter, served as chief justice of the county court, published a newspaper, and helped found the University of Michigan. Her father had maintained the family legal tradition and the tie with New England when he took a schoolteacher from Springfield, Massachusetts, as his bride. He led the rebuilding of Chicago after the great fire as a pillar of the Committee to Restore Law and Order and of the Committee to Rebuild Chicago.

After her husband's premature death from a heart attack, Josephine Moore Dexter returned to Massachusetts with her daughter, establishing a proper Brahmin home on Commonwealth Avenue, close to the Massachusetts Institute of Technology, where Katharine studied for three years as a special student in preparation for the entrance examinations. Having remedied the deficiencies left by a lady's education in the fine arts, Katharine entered MIT in 1900 and finished in 1904 with a senior thesis entitled "Fatigue of the Cardiac Muscles in Reptilia."

While attending MIT, Katharine was courted by Stanley McCormick, the son of Cyrus, the founder of the International Harvester Company. An heir to the fabulous new wealth of the Midwest, young McCormick was a varsity tennis player at Princeton and a gifted amateur painter, and he had shown considerable executive ability as comptroller of his father's company. In 1904 the two beautiful people were married in the château at Prangrins on Lake Geneva, Switzerland, a former home of Joseph Bonaparte which Josephine Dexter had bought after her husband's death.

The future looked bright for the McCormick-Dexter line. The newlyweds, both enthusiastic outdoor athletes and admirers of the French Impressionist painters, had the rich promise that life seemed to offer tragically snatched from them. Stanley became mentally ill two years after their marriage, and he remained a schizophrenic until his death in 1947 at the age of 73.

Alone but not free for forty years, Katharine McCormick fought and won a legal battle with Cyrus McCormick for control of her husband's estate. After Stanley McCormick was declared legally incompetent in 1909, Katharine found a new focus for her life in the woman's suffrage movement. When the College Equal Suffrage League of Massachusetts was formed (1909), notices put up by suffragists at MIT were immediately torn down by male students. McCormick showed that MIT women were behind their sisters by speaking at the state's first open-air suffrage demonstration on the Bedford Common. Mary Ware Dennett, Margaret Sanger's rival for leadership of the birth control movement after World War I, joined McCormick on the platform that day. In all, ninety-seven rallies were conducted by a small group of about fifteen women. "The campaigners were resourceful. At Nantasket, when forbidden to speak on the beach, they went into the water with their Votes for Women banner and spoke from the sea to the women on the shore."[2]

McCormick testified for a suffrage bill before a Massachusetts legislative committee in 1911 and began her long service as one of Carrie Chapman Catt's lieutenants in the National American Woman Suffrage Association, providing $6,000 to make up the deficit of the *Woman's Journal,* and serving as treasurer and as vice-president of the association. During World War I she worked as chairman of the association's War Service Department and as a member of the Women's Committee of the Council of National Defense. She opposed cooperation with the militant Congressional Union (later National Woman's Party) which insisted on opposing all Democratic candidates for office because their party had not adopted a prosuffrage plank in its platform, and she introduced a resolution at the Suffrage Association's 1919 convention thanking President Wilson for his cooperation and help. Since McCormick later gave the same allegiance to Margaret Sanger that she gave to Carrie Catt, she and Mary Ware Dennett provide an example of continuity between the suffrage and birth control movements, a continuity that is somewhat obscured by Catt's indifference to Sanger's cause and by Sanger's frequently voiced contempt for suffrage, which she considered a superficial reform.[3]

While battling for ratification of the Nineteenth Amendment, McCormick worked for the International Suffrage Alliance, along with Catt and the Dutch birth control pioneer, Dr. Aletta Jacobs. Many suffrage meetings were held in the château at Prangrins. This mansion also provided the setting for a lavish reception for the 300 delegates to the 1927 World Population Conference called by Sanger in an effort to attract the attention of the League of Nations. The meeting did not win the League of Nations for birth control. Indeed, Sanger's name had to be removed from the conference program in order to avoid a walkout of Catholic delegates, but formation of the International Union for the Scientific Investigation of Population, the first international association of demographers, resulted from Sanger's Geneva conference.[4]

It is unclear exactly when McCormick's financial support of Sanger began, although she was probably contributing before placing her château at Sanger's disposal in 1927. McCormick first met Sanger in 1917. During the 1920s, McCormick was one of the European travelers who helped keep Sanger's Clinical Research Bureau in operation by smuggling diaphragms into the United States.[5]

Although McCormick was often generous in her gifts, several factors limited her aid to Sanger. Expenditures from her husband's estate had to be approved by the probate court in Chicago. Perhaps because of her struggle to maintain control of this money, McCormick had an intense sense of stewardship and limited her contributions to projects of which she had firsthand knowledge. Her lawyer remembered her insistence that,

> . . . she must understand each problem and all of its details. Details were an all-important thing to Katharine. She welcomed ad-

337

vice, listened to the opinions of others, spent endless hours going over every aspect of each problem to make sure that the ultimate result, regardless of time and expense, would measure up to her conception of what should be a fitting memorial to Stanley. I am sure that no professional trustee ever gave the tenacious and conscientious attention to his duties that Katharine gave to her own self-imposed rules.[6]

McCormick generally limited her birth control gifts to contraceptive research and to Sanger's international work, the two areas in which she felt that she had some expertise. Sanger understood her patron's interests, and she kept McCormick informed of research projects. McCormick, in turn, wrote of her concern over the low priority given to contraceptive research and wished "very much that I could enter that field in a definitely constructive way," but the major part of her fortune was still under the control of the courts, and perhaps she felt that Sanger had not yet turned up the right project. Nevertheless, they intermittently corresponded over the prospects for a major scientific breakthrough for twenty years.[7]

Until her husband's death, McCormick spent a great deal of money in a vain search for a cure to his illness. After psychoanalysts failed to help him, she turned to Roy G. Hoskins, a Harvard endocrinologist, who had been investigating the role of adrenal cortex malfunction in schizophrenia. Perhaps schizophrenia was a matter of biochemistry, a result of adrenal hormone deficiency that undermined the individual's ability to deal with stress, forcing a retreat into an unreal but more secure world.

In 1927, McCormick established the Neuroendocrine Research Foundation to support Hoskins' research. The foundation's office and animal research program were in the department of physiology at the Harvard Medical School, but its main activity centered on clinical research at the Worcester State Hospital. Beginning in the 1930s, Hudson Hoagland collaborated with Hoskins in a number of attempts to treat schizophrenics with adrenal steroids, but they were never able to develop an effective therapy.[8]

In 1947, the year Stanley McCormick died, the Neuroendocrine Research Foundation closed, after Mrs. McCormick withdrew her support. Nevertheless, she had a high opinion of Hudson Hoagland and of the Worcester Foundation because of the cooperation with the Hoskins project. One day in the early 1950s, she burst into Hoagland's office demanding to know, "What are we going to do about it?" Hoagland, eager to encourage a potential donor, assumed she wanted to know about the progress of his schizophrenia work and began to outline a plan of research in the biology of madness, only to be informed that McCormick did not mean *that* problem, but the impending world population crisis! Happily he could call in another expert, Gregory Pincus, to explain what the foundation needed in order to push forward on population control.[9] McCormick already knew about Pincus' work, however, and apparently her stop at Hoagland's office was just a courtesy call.

More than half of Stanley McCormick's estate had to be liquidated to pay federal inheritance taxes. This required the selling of five residences, including the baronial mansion at Santa Barbara, California, where Stanley had been attended by a staff of forty gardeners and by six musicians who played for him at dinner.[10] Having paid her taxes and reduced her fixed expenses, McCormick wrote Sanger in October 1950, asking about the prospects in contraceptive research. Sanger recommended a crash program of $100,000 a year to be distributed through the National Research Council's new Committee on Human Reproduction to several university laboratories. Financial reverses prevented McCormick from making this commitment in 1951, and the Committee on Human Reproduction died for lack of support.[11] By January 1952, however, she was finally able to concentrate her considerable intellectual and financial power on the problem, and Sanger journeyed to Santa Barbara to confer with her. On the verge of action after years of enforced equivocation, McCormick could hardly control her excitement over the prospect of having Sanger with her, explaining that she was "feeling pretty desperate over the research end of our work." She had been sending all she could to the Planned Parenthood Federation's small research fund [Robert Dickinson Memorial], "but it does not make me feel any better about the vitally constructive effort necessary to achieve a fool-proof contraceptive, which is the main end I hold in view at present, and over which I chafe constantly."[12]

While Sanger had done everything within her power throughout her career to promote contraceptive research, her plans for use of McCormick's money now had a concreteness that they had formerly lacked. Through Abraham Stone, who had taken over his wife's work as director of the Margaret Sanger Research Bureau after her death, Sanger had been introduced to Gregory Pincus, and in 1951 she had conferred with Pincus about the possibility of using steroids as contraceptives.[13] Pincus had received a total of $14,500 in 1948 and 1949 from the Planned Parenthood Federation of America for study of the early development of mammalian eggs, but this research had not led to any concrete plans for a new contraceptive, and the grant expired in 1949. Following his conference with Sanger, Pincus reapplied to the PPFA for support of "Studies in Hormonal Contraception," and he received $3,100 in 1951 and $3,400 in 1952.[14] These funds, however, were only a fraction of what he would need if he was to make the concerted effort necessary to develop a hormonal contraceptive.

Sanger knew where to find the money to pay Pincus. In March 1952 she wrote McCormick asking if she had heard about Pincus' research from the federation. McCormick had not and Sanger remedied that oversight.[15] By May, McCormick had moved from Santa Barbara into her house in Boston, closer to the Worcester Foundation, the new focus for her energies during the next five years. Through Roy Hoskins, the former director of the Neuroendocrine Research Institute and a trustee of the WFEB, McCormick arranged for a meeting with Pincus.[16] On June 8, 1953, McCormick, Sanger, and Mrs. Hoskins visited the Worcester Foundation, and McCormick promised $10,000 a year on the spot, a commitment that grew as fast as Pincus could rewrite his budget.[17] McCormick gave from $150,000 to $180,000 a year to the foundation for the rest of her life, and left the foundation $1 million in her will.[18] The only remaining question in regard to money was whether the Planned Parenthood Federation would continue to administer Pincus' grants for contraceptive research.

While the federation had supported Pincus' research, his work had not been singled out for special consideration. In his January 1952 progress report to the PPFA, Pincus had explained that after injections of progesterone had suppressed

340

ovulation in rabbits, he had tested the hormone's oral effectiveness and had found that a single dose of 10 milligrams was effective in 90 percent of the rabbits tested. He concluded, "These data demonstrate definitely the contraceptive ovulation-inhibiting activity of an oral progestin, and suggest that with proper dosage and regimen of administration control of ovulation may be effective." Pincus immediately began seeking a clinician to extend his investigation to humans. His modest PPFA grant was renewed for 1952, but the project did not arouse much excitement in PPFA's New York office. In September, Sanger conferred with William Vogt, the federation's director, but she found that "they have evidently not been sold on the Pincus research." McCormick was "rather surprised that the Pincus plan does not receive more attention." [19]

Relations between the two indomitable old feminists and the Planned Parenthood Federation quickly deteriorated. Sanger's quarrel with the New York office dated from the late 1920s, but she was especially irritated by the federation's insistence on taking a 15 percent cut out of all donations for international work, a practice that Lady Rama Rau also found galling.[20] Sanger's first letter renewing ties with McCormick in 1950 had included a warning that the federation had to be prodded to get results.

> They have done an excellent job in holding groups together but they have rather abandoned the project of getting our Public Health units interested and insisting contraceptive supplies and advice be given to the element of the population over which they, the Public Health officials, preside. As I see the PPF they are rather marking time and just holding their own.[21]

Sanger helped create a critical attitude toward the federation on McCormick's part, but McCormick did not need much help in finding fault. A woman who "chafed constantly" over the lack of a foolproof contraceptive was sure to have problems with the house that Kenneth Rose had built. Director William Vogt was a conservationist who was hired on the strength of his best seller, *The Road to Survival*, one of the first textbooks of the ecology consciousness movement. Crippled by polio in adolescence, Vogt was more of an artist than a dynamic leader.

His original interest in conservation had grown out of bird watching. Vogt had argued in his book,

> If the United States had spent two billion dollars developing . . . a contraceptive, instead of the atom bomb, it would have contributed far more to our national security while, at the same time, it promoted a rising living standard for the entire world. If such an amount is required to develop a satisfactory contraceptive, it will be a sound investment.[22]

But Vogt infuriated McCormick with his apparent indifference to Pincus' work. One of McCormick's first gifts to the Worcester Foundation had been $50,000 for a new animal house, a necessity if Pincus was to expand the animal testing of steroids. Vogt told McCormick that he did not think it was a necessary expenditure. He had never been to Worcester. He submitted no concrete plans to her for promoting research, and when she called at the New York office she got only "desultory conversation" rather than the hard facts and large plans that she craved. McCormick, who was fast becoming an expert on endocrinology, was offended both as a feminist and as a careful spender when Paul Henshaw, the federation's part-time director of research, "offered to show me the office layout which Mr. Vogt said they were rapidly outgrowing, so I looked into two or three smaller rooms, was introduced to two office women and then took my leave."[23]

The confusion at headquarters partly resulted from indecision as to whether the federation should continue supporting research. The Population Council was beginning to spend half a million dollars a year, and it seemed to Vogt that the federation's role should be in education and clinic organization.[24] When McCormick walked into the federation office, Henshaw's resignation had already been accepted as part of the reorganization. A blunt explanation of the situation might have won her respect. Vague appeals for continued support seemed like the gold digging of incompetent bureaucrats. McCormick wrote Sanger,

> It appears to me that no one there . . . is really concerned over achieving an oral contraceptive and that I was mistaken originally in thinking they were. If I assume that they are entirely satisfied with the present contraceptives then everything they do appears

logical and clear—otherwise it is to me vague and puzzling,— really mystifying. [25]

McCormick wanted to channel all of her money directly to the Worcester Foundation, but Hoagland and Pincus convinced her that "it would probably be wiser for you to continue to pay the Planned Parenthood organization the funds which have been earmarked for us, as in the past. To cut them out of the picture would perhaps cause a loss of prestige and we would not like to weaken them in any way." [26] Some McCormick money continued to come to the foundation through the PPFA, but increasingly McCormick dealt directly with her experts. After synthetic steroids supplied by G. D. Searle were adopted as the contraceptive in the pill, Pincus agreed with McCormick that all of her contributions should be made directly to the foundation, and the federation's role was reduced to a token contribution. [27] It was a simpler arrangement, and the federation would usually be given ample credit in future accounts of the pill's development, but the direct connection with McCormick also avoided any legal embarrassment that might have resulted from a clause in the federation's grants-in-aid application which gave the federation control over all patents resulting from research it sponsored.

> Unless otherwise arranged at the time the grant is made, the investigator shall execute absolute and unconditional assignments of all such patents, copyrights, trademarks and documents of title to the Federation. The Federation, unless otherwise arranged, shall have exclusive right to determine the exploitation and use of all investigations, and of the products and results of investigations and to keep all of the proceeds thereof. . . . [28]

G. D. Searle and Company was only able to patent the specific steroids developed in its laboratories, not the term "The Pill" or the concept of using steroids as contraceptives. And Searle never would have supplied Pincus with the experimental drugs he needed if in doing so they had risked their right to exclusive control over compounds they developed. Nevertheless, Pincus only encouraged McCormick to make all of her contributions directly to the foundation after G. D. Searle had begun supporting the pill project with both experimental drugs and specific research grants.

343

McCormick apparently never understood that Searle had paid a large portion of Pincus' salary for years. Rather, as McCormick explained to Abraham Stone, Pincus was "acquainted with some one [sic] in the Searl [sic] Company."[29] Exactly how he was able to convince them to provide free experimental drugs for the project on a large scale was never explained.

In fact, Searle's steroid chemists played an important role in the pill's development. Although similar feats were being duplicated in a number of competing industrial laboratories, the large number of synthetic hormones that they were producing gave Pincus an essential variety of compounds with a wide range of effects that he could try on animals, selecting for clinical trial only a few of the most promising out of the dozens that had some contraceptive effect.[30] But McCormick was shielded from the commercial aspects of the project she was subsidizing.

Nevertheless, her contribution was vital. She provided the funds that turned a desultory PPFA project into a crash program to develop an oral contraceptive. Pincus asked Searle for substantial help on the project only after he had suppressed ovulation in women with a progesterone regimen. By then he knew that he could develop an oral contraceptive. Searle's cooperation simply hastened the process.

When the first successful use of synthetic steroids as an oral contraceptive in women was announced in *Science* in 1956, Sanger wrote McCormick:

> You must, indeed, feel a certain pride in your judgment. Gregory Pincus had been working for at least ten years on the progesterone of reproductive process in animals. He had practically no money for this work and Dr. Stone and I did our best to get a few dollars for him and I think that that amount we collected went to pay the expenses of Chang [senior scientist, WFEB]. Then you came along with your fine interest and enthusiasm and with your faith and . . . things began to happen and at last the reports . . . are now out in the outstanding scientific magazine and the conspiracy of silence has been broken.[31]

Although "conspiracy of silence" may have been an exaggeration, throughout the late 1950s few scientists believed an oral contraceptive was at hand.[32] Sanger and McCormick iden-

The Lady Bountiful

tified and supported a project that led to a major breakthrough because they had an intense personal interest in relieving other women of unwanted pregnancies. They were able to communicate their vision to Gregory Pincus, who translated it into the rationality of commercial technology. A later generation of feminists would point out that the pill placed all of the responsibility for contraception on women. That, however, is where Sanger and McCormick wanted it. For them absolute security in contraceptive practice seemed a fabulous achievement.

CHAPTER 27 **The Product Champion**

IN 1967 the National Science Foun-
dation commissioned a study of the relationship between
basic research and technological innovation. What role did
"nonmission" research, research motivated solely by a desire
for knowledge, play in the development of new products of
great economic and social significance, such as the electron mi-
croscope, the videotape recorder, and the oral contraceptive
pill? Since the National Science Foundation existed to promote
research, it was not surprising when the study revealed that 70
percent of the key events leading to technological innovation
resulted from so-called nonmission research. Seventy-six percent of this basic work was done in university laboratories; 14
percent in research institutes and government laboratories. Industrial laboratories made only 10 percent of the original discoveries that advanced knowledge.[1]

Large diagrams were provided on which the red dots representing basic research stretched far into the past, while the
blue symbols for "mission-oriented research" and the green
symbols for "development and application" were clustered
near the present. In the diagram explaining the origins of the
pill, Arnold Berthold's 1849 demonstration that castrated
roosters do not behave like roosters was given equal billing
with key events in the development of twentieth century endocrinology. The overall impression was one of a long chain of
basic researches leading inevitably to an oral contraceptive.[2]

346

The National Science Foundation continued its research into "The Interactions of Science and Technology in the Innovative Process," and, as knowledge accumulated, the foundation's interpretation of events became increasingly sophisticated. Further study revealed that scientific discoveries were not inevitably, quickly, or easily translated into technology. Rather, in nine out of the ten cases studied, one person, a "technical entrepreneur," had been responsible for innovation, sometimes in the face of the indifference of scientists or predictions by businessmen that his product would be a commercial failure. Indeed, the importance of the scientific entrepreneur or "product champion" was the "strongest conclusion" that emerged from the NSF study. Massive investment in basic research did not necessarily translate into useful products because "the actions of the technical entrepreneur, or the role of such motivational forces as recognition of need and recognition of technical opportunity, involve inventive or creative activities that do not lend themselves to detailed planning."[3]

The role played by Gregory Pincus in the development of the pill fits perfectly the model outlined in the later NSF studies. He drew G. D. Searle and Company into the project while other drug houses were refusing to consider marketing a contraceptive or assumed that an ovulation-suppressing drug would not be an acceptable contraceptive. Pincus also selected and supervised the key personnel for clinical trials of the product. His choices were crucial in gaining acceptance of oral contraception by the Food and Drug Administration and by the general public. Finally, he traveled all over the world spreading the good news of his invention while many scientists and physicians were still skeptical.

Contraceptive research, despite recognized social need and large subsidies from foundations and from government, has not produced a new contraceptive for general use since the Pincus pill and the plastic intrauterine devices, and the best informed guesses are that there will not be a comparable breakthrough in the near future.[4] It may be that Pincus seized a unique opportunity and exploited it just in time. Both the ethics of the marketplace and scientific experimentation with humans came under increasing critical scrutiny in the early 1970s in response to appalling abuses of power and of privilege. Horror stories of mentally retarded children being deliberately exposed to hepatitis or of Alabama Negroes being allowed to die of syphilis as part of a United States Public Health Service experiment[5] found a counterpart in the drug industry when Richardson-Merrell, Inc., the Cincinnati-based maker of Vicks VapoRub, marketed a steroid to suppress cholesterol biosynthesis and in the process caused 500 Americans to develop cataracts. Having concealed their own laboratory data on animals that should have prevented the cholesterol suppressant from being marketed, Richardson-Merrell then tried to strong-arm the Food and Drug Administration into releasing Thalidomide, the fetus-deforming tranquilizer. They remained in business despite these actions.[6]

While scientists and businessmen need one another, and society needs the products resulting from their ethical collaboration, in the 1970s the development of new physiological contraceptives was made increasingly difficult by governmental regulation, reflecting a growing public distrust of big business. Gregory Pincus had to overcome many obstacles in his role as product champion. The question remains whether another scientific entrepreneur will be able to repeat his performance in the future. The problems of a product champion in the 1950s and early 1960s were in some respects analogous to those of the scientific entrepreneur of today, but it was also a simpler world in which both the scientist and the businessman had the benefit of the doubt.

The spare prose of scientific papers often obscures the difficulties overcome by researchers in gathering and analyzing their data. Gregory Pincus was a master of the approved style in which results are concisely presented and concepts advanced, while the personality of the researcher, his uncertainties, wrong turns, and failures are excluded, thereby giving a logic and elegance to the presentation that transcends reality. As another scientist has noted, "our papers rarely recount the truth of what actually transpired . . . a logical answer is provided to a logical question, often composed retrospectively."[7] The development of the pill was described in a series of model publications that not only established the effectiveness of oral contraception but also did much to mitigate criticism of the possible side effects of the method. As Dwight Ingle has pointed out,

> At least twice in his life he [Pincus] had authored research reports in which the conclusions were not documented by well-controlled experiments. He knew that he had been criticized and was now determined that each step forward should be supported by unassailable evidence. The long-term effects of anti-fertility agents are not yet known with certainty and now and then there are sobering claims for pathogenesis in a small number of patients, but in general the laboratory and clinical testing of these agents was done in the best possible way.[8]

In order to ensure the success of the pill project, Pincus had to orchestrate the efforts of a number of specialists, including biologists at the Worcester Foundation, Searle's steroid chemists, university professors of medicine, and the clinicians and social workers who carried out the large-scale field trials of the product. The success story told in scientific monographs revealed little of the human drama involved, but the lack of disruptive conflict and the unity of purpose among the variety of personalities essential to the project's completion testify to Pincus' ability as a scientific executive. In the end there was credit for everyone, and the needs of sponsors, laboratory workers, and doctors were satisfied. Perhaps success bred loyalty. The key to success, however, was the high competence of the team Pincus recruited.

Min-Chueh Chang (born 1908) was the first key personality drawn into the project by Pincus. Today recognized as one of the world's outstanding investigators of mammalian reproduction, Chang had worked at the Worcester Foundation for six years when Pincus asked him to begin testing the contraceptive effects of progesterone on animals in April 1951.[9] A lean Chinese intellectual whose keen, and occasionally sardonic, wit finds expression in English that remains a very second language, Chang's relationship with Pincus was warm but not without conflict. Chang once joked that in his first years at the Worcester Foundation his contributions were so poorly understood by outsiders that a rumor circulated about a Chinaman who was being kept chained up in a cellar for experimental purposes.[10] His first difference of opinion with Pincus arose not because Pincus wanted to chain him in the cellar, but because Pincus wanted him to work for Tom Slick, a Texas cattleman. As a new Cambridge University Ph.D., whose work had centered on mammalian spermatozoa, Chang came to Worcester to learn more about mammalian eggs and expected to stay only a year when he arrived in 1945. Cattle are large and expensive animals, inappropriate for basic research, and Chang was "quite startled" when, on his first morning at the foundation, Pincus asked him to begin working on artificial insemination of cattle. Goaded by one of his British professors, Chang asked for other work related to his primary interests. Pincus looked over Chang's plan of research and promised to find him some rabbits, but insisted, "You can carry on your study according to your plan in your spare time."[11]

Pincus found the rabbits. Chang divided his time between rabbits and cows, and he stayed on. The foundation was an exciting place to work, and Pincus proved an efficient raiser of funds for Chang's research. In 1950, Warren Weaver of the Rockefeller Foundation took exception to Chang's divided attention. Weaver did not want to pay $5,500 a year toward Chang's keep if he was going to be in Texas for six months, since the Rockefeller Foundation had "a clean-cut policy . . . of supporting laboratory research and of not investing funds in programs seeking to apply existing knowledge to commercially attractive problems." Pincus agreed over protest to have the Rockefeller grant postponed until Chang could return to Worcester.[12]

Chang seems to have been less affected than his bosses by the tensions resulting from the need to find funds from diverse sources. When a project to breed minks collapsed because a key lab technician became pregnant and quit, Chang wrote Pincus that Hoagland seemed to be suffering from excessive adrenal output. Chang thought that they should not become so involved with businessmen since real science rarely yielded quick cash return.[13] But commerce and science proved compatible. Chang regularly published original contributions to knowledge, and in 1950 he received an award for distinguished achievement from the American Society for the Study of Sterility. By the early 1950s his work commanded generous support from both the Rockefeller Foundation and the Population Council.[14] The Worcester Foundation's lean years were over, and Hoagland, Pincus, and Chang were able to turn away from ordinary commercial work.

After Pincus' interest in contraceptive research was renewed in 1951, Chang quickly provided impeccable data on the contraceptive properties of progesterone.[15] Pincus' attention then shifted to clinical trials of progesterone, but when he began looking for more effective ovulation suppressants among the synthetic steroids, Chang again played a key role as the head of the laboratory team that did the animal testing of several hundred compounds.[16]

According to Chang, his contribution was not understood by the project's sponsors. When Pincus brought Sanger and McCormick to inspect Chang's laboratory, one of the women remarked, "I do envy you working in the laboratory; you must have lots of fun." Chang, apparently unaware of McCormick's genuine interest, resented what he interpreted as condescension and replied, "Sure enough, but I hope it can be useful!" Officials at Searle also seemed to equate Pincus with the Worcester Foundation, overlooking the fact that Pincus' efficiency depended on the exceptional skills of other scientists. Chang notes that in the autumn of 1967 the people at Searle still did not know of his contribution to the pill's development. "Confucius said, 'Do not get upset when people do not recognize you.' I hope Chairman Mao will say the same."[17] Pincus, however, often mentioned Chang's contribution. Chang's salary was among the highest paid by the foundation.[18] It came out of money raised by Pincus. Chang's difficulty with English limited his prospects for an academic teaching career, but at the foundation he was better paid than academicians, and he was able to spend his time in the laboratory pursuing his interests, while Pincus took the responsibility for satisfying donors and finding supplies, as well as overall direction of the foundation's programs.

The second key expert Pincus recruited for the project was John Rock (born 1890), a Roman Catholic gynecologist. Pincus had considered both Abraham Stone and Alan Guttmacher for the job of working out a contraceptive regimen in women, but Rock proved an ingenious choice. While Stone and Guttmacher were Jews, leaders of the birth control movement, and overburdened with their own work, Rock bore none of the anti-Semitic or antinatalist stigmata, and he was about to retire from his professorship at Harvard (1956), so he was able to give adequate time to a demanding new investigation.

Margaret Sanger originally opposed bringing Rock into the project, arguing that "he would not dare advance the cause of contraceptive research and remain a Catholic."[19] Pincus insisted that Rock was the right man. Rock, McCormick explained to Sanger, was a "reformed Catholic" whose "position is that religion has nothing to do with medicine or the practice of it and that if the Church does not interfere with him he will not interfere with it—whatever that may mean!"[20] Sanger eventually changed her mind about Rock and marveled at his ability to win support for the cause. "Being a good R.C. and as handsome as a god, he can just get away with anything."[21]

Some Catholic officials were outraged by Rock's habit of proclaiming his faith while he was violating Catholic dogma in his medical practice. In telling the world that the pope would surely accept a "natural" contraceptive of synthetic hormones as soon as he was able to review the facts, Rock provided a rationale for Catholic contraceptors.[22] By the time Catholic spokesmen decided that the pill was no more natural than other contraceptives, many Catholic laymen had found the pill acceptable to them, regardless of the hierarchy's attitude. Rock sincerely believed himself a good Catholic, however, and his changing attitudes toward contraception were those of a conservative seeking to preserve stable family life.

Rock first spoke out on the issue of contraception in a 1931 article criticizing the poor obstetrical training of Massachusetts physicians. The Harvard associate professor of obstetrics listed laws prohibiting contraceptive advice as a minor factor in the state's high maternal mortality rate, but he was quick to distinguish "medical contraception," prescribed only when a woman's life would be endangered by pregnancy, from "birth control." Indeed, all efforts to separate sex from procreation were fraught with social risk, since only child rearing provided the discipline and purpose essential to happy marriage. As late as 1943, in an article advocating repeal of legal restrictions on "medical birth control advice," Rock noted:

I hold no brief for those young or even older husbands and wives who for no good reason refuse to bear as many children as they can properly rear and as society can properly engross. Ignorant of the fact that sustained happiness comes only from dutiful sacrifice, such deluded mates are perhaps doing society a backhanded favor. Whatever genetic trait may contribute to the intellectual deficiency which permits them selfishly to seek more immediate comfort, is at least kept from the inheritable common pool, and in time their kind is thus bred out.[23]

Thirty years later Rock told a reporter, "I think it's shocking to see the big family glorified."[24] Despite the apparent contradiction in his views over time, Rock's attitudes toward the family and its place in society were consistent. Rock considered himself a humanist, in contrast to the contemplative "egoist" who saw man as part of a transcendental unit or the hedonist-naturalist who believed life had no spiritual purpose. In Rock's view life's meaning derived from social interaction, and especially from service to others.[25] Man was an animal, evolved from lower life forms. Cultural values, derived from centuries of trial and error, made man human.[26]

Sexuality was an immutable part of man's biological heritage. "Unprejudiced observation of so-called civilized man discloses that his fundamental coital pattern . . . is that of other primates, however his coital behavior may appear to be modified by social and spiritual factors." The family provided an essential social focus for sexual expression. For centuries society had needed all of the young that women could bear. Thus, the immutable coital urge, when expressed in marriage, was compatible with, if not essential to, social well-being.[27]

Rock, the father of five, shared the dominant pronatal values of American culture during the first half of the twentieth century. Experience as a gynecologist made it clear, however, that human fertility would have to be controlled if the family were to remain a strong institution. Rock did not believe that most men and women could live together happily without frequent coitus.

Suppression of the coital urge directed towards his wife is possible for the intelligent considerate husband aware of a good reason why she should not become pregnant. But the urge is still there, and unless, by appropriate and effective taboos, it can be sublimated into a sexual martyrdom of which few Americans, including all colors and creeds, are capable, it will express itself in any of the innumerable aberrancies of the primate sex function; for those too are "natural."[28]

Social order depended on sexual expression within marriage, yet frequent coitus without contraception led to more children than most American breadwinners could support. Too often, Rock believed, physicians failed to provide the contraceptive advice necessary to protect the family from excessive fertility.[29]

Rock associated his respect for the family with a Catholic heritage, but his views were widely shared by Protestants and Jews. He originally accepted contraception as an aid to marital sexual adjustment, while disapproving of those who were able to raise large families but refused to do so. When it became clear to him after World War II that rapid population growth was a threat to a well-ordered society, then he became an advocate of population control and of the small family. Changes in Rock's views mirrored the redefinition of "the population problem" that was taking place among social scientists. Rock was an invaluable ally for family planners because his background and competence gave him an aura of objectivity that they lacked. But his presence in their ranks was symbolic of a broad change in educated opinion, the decline of pronatalism as birth rates ceased to fall and a more critical attitude toward population growth developed. Rock was no less of a humanist in 1973 than he had been in the 1930s. His view of what mankind needed had simply changed.

Gregory Pincus and John Rock had known one another since the 1930s. Pincus had followed Rock's efforts to develop better methods for detection of ovulation, and he had placed several of Searle's experimental compounds with Rock for clinical testing.[30] When Rock decided to attempt *in vitro* fertilization of human ova in the early 1940s, he sent his research assistant, Miriam Menkin, to Pincus for instruction in how to retrieve and preserve mammalian eggs.[31] Rock, a leader in the application of discoveries by endocrinologists to clinical gynecology, was using large injections of progesterone in the early 1950s to strengthen the reproductive organs of sterile women. His re-

354

search was funded by some of the same organizations that supported Pincus, including the National Research Council and the Planned Parenthood Federation of America. From 1948 to 1951, Rock received a total of $17,064 from the federation for statistical evaluation of his sterility cases.[32]

Thus, in April 1953, Pincus asked Paul Henshaw, the federation's research director, to approach Rock about cooperating in a study of progesterone as a contraceptive, with funds supplied by Katharine McCormick.[33] Rock was willing. He had helped a remarkable 16 percent of one series of patients to become pregnant by a hormone regimen that suppressed ovulation but also strengthened the reproductive system. When the medication was stopped, pregnancy sometimes followed. Patients were upset, however, by the complete absence of menstruation, which led some to believe that they were pregnant despite Rock's assurances to the contrary. Rock needed a therapy that would imitate the normal menstrual cycle.[34]

At Pincus' suggestion, he tried a twenty-day cycle of progesterone that was interrupted to allow menstruation. This regimen suppressed ovulation while leaving the patient with a greater sense of normality. When the therapy stopped, a significant number of formerly sterile women became pregnant. Thus, progesterone could be used as a contraceptive or to treat sterility, but large doses were required, resulting in high cost and unpleasant side effects. Further progress required a less expensive drug that would be effective at lower dosage. At this point G. D. Searle joined the project.[35]

The progesterone used in the first Rock-Pincus study was purchased from Syntex's American sales manager.[36] Syntex's synthetic progesterone, although much less expensive than natural progesterone, was only effective when given in doses so high that too many side effects occurred to allow the drug to be given to normal women. One of the promising discoveries of steroid chemists in the 1940s, however, was that analogues of progesterone (slightly altered molecules) produced specific effects many times greater than those of the natural hormone. In 1950, Carl Djerassi, a Syntex chemist, began to develop a commercially feasible process for synthesizing orally active analogues of progesterone, and, in April 1952, he announced his success at a meeting of the American Chemical Society.

Djerassi's wonder drug was a 19-nor progestin, so named because it lacked a side chain of one carbon and three hydrogen atoms (a so-called methyl group) at the number 19 position in the progesterone molecule. Rapid clinical evaluation of 19-nor steroids followed under the auspices of Syntex. The commercial value of Djerassi's discovery, quite aside from its contraceptive possibilities, was apparent to Searle's chemists, and by November 1955 they managed to synthesize an analogue of progesterone which differed enough from Djerassi's to be patented.[37]

As Searle chemists developed new compounds, they were sent to Pincus for evaluation. Several of Searle's 19-nor progestins had much higher antiovulatory effects on animals than progesterone, and Pincus wanted Searle to give priority to development of a contraceptive.[38] Searle's chief chemist, Francis Saunders, thought that Pincus was working on another dead end. In December 1954, when Pincus asked for increased supplies of progestin so that Rock's clinical trials could continue, Saunders explained his reservations about the project to Victor Drill, Searle's new director of biological research. He argued that any compound that interrupted the reproductive cycle on such a large scale as to suppress ovulation and induce pseudopregnancy would be unacceptable for regular use by healthy women. Saunders wanted compounds that interfered with the menstrual cycle to be eliminated from further contraceptive testing.[39]

Pincus thought that Saunders was too cautious. Rock had been giving massive doses of ovulation inhibitors to women for some time without dangerous side effects. Rock's new regimen allowed regular menstruation. Moreover, Pincus argued, synthetic progestins could be given in small doses close to the levels manufactured by the body in the course of a normal cycle. Rock's reputation as a clinician and his willingness to continue the project provided Pincus with an effective rebuttal to Saunders, and Searle's management agreed to collaborate in the project while cautioning Pincus not to publicize their involvement.[40]

In addition to some skepticism about the acceptability of using ovulation suppressants in normal women, Searle management was troubled by the cost of supplying Pincus with drugs. Searle had no guaranteed source of plant steroid from which to make large quantities of 19-nor progestins.[41] Syntex had a monopoly on the Mexican root supply. Efforts by other American interests to establish root processing plants in Mexico had been frustrated by the opposition of Syntex lobbyists, who convinced Mexican officials that competition would not be good for the Mexican economy.[42]

Syntex was vulnerable to prosecution under American antitrust laws, however. Several of the key processes in steroid manufacture were covered by American patents that had belonged to the Schering Corporation, a German-owned drug house whose assets were confiscated under the Alien Property Act during World War II. Thus, Syntex's operations depended on a licensing agreement with the attorney general of the United States.[43]

In 1956, American drug manufacturers brought Syntex's monopolistic practices to the attention of the Senate's Subcommittee on Patents, Trademarks, and Copyrights. Syntex had clearly inflated the price of plant steroids by suppressing competition, thereby unfairly exploiting the need of citizens of the United States for cortisone and other steroid wonder drugs. Moreover, the Mexican owners of Syntex had recently sold controlling interest in their company to the Ogden Corporation of New Jersey. Under the threat of antitrust prosecution, Syntex stopped opposing the granting of Mexican licenses for the gathering and processing of roots to other companies, and alternative sources of plant steroids were soon available.[44]

One of Syntex's chief competitors was Productos Esteroides, founded in 1955 by Irving V. Sollins, former sales manager for Syntex in the United States.[45] Sollins was a personal friend of Pincus. He had provided Pincus with the progesterone for Rock's clinical studies. Pincus was one of the original shareholders of Root Chemicals, the corporation established by Sollins as a marketing agent for Productos Esteroides in the United States.[46]

In January 1957, Pincus pointed out to Searle's president that a cheap and reliable supply of plant steroids was essential if Searle was going to market a birth control pill.[47] Searle bought both Root Chemicals and Productos Esteroides in 1957.[48] Syntex had no retail marketing organization in the United States, but sold its products through contracts with American drug manufacturers. None of the American drug houses controlled sources of plant steroids, so Searle was in a unique position to exploit the developing mass market for synthetic hormones. Henceforth, Pincus had the complete cooperation of Searle's chemistry department. His main concern then was to conduct careful clinical trials of oral contraceptives, in the face of pressure from Chicago to hurry.[49]

Rock had first tested Pincus' progesterone regimen on sterile women who ovulated regularly. Accurate evaluation of the drug's effects required a great deal of the patients, including willingness to keep records of their temperature, provide urine samples, and show up at Rock's office for frequent examination and endometrial biopsies, in addition to enduring nausea, dizziness, and tender breasts. Only sterile women who badly wanted to become pregnant had the required motivation. The necessarily tedious tests were also hard on the physician and his sponsor. McCormick continued to chafe constantly over the time required to gain mastery over "that 'ol devil' the female reproductive system!" She asked Sanger, "How can we get a 'cage' of ovulating females to experiment with," and spent hours going over the details of the work with Rock. When Rock returned from a vacation, McCormick wrote, "I was able to get hold of Dr. Rock today. . . . I did not want to leave him for fear that he would escape!" But Rock held up under the strain, and McCormick showed her gratitude by convincing him to move into larger quarters where he could handle more patients. "I do dislike to put money into bricks and mortar rather than into brains and experiments, but in this exceptional case it appears necessary." In February 1955, McCormick wrote Sanger that she was freezing in Boston for the pill. In June she regretted paying Pincus' way to the International Planned Parenthood Federation's Tokyo conference because it took him away from the work, but she felt better when Rock finally allowed her to put an air-conditioner in the attic of his new clinic so that his medical student assistants would sleep better and work more efficiently.[50]

The effort was paying off. Rock and Pincus had found a

Searle compound that surpassed all others as an ovulation suppressant, allowing lower dosage and decreased side effects.[51] Moreover, a fortunate accident revealed a regimen that greatly reduced the incidence of breakthrough bleeding. A batch of 19-nor progestin manufactured in Chicago was contaminated by a tiny amount of estrogen. After this "defect" was remedied, the researchers found that there was a higher incidence of breakthrough bleeding toward the end of the ovulation-inhibiting cycle of medication. After some debate over the wisdom of combining two hormones in the daily dosage, it was decided to include estrogen in controlled quantities. Armed with Enovid (norethynodrel with 1.5 percent mestranol as the estrogenic component), Searle's combination regimen that would become famous as the first pill for general contraceptive use, Pincus was ready to begin large-scale trials.[52]

Contraceptive advice by a physician was still prohibited by law in Massachusetts. Moreover, Rock had been working with highly motivated, sterile, middle-class women. The researchers needed a population of fertile women in a clearly overpopulated area. Ideally, it would be an area where the acceptability of a pill regimen among poorly educated or illiterate women could be tested. The subjects would have to be easily accessible and unlikely to move, so that careful records could be kept. Puerto Rico, for its size and population by far the most studied "underdeveloped" area in the world, was an ideal site.

Pincus and Rock had contacts with officials of the University of Puerto Rico Medical School. Dr. Edris Rice-Wray was a member of the University faculty and director of the Public Health Department's Field Training Center for nurses, as well as medical director of the Puerto Rico Family Planning Association. She knew of a new housing project in Rio Piedras, a suburb of San Juan, where nontransient, medically indigent women could be recruited. The superintendent of the housing project was a friend of family planning, and a former social worker with the Housing Authority was available and already familiar with the local people.[53]

The social worker began recruiting married mothers in April 1956 and quickly filled her quota of 100 volunteers. Despite careful plans, however, many women dropped out of the project during the first fourteen months. A scare story in a local newspaper on the "neomalthusian campaign" caused some problems."We have had some trouble with patients stopping the tablet," Dr. Rice-Wray reported to Pincus.

> Some gave it up because of the article in the paper which produced a very negative reaction. The Secretary of Health accused me of using the Health Department as bait for this program. That got some people excited. A few cases had nausea, dizziness, headache and vomiting. These few refused to go on with the program. Two were sterilized. One husband hung himself because of desperation over poverty. Several patients found they were pregnant before starting the tablet.[54]

In all, 30 of the first 100 recruits were lost, but the secretary of the Family Planning Association wrote Pincus:

> . . . there is one thing that I can assure you . . . in this housing project we have more cases than what we can take for our study. Continuously they are ringing this office asking for the pill, going to see Dr. Rice-Wray and calling on me when I make the visits.[55]

Not only were there replacements waiting in line, but dropouts who had taken the pill for several months quickly became pregnant when they stopped. And children conceived by these women were normal. A few even returned to the project after delivery. To the relief of the researchers, a normal ratio of boys and girls was born to their "failures."

The secretary of health continued to oppose Dr. Rice-Wray's involvement in the pill project. She told him that she was doing it on her own time, apart from her public health duties. He did not see how her several jobs could be separated, and in December 1956, Dr. Rice-Wray left Puerto Rico for a position with the World Health Organization in Mexico. Before she left, however, she furnished Pincus with data on 221 patients representing 47 years of pill taking. "Of this number," she reported, "we have not had one single pregnancy which could be attributed to method failure."[56]

The pill prevented pregnancy, but Dr. Rice-Wray was concerned over the high incidence of side effects (17 percent). With characteristic single-mindedness, Pincus set out to solve the problem. He found that over 80 percent of these complaints could be "cured" among one sample of patients by including an antacid in the regimen. With the cooperation of Dr. Manuel E. Paniagua, Rice-Wray's replacement as medical director of the Family Planning Association, Pincus began a study of the part played by anxiety over taking an experimental drug in the incidence of unpleasant reactions. The social workers had warned recruits that they might experience side effects and had described them in detail. A new group of volunteers who were using conventional contraceptives were asked to continue their customary practice during the first three months of pill taking. Half of these women were given placebos, and half were given the pill. A slightly higher incidence of side effects was reported by those receiving sugar tablets than by those receiving Enovid. In another group taking the pill, Pincus substituted placebos for antacid tablets in response to complaints. The placebos were 70 percent as effective as the antacid tablets in curing reported side effects. Moreover, "reactions" declined among all patients after the first few months of medication.[57]

After the success of Dr. Rice-Wray's project seemed assured, Pincus began efforts to expand the Enovid trials. Clarence Gamble had been excited by the initial report of the Rock-Pincus experiment in *Science,* and he sent a reprint of the article to the director of Ryder Memorial Hospital in Humacao, a community of 35,000 some thirty miles from San Juan. The Ryder was operated by the Board of Home Missions of the Congregational Christian Churches, and in the 1930s, Ryder officials had cooperated with Gamble in one of his studies. Was there a clinician at the Ryder who was interested in helping test the pill under Gamble auspices?[58]

Gamble's query was referred to Adaline Pendleton Satterthwaite, a Quaker and former medical missionary in China, who performed most of the deliveries and gynecological operations in the overburdened little hospital. A physician who had dedicated her life to the care of indigent women and children, Dr. Satterthwaite had also been a one-woman family planning clinic in Humacao. She agreed to participate in the pill project, with Gamble paying for a social worker and statistical evaluation of the case records. Pincus was delighted to have a person of Satterthwaite's stature on the team, and

Searle provided a free supply of Enovid. A steady stream of letters from Gamble asking for details of the project's progress tested the patience of both Satterthwaite and the social worker, but the women kept the project moving as quickly as possible. When Pincus reported on the expanded trials in 1959, 243 out of 830 patient histories were provided by Dr. Satterthwaite, who left Ryder Memorial Hospital in 1963 after conflict developed over her divided attention between research and clinical service. She became a research associate in the department of obstetrics and gynecology at the University of Puerto Rico Medical School, where she conducted studies of the pill's long-term effects. In 1971, she joined the Population Council's technical assistance field staff, and has since helped set up family planning programs all over the world.[59]

While studies of Enovid as a contraceptive were continuing in the late 1950s, Pincus twice conferred with Searle competitors who had similar drugs. Parke, Davis and Company had been urged by Warren Nelson of the Population Council to get into fertility research but feared antagonizing Catholics. After a conference with Pincus, Parke, Davis contributed $5,000 to the Worcester Foundation and announced that it was their policy to keep out of the contraceptive field.[60] The Upjohn Company contacted Dr. Manuel Paniagua about the possibility of having one of their products included in the Puerto Rican trials, but after a conference with Pincus, they dropped the idea.[61] Carl Hartman, the distinguished endocrinologist, was then a research director for Ortho Pharmaceutical Corporation and on the medical advisory committee of the PPFA, but Hartman was skeptical about the possibilities for an oral contraceptive, and Ortho would not attempt to market an oral contraceptive until after Searle had proven that it would be accepted.

Clinicians all over the United States were being introduced to Enovid, as well as similar drugs distributed by Parke, Davis and Company and E. R. Squibb and Sons, for treatment of threatened or habitual abortion, dysfunctional uterine bleeding, painful menstruation (endometriosis), and infertility. The new synthetic hormones offered relief for conditions that had formerly been treated by more radical therapies, including hysterectomy. The Food and Drug Administration approved

Enovid for treatment of pathological conditions in 1957, so the drug was well known to physicians by 1960.[62]

Nevertheless, few drug industry watchers expected an oral contraceptive to be marketed. *Fortune* told its readers in April 1958:

> . . . there is a vast difference between dispensing the drug as a safe means of inducing temporary sterility for therapeutic purposes, and dispensing it for 'habitual use' as a standard contraceptive. It will take perhaps five years of research to satisfy any drug firm that it is ready to apply to the Food and Drug Administration for permission to so label its product; and it would probably take five years after that before the FDA—which says it may well require clinical data on 'thousands of women,' not 500—would approve such applications.[63]

Gregory Pincus did not think oral contraception was so far away. Beginning in 1955 with a trip to the International Planned Parenthood conference in Tokyo, he traveled all over the world, first class, with his wife, at Katharine McCormick's expense, announcing that the pill was on its way. Attempts by officers of the Planned Parenthood Federation of America and of the Population Council to quell the excitement generated by Pincus' statements to the press aroused his ire and led to brisk exchanges between Pincus, Alan Guttmacher, and Christopher Tietze.[64] Even some of Searle's foreign representatives were taken by surprise when Pincus told their customers that an effective oral contraceptive was available from Searle, before Searle salesmen had been informed that Enovid was going to be marketed as a contraceptive.[65]

By December 1958, Pincus had decided that after one more year of testing the pill could be marketed. He saw no reason to continue testing indefinitely simply to satisfy "the qualms of officialdom."[66] Clinical trials would have to go on for years before all possibility of dangerous side effects could be definitely disproven. Further study did show that the progestin-estrogen combination had a blunderbuss effect, suppressing not only ovulation but a number of other reproductive mechanisms. Pincus and Rock believed that the pill worked by suppressing ovulation, but in fact no one knew precisely why it worked.[67] Nevertheless, by 1959 they were both convinced that Enovid was safe for long-term use by normal women.

Rock's personal intervention was required, however, in order to gain Food and Drug Administration approval of Enovid as a contraceptive. Government officials were still hesitant, because no drug of such potency had ever been released for general use by perfectly healthy women. For years Rock had been administering doses of steroids much larger than the 10-milligram-a-day regimen of Enovid that Searle wanted the FDA to approve. In the spring of 1960, Rock and Searle's medical research director called on the physician in charge of evaluating Enovid as a contraceptive. Rock was irritated when he arrived exactly on time at the FDA's Washington office and was kept waiting for thirty minutes. When he was finally ushered in and discovered that the government's expert was a general practitioner who had no experience as a gynecologist or as an endocrinologist, Rock was "livid" and let a number of high officials know how he felt about the way he was treated.[68] The application was approved in May 1960.

It might be argued that Enovid should not have been released as a contraceptive in 1960, since the next year Searle reduced the progestin in the pill to 5 milligrams per day and further reductions followed. Thus, many healthy women ingested much larger doses of synthetic steroids than were necessary to prevent conception. Moreover, more potent progestins were developed in the early 1960s that were effective at dosages of 2 milligrams per day or less. The estrogen content of the pill was also reduced, although attempts to do away with it entirely failed.[69]

By January 1961, Pincus had announced that the pill might inhibit tumors of the breast, a claim that has been substantiated by further research. Public response to oral contraception was better than even Searle's marketing executives had hoped. In two years Enovid boosted annual sales of medically prescribed contraceptives from around $20 million to $40 million. Searle's total sales rose 27 percent, to a record high of $56.6 million in 1962. Although before the pill fewer than 20 percent of fertile women went to doctors for contraceptive advice, suddenly physicians had a much-sought-after service that commanded good fees, lent the prestige of science to the general practitioner, and involved none of the awkwardness of diaphragm fitting.[70]

After the Thalidomide scare of 1962, a number of claims were made against the pill. A vast literature quickly accumulated in which various investigators linked the pill to deep-vein thrombosis (blood clots that can be fatal if they lodge in the lung), and increased risk of heart attack, hypertension, gall-bladder disease, liver tumor, and even profound depression. Defenders of the pill pointed out that the risk to a healthy woman was statistically quite small. For example, the projected number of deaths from clotting disease in the lungs, the most serious risk, is 1.3 in 100,000, or 13 women in a million. After surveying the literature on side effects, the head of the National Medical Committee of the Planned Parenthood Federation of America concluded in 1975 that:

> . . . the risk of developing serious illness as a consequence of taking the pill is small; that mortality associated with the orals is of a very low order of magnitude, much lower than that associated with pregnancy; and that the pill's long term effects must continue to be monitored closely. . . . there are significant health benefits associated with use of the combined pill: It protects women from the development of benign breast disease and ovarian cysts, both common conditions; it regularizes previously irregular menstrual cycles; it reduces premenstrual tension; and it reduces blood loss and protects women from anemia. Perhaps its major asset is its contribution to the enhancement of maternal health, since the ability to plan the timing of pregnancy has a profound effect on the health and well-being of women and their children.[71]

This position was hotly contested by the journalist Barbara Seaman and others, but the consensus of scientific opinion in 1975 was that the pill was safe for healthy women under thirty-five when taken under competent medical direction.[72]

Despite the claims against the pill, women continued to buy them. By 1974, 10 million American women and 50 million women worldwide were using the pill. Tidy, scientific, effective, and even inexpensive, the pill convinced more people than ever before that effective contraceptive practice was possible. Ironically, its "use effectiveness" was not much higher than conventional contraceptives despite a theoretical failure rate of only 0. 1 per woman per year. Six percent of married pill users became pregnant during their first year, and dropout rates in family planning programs ranged from 25 percent to 45 percent.[73] The motivation of the contraceptor remained the key factor in the effectiveness of even a theoretically near-perfect method.

PART VIII

THE TROUBLE
WITH FAMILY
PLANNING

PAUL EHRLICH, the Stanford biologist and prophet of environmental apocalypse, told an interviewer for *Playboy* magazine in 1970: "Despite the fact that family planning has existed in many countries for well over 60 years, we still have rapid population growth. We've tried family planning and we know it doesn't work."[1] Ehrlich's dismissal of family planning as too little and too late echoed the position outlined in the late 1960s by the University of California demographers Kingsley Davis and Judith Blake (husband and wife), the two leading critics of population control through voluntary programs designed to maximize individual free choice. According to Davis and Blake, population grew quickly because people wanted more children than population maintenance required. Only a direct attack on pronatal values could change the millions of individual decisions that resulted in high fertility. Because family planners sought to work within the consensus of accepted values, they were doomed to failure. Successful population control required a revolutionary ideology.[2]

Margaret Sanger had been dead for less than a year (September 1966), when Davis denounced family planning as "an escape from the real issues" at the annual meeting of the National Research Council (March 1967). After years of trying to disassociate contraception from abortion, feminism, low fertility among the middle classes, sexual promiscuity, and medical socialism, birth controllers were suddenly being criticized for failing to face the fact that fundamental changes in social organization were necessary before population growth could be stopped. Davis observed:

> Changes basic enough to affect motivation for having children would be changes in the structure of the family, in the position of women, and in the sexual mores. Far from proposing such radicalism, spokesmen for family planning frequently state their purpose as "protection" of the family—that is, closer observance of family norms. In addition, by concentrating on *new* and *scientific* con-

traceptives, the movement escapes taboos attached to old ones (the Pope will hardly authorize the condom, but may sanction the pill) and allows family planning to be regarded as a branch of medicine: overpopulation becomes a disease, to be treated by a pill or a coil.[3]

While Davis correctly pointed to the fact that social values are more important factors than contraceptive technology in determining birth rates, his critique of the efforts of birth controllers reflected his academic orientation. Birth controllers had to work within the value systems of the societies they sought to change because their programs required the support of government and professional elites. They believed that their reform, if adopted, would have subtle but profound effects on social mores. The changes required in order to deliver contraceptive services to everyone were revolutionary. That is the major reason why they were not accepted.

A strategy for change cannot be proven a failure unless it has been tried, just as a reform program cannot be implemented in a free society if it is in conflict with basic social values. Contrary to Ehrlich's assertion, family planning as a national policy had only recently been adopted in the United States in 1970, and it had hardly begun to be implemented. Political necessity required that contraception be offered as a medical service intended to strengthen the family. And no one knew what the birth rate would be if highly effective contraceptives were available to everyone because that modest experiment had not been tried.

Contraception failed to gain a significant place in state or federal social welfare programs before the 1960s for several reasons. Birth control lacked the commanding rationalization or social purpose necessary to neutralize the militant and well-organized opposition of the Roman Catholic hierarchy in the United States.[4] While the great majority of Americans practiced contraception because personal well-being required it, fears of depopulation and of economic stagnation reflecting the experience of the 1920s and 1930s persisted into the 1960s. In June 1958, the cover of *Life* magazine showed several dozen infants modeling expensive walkers, rockers, and other "kiddie-care" paraphernalia under the headline "Kids: Built-in Recession Cure."[5] Even after the discovery of the "population explosion" in the 1950s, it took some time before significant numbers of Americans began to question the need for population growth in the United States, in contrast to India, China, or other "backward" countries where overpopulation provided a simple explanation for complex problems.

Moreover, social definitions of male and female (sex roles), based upon the belief that large families were essential to individual and social well-being, seemed like the foundation of morality to most Americans, even as these attitudes lost their original purpose. Only as "patriarchal" attitudes began to be questioned by a post–World War II generation raised in an affluent and crowded society did it become possible to ask whether most women needed to devote their lives to motherhood. Thus, the decline of pronatalism as a religious and social value, a process that social scientists only began to study in the 1960s, was necessary before population control could become a concern of government. Family planning, a vague term that could also imply help for the sterile, was the most innocuous synonym for population control, but more rigorous concepts aroused Catholic opposition and stood outside the consensus of the politically acceptable even in the 1960s.

Until the 1960s, only three groups perceived the spread of contraceptive practice as an essential reform. Margaret Sanger represented the aspirations of many women—feminists, club women, working women—for whom autonomy, security, leisure, or a better life depended upon female birth control methods. Whether a woman aspired to a professional career, wanted time for her garden and bridge club, or simply hoped to supplement her husband's income by working, her chances for a fuller existence were contingent upon access to sound contraceptive advice. Although Sanger received contributions from foundations and from male admirers, most of her support, financial and spiritual, came from women, just as almost all of the doctors working in birth control clinics were women, despite their dwindling numbers in the medical profession during the middle decades of the twentieth century.

Some physicians and social workers were convinced by work experience of the need to include contraception among the services they offered. The career of Robert Dickinson symbolized the second motive for supporting birth control, the

371

growing awareness that the viability of the family, economic and psychological, often depended upon successful contraceptive practice. Organized medicine recognized contraception as a legitimate service for the married mother in 1937, but doctors found it difficult to accept the idea that social problems were the responsibility of the profession. A steady stream of clients were referred to birth control clinics by social agencies that had learned from bitter experience that the poor could not get contraceptive advice through hospital outpatient departments and other regular medical services.[6] Whatever the justification for birth control clinics, organized medicine was opposed to all special care clinics, as well as to group practice, services provided at reduced rates, or lay control of medical practice. Moreover, the status of the profession depended on public support, support which, in turn, required that physicians uphold the highest moral standards of the community. As long as most social scientists, politicians, and the general public agreed that the country needed four children from every fertile woman in order to keep the economy growing and to show the world that democracy was virile, then support of contraception from physicians would be cautious. A minority of socially conscious physicians and their lay allies gradually won a limited place for birth control in medicine, but further progress required changes in social values that doctors shared with laymen.

The third motive for advocating the spread of contraceptive practice was fear that the quality of the population would decline if those least able to support children continued to have most of them. While eugenicists believed that differential fertility was a threat to social order and some of them supported the birth control movement, concern over differential fertility antedated the naive Mendelianism of the early twentieth century and survived the decline of hereditarianism in American thought during the 1930s. Clarence Gamble's simple methods approach to the delivery of contraceptives epitomized the desire of many Americans to find an easy solution to the problem of social dependency. The impulse to teach the indigent to control their fertility was based on no particular biological theories. It was a "commonsense" response by taxpayers to the high cost of welfare, a protest against the emergence of an industrial society in which professional social services and cash income necessarily replaced the person-to-person, service altruism of a simpler time.

No one of these three concerns—autonomy for women, better sexual adjustment within marriage, differential fertility between classes—commanded enough allegiance from Americans to make the spread of contraceptive practice a goal of government. Not until the 1960s did publicity given to the population explosion in the Third World draw attention to the possible economic disadvantages of rapid population growth. The deterioration of the American habitat provided a focus for criticism of the quality of life in a mass society. Social order everywhere suddenly seemed threatened by human fertility. The prospect of political upheaval, famine, and ecological catastrophe gave birth control the overriding social justification it had lacked.

In retrospect then, could birth controllers have achieved more if they had individually or collectively used different tactics? Did Margaret Sanger's ego, Robert Dickinson's concern for professional proprieties, or Clarence Gamble's unwillingness to share the power of his money retard the progress of the movement? The answer is probably no. The assertion by historian David M. Kennedy, Sanger's most critical biographer, that the whole course of the birth control movement in America would have been different if Sanger had handed over the Clinical Research Bureau to Dickinson in 1925 has no basis in fact.[7] Sanger's aggressiveness and flamboyance, as well as her habit of paying for some of her high living out of money she raised for the cause, led to divisions in the movement, but the competition between groups was often a source of progress. For example, Morris Ernst, acting on behalf of Sanger, won the *One Package* decision (1936) at a time when the American Birth Control League was claiming that no further legal changes were necessary. Sanger's accomplishments over a long career from her establishment of the first birth control clinic in the United States to her introduction of Katharine McCormick to Gregory Pincus, were more significant than might have been expected given the social context in which she worked. In her last years—drug dependent, obsessed with her appearance, hungry for flattery—she became a parody of the woman she had once been.[8] But even Robert Dickinson in his old age became an embarrassment to colleagues who did not share his enthusiasm for simple sterilization operations, intrauterine contraceptive devices, or Alfred Kinsey. Many medical researchers regarded contraception as a banal subject, unworthy of a first-class researcher, and it remained so until society reordered its priorities.[9]

Clarence Gamble was clearly a disruptive force in the American Birth Control League, but after Kenneth Rose forced Gamble out of the national organization and changed its image, the movement did not attract much greater support or reach many more indigent women. By the mid-1950s the Planned Parenthood Federation of America had begun to reconsider Gamble's simple methods approach.[10] The rediscovery of the IUD in the late 1950s and the development of the pill ended, at least for a time, the reevaluation of the role of contraceptives requiring no medical prescription, but Gamble and Dickinson had tried to promote investigation of the IUD in the late 1940s and Gamble helped Gregory Pincus gather the data that got the pill on the market. Twice during the 1960s the Population Council prevented Gamble from obtaining supplies of experimental IUDs out of fear that he would distribute them to physicians without training in gynecology or statistical analysis, leading to possible unnecessary side effects or shoddy publications that might discredit the method.[11] Nevertheless, after Gamble's death, the Pathfinder Fund, his family foundation for support of contraceptive field trials, acquired a highly competent professional staff that cooperated with the Population Council and became one of the private organizations to which the United States Agency for International Development turned for expertise.[12]

By the early 1960s the efforts of individual philanthropists and of private foundations had provided the world with two superior contraceptives, the IUD and the pill. As soon as these methods became available, many spokesmen for the planned parenthood movement became contemptuous of "the back-fence methods."[13] Gregory Pincus was "profoundly uninterested" in participating in evaluation of conventional barrier methods, and the IUD remains the butt of jokes at the Worcester Foundation, while representatives of the Population Council make vague references to "the commercial interests" that control distribution of the pill; the Population Council resisted including oral contraceptives in its programs long after it was clear that many women preferred them to any other method.[14] Aside from the need to boost their newest products, the desire of population controllers to disassociate themselves from the low status, messy-method past of the movement is understandable. For years critics had used "the culture of poverty argument," the idea that the poor did not have sufficient desire to control their fertility to make use of contraceptives, as a means of dismissing as impractical plans to extend contraceptive services to them.[15] New methods could not be dismissed unless they were tried, and initial studies showed a very high acceptance rate among the poor. Birth controllers could blame the failures of the past on a lack of technology.

From a historical perspective, however, *coitus interruptus,* douching, condoms, and diaphragms deserve more respect. Although the question of whether sexual repression, abortion, or contraceptive practice played the key role in the nineteenth century fertility decline in the United States may never be answered, the fact remains that Americans dramatically lowered their fertility without high-powered contraceptive technology. The birth rate reached the replacement level in the early 1930s before the AMA accepted contraception as a service. Clearly diaphragms did not account for the historic decline in fertility, so even the aid of doctors was not required. Probably Americans paid a high cost for limiting their families in the past. Sexual repression, called self-control by earlier generations, might be viewed as a valuable habit by future historians, but it represented a tremendous psychological burden and was a factor in the "angel-bitch" syndrome that has perverted male attitudes toward women in Western culture. Pelvic inflammatory disease resulting from abortions and from the use of dangerous contraceptives such as the wishbone pessary also damaged bodies and minds. Douching, while not a threat to life, perhaps symbolized the psychological barriers to sexual expression in a society where the genitals were considered unclean and the need of married couples to separate sex from procreation was not recognized. Despite the obstacles they faced, many Americans controlled their fertility and enjoyed happy marriages while using simple methods or self-control.

In the 1970s the pill and the IUD still had not made contraception stress or risk free, and interest remains high in the prospects for still better technology. [16] Perhaps the hope for a new technological fix, the persistent desire to separate contraception from coitus, reflects a naive attitude toward sex, the need to avoid responsibility or to maintain some myth of spontaneity. No one ever died from using a condom. Nor do diaphragms cause excessive menstruation or pelvic infections. In a rational society fertility could be controlled without "physiological" contraception or sexual repression. Society's need for the pill and the IUD might then be regarded as symbols of our lack of sex education, a measure of the persistence of dysfunctional attitudes from the past.

The development of the pill and of the IUD depended more on changes in social values than on technological opportunity. A generation earlier the pill would have been dismissed as a dangerous interference with intricate natural processes; the IUD would have been banned as an abortifacient. These contraceptives represented great improvements in mankind's prospects because they offered hope that the vital transition to a new biological economy of low death rates and low birth rates could be completed before population growth brought social or environmental catastrophe. The middle classes in industrial nations had shown that an end to population growth was possible among certain highly motivated groups, but it had become imperative that all classes control their fertility, not just temporarily but permanently. Conventional contraceptives had made possible the transition from the seven-child to the three-child family, but they were not adequate to the task of ending population growth in free societies. The new contraceptives might serve as a stopgap measure until further changes in values would make accidental parenthood the rare exception rather than a normal experience. They did more than lower birth rates; they also changed attitudes. Once people learned that they could control their fertility, then specific methods became less important. Many married couples who began controlling their fertility in the 1960s with the pill or IUD rediscovered the condom and the diaphragm in the 1970s. Margaret Sanger's generation of women activists accepted contraception as woman's problem, but the revival of feminism in the 1970s led to a new emphasis on male responsibility and mutuality in sexual relations. Suddenly, condoms became respectable; they even had sex appeal.

What are the prospects for controlling human fertility in the last decades of the twentieth century? Measured by recent changes in attitudes the prospects look good in the United States. The first post–World War II changes in the law came in 1965 and 1966 when New York, Ohio, Massachusetts, Minnesota, and Missouri repealed restrictions on the dissemination of contraceptive information, and the United States Supreme Court, in *Griswold* v. *Connecticut,* struck down an "uncommonly silly law" that prohibited contraceptive practice. In 1970, Congress rewrote the Comstock Act, taking contraceptive information and appliances off the obscene list. Finally, in 1972, the Supreme Court, in *Eisenstadt* v. *Baird,* decided that the unmarried have the same right to contraceptives as the married.[17]

The effort to give family planning a recognized place in federal policy began in the Senate in the mid-1960s under the leadership of Ernest Gruening (Democrat of Alaska and M.D.). As a medical student at Harvard before World War I, Gruening wanted to offer birth control to the city's poor but found it was illegal and not a recognized part of medicine. As a crusading journalist in Boston, he tried to write about Margaret Sanger but found that his bosses did not approve. As an administrator of federal programs in Puerto Rico during the depression, he attempted to include family planning in the maternal and child-health programs of the Puerto Rico Reconstruction Administration but had his plans vetoed by New York's Cardinal Spellman, who personally intervened with James A. Farley, Democratic National Committee chairman, in the midst of the 1936 election campaign. Gruening later commented, "Who was I to jeopardize F.D.R.'s campaign for reelection? The following November he would carry only 46 out of 48 states." Gruening got a measure of revenge by encouraging Clarence Gamble to support the private efforts of Puerto Ricans to establish a family planning association.[18]

Senator J. William Fulbright (Democrat of Arkansas) raised the question of whether foreign aid for economic development was wasted in the absence of population control in the early 1960s. An amendment was written into the foreign aid bill of 1963 allowing the Agency for International Development to fund "research into the problems of population growth." Gruening seized the opportunity to introduce, along with Joseph S. Clark (Democrat of Pennsylvania), a resolution calling for the National Institutes of Health to support contraceptive research and for the creation of a presidential commission on population. Gruening intended the resolution to serve as a call for debate rather than for immediate legislation, but it was forgotten in the aftermath of the assassination of President Kennedy.[19]

As Lyndon Johnson's War on Poverty emerged from Congress in 1964, a number of Planned Parenthood affiliates successfully applied to the Office of Economic Opportunity for funds under the "local option" policy that allowed community groups to initiate welfare programs. One result of considerable lobbying by John D. Rockefeller III and William H. Draper, Jr. (who had chaired a study committee on foreign aid during the Eisenhower administration that had aroused controversy with a recommendation that population control be recognized as an important factor in economic development) was a single statement in President Johnson's 1965 State of the Union Message: "I will seek new ways to use our knowledge to help deal with the explosion in world population and the growing scarcity in world resources."[20]

Again Gruening seized the initiative and began hearings on the population crisis before the Subcommittee on Foreign Aid Expenditures, of which he was chairman. The excuse for the public debate he orchestrated was a bill that would have established an Office of Population Problems, with assistant secretaries in both the State Department and the Department of Health, Education, and Welfare. From June 1965 through February 1968, 120 witnesses were in the news testifying before Gruening's committee about the threat posed by population growth to world peace and to individual well-being. The most important aspect of the Gruening hearings, however, was the emphasis placed on personal freedom of choice and equal

378

access to medical services. Whereas birth controllers had for years been stopped by the problem of justifying use of taxpayers' money for a purpose that many citizens considered immoral, in the context of Lyndon Johnson's War on Hunger abroad and War on Poverty at home, the question became, how can we justify withholding from the poor contraceptive services that the middle classes already enjoy?[21]

In 1967 contraceptives were removed from the list of articles that could not be purchased with United States foreign-aid funds, and the Agency for International Development began supporting population control programs abroad through grants to the International Planned Parenthood Federation, the Population Council, and the Pathfinder Fund. At home, the Social Security Amendments of 1967 specified that no less than 6 percent of funds for maternal and child-health services were to be spent on family planning and marked the practical inclusion of family planning in federal welfare policy.[22]

The question remained, would the removal of legal restrictions on the distribution of contraceptives and strong government support of family planning lead to dramatic declines in fertility? Given the opportunity to control their fertility, would the great majority of Americans choose the two-child family? Even if a zero-growth birth rate were achieved in the 1970s, population growth would continue for sixty to seventy years, the period of time required for the population age structure to assume a stationary pattern, and the population of the United States would still increase by at least 40 percent. To achieve zero population growth immediately, it would be necessary for the average family to limit itself to one child for about twenty years, with two-child families not permissible until after the year 2000.[23] A distinction must be made then between a birth rate that will eventually result in a stable population and the goal of an end to population growth in the near future.

A careful study of the incidence of unwanted births in the United States between 1960 and 1965, based on the 1965 National Fertility Survey, revealed that 22 percent of births were unwanted by at least one spouse, 17 percent by both. Among the poor, 34 percent of the births were unwanted, compared with 15 percent among the nonpoor. In 1960–65 there were 4.7 million births that would have been prevented by the use of a perfect contraceptive. Since the women questioned in the survey were raised in a period of strong pronatalist conditioning, they probably underreported the incidence of unwanted births. Future generations of American women raised at a time when alternatives to motherhood were being encouraged would probably want fewer children, and, with the aid of better contraceptives, there is every reason to expect them to be more successful contraceptors. In 1960–65 perfect contraception would have reduced the fertility of American women from 3.0 births to 2.5 births per woman. The study of unwanted births concludes, "Since an eventual zero rate of population growth would require cohort fertility of about 2.25 births per woman, the elimination of unwanted births would not have been sufficient to establish exact replacement for this cohort, but it would have resulted in considerable progress toward that objective." [24]

The growth of population in the United States in the early 1970s was following the lowest of four possible scenarios projected by the United States Census Bureau in 1969. This lowest prediction would yield a population of 266 million by the year 2000, a number easily supportable by the American habitat if reforms in the system of production, consumption, and income distribution are made. [25] The changes necessary in order to manage population growth without coercion are changes that need to be made if our society is to live up to its ideals of equality of opportunity for all. The poor will have fewer children when they are provided with the same access to medical care that the wealthy now enjoy. Not only justice but survival requires that the health system in the United States be reorganized so that core services for the many can replace the present system of high-quality services for the few. The end of sexual discrimination, by providing rewarding alternatives to parenthood, will undoubtedly have a profound effect on birth rates. Finally, elimination of the appalling waste of natural resources built into our throw-away economy will make it possible to support the population growth that will come before we can make the psychological and institutional adjustments essential to our survival. [26]

Some have argued that more aggressive measures than offering voluntary contraception are essential to controlling population growth, especially in the Third World. Bernard Berelson, president of the Population Council, has analyzed twenty-nine policies which governments have been urged to adopt in order to go "beyond" family planning. These proposals range from abortion on demand to the addition of sterilants to the water supply. Berelson concluded, however, that, given the technology available, the political situation in the less developed countries, and the ethical standards essential to the maintenance of free society, there is no alternative to voluntarism.[27] In view of the tremendous progress made in the last decade in establishing national family planning programs all over the world, there is some basis for hope that population growth can be controlled in time to avert catastrophe. Frank Notestein has observed:

> I am aware that values influence behavior, but I am also aware that behavior influences values. It seems to me that the example of successful fertility limitation set by those now motivated is probably the most effective means of fostering both new values and innovative behavior. Moreover, I am greatly impressed by the speed with which the restrictive behavior has spread where family planning programs have been skillfully introduced.[28]

Family planning is no substitute for social justice, but successful birth control programs require a high level of health care for the masses. The trouble with family planning in the United States and in the Third World is that it has not been tried. One can only hope that it will be, because the human race has no other acceptable choice.

Abbreviations Used in
the Notes

ABCL-Houghton	American Birth Control League Papers, Houghton Library, Cambridge, Massachusetts
AJOG	*American Journal of Obstetrics and Gynecology*
AJPH	*American Journal of Public Health*
AS-CL	Abraham Stone Papers, Countway Library, Boston
BMSJ	*Boston Medical and Surgical Journal*
CJG-CL	Clarence J. Gamble Papers, Countway Library, Boston
CMH	Minutes of the Committee on Maternal Health, Robert L. Dickinson Papers, Countway Library, Boston
GP-LC	Gregory Pincus Papers, Library of Congress, Washington, D.C.
HF	*Human Fertility*
JAMA	*Journal of the American Medical Association*
JOC	*Journal of Contraception*
ME	*Mother Earth*
MS-LC	Margaret Sanger Papers, Library of Congress, Washington, D.C.
MS-SS	Margaret Sanger Papers, Sophia Smith Collection, Smith College, Northampton, Massachusetts
MMFQ	*Milbank Memorial Fund Quarterly*
NH-CL	Norman Himes Papers, Countway Library, Boston

PPFA-SS   Planned Parenthood Federation of American Papers, Sophia Smith Collection, Smith College, Northampton, Massachusetts

PPLM-SS   Planned Parenthood League of Massachusetts Papers, Sophia Smith Collection, Smith College, Northampton, Massachusetts

RLD-CL   Robert L. Dickinson Papers, Countway Library, Boston

Notes

Chapter 1

1. For an excellent critique of the conventional models of demographic transition, see Robert V. Wells, "Family History and Demographic Transition," *Journal of Social History* 9 (Fall 1975), pp. 1–19. Ronald Freedman gives a summary of demographic theories of fertility in *The Sociology of Human Fertility* (New York, 1963). Edward Meeker shows in "The Improving Health of the United States, 1850–1915," *Explorations in Economic History* 9 (Summer 1972), that the fundamental improvements in life expectancy in the United States occurred *after* 1880 and were a function of general advances in public health that were associated with the diffusion of sanitary sewers, clean water supplies, and other general advances in the standard of living.

2. Ansley J. Coale and Melvin Zelnik, *New Estimates of Fertility and Population in the United States: A Study of Annual White Births from 1855 to 1960 and of Completeness of Enumeration in the Censuses from 1880 to 1960* (Princeton, N.J., 1963), pp. 36, 40.

3. Maris A. Vinovskis, "Demographic Changes in America from the Revolution to the Civil War: An Analysis of the Socio-Economic Determinants of Fertility Differentials and Trends in Massachusetts from 1765 to 1860" (Ph.D. dissertation, Harvard, 1975), p. 12.
The ratio of children under 10 to women of childbearing age declined by 29 percent between 1800 and 1860.

4. Wilson H. Grabill, Clyde V. Kiser and Pascal Whelpton, *The Fertility of American Women* (New York, 1958), pp. 15–19; Vinovskis, pp. 12–14, 85–86, 94–95; John Modell, "Family and Fertility on the Indiana Frontier, 1820," *American Quarterly* 23 (December 1971), pp. 615–32.

5. Brown, "Modernization and the Modern Personality in Early America, 1600–1865: A Sketch of a Synthesis," *Journal of Interdisciplinary History* 2 (Winter 1972), pp. 201–28, and "The Emergence of Urban Society in Rural Massachusetts, 1760–1820" *Journal of American History* 111 (June 1974); Wells, "Family History and Demographic Transition"; Vinovskis, chs. 7 and 8.

6. "Socioeconomic Determinants of Interstate Fertility Differentials in the United States in 1850 and 1860," *Journal of Interdisciplinary History* 6 (Winter 1976), pp. 375–96.

7. Mary Ryan, "American Society and the Cult of Domesticity, 1830–1860" (Ph.D. dissertation, University of California, Santa Barbara, 1971), pp. 222–23.

8. Yasukichi Yasuba, *Birth Rates of the White Population in the United States, 1800–1860* (Baltimore, 1962), p. 119 and passim. In his study of fertility in Massachusetts, Maris Vinovskis found no significant increase in the mean age of marriage for women in the first half of the nineteenth century and concluded that Yasuba's thesis did not hold for Massachusetts. Yasuba underestimated the age of marriage in the late eighteenth century and overestimated the age of marriage in the antebellum period. See "Demographic Changes in America from the Revolution to the Civil War," p. 44.

9. Arthur W. Calhoun, *A Social History of the American Family* (New York, 1945; three volumes in one; first editions 1917, 1918, 1919, same pagination), vol. 3, p. 236. On the history of abortion, see also R. Sauer, "Attitudes to Abortion in America, 1800–1973," *Population Studies* 28 (March 1974), pp. 53–67.

10. Peter Fryer, *The Birth Controllers* (New York, 1966), chs. 4–9. Norman Himes

reproduced samples of these handbills in *Medical History of Contraception* (Baltimore, 1936), pp. 214–17.

11. Fryer, ch. 9; Richard W. Leopold, *Robert Dale Owen* (Cambridge, Mass., 1940), pp. 60–61, 76–78. *Every Woman's Book* was written by Richard Carlile and was a revision of his 1825 essay "What Is Love." See Himes, *Medical History*, pp. 220–22, 440, and Fryer, chs. 6–7.

12. Leopold, pp. 144–45; Sidney Ditzion, *Marriage, Morals, and Sex in America* (New York, 1953), p. 120. For a list of editions of *Moral Physiology*, see Himes, *Medical History*, pp. 473–75.

13. Knowlton's autobiography, which only describes his life until 1829, was published in *The Boston Medical and Surgical Journal* 45 (September 10, 1851), pp. 111–20 and (September 24, 1851), pp. 149–57. Hereafter cited as *BMSJ*. On Knowlton's appearance at the Hall of Science and the exchange of literature with Owen, see Mary Lee Esty, Charles Knowlton, unpublished manuscript. Knowlton acknolwedged his debt to Owen in *Fruits of Philosophy* (Philadelphia, 1839), p. 86. Norman Himes discussed the various editions of *Fruits* in *Medical History*, pp. 460–64.

14. Knowlton, *Fruits*, pp. 87–88.

15. Ibid., pp. iii–v, 88–89; Charles Knowlton, *History of the Recent Excitement in Ashfield* (n.p., n.d.), copy in Houghton Library, pp. 1, 18, 23; Frederick Howes, *Illustrated History of the Town of Ashfield* (Ashfield, Mass., 1914), p. 368.

16. Knowlton, *History of the Recent Excitement in Ashfield*, pp. 18–22.

17. Ibid.; *Boston Investigator* (April 19, 1833), pp. 19–20.

18. Howes, pp. 162–64. In *History of the Recent Excitement*, Knowlton claimed that this minister had purchased a copy of *Fruits* "a year before—as he was then lately married!" Attacks on Knowlton's book only began after the minister attended a local synod and was warned about the evil tendency of Knowlton's book by his colleagues.

19. S. J. W. Tabor, "The Late Charles Knowlton, M.D.," *BMSJ* 45 (September 10, 1851), pp. 109–10; *The Massachusetts Medical Society, A Catalogue of the Officers, Fellows, and Licentates, 1781–1893* (Boston, 1894), p. 133. For articles and notices by Knowlton, see *BMSJ*, 28 (June 14, 1843), pp. 369–73; 29 (December 13, 1843), pp. 379–82; 30 (March 6, 1844), pp. 89–95; 30 (April 24, 1844), pp. 233–37; 30 (June 12, 1844) pp. 380–81; 32 (February 26, 1845), pp. 69–73; 34 (April 8, 1846), pp. 194–95. For Knowlton's attack on Thomsonianism, see "Quackery," *BMSJ* (April 1, 1846), pp. 169–80.

20. Howes, p. 368. Norman Himes, "Charles Knowlton's Revolutionary Influence on the English Birth Rate," *New England Journal of Medicine* 199 (September 6, 1928), pp. 461–65.

21. Ronald Freedman, Pascal K. Whelpton, and Arthur A. Campbell, *Family Planning, Sterility, and Population Growth* (New York, 1959), pp. 174–75, 408–10. The authors concluded that although appliance methods were more effective than withdrawal or rhythm, and some appliance methods (condom, diaphragm) more effective than douching, "most couples can restrict their children to a relatively small number by using any of these six methods (condom, diaphragm, rhythm, douche, withdrawal, jelly) regularly and carefully." (p. 211).

In the 1930s medical authors still described proper contraceptive douching technique, while warning of the ineffectiveness of the method compared to the diaphragm or to the condom. See Robert L. Dickinson, *Control of Conception* (2nd ed., Baltimore, 1938), ch. 10, "Douche," pp. 159–71.

The Freedman, Whelpton, and Campbell study attempted to examine more closely several of the hypotheses developed in "The Indianapolis Survey," a classic attempt to discover the social and psychological factors affecting fertility that was conducted between 1938 and 1941. The 1955 study found that there had been a sharp decline in contraceptive douching since the early 1940s. For a brief review of the Indianapolis survey, see Clyde V. Kiser, ed., *Research in Family Planning* (Princeton, N.J., 1962), pp. 149–66. The earlier findings on specific methods of contraception were reported in volume 4 of *Social and Psychological Factors Affecting Fertility*, ed. Pascal Whelpton and C. V. Kiser (New York, 1954), pp. 885–951.

22. Knowlton, *Fruits*, p. 82. "*A female syringe*, which is a simple and cheap in-

strument, will be required, and one can be obtained in any apothecary's shop. Arrangements are in contemplation for furnishing them, with other facilities, in connection with this book, and better ones than are generally made." For illustrations of syringes, see Charles Goodyear, *The Applications and Uses of Vulcanized Gum-Elastic,* vol. 2 (New Haven, Conn., 1853), pp. 172–73.

23. Knowlton, *History of the Recent Excitement in Ashfield,* p. 17; *Fruits,* pp. 8, 85.

24. Geoffrey Hawthorn, *The Sociology of Fertility* (London, 1970), pp. 33–39.

25. Withdrawal prevented more than 94 percent of expected pregnancies among couples using the method in the 1955 survey. Great Britain's first Royal Commission on Population reported in 1949 that there was no significant difference in the effectiveness of fertility planning between couples using vaginal diaphragms and those using withdrawal. Those using diaphragms averaged 2.6 children while those using withdrawal averaged 2.7 children.

Family Planning, Sterility, and Population Growth, pp. 212–213, 410; Ernest Lewis-Faning, *Report on an Enquiry into Family Limitation and Its Influence on Human Fertility during the Past Fifty Years: Papers of the Royal Commission on Population,* I (London, 1949), pp. 70, 160.

All nineteenth century birth control methods demanded a great deal of the contraceptor. The most important factor governing the number of pregnancies prevented by these methods was the strength of the motivation of the individuals using them. Most twentieth century studies of the effectiveness of contraceptives use medically indigent or working-class populations and show high failure rates for simple methods like withdrawal, douching, or the condom. While the effectiveness of barrier and chemical contraceptives is a complex problem that has inspired a vast literature, it should be noted that most studies of these methods do not use middle-class subjects and the more recent ones are influenced by the high standard of effectiveness set by the modern intrauterine devices and by the anovulant pill. The socially ambitious middle classes, including farmers, villagers, and city dwellers, provided the audience for the nineteenth century birth control tracts. And these middle groups did significantly lower their fertility. Whether or not contraceptive practice was the cause of this phenomenon, I believe that sufficient contraceptive technology was available to account for it.

The classic studies of working-class attitudes toward women, children, sex, and contraception are Lee Rainwater, *And the Poor Get Children* (Chicago, 1960) and *Family Design* (Chicago, 1965). The poor couples that Rainwater studied had a vague knowledge of contraceptives, but they were often unable to use what they did know in an effective way. Their failures as contraceptors reflected both the strength of competing values (i.e., good women are mothers) and the general inability of the poor to control their lives. For a summary of the literature on sociological factors and fertility, see Hawthorn, *The Sociology of Fertility.*

Christopher Tietze's *Selected Bibliography of Contraception* (National Committee on Maternal Health, Inc., Publication No. 6, n.p., 1960) lists dozens of studies of simple methods, some of which are discussed in Part V.

26. *The Relations of the Sexes* (New York, 1876), p. 265.

27. Personal communication with Mary Lee Esty.

28. Frederick Hollick, *The Marriage Guide or Natural History of Generation: A Private Instructor for Married Persons and Those about to Marry* (New York, 1850), p. 219.

29. Frederick Hollick, *The Diseases of Women* (New York, 1847), pp. xiv, 271–82; *The Origin of Life: A Popular Treatise on the Philosophy and Physiology of Reproduction, in Plants and Animals, with a Detailed Description of Human Generation* (New York, n.d. [1872]), pp. v–vii.

30. *The Origin of Life,* p. xiii.

31. *The Marriage Guide,* p. 213.

32. Modern researchers have established that the ovum is only available for fertilization for twenty-four hours. Spermatozoa, once they have entered the uterus, can remain viable for only forty-eight hours. Thus, there is a period of only three days in each cycle during which conception is possible. Calculation of the safe period is com-

plicated by the uncertainty of the precise day of ovulation in even the most regular menstrual cycles. For practical purposes a fertile period of eight days is assumed, and the prediction of this eight-day period must take into account a normal variation of three or four days in the length of the cycle. Thus, in a twenty-four day cycle, counted from the *first day of menstruation* to the assumed onset of menstruation on the twenty-fifth day, the fertile period should fall between the seventh and fourteenth days; for a thirty-day cycle, between the thirteenth and twentieth days. The theoretical range in fertile days for a cycle that varied by as much as twenty days would be from day six to day twenty.

In Hollick's static and thus imprecise system, this fertile period for twenty- to thirty-day cycles corresponds to days one through fifteen. Hollick counted his days from the *end* of menstruation. Thus, a woman whose cycle did not fluctuate beyond thirty days would be protected if she followed Hollick's advice. During a thirty-one day cycle the chance of conception would be slight, but for longer cycles the probability of conception would be quite high. For a succinct discussion of the fertile period, see John Peel and Malcolm Potts, *Textbook of Contraceptive Practice* (Cambridge, Great Britain, 1969), pp. 81–84 and the Ovulation Chart for Cycles of 20 to 40 days (p. 14) which I have adapted from Peel and Potts, p. 82.

33. John T. Noonan, Jr., *Contraception: A History of Its Treatment by the Catholic Theologians and Canonists* (Cambridge, Mass., 1965), pp. 522ff. For confused discussions of the fertile period, see Elizabeth Blackwell, *Essays in Medical Sociology* vol. 1 (London, 1902), p. 77, and Augustus Gardner, *Conjugal Sins* (New York, 1870), p. 97. See also Vern Bullough and Martha Vought, "Women, Menstruation, and Nineteenth-Century Medicine," *Bulletin of the History of Medicine* 47 (January-February 1973), pp. 66–82.

34. Thomas Low Nichols, *Esoteric Anthropology* (London, n.d.; reprint, New York, 1972), p. 113; William A. Alcott, *The Physiology of Marriage* (Boston, 1866; reprint, New York, 1972), p. 191; The Editorial Staff of the Alkaloida Clinic, *Sexual Hygiene* (Chicago, 1902), p. 97.

35. Ralph F. Wolf, *India Rubber Man: The Story of Charles Goodyear* (Caldwell, Idaho, 1939); P. Schidrowity and T. R. Dawson, eds., *History of the Rubber Industry* (Cambridge, Great Britain, 1952), pp. 263–69; 303–4; William Woodruff, *The Rise of the British Rubber Industry during the Nineteenth Century* (Liverpool, 1958), pp. 74–76, 79, 156.

36. T. J. B. Buckingham, "The Trade in Questionable Rubber Goods," *The India Rubber World* 5 (March 15, 1892), pp. 164–65.

37. Norman Himes, *Practical Birth Control Methods* (New York, 1938), pp. 74–75, and figure 12, p. 69.

38. Charles Goodyear, *The Applications and Uses of Vulcanized Gum-Elastic*, vol. 2 p. 173.

39. Edward Bliss Foote, *Medical Common Sense* (New York, 1864), pp. 335–37.

40. Ibid., p. 380, note 2. For a discussion of the various editions of *Medical Common Sense*, see Vincent J. Cirillo's articles on Foote in *Journal of the History of Medicine* 25 (July 1970), pp. 341–45 and *Bulletin of the History of Medicine* 47 (September-October 1973), pp. 471–79.

41. Norman Himes, *Medical History of Contraception*, pp. 279, 318–19.

42. W. D. Buck, "A Raid on the Uterus," *New York Medical Journal* 5 (August 1867), pp. 464–65.

Although there is no means of estimating the extent to which contraceptive pessaries were used in the nineteenth century, in 1886, in an article attacking the campaigns of the New York Society for the Suppression of Vice against the vendors of contraceptives, Edward Bond Foote complained that a raid "was made in the fall of 1885, upon half a dozen of the hundreds of druggists in New York who were selling closed-ring-pessaries. Following the prophecy 'one shall be taken and the other left,' one prominent Broadway druggist was arrested while another equally *Hazard*-ous was not, but this was not so surprising, after all, when the name of the latter was found to appear on the subscription list of the Vice Society while the former did not." See Edward Bond Foote, *The Radical Remedy in Social Science* (New York, 1886), p. 89, footnote.

43. "The New England Family," *New Englander* (March 1882), p. 151.
44. Coale and Zelnik, *New Estimates of Fertility*, pp. 40–41.

Chapter 2

1. Two Ph.D. dissertations relate the domestic literature of the middle decades of the nineteenth century to the social changes that were transforming American society: Kirk Jeffrey, Jr., "Family History: The Middle-Class American Family in the Urban Context, 1830–1870" (Stanford, 1971) and Mary Ryan, "American Society and the Cult of Domesticity, 1830–1860" (University of California, Santa Barbara, 1971). Kathryn Sklar's *Catharine Beecher: A Study in Domesticity* (New Haven, Conn., 1973) analyzes the place in American history of one of the most important "household divinities."

The best attempts to place the nineteenth century literature on sexuality in a broad social context are: Charles Rosenberg, "Sexuality, Class, and Role in Nineteenth Century America," *American Quarterly* 25 (May 1973), pp. 131–53; Ronald Walters, "The Family and Antebellum Reform: An Interpretation," *Societas* 3 (Summer 1973), pp. 221–33 and Walters' introduction to *Primers for Prudery: Sexual Advice to Victorian America* (Englewood Cliffs, N.J., 1974); Carl Degler, "What Ought to Be and What Was: Women's Sexuality in the Nineteenth Century," *American Historical Review* 79 (December 1974), pp. 1467–90.

2. William Goode, *World Revolution and Family Patterns* (New York, 1963), pp. 6–7.

3. Philip Greven, Jr., *Four Generations: Population, Land, and Family in Colonial Andover, Massachusetts* (Ithaca, N.Y., 1970); John Demos, *A Little Commonwealth, Family Life in Plymouth Colony* (New York, 1970).

4. Jeffrey, "Family History," pp. 24–30, 68–69.

5. Ibid., pp. 139–51, 160–67.

6. Ibid., pp. 167–87; Henry Clarke Wright, *The Reproductive Element* (Warrington, N.Y., 1858), p. 74.

7. Jeffrey, pp. 34–38, 203–9; Alexis de Tocqueville, *Democracy in America* (New York, 1945; the Henry Reeve text as revised by Francis Bowen and further corrected and edited by Phillips Bradley), II, pp. 222–23.

8. Sklar, *Catharine Beecher*, pp. 155–63; Jeffrey, pp. 202–9.

9. Geoffrey Hawthorne, *The Sociology of Fertility* (London, 1970), pp. 12–14.

10. *The Physiology of Marriage* (Boston, 1866; first edition, 1855), pp. 12–19. Alcott's popularity is reflected in the thirty-two titles under his name in the Harvard College Library. There are seven copies of *The Physiology of Marriage* in the Harvard Medical School Library (Countway). For a biographical sketch of Alcott, see *Dictionary of American Biography*.

11. Ibid., pp. 16–17, 91.

12. Ibid., pp. 116–17. For discussion of Graham and his place in American history, see Stephen Nissenbaum, "Careful Love: Sylvester Graham and the Emergence of Victorian Sexual Theory in America: 1830–1840" (Ph.D. dissertation, University of Wisconsin, 1968).

13. Ibid., pp. 118–19, 136–41.

14. Ibid., pp. 180–81.

15. Ibid., pp. 190–91, 198–99.

16. Reprint New York, 1972, ch. 9, "Morals of the Sexual Relation," pp. 112–21. There is a description of Nichols' career in Harry B. Weiss and Howard R. Kemble, *The Great American Water-Cure Craze* (Trenton, N.J., 1967), pp. 72–80. See also *Dictionary of American Biography*.

17. John Cowan, *The Science of a New Life* (New York, 1874). The endorsements are on pp. 407–10.

18. Ibid., p. 111.

19. Sklar, pp. 152–55; Jeffrey, pp. 215–28.

20. Cowan, pp. 108–13.

21. Alcott, p. 55.

22. Richard D. Brown, "Modernization and the Modern Personality in Early America, 1600–1865: A Sketch of a Synthesis," *Journal of Interdisciplinary History* 2 (Winter 1971), p. 220.

23. For recent recitations of this myth, see Ann D. Wood, " 'The Fashionable Diseases': Women's Complaints and Their Treatment in Nineteenth Century America," *Journal of Interdisciplinary History* 4 (Summer 1973), pp. 33–34; Linda Gordon, "Voluntary Motherhood: The Beginnings of Feminist Birth Control Ideas in the United States," *Feminist Studies* (Winter-Spring 1973), p. 9. Cf. Andrew Sinclair, *The Better Half : The Emancipation of the American Woman* (New York, 1965), ch. 11, "The Unmentionable Fears."

24. Carroll Smith-Rosenberg describes the mid-nineteenth century campaign to outlaw abortion in "H. R. Storer and the Crazy Kangaroo," a paper presented to the conference Two Hundred Years of American Medicine, University of Pennsylvania, December 3, 1976. See also Cyril Means, Jr., "The Law of New York Concerning Abortion and the Status of the Fetus: A Case of Cessation of Constitutionality," *New York Law Forum* 14 (Fall 1968), pp. 411–515, and R. Sauer, "Attitudes to Abortion in America, 1800–1973," *Population Studies* 28 (March 1974), pp. 53–67.

25. The use of disease sanctions and scientific terminology to reinforce feminine sexual stereotypes is discussed by Wood, " 'The Fashionable Diseases': Women's Complaints and Their Treatment in Nineteenth Century America," and by Carroll Smith-Rosenberg and Charles Rosenberg, "The Female Animal: Medical and Biological Views of Woman and Her Role in Nineteenth-Century America," *Journal of American History* 60 (September 1973), pp. 332–56.

26. Seale Harris describes the development of the operation in *Woman's Surgeon: The Life of J. Marion Sims* (New York, 1950), chs. 10–11. For the spring-loaded pessary, see Sims' *Clinical Notes on Uterine Surgery* (New York, 1866), p. 269 and figure 11.

27. Autobiographical notes by Thomas Longshore, Archives of the Medical College of Pennsylvania. For a sketch of Hannah Longshore, see *Notable American Women*. Dr. Longshore was a member of the first class of the Women's Medical College of Pennsylvania and the first woman to hold a teaching position in a medical school in the United States.
   I am indebted to Regina Morantz of the University of Kansas for this citation.

28. Lester Ward, *Young Ward's Diary*, ed. Bernhard J. Stern (New York, 1915).

29. Ibid., p. 35 (February 9, 1861).

30. Ibid., pp. 41, 44–45, 58–59, 81 (March 3, March 18, May 7, October 25, 1861).

31. Ibid., p. 140 (March 13, 1864).

32. Ibid., p. 145 (June 19, 1864).

33. Ibid., pp. 150–52 (October 23, November 6, November 13, December 4, 1864).

34. Ibid., pp. 238, 246 (September 1, 1867; January 5, 1868).

35. I have not been able to examine Dr. Mosher's sex histories. My information on them is drawn from Carl Degler's "What Ought to Be and What Was: Women's Sexuality in the Nineteenth Century" and Caroll Smith-Rosenberg, "A Gentler and a Richer Sex: Female Perspectives on Nineteenth Century Sexuality," Paper given in the Third Berkshire Conference on the History of Women," June 11, 1976. The Mosher Papers are in the Stanford University Archives.

36. Degler, pp. 1480–81.

37. Smith-Rosenberg, "A Gentler and a Richer Sex." Handout distributed to audience.

38. Case 50, Mosher Survey. I am indebted to Barbara Campbell of the University of Illinois, Chicago Circle, for copies from several of Mosher's histories of the responses to the question on contraceptive practice.

39. *The Relations of the Sexes* (New York, 1876), p. 266.

40. Robert Wells, "Family Size and Fertility Control in Eighteenth-Century America: A Study of Quaker Families," *Population Studies* 25 (1971), pp. 73–82.

41. Daniel Scott Smith, "Family Limitation, Sexual Control, and Domestic Feminism in Victorian America," *Feminist Studies* 1 (Winter-Spring 1973), pp. 40–57.

Chapter 3

1. Mary Ware Dennett, *Birth Control Laws* (New York, 1926), p. 10. Most of the state laws classifying information on contraception as obscene were passed in the 1870s and were modeled on the Comstock Act of 1873, a federal statute passed for the purpose of restricting the circulation of obscene material by mail. The law was intended to close loopholes in the postal code of 1872. Under the 1873 "Act for the Suppression of Trade in and Circulation of, Obscene Literature and Articles of Immoral Use" it was a felony to:

> Sell or lend, or give away, or in any manner exhibit, or . . . offer to sell, or lend or give away, or in any manner exhibit . . . publish or offer to publish in any manner, or . . . have in [one's possession], for any purpose or purposes, any obscene book, pamphlet, paper, writing, advertisement, circular, print, picture, drawing or other representation, figure, or image on or of paper or other material, or any cast, instrument or other article of an immoral nature, or any drug or medicine, or any article whatever, for the prevention of conception, or for causing unlawful abortion, or . . . advertise same for sale. . . . (*Congressional Globe*, 1873, p. 297)

In 1926 anticontraception laws modeled on the Comstock Act existed in 24 states. In 22 other states obscenity laws that did not specifically mention contraception were interpreted to include it because of the federal law. Although more or less nullified by a series of court decisions in the 1930s, the Comstock Act's clause on contraception was not repealed until 1971.

For a typical denunciation of contraception by a representative of organized medicine, see John P. Reynolds' presidential address to the American Gynecological Society, *Transactions* 15 (1890), pp. 3–24.

2. David J. Pivar, "The New Abolitionists: The Quest For Social Purity, 1876–1900" (Ph.D. dissertation, University of Pennsylvania, 1965). Pivar's dissertation has been published as *Purity Crusade: Sexual Morality And Social Control, 1868–1900* (Westport, Conn., 1973), but I cite his dissertation below because many of the documents I cite are quoted extensively in the dissertation, where I first read them.

3. Pivar, pp. 33–38, 65, 97–101.

4. Ibid., pp. 102–26. See also Constance Rover, *Love, Morals, and the Feminists* (London, 1971) and Carroll Smith-Rosenberg, "Beauty, the Beast, and the Militant Woman: A Case Study in Sex Roles and Social Values in Jacksonian America," *American Quarterly* 23 (October 1971), pp. 562–84.

5. *Buffalo Medical Journal* (April 1856), p. 680. Quoted in Pivar, p. 46.

6. "The Social Evil and Its Remedy," *The Nation* 4 (March 4, 1867), pp. 153–54; Pivar, p. 59; John Burnham, "The Medical Inspection of Prostitutes in America in the Nineteenth Century," *Bulletin of the History of Medicine* 45 (1971), pp. 203–18.

7. Pivar, pp. 104–26.

8. Charles H. Kitchell, *The Social Evil; Its Cause and Cure; Read before the Society of Medical Jurisprudence and State Medicine . . . New York, May 13, 1886* (New York, 1886); "Scientific Cookery," *Journal of the American Medical Association* (June 2, 1894), p. 857. Quoted in Pivar, pp. 108, 264, 267.

9. Heywood Broun and Margaret Leech, *Anthony Comstock: Roundsman of the Lord* (New York, 1927), pp. 75–83; Paul Boyer, *Purity in Print: The Vice-Society Movement and Book Censorship in America* (New York, 1968), pp. 3–5. Comstock's belief that social mobility depended on clean living is explained in R. Christian Johnson, "Anthony Comstock: Reform, Vice, and the American Way" (Ph.D. dissertation, University of Wisconsin, 1973).

10. For an excellent analysis of the social origins and position of Comstock's supporters, see Boyer, pp. 5–15, 277 note 8.

11. Broun and Leech, ch. 10, pp. 128–44.

12. Ibid., pp. 148, 151, 153.

13. Anthony Comstock, *Frauds Exposed* (New York, 1880), p. 542.

14. Broun and Leech, pp. 158–60, 167–68.

15. Charles Walter Clarke, *Taboo: The Story of the Pioneers of Social Hygiene* (Washington, 1961), pp. 45–46 and passim. The Wasserman test for syphilis was developed in 1906. There is still no blood test or easy serological means of detecting gonorrhea.

16. Augustus K. Gardner, *Conjugal Sins against the Laws of Life and Health* (New York, 1870), p. 109.

17. Henry Maudsley, *Sex in Mind and in Education* (New York, 1874).

18. Edward Clarke, *Sex in Education; or, A Fair Chance for the Girls* (Boston, 1873), pp. 63, 89–90. Quoted in Maudsley, p. 19.
Clarke's book provoked four replies from supporters of equal educational opportunity for women. Julia Ward Howe, ed., *Sex and Education: A Reply* (Boston, 1874); George and Ann Comfort, *Woman's Education and Woman's Health* (Syracuse, 1874); Eliza B. Duffey, *No Sex in Education, or An Equal Chance for Boys and Girls* (Philadelphia, 1875); Mary Jacobi, *The Question of Rest for Women During Menstruation* (New York, 1877). Jacobi's book won the Harvard Boylston Medical Prize.

19. Quoted in Maudsley, p. 30. For an analysis of the debate over the effects of higher education on the health of women, see Vern Bullough and Martha Voght, "Women, Menstruation, and Nineteenth Century Medicine," *Bulletin of the History of Medicine* 47 (January 1973), pp. 66–82.

20. Alexander J. C. Skene, *Education and Culture as Related to the Health and Diseases of Women* (Detroit, 1889).

21. Emelius C. Dudley, *The Medicine Man; Being the Memoirs of Fifty Years of Medical Progress* (New York, 1927), pp. 166–67.

22. Skene, *Education and Culture*, pp. 26, 29, 30, 38.

23. Ibid., p. 39.

24. "Present Tendencies in Women's College and University Education," *Publications of the Association of Collegiate Alumnae* 3 (February, 1908). Quoted in William L. O'Neill, ed., *The Woman Movement: Feminism in the United States and England* (Chicago, 1971), pp. 168–69.

25. Henri Ellenberger, *The Discovery of the Unconscious: The History and Evolution of Dynamic Psychology* (New York, 1970), p. 291 and passim. See also the description of the early career of Robert L. Dickinson, Part III of this work; Edward M. Brecher, *The Sex Researchers* (Boston, 1969), chs. 1–4; Nathan Hale, Jr., *Freud and the Americans: The Beginnings of Psychoanalysis in the United States, 1876–1917* (New York, 1971).

26. Carl Degler has shown that many nineteenth century physicians did not view women as lacking in sexual desire or generally incapable of sexual fulfillment. That stereotype of medical opinion was created by historians who failed to read widely or carefully in the medical literature. See, "What Ought to Be and What Was: Women's Sexuality in the Nineteenth Century," *American Historical Review* 79 (December 1974), pp. 1467–79.

27. The Editorial Staff of the Alkaloida Clinic, *Sexual Hygiene* (Chicago, 1902), "Preface" and pp. 10–15. There are two copies of *Sexual Hygiene* in the Countway Library of Medicine.

28. Ibid., p. 95.

29. Ibid., p. 184.

30. Ibid., pp. 188, 190.

31. Ibid., pp. 186–87, 189–90.

Chapter 4

1. For a representative list of articles on birth control in *Critic and Guide,* see Julia E. Johnson, ed., *Selected Articles on Birth Control* (New York, 1925), pp. lxviii–lxix; Norman Himes, *Medical History of Contraception* (Baltimore, 1936), pp. 310–11.

2. Robert Dickinson to Margaret Sanger, November 7, 1945, MS-SS; Sanger to Dickinson, November 9, 1945, RLD-CL. Dickinson wrote Sanger about this incident while he was preparing a paper for the New York Academy of Medicine on "Personal Recollections Concerning the Early Days of Contraception."

3. *ME* 11 (April 1916): 457–60.

4. Emma Goldman, *Living My Life* (New York, 1934; 1st ed., 1931), pp. 122–48, 161–62, 169–74.

5. Ibid., pp. 185–86.

6. Ibid., p. 187.

7. Ibid., pp. 187, 227, 229, 271–73.

8. Ibid., pp. 320, 335, 337; Richard Drinnon, *Rebel in Paradise: A Biography of Emma Goldman* (Chicago, 1961), chs. 16–18.

9. *Living My Life,* pp. 415–16; 420–23.

10. Ben Reitman, "Prisons in My Life," *Phoenix* (The University of Chicago Student Magazine) (May 1937), copy in NH-CL; Goldman, *Living My Life,* pp. 434, 469. There are some biographical notes as well as Reitman's manuscript autobiography at the University of Illinois, Chicago Circle.

11. *Living My Life,* pp. 434, 469.

12. Ibid., pp. 552–53.

13. Margaret Sanger, *An Autobiography* (New York, 1938), chs. 7, 8, pp. 176–77. In view of Sanger's later efforts to renounce her radical past, it should be noted that she began her reform career as an organizer for the International Workers of the World, was a friend of Emma Goldman's, and a lover of Alexander Berkman's. See, Alexander Berkman to Sanger, December 9, 1915, MS-SS. For Sanger's arrest while working as an IWW organizer in Hazelton, Pennsylvania, see Scrapbook II, MS-LC. On her relationship with Goldman, see Goldman to Sanger, December 8, 1915, and December 16, 1915, MS-LC; *ME* 10 (April 1915), pp. 75–78; *Woman Rebel* (June 1914), p. 27; William Sanger to Margaret Sanger, September 3, 1913, January 28, 1914, and February 6, 1914, MS-SS.

14. Louise Bryant, "A New Adventure in Arcadia," *ME* 10 (September 1915), pp. 235–38; Ben L. Reitman, "The 1915–1916 Tour," *ME* 11 (October 1916), pp. 643–48; *ME,* Birth Control Number, 11 (April 1916); "Emma Goldman Before the Bar," 11 (May 1916), pp. 496–507 and "Pinched," pp. 507–8; "Ben L. Reitman Before the Bar," 11 (June 1916), pp. 508–516. For a description of Reitman's arrest and imprisonment in Ohio, see *ME* 11 (January 1917), pp. 730–32 and Ben Reitman, "The Cleveland Myth," 11 (February 1917), pp. 761–66. Goldman described her conflict with comrades over the homosexuality lectures in *Living My Life,* p. 555.

15. *ME* 11 (October 1916), p. 647; Ben Reitman, "Why You Shouldn't Go to War—Refuse to Kill or Be Killed," *ME* 12 (April 1917), pp. 41–44 and "Conscription," *ME* 12 (June 1917), pp. 108–12; Emma Goldman, "The No Conscription League," *ME* 12 (June 1917), pp. 112–14 and "Between Jails" *ME* 12 (August 1917), pp. 207–12; Reitman to Norman Himes, April 1, 1937, NH-CL; Edwin A. Lahey, "Ben Reitman Pushes into Field of Social Pathology!" newspaper clipping, NH-CL; Reitman obituary, *Christian Century* 59 (December 2, 1942), p. 1499.

16. Reitman to Norman Himes, February 13, 1938, NH-CL.

17. Although Himes wrote "@ 1910" on the leaflet, Reitman stated in his unpublished autobiography, "Following the Monkey," that he wrote it in 1913 (pp. 328–32). Copy in Reitman Papers, University of Illinois, Chicago Circle. For comparison of "How and Why" with representative medical literature, pick any

of the articles cited under contraception in the *Index Catalogue of the Library of the Surgeon General's Office.*

Chapter 5

1. Agnes Repplier, "The Repeal of Reticence," *Atlantic Monthly* 103 (March 1914), pp. 293–304; "Sex O'Clock in America" *Current Opinion* 55 (August 1913), pp. 113–14. Both Repplier and *Current Opinion* are quoted in James R. McGovern, "The American Woman's Pre–World War I Freedom in Manners and Morals," *Journal of American History* 55 (September 1968), p. 316.

2. Daniel Scott Smith, "Family Limitation, Sexual Control, and Domestic Feminism in Victorian America," *Feminist Studies* 1 (Winter–Spring 1973), pp. 40–57. See also, Herman R. Lantz and Jane Keyes, "The American Family in the Preindustrial Period: From Base Lines in History to Change," *American Sociological Review* 40 (February 1975), pp. 21–36.

3. John Scanzoni, *Sexual Bargaining: Power Politics in the American Marriage* (Englewood Cliffs, N.J., 1972), pp. 31–46.

4. Andrew Sinclair, *The Emancipation of the American Woman* (New York, 1965), p. 100; Dee Garrison, "The Tender Technicians: The Feminization of Public Librarianship, 1876–1905," *Journal of Social History* (Winter 1972–73), pp. 131–59; Margery Davies, "Woman's Place Is at the Typewriter: The Feminization of the Clerical Labor Force," *Radical America* 8 (July–August 1974), pp. 1–28.

5. Jill K. Conway, "Women Reformers and American Culture, 1870–1930," *Journal of Social History* 5 (Winter 1971–72), pp. 164–77.

6. See "The Rise of the Companionate Family," Chapter 2 of this work; Alexis de Tocqueville, *Democracy in America* (New York, 1945; the Henry Reeve text as revised by Francis Bowen and further corrected and edited by Phillips Bradley), vol. 2, book 3, chs. 8–12; Frank J. Furstenberg, Jr., "Industrialization and the American Family: A Look Backward," *American Sociological Review* 31 (June 1966), pp. 326–37.

7. For discussion of the quality of husband-wife relations in the late nineteenth century, see Carl Degler, "What Ought to Be and What Was: Women's Sexuality in the Nineteenth Century," *American Historical Review* 79 (December 1974), pp. 1479–90. Degler's essentially positive evaluation is questioned by Carroll Smith Rosenberg, "A Gentler and a Richer Sex: Female Perspectives on Nineteenth-Century Sexuality," Paper Presented to the Third Berkshire Conference on the History of Women, June 11, 1976.

On the emergence of psychotherapy in the United States, see Nathan G. Hale, Jr., *Freud and the Americans: The Beginnings of Psychoanalysis in the United States, 1876–1917* (New York, 1971), pp. 116–50.

On prostitution, see David J. Pivar, *Purity Crusade: Sexual Morality and Social Control, 1868–1900* (Westport, Conn., 1973), pp. 30–32, and Howard B. Woolston, *Prostitution in the United States: Prior to the Entrance of the United States into the World War* (New York, 1920).

8. John C. Burnham, "The Progressive Era Revolution in American Attitudes toward Sex," *Journal of American History* 59 (March 1973), pp. 885–908; Charles W. Clarke, *Taboo: The Story of the Pioneers of Social Hygiene* (Washington, 1961), ch. 8; James F. Gardner, Jr. "Microbes and Morality: The Social Hygiene Crusade in New York City, 1892–1917" (Ph.D. dissertation, Indiana University, 1973), ch. 3.

9. Brand Whitlock, *Forty Years of It* (New York, 1914), pp. 278–79. Quoted in Louis Filler, *The Muckrakers: Crusaders for American Liberalism* (New York, 1939), p. 292; Egal Feldman, "Prostitution, the Alien Woman and the Progressive Imagination, 1910–1915," *American Quarterly* 29 (September 1967), pp. 192–206. On the close relationship between municipal reform and social hygiene, see Gardner, "Microbes and Morality," pp. 46–105.

10. McGovern, "The American Woman's Pre–World War I Freedom," pp. 318–22; Simon N. Patten, *The New Basis of Civilization* (Cambridge, Mass., 1968; 1st ed., 1907), ed. Daniel M. Fox.

11. William H. Chafe, *The American Woman: Her Changing Social, Economic, and Political Role, 1920–1970* (New York, 1972), pp. 55–56.

12. Richard N. Wertz and Dorothy C. Wertz, *Lying In: A History of Childbirth in America* (in press), ch. 6; Tom Mahoney and Leonard Sloane, *The Great Merchants* (New York, 1966), p. 249.

13. Wertz and Wertz, ch. 6; Brochure of the New England Twilight Sleep Association, Eliza Taylor Ransom Papers, The Schlesinger Library; Hannah Rion, *The Truth about Twilight Sleep* (New York, 1915); Marguerite Tracy and Mary Boyd, *Painless Childbirth* (New York, 1915).

14. Vern L. Bullough, *The Subordinate Sex: A History of Attitudes toward Women* (Urbana, Ill., 1973), p. 345.

15. Charlotte Teller, "The Neglected Psychology of Twilight Sleep," *Good Housekeeping* 61 (July 1915), pp. 18–23. Quoted in Wertz and Wetz.

16. Quoted in McGovern, p. 323.

17. Lewis A. Erenberg, "Everybody's Doin' It: The Pre–World War I Dance Craze, the Castles, and the Modern American Girl," *Feminist Studies* 3 (Fall 1975), pp. 158–59.

18. Alfred Kinsey et al., *Sexual Behavior in the Human Female* (Philadelphia, 1953), pp. 267–69, 300, 330–32. The changes Kinsey described among the upper-middle class might have begun much earlier among the lower-middle and working classes. See, Daniel Scott Smith, "The Dating of the American Sexual Revolution: Evidence and Interpretation" in *The American Family in Social-Historical Perspective*, ed. Michael Gordon (New York, 1973), pp. 328, 330–32. Unfortunately, Kinsey's study is the only comprehensive, large-scale analysis we have of sexual behavior among American women in the first half of the twentieth century.

19. Ira L. Reiss, *Premarital Sexual Standards in America* (Glencoe, Ill., 1960), pp. 126–45.

20. Reiss, pp. 183–92; Kinsey, pp. 358–59, 371–73.

Chapter 6

1. Harold Hersey, *Margaret Sanger: The Biography of the Birth Control Pioneer* (New York, 1938), p. 73. Hersey was a poet and journalist who fell in love with Margaret Sanger in 1917 and contributed much time and effort to her various publications. From the autumn of 1920 to the autumn of 1921 he was the anonymous managing editor of *Birth Control Review*. After Sanger ended their affair in 1921, Hersey began gathering materials for a biography of her. He interviewed many of her old radical friends, her neighbors in Hastings-on-Hudson, and most of her relatives, and was a personal friend of William Sanger, her first husband. In 1938, Hersey had completed his monument to unrequited love and sought Sanger's permission to publish the book. She was vehement in her opposition to the book both because she wanted to suppress knowledge of much of her past and because her autobiography was ready for press, and she did not want any competition. Hersey copyrighted his manuscript, and it was put into typescript, but the publisher, Pulp Press, went broke, and the book was never published. One suspects that Hersey really did not have his heart in getting the book published after Sanger unequivocally expressed her opposition.

Hersey's biography is an important source of information on Margaret Sanger and her experiences as a participant in the prewar cultural ferment. There are copies of the manuscript in the Sophia Smith Collection and the Manuscript Reading Room of the Library of Congress. For Hersey's personal relationship with Sanger, see Hersey to Margaret Sanger, November 27, 1920, and ff., MS-SS.

2. Margaret Sanger, *An Autobiography* (New York, 1938), pp. 18, 20–21, 31–32. Henceforth cited as *Autobiography*.

3. *Autobiography*, pp. 11, 28–29. For a specific reference to her father's longevity in comparison to her mother, see Helen Smith's interview with Sanger in *The New Yorker* (July 5, 1930), copy in MS-SS.

4. *Autobiography*, pp. 28, 24; Hersey, pp. 2, 43. Margaret Sanger often told Harold Hersey, "I never look back on my childhood with joy."

5. *Autobiography*, p. 35; in "Girlhood," manuscript notes written in preparing her autobiography, Sanger wrote that during her first weeks at Claverack, "I was lonely and homesick, but I never wanted to return home." MS-SS.

6. *Autobiography*, pp. 37, 40, 41–42; Hersey, p. 85.

7. Ibid., pp. 13, 16, 17, 20, 30, 38, 43–45.

8. Ibid., pp. 41–45.

9. Ibid., pp. 49, 53; Margaret Sanger to Philip Burke, feature editor of *The Fluoroscope*, June 5, 1935, MS-LC. (Hersey, pp. 71, 75.)

10. Ibid., pp. 56–57, 58–61. Cf. Hersey, p. 81.

11. Margaret Sanger to Mary Higgins, May 12, 1902, MS-LC.

12. Margaret Sanger to Nan Higgins, n.d. (August 1902); William Sanger to Mary Higgins, August 18, 1902, MS-LC.
They were married on August 18, 1902. Margaret's two older sisters, Mary and Nan, never married, and they had sacrificed to send her to Claverack. The tone of her letters to them in part reflected her need to justify an act which they might believe was making their efforts on her behalf useless. Still, Margaret's resentment at being "forced" into marriage was real and was increased by her sense of having let her sisters down.

13. *Autobiography*, pp. 58–61.

14. Ibid., pp. 62, 64.

15. Hersey, pp. 86, 92; *Autobiography*, pp. 66, 435.

16. Hersey, p. 92; Hutchins Hapgood, *A Victorian in the Modern World* (New York, 1939), p. 170.

17. *Autobiography*, pp. 66–67.

18. *Autobiography*, pp. 68–73; Alexander Berkman to Margaret Sanger, December 9, 1915, and September 26, 1924, MS-SS; William Sanger to Margaret Sanger, September 3, 1913, and December 8, 1914, MS-SS.

19. Margaret Sanger, "What Every Girl Should Know: The Censored Article," Scrapbook II, MS-LC.

20. Nineteenth century feminists used the term "sex slavery" to denote the separation of human activities into two separate spheres on the basis of gender. Woman was a "sex slave" not only because she was forced to marry and have sexual relations with man to support herself, but because she was denied any alternative by the belief that women were not suited for most kinds of useful work. Charlotte Perkins Gilman's *Woman and Economics* (New York, 1966; first published 1898) is the classic exposition of the denial of woman's humanity through her exclusion from equal opportunity to work.

21. Margaret Sanger, "Comstockery in America," speech delivered in England, 1915, MS-LC.

22. Clippings from Hazelton newspapers, Scrapbook II, MS-LC.

23. David A. Shannon, *The Socialist Party of America* (New York, 1955), pp. 70–71; Patrick Renshaw, *The Wobblies: The Story of Syndicalism in America* (New York, 1967), pp. 98–103; *Autobiography*, pp. 80–84.

24. Renshaw, pp. 109–11; Clippings in Scrapbook II, MS-LC; *Autobiography*, pp. 81–83.

25. Renshaw, pp. 112–18; Mabel Dodge Luhan, *Movers and Shakers* (New York, 1936), pp. 200, 212; Henry May, *The End of American Innocence* (New York, 1959), pp. 313–14.

26. *Autobiography*, p. 85; William Sanger to Margaret Sanger, September 3, 1913, MS-SS; M. S. Boyd quoted in Hersey, p. 110.

27. *Autobiography*, pp. 79, 85; Sanger, *Pivot of Civilization* (New York, 1922), p. 5.

28. *Pivot of Civilization*, pp. 6–8, 163.

29. *Autobiography*, pp. 14–15, 21, 22, 27.

30. *Woman and the New Race* (New York, 1920), p. 234; *Autobiography*, pp. 21–22, 71–72, 75. In her "Journal" (MS-SS) Sanger noted on October 1, 1928: "Hoover and Smith in race [for] Presidency. Much excitement and interest. We are for Hoover—tho ordinarily I'd be for Norman Thomas—except that Al Smith must be kept out." In 1960, Margaret Sanger made headlines by announcing she would leave the country if the Roman Catholic, John F. Kennedy, was elected president. The incident began when Norman Thomas wrote Sanger suggesting she raise the issue of birth control and Senator Kennedy's position as a Catholic candidate for president. Thomas, then, was the instigator of what turned out to be a most embarrassing incident for Sanger. There is a whole box of material on the incident at Smith. See Norman Thomas to Margaret Sanger, January 5, 1960.

31. *Autobiography*, pp. 72, 86–87.

32. See clippings in Scrapbook II, MS-LC; *Autobiography*, pp. 76–79; Lawrence Lader, *The Margaret Sanger Story* (New York, 1955), pp. 36–37.

33. *Autobiography*, p. 55; *Woman and the New Race* p. 213.

34. *Autobiography*, pp. 86–92.

35. Morris Kahn, "A Municipal Birth Control Clinic," *New York Medical Journal* 54 (April 28, 1917). Reprint MS-LC.

36. *Autobiography*, pp. 86–92.

37. David M. Kennedy, *Birth Control in America: The Career of Margaret Sanger* (New Haven, Conn., 1970), pp. 17–18.

38. Hutchins Hapgood, *The Spirit of the Ghetto* (New York, 1902); Moses Rischin, *The Promised City: New York Jews, 1870–1914* (Cambridge, Mass., 1962); Hersey, p. 81; *Autobiography*, pp. 89, 106.

39. Compare "How and Why the Poor Should Not Have Many Chilren" circa 1913, NH-CL, or Margaret Sanger, *Family Limitation*, first edition, 1914, MS-SS, with any of the articles listed in the *Index Catalogue of the Library of the Surgeon General's Office*. The addition of illustrations to Sanger's pamphlet circa 1915 made it by far the most authoritative work on contraception available until Robert Latou Dickinson published a well-illustrated article in the *American Journal of Obstetrics and Gynecology* 8 (November, 1924) pp. 583–604.

40. *Autobiography*, p. 96; Margaret Sanger, "Diary, November 1914, January 1915." See entries for December 16, 17, 1914, MS-LC.

41. William Sanger to Margaret Sanger, September 3, 1913; December 28, 1913; January 14, 1914; January 20, 1914; January 22, 1914; January 28, 1914, MS-SS. For a discussion of Sanger's painting, see Harold Hersey, "William Sanger, Man and Artist," *The Call* (November 9, 1919).

42. Mabel Dodge Luhan, *Movers and Shakers* (New York, 1936), pp. 69–71.

43. "Cannibals," *The Woman Rebel* 1 (May 1914), p. 1.

44. *The Masses* (May 1914), p. 5; Emma Goldman to Sanger, May 26, 1914, and December 7, 1915, MS-LC.

45. "Fabian Hall Address: July 5, 1915," MS-LC.

46. Ibid.

47. For attacks on Davis, see clipping dated August 11, 1914, MS-LC; for Davis's later cooperation, see Davis to Sanger, October 6, 1925, MS-LC and Chapter 9 below.

48. *Autobiography*, pp. 109–20.

Chapter 7

1. F. H. Amphlett Micklewright, "The Rise and Decline of English Neo-Malthusianism," *Population Studies* 15 (1961), pp. 32–51.

2. Ibid.; Peter Fryer, *The Birth Controllers* (New York, 1966), Parts 2 and 3, pp. 43–192. The two most important American physicians inspired by Owen were Charles Knowlton and Frederick Hollick.

3. Keynes thought England was overpopulated. Important Fabians including George Bernard Shaw and H. G. Wells supported population control through the spread of contraception. Marx never attacked contraception but only the pessimism he believed Malthus inspired. Lenin made a careful distinction between contraceptive practice as a means of freeing women and neo-Malthusian propaganda which he deplored. Nevertheless, proponents of Fabianism, Marxism, and Keynesianism generally dismissed the idea that controlled population growth was essential if living standards for everyone were to be raised. Richard Symonds and Michael Carder, *The United Nations and the Population Question* (New York, 1973), pp. 6, 20–21.

4. *Margaret Sanger, My Fight for Birth Control,* (New York, 1931), pp. 98–101, 103–4.

5. Edward Brecher, *The Sex Researchers* (Boston, 1969), ch. 1; Joseph Wortis, *Fragments of an Analysis with Freud* (New York, 1954), pp. 11–12, 65, 91–92, 113, 171–79; "Havelock Ellis," *Recent Advances in Biological Psychiatry* (New York, 1960), pp. 186–99; Havelock Ellis, *My Life* (Boston, 1939), pp. 76–77.

Wortis provides an admirable critique of Freud which reflects many of Ellis' views in "Retrospect and Conclusions," *Fragments of An Analysis*, pp. 185–203. Sanger described her meeting with Ellis in *My Fight*, p. 102, and *Autobiography*, pp. 133–35. The "supreme triumph of human idealism" is the last line in *Erotic Symbolism* (Philadelphia, 1906).

6. Havelock Ellis, *Sex in Relation to Society* (Philadelphia, 1911), pp. 116, 176–77, 213, 216; "Morality as an Art," *Atlantic Monthly* 114 (November 1914), pp. 700–7.

7. Brecher, pp. 37–38; Ellis, *Auto-Erotism* (Philadelphia, 1900), p. 203. Paul Robinson provides an excellent analysis of Ellis' place in the history of sex research in *The Modernization of Sex* (New York, 1976). Unfortunately this work came to my attention too late for me to incorporate his insights.

8. Ellis, *My Life*, pp. 84–86.

9. Ellis, *Impressions and Comments, 1920–1923* (London, 1924), p. 60.

10. Ellis, *My Life*, p. 106.

11. Françoise Delisle, *Friendship's Odyssey* (London, 1946), pp. 277–79.

12. Margaret Sanger to Vincent Brome, January 6, 1954, MS-SS.

13. Havelock Ellis to Margaret Sanger, February 2, 1915; January 27, 1915, MS-LC.

14. Ellis, *My Life*, p. 521.

15. Sanger, *My Fight*, pp. 107–16; Fryer, *The Birth Controllers*, p. 318, n. 24; Aletta Jacobs, "A Generation of Birth Control in Holland," in *International Aspects of Birth Control*, ed. Margaret Sanger (New York, 1925), pp. 85–94. Margaret Sanger's claim that she learned that better conditions existed in Holland while studying in the British Museum is contradicted by an article in *The Woman Rebel* (May 1914), p. 18, which claimed great benefits to the poor in Holland through birth control centers. This was a common point in neo-Malthusian propaganda. The Dutch league was begun after a visit by C. R. Drysdale in 1879. For an accurate description of the Dutch system of birth control "clinics," see Robert L. Dickinson, "Contraception: A Medical Review of the Situation," *American Journal of Obstetrics and Gynecology* 8 (November 1924), pp. 597–98.

16. Sanger, *My Fight*, pp. 110, 113.

17. *Family Limitation* (1st ed., 1914), p. 6. Copy in MS-SS.

18. William D. Haywood to Margaret Sanger, February 1, 1919, MS-SS.

19. Quoted in Harold Hersey, *Margaret Sanger*, p. 110. Hersey was for the war and had just been commissioned a lieutenant in the army. When he showed up for a meeting at her home in his uniform, she told him, "I don't know what to say about your entrance into the army. You are the first man in uniform to enter my house. I'm against all war, just as my father is—just as all my friends and associates are—but if I take a stand against it, become an active pacifist, the Birth Control movement will suffer. I cannot let this happen just as I have gotten order out of chaos."

Chapter 8

1. Margaret Sanger, *Autobiography* (New York, 1938), pp. 107–8.
2. Sanger, *My Fight for Birth Control* (New York, 1931) pp. 119–21, 123, 128; William Sanger to Margaret Sanger, January 17, January 21, September 3, September 10, September 12, September 14, September 27, October 6, 1915; Margaret Sanger to William Sanger, October 13, 1915, MS-SS.
3. Sanger, *My Fight*, pp. 126–28, 137–40.
4. Mary Ware Dennett, *Birth Control Laws* (New York, 1926), p. 67. Margaret Sanger's claim that she founded the National Birth Control League before she left in 1914 is specious; Francis Vreeland, "The Process of Reform" (Ph.D. dissertation, University of Michigan, 1929), pp. 66–77. For plans for a birth control league, see *The Woman Rebel*, March, May, and July, 1914. For a list of members of the National Birth Control League, see *Survey* 34 (April 1915), p. 5 Cf. Sanger, *Autobiography*, p. 108.
5. Chrisopher Lasch, "Mary Ware Dennett," *Notable American Women*, vol. 1 (Cambridge, Mass., 1971), pp. 463–65.
6. Sanger, *My Fight*, pp. 124–25.
7. Ibid., pp. 141–42.
8. Margaret Sanger to Lawrence Lader, December 3, 1953, MS-SS.
9. Dennett, *Birth Control Laws*, p. 73.
10. Ibid., pp. 74, 88–89, 115, 180.
11. Ibid., pp. 74, 176–80; Sanger quoted p. 188.
12. Ibid., pp. 88–89.
13. Ibid., pp. 94–96, 164–65.
14. Ibid., pp. 80–81; Lasch, "Mary Ware Dennett"; Vreeland, "Process of Reform," pp. 98–99.
15. Ibid., pp. 212, 255.
16. C. Thomas Dienes, *Law, Politics, and Birth Control* (Urbana, Ill., 1972), pp. 189–91, 195–96.
17. For discussion of the one exception that proves the rule, see *Autobiography*, pp. 426–27.
18. *Birth Control Review* (January 1919), p. 2. Quoted in Dienes, p. 82.
19. Margaret Sanger, *Birth Control: The Proceedings of the First American Birth Control Conference* (New York, 1922), pp. 91–92. Quoted in Dienes, p. 82.
20. In the *One Package* decision of 1936, discussed in the next chapter.
21. This document is among the papers of the American Birth Control League at Houghton Library (Harvard University) and is titled "Congressional Report: January 1 to May 1, 1926." Included in it is a 68-page "Short Synopsis of Interviews with Senators." All of the quotes below are from the "Short Synopsis."
22. G. Stanley Hall to Mary Lawrence East (Mrs. Edward M. East), December 13, 1916, Blanche Ames Papers, Sophia Smith Collection.

Chapter 9

1. Margaret Sanger, *My Fight for Birth Control* (New York, 1931), p. 157; *People of New York* v. *Margaret Sanger*, p. 5, MS-SS.
2. *People of New York* v. *Margaret Sanger*, pp. 4, 5, 25; "Original Speech Given by Margaret Sanger in 1916," MS-LC, p. 19; Elizabeth Steyvesant, "The Brownsville Birth Control Clinic," *Birth Control Review* (March 1917), p. 8. Steyvesant served as baby-sitter at the clinic. She claimed that the police matron, whom both she and Fania Mindell recognized, had inisted on paying two dollars for a pessary, and "No one else purchased anything but friendly advice, counsel and instruction, which was 'sold' for the

nominal registration fee of ten cents—to such as could pay that much." Sanger apparently deliberately sold the pessary to the policewoman in order to insure police intervention.

3. 179 Appellate Division New York 939.

4. Sanger, *The Case for Birth Control* (New York, 1917).

5. *People of New York* v. *Margaret Sanger*, p. 26.

6. 222 New York, pp. 192–95; "Minutes of Executive Meeting," Appendix B, Committee on Maternal Health, June 11, 1929, RLD-CL.

7. C. Thomas Dienes, *Law, Politics, and Birth Control* (Urbana, Ill., 1972), p. 87.

8. Sanger, *My Fight*, pp. 162–66, 170, 178, 185–86; Francis Vreeland, "The Process of Reform with Especial Reference to Reform Groups in the Field of Population" (Ph.D. dissertation, University of Michigan, 1929), p. 85.

9. The best sellers were *Woman and the New Race* (New York, 1920) and *The Pivot of Civilization* (New York, 1922). On the founding of the *Birth Control Review*, see *My Fight*, pp. 191–92; on founding of American Birth Control League, see *My Fight*, p. 212. On the banned movie, see *Message PhotoPlay* v. *George Bell*, MS-SS. Sanger discusses her marriage to J. Noah Slee in *Autobiography*, pp. 355–57. On the Far East tour, see *My Fight*, pp. 238–70.

10. Sanger, *My Fight*, p. 190.

11. William Sanger to Margaret Sanger, September 14, 1915; September 21, 1915; September 27, 1915, MS-SS; Sanger, *My Fight*, p. 191; Sanger, *Autobiography*, p. 232; Vreeland, pp. 86–87.

12. Ethel Byrne to Margaret Sanger, n.d., MS-SS.

13. Dorothy Brush, "Impressions of Margaret Sanger," MS-SS.

14. Ibid.

15. Sanger, *My Fight*, pp. 191–94; *Autobiography*, pp. 253–54, 260–61; Vreeland, pp. 88, 92, 251–52. For Blossom's appeal to the Socialist Party and Sanger's response, see the material in MS-SS; Sanger, *Woman and the New Race*, p. 216.

16. *My Fight*, pp. 211–13; *Autobiography*, pp. 299–301.

17. *My Fight*, pp. 212–18; *Autobiography*, pp. 302–5.

18. *My Fight*, pp. 221–25; *Autobiography*, pp. 307–9.

19. *My Fight*, pp. 219–20, 237.

20. Ibid., pp. 238–54.

21. Keith Briant, *Passionate Paradox: The Life of Marie Stopes* (New York, 1962), pp. 116–17, 134, 138–39, 151–52; Mary Ware Dennett, *Birth Control Laws* (New York, 1926), pp. 201, 206, 208, 254; Mary Ware Dennett to Alice Park, May 17, 1925, Suffrage Collection-Sophia Smith; Margaret Sanger to Norman Himes, December 28, 1931, MS-LC. There is an interesting attack on Marie Stopes in Emily T. Douglas, *Pioneer of the Future: Margaret Sanger* (New York, 1970), pp. 152–53.

22. Dorothy Brush, "J. Noah Slee" MS-SS; *Autobiography*, p. 357. Joan Dash provides a detailed account of Sanger's second marriage in *A Life of One's Own: Three Gifted Women and the Men They Married* (New York, 1973), pp. 69–113.

23. For analysis of the ABCL's early financial records, see Vreeland, pp. 249–52.

24. "Resume-Dorothy Bocker," MS-LC; Cablegram, Clinton Chance to Margaret Sanger, Nobember 3, 1922; Margaret Sanger to Dorothy Bocker, October 17, 1922, MS-LC; J. Noah Slee to Dorothy Bocker, December 29, 1922, MS-LC; *My Fight*, pp. 312–15; *Autobiography*, pp. 358–60.

25. Dorothy Bocker, *Birth Control Methods* (printed privately, New York, 1924), p. 1; Unsigned memorandum, J. Noah Slee, November 25, 1925, MS-LC.

26. "Reminiscences of Herbert R. Simonds," pp. 44, 83, MS-SS; Anne Kennedy, "History of the Development of Contraceptive Materials in the United States," *American Medicine* 41 (1935), pp. 159–61; Sanger, *Autobiography*, pp. 363–64.

27. "Contraception: A Medical Review of the Situation," *American Journal of Obstetrics and Gynecology* 8 (November 1924), p. 587; Ettie Rout to Margaret Sanger, December 26, 1924, MS-SS.

28. Margaret Sanger, "Journal," January 1, 1925, MS-SS.

29. Bocker, *Birth Control Methods*, pp. 23–24; Anne Kennedy, "History of Contraceptive Materials," p. 159; Hannah Stone, "Therapeutic Contraception," *Medical Journal and Record* 6 (March 21, 1928), pp. 8–17; "Hannah Stone—In Memorium," *Human Fertility* 6 (August 1941), pp. 108–13; Sanger, *Autobiography*, p. 360; *My Fight*, p. 291. Hannah Stone to Margaret Sanger, March 27, 1932, MS-LC, describes one failure to gain membership in the County Medical Society. There is an interesting description of a fictional Hannah Stone in Mary McCarthy, *The Group* (New York, 1963), ch. 3.

30. Margaret Sanger to J. Noah Slee, February 22, 1925, MS-LC.

31. S. Adolphus Knopf, "James F. Cooper," *Medical Journal and Record* (May 20, 1931), reprint MS-LC; James F. Cooper to Clara L. Rowe, July 19, 1933, and to Margaret Sanger, September 14, 1923, ABCL-Houghton. For itineraries and reports of Cooper's nationwide tours, see boxes 4, 5, 6, 11, 12, ABCL-Houghton.

32. Reply to Questionnaire on Birth Control Movement Compiled for John Price Jones Corporation: 1930, MS-LC.

33. Katharine B. Davis to Margaret Sanger, October 6, 1925, MS-LC; Margaret Sanger to Raymond Fosdick, March 24, 1931, MS-LC.

34. Most of the testing of new methods, as well as the analysis of the social and economic position of those seeking contraceptive advice, was conducted by the Clinical Research Bureau, but as Sanger explained in 1937 to a conference on contraceptive research sponsored by the clinic, although she was proud of the clinic's thirteen-year record as a teaching and research facility, "the outstanding achievement of this bureau has been to . . . give contraceptive advice to more than 56,000 women who voluntarily appealed to us for the advice." See "Conference on Contraceptive Research, December 29–30, 1936," CJG-CL; Margaret Sanger to Raymond Fosdick, January 10, 1931, MS-LC; "Minutes of Board of Managers of the Clinical Research Bureau," January 7, 1931, MS-LC.

35. "Annual Report of the Birth Control Clinical Research Bureau, December 1, 1929–November 1, 1930," MS-LC; Margaret Sanger to Raymond Pearl, August 28, 1923, ABCL-Houghton; Important studies based on the clinic's records include, Marie Kopp, *Birth Control in Practice* (New York, 1934), and Regine K. Stix and Frank Notestein, *Controlled Fertility* (Baltimore, 1940); *Birth Control Clinical Research Bureau's List of Clinics and Centers*, CJG-CL.

36. Margaret Sanger to Michael Davis, March 24, 1931 and June 30, 1931, MS-LC; "Harlem Birth Control Bureau Officially Opens," News release MS-LC; Clipping from *Amsterdam News*, March 5, 1938, MS-LC; Memo by E. D. Jenkins, social worker at the Harlem Clinic, n.d., MS-LC; Margaret Sanger to Nathan Lewis, comptroller of the Julius Rosenwald Fund, February 18, 1932, MS-LC.

37. Charles Johnson to Margaret Sanger, November 17, 1921, and May 16, 1922; "Application for Dispensary License," May 12, 1922, and Nobember 21, 1925, MS-LC.

38. "Minutes of the Staff Meeting of the Clinical Research Bureau," April 29, 1929; Margaret Sanger to Hannah Stone, January 31, 1933, MS-LC.

39. *New York Times*, January 23, 1973, p. 1; Marjorie A. Prevost, Assistant Director, BCCRB, to Margaret Sanger, February 15, 1932, MS-LC.

40. "Report to Executive Committee, Committee on Maternal Health, June 11, 1929," RLD-CL; Sanger, *My Fight*, p. 321.

41. "Academy Action in Present Birth Control Seizures," *Bulletin of the New York Academy of Medicine*, Second Series 5 (1929), pp. 461–66; Sanger, *My Fight*, p. 322.

42. Sanger, *My Fight*, p. 321.

43. Margaret Sanger to Michael Davis, April 29, 1930, MS-LC.

44. Sanger, *Autobiography*, p. 427.

45. Ibid., pp. 404, 406; *A New Day Dawns for Birth Control: Concluding Report of the National Committee on Federal Legislation For Birth Control* (n.p., July 1937), pp. 9, 41.

46. 13 F. Supp. 334 (E.D.N.Y. 1936), affirmed 86 F. 2d 737 (2d Cir. 1936); Morris Ernst, quoted in *National Birth Control News* (February 1937), p. 6; C. Thomas Dienes, *Law, Politics, and Birth Control*, pp. 108–15.

47. Margaret Sanger to Penelope Huse, September 25, 1938, MS-SS.

48. Ansley J. Coale and Melvin Zelnik, *New Estimates of Fertility and Population in the United States* (Princeton, N.J., 1963), p. 36; Wilson H. Grabill, Clyde V. Kiser, and Pascal Whelpton, *The Fertility of American Women* (New York, 1958), pp. 38–39, 381.

49. Margaret Sanger to Robert L. Dickinson, February 20, 1942, RLD-CL. Part of this paragraph is based on a newsreel pitch for birth control given by Margaret Sanger in the 1930s during which she specifically named epileptics as a group which should not have children. Her views on qualification for parenthood are, however, succinctly stated in *Woman and the New Race*, pp. 78–90. She concluded, "No matter how much they desire children no man and woman have the right to bring into the world those who are to suffer mental or physical affliction." "In brief, a woman should avoid having children unless both she and the father are in such physical and mental condition as to assure the child a healthy physical and mental being."

In *Pivot of Civilization*, pp. 188–89, she argued, "Our problem is not that of 'Nature vs. Nurture,' but rather of Nature × Nurture, of heredity multiplied by environment. The Eugenicist who overlooks the importance of environment as a determining factor in human life is as short-sighted as the Socialist who neglects the biological nature of man. We cannot disentangle the two forces, except in theory." Sanger's relationship to the eugenics movement is discussed in the next chapter.

50. "Process of Reform," pp. 271–72, 275–76.

51. William J. Robinson, the muckraking physician, and Judge Ben Lindsey, the juvenile court pioneer from Denver, both noted receiving large numbers of letters asking for contraceptive information. See Victor Robinson, *Pioneers of Birth Control* (New York, 1919), pp. 68–69; Charles Larsen, *The Good Fight: The Life and Times of Ben B. Lindsey* (Chicago, 1972), pp. 178–79; Vreeland, p. 273; Sanger, *Motherhood in Bondage* (New York, 1928); *Autobiography*, pp. 361–62; Margaret Sanger to Mary Compton, March 17, 1942, MS-SS.

52. I am indebted to Paul H. Gebhard and Alan B. Johnson of the Institute for Sex Research for providing me with this data. Any errors in interpretation are my own. An excellent description of how the Kinsey team collected their data is provided by Wardell B. Pomeroy, *Dr. Kinsey and the Institute for Sex Research* (New York, 1972), pp. 106–37, 369–71.

I have not made use of the data from all of the sex histories gathered by the Kinsey team but only data on the married, white women who were not in prison (nondelinquents). Some subjects reported "much use" of more than one method.

It is not possible to determine when the contraceptive practice reported in these interviews took place. Thus, women born before 1899 might have been referring to contraceptive practice throughout their fertile years or during the 1920s or during any time in their lives. This data does give an indication of how contraceptive practice changed among four cohorts of married women. Although women born before 1899 might have had all of their experience with the diaphragm in any span of time before they were interviewed, they clearly had less experience with this method than younger women and more experience with douching and withdrawal.

53. Only 3 of the 323 women born before 1899 reported "much use" of rhythm; 12 of 560 born 1900–09; 23 of 867 born 1910–19; 8 of 578 born 1920–29.

Only 13 of the 323 women born before 1899 reported "much use" of jelly or suppositories; 18 of 560 born 1900–09; 17 of 867 born 1910–19; 8 of 578 born 1920–29.

54. See "Policing the Market Place," ch. 18 below, pp. 244–45.

55. These figures are drawn from a monograph written after Kinsey's death by the staff of the Institute for Sex Research. See Paul Gebhard et al., *Pregnancy, Birth, and Abortion* (New York, 1958), Table 46, p. 131.

56. On the representativeness of Kinsey's subjects, see William C. Cochran, Frederick Mosteller, and John Turkey, *Statistical Problems of the Kinsey Report* (Washington, 1954) and ch. 2, "The Sample," in Gebhard et al., *Pregnancy, Birth, and Abortion*, pp. 11–29.

57. Gebhard et al., *Pregnancy, Birth, and Abortion*, pp. 22–23 and Table 7, p. 22.

58. Dr. Mudd's oral history, taped between May 21 and August 3, 1974, has been transcribed and is available to scholars at The Schlesinger Library, Radcliffe College.

59. Mudd interview, p. 23.

60. Ibid., p. 28.

61. Ibid., p. 30.

62. Ibid., pp. 156–61.

63. For interesting studies of the clientele of the Clinical Research Bureau, see Marie Kopp, *Birth Control in Practice* (New York, 1934) and Regine K. Stix and Frank W. Notestein, *Controlled Fertility: An Evaluation of Clinic Studies* (Baltimore, 1940). Christopher Tietze's *Selected Bibliography of Contraception, 1940–1960* (National Committee on Maternal Health, Publication No. 6, 1960) provides the historian with a convenient source for studies of clinic patients before 1960.

Chapter 10

1. Quoted from William Morehouse, "The Speaking of Margaret Sanger in the Birth Control Movement from 1916 to 1937" (Ph.D. dissertation, Purdue University, 1968), p. 38.

2. *The Works of Robert G. Ingersoll* (New York, 1900), vol. 4, pp. 502–4. Quoted in Herman E. Kittredge, *Ingersoll: A Biographical Appreciation* (New York, 1911), pp. 330–31.

3. John L. Thomas, "Utopia for an Urban Age: Henry George, Henry Demarest Lloyd, Edward Bellamy," *Perspectives in American History*, ed. Donald Fleming and Bernard Bailyn, 6 (1972), pp. 135–63.

4. Arthur Calder-Marshall, *Havelock Ellis* (London, 1959), p. 86.

5. Charlotte Perkins Gilman, "Progress through Birth Control," *North American Review* 224 (December 1927), pp. 627, 628.

6. *Everyone Was Brave: A History of Feminism in America* (Chicago, 1969), pp. 313, 342–43.

7. Donald K. Pickens, *Eugenics and the Progressives* (Nashville, Tenn., 1968), ch. 5, pp. 69–85.

8. Crystal Eastman, "Birth Control in the Feminist Program," *Birth Control Review* (January 1918), p. 3.

9. Harriet Stanton Blatch to Margaret Sanger, October 27, 1923, ABCL-Houghton.

10. "Progress through Birth Control," pp. 622–29.

11. Carrie Chapman Catt to Margaret Sanger, November 24, 1920, MS-LC.

12. Vida Scudder to Margaret Sanger, June 21, 1952, MS-SS.

13. Margaret Sanger to Vida Scudder, July 13, 1952, MS-SS.

14. Margaret Sanger to Kitty Marion, January 18, 1935, MS-LC.

15. Margaret Sanger to Carrie Chapman Catt, February 12, 1940, MS-LC; Margaret Sanger, "Hotel Commodore Luncheon Speech," MS-LC.

16. Margaret Sanger to James A. Field, June 5, 1923, ABCL-Houghton; Anna Lifshiz to J. Noah Slee, September 12, 1928, MS-LC.

17. Minutes of the Committee on Maternal Health, November 10, 1924, RLD-CL; Mark Haller, *Eugenics: Hereditarian Attitudes in American Thought* (New Brunswick, N.J., 1963), pp. 91, 221, n. 50; Harry H. Laughlin to Margaret Sanger, March 24, 1923, ABCL-Houghton.

18. Clarence Gamble to Board of Directors, Planned Parenthood Federation of America, March 16, 1946, MS-SS; Margaret Sanger to Clarance Gamble, March 29, 1946, MS-SS; Edward East to Margaret Sanger, May 15, 1925, ABCL-Houghton.

19. By the early twenties professional geneticists had become alarmed by the misuse of science by the eugenicists, most of whom were ignorant of the latest advances in genetics which showed the complexity of human inheritance. See Kenneth M. Ludmerer, "American Geneticists and the Eugenics Movement: 1905–1935," *Journal of the History of Biology* 2 (1969), pp. 337–65 and *Genetics and American Society* (Baltimore, 1972).

20. Haller, *Eugenics*, pp. 64–66; *Autobiography*, pp. 374–75.

21. *Woman and the New Race,* p. 68.

22. *The Pivot of Civilization,* pp. 24–27, 179–89.

23. Round Table Discussion, "The Eugenic Effect of Contraception: The Significance of the Decline in the Birth Rate," National Committee on Maternal Health, May 13, 1937, RLD-CL; Haller, *Eugenics,* pp. 174–75.

24. Margaret Sanger to Cecile Damon, December 24, 1939; Margaret Sanger to Mary Lasker, January 8, 1943, MS-SS. From the perspective of the 1970s the caution of some members of the Planned Parenthood Federation does seem extreme. The following quote from the Minutes of the Executive Committee, December 1, 1942, is representative. "Dr. Eastman felt that there had been criticism of too liberal standards for clinics, in that they will give contraceptive advice to any married woman." He had, therefore, prepared a more restrictive set of medical indications for distribution to affiliated clinics.

25. William Morehouse, "The Speaking of Margaret Sanger in the Birth Control Movement from 1916 to 1937," p. 160.

26. For late love affairs, see Sanger's correspondence with Angus S. Macdonald and with Hobson Pitman, MS-SS; *Woman and the New Race,* pp. 116–17 and passim.

27. *The Pivot of Civilization,* pp. 189, 218–19; *Woman and the New Race,* pp. 34–36.

28. David M. Kennedy provides a searching critique of the limitations of Sanger's vision and of her fellow traveling with eugenicists, nativists, and conservatives in Chapter 4, "Revolution and Repression," of *Birth Control in America: The Career of Margaret Sanger* (New Haven, Conn., 1970), pp. 108–26.

Chapter 11

1. For critiques of some of the effects of professionalism, see Gerald E. Markowitz and David Karl Rosner, "Doctors in Crisis: A Study of the Use of Medical Education Reform to Establish Modern Professional Elitism in Medicine," *American Quarterly* 25 (March 1973), pp. 83–107.

2. George W. Kosmak, "Birth Control: What Shall Be the Attitude of the Medical Profession toward the Present-Day Propaganda?" *Medical Record* 91 (1917), pp. 268–73.

3. *Medical Follies* (New York, 1925), p. 142. For an excellent discussion of the Sheppard-Towner Act and its opponents, see J. Stanley Lemons, "The Sheppard-Towner Act: Progressivism in the 1920's," *Journal of American History* 55 (March 1969), pp. 776–86.

For insights into Fishbein's attitude toward women, see the oral history interview of Emily H. Mudd, Ph.D., in the Schlesinger Library, Radcliffe College, pp. 124–27.

4. David M. Kennedy, *Birth Control in America: The Career of Margaret Sanger* (New Haven, Conn., 1971), pp. 176–79.

5. *Medical Follies,* pp. 55–58, 218–20.

6. Ibid., pp. 142–49.

7. *Technique of Contraception* (New York, 1928), pp. 23–24.

8. A discussion of the involvement of doctors in social reform is provided by John C. Burnham, "Medical Specialists and Movement toward Social Control in the Progressive Era: Three Examples," in *Building the Organizational Society,* ed. Jerry Israel (New York, 1971). See also Charles W. Clarke, *Taboo: The Story of the Pioneers of Social Hygiene* (Washington, 1961); Richard H. Shryock, *National Tuberculosis Association, 1904–1954; A Study of the Voluntary Health Movement in the United States* (New York, 1957); James H. Cassedy, *Charles V. Chapin and the Public Health Movement* (Cambridge, Mass., 1962); Greer Williams, *The Plague Killers: Untold Stories of the Great Campaigns Against Disease* (New York, 1969).

9. Burnham, "Medical Specialists and Movements toward Social Control"; Williams, *The Plague Killers,* Part 1.

10. Robert L. Dickinson and Lura Beam, *The Single Woman: A Study in Sex Education* (New York, 1934), p. 4.

11. Robert L. Dickinson, "Medical Notes on the Sex Life of the Unmarried Adult" in *The Sex Life of the Unmarried Adult*, ed. Ira S. Wile (New York, 1935). Reprint RLD-CL.

12. Lura Beam to George Barbour, November 18, 1960. RLD-CL.

13. Interview with Dorothy Dickinson Barbour (Mrs. George Barbour), Cincinnati, Ohio, June 2, 1971. Mrs. Barbour was Dickinson's eldest daughter.

14. This section is based on two documents: Incidents in a Happy Life, Dickinson's reminiscences, recorded in December 1949 by his son-in-law, George Barbour, and transcribed, and R. L. D.: The Life of Robert Latou Dickinson, 1861–1950, a biography in manuscript by Barbour covering the period to roughly 1900. R. L. D. contains generous abstracts from Dickinson's early diaries and correspondence. These documents are not among the Dickinson Papers in Countway Library but have been retained by his family. Two copies of both Incidents and R. L. D. have been deposited in Countway Library by Barbour. Barbour, R. L. D., pp. 7–9. Hereafter cited as Barbour. Incidents in a Happy Life, p. 1. Hereafter cited as Incidents.

15. Incidents, pp. 4–5; Interview with Dorothy Dickinson Barbour, June 2, 1971. Cf. Barbour, pp. 5–6.

16. Interview with Lura Beam, Bronxville, New York, November 30, 1970; Interview with Dorothy Dickinson Barbour, June 2, 1971.

17. Emelius C. Dudley, *The Medicine Man: Being the Memories of Fifty Years of Medical Progress* (New York, 1927), pp. 166–67; Barbour, pp. 18, 120–21; Incidents, p. 5.

18. James L. Walsh, *History of Medicine in New York* II (New York, 1919), pp. 506–27; *Medical Education in Brooklyn: The First Hundred Years* (A brochure put out in 1960 by the publicity department of Down State Medical Center to celebrate the centennial of its founding), RLD-CL.

19. Walsh, pp. 517–18; Barbour, p. 21; *Medical Education in Brooklyn*, p. 13.

20. *American Journal of Obstetrics* 42 (1900), pp. 712–14. Dudley, p. 159; Harold Speert, "Alexander Skene and the Paraurethral Ducts," *Obstetric and Gynecologic Milestones: Essays in Eponymy* (New York, 1958), pp. 53–58.

21. Interview with Dr. Jean Curran, September 14, 1970, Boston. On Dickinson's friendship with Skene, see Barbour, pp. 21–22; Dickinson, Incidents, pp. 13–14.

22. Barbour, p. 21; *Treatise on the Diseases of Women* (New York: 1st ed., 1888, reprinted, 1889, 1890; 2nd ed., 1892, reprinted, 1893, 1895; 3rd ed., 1898).

23. Harold Syrett, *The City of Brooklyn, 1865–1898: A Political History* (New York, 1944), pp. 11–24; Barbour, p. 23; Incidents, pp. 9–11; Lura Beam to George Barbour, November 18, 1960, RLD-CL.

24. Syrett, pp. 16–17, 25, 33, 86, 90–91, 133.

25. For two statements of this idealism see Edward F. Shepard, "The Brooklyn Idea in City Government," *Forum* 16 (September 1893), pp. 38–47; Robert L. Dickinson, "What Is a Reasonable Standard in the Medical Civil Service Examination for Policemen and Firemen?" *Brooklyn Medical Journal* 8 (1894), pp. 550–60; Incidents, p. 10; Barbour, p. 51.

26. Barbour, pp. 44–47.

27. Incidents, pp. 13–14; Barbour, pp. 33, 61; Interview with Dr. and Mrs. John Truslow, November 28, 1970, Biddeford, Maine.

28. Barbour, p. 36.

29. This quote is taken from an earlier version of the Barbour biography titled Wide Horizons, Chapter 5, p. 10.

30. Barbour, pp. 38, 40–41.

31. Interview with Lura Beam; Interview with Dorothy Dickinson Barbour; Obituaries, Sarah Truslow Dickinson, *New York Times* and New York *Herald Tribune*, October 1, 1938.

32. Barbour, p. 25.

33. Bibliography of Robert Latou Dickinson, Bibliographical Department of the New York Academy of Medicine Library (June, 1953), RLD-CL.

"The Diagnosis of Pregnancy Between the Second and Seventh Weeks by Bimanual Examination: Thirty Five Cases" and "Further Studies of the Bimanual Signs of Early Pregnancy," *New York Journal of Gynaecology and Obstetrics* 2 (1892), pp. 544–55 and 3

(1893), pp. 985–1105; "Ridges, Furrows, and Prominences on the Imparous Uterus," *American Gynaecological and Obstetrical Journal* 19 (1901), pp. 45–51.

34. For articles on efficiency engineering see Bibliography of Robert Latou Dickinson, pp. 9–11. "Medical Needs and Conditions of the National Army," *Long Island Medical Journal* 12 (1918), pp. 54–57; "Army Hospital Histories," manuscript in the library of the New York Academy of Medicine, n.d. A collection of annotated record forms.

35. Barbour, p. 45.

36. Eugene Gehrung, "Remarks on the Local Treatment of the Unmarried," *American Journal of Obstetrics* 22 (1889), pp. 927–31.

37. Censored to Robert Latou Dickinson, May 9, 1950, RLD-CL.

38. Interview with Lura Beam; Robert Dickinson and Lura Beam, *A Thousand Marriages: A Medical Study of Sex Adjustment* (Baltimore, 1931), p. 11.

39. *American Journal of Obstetrics* 22, pp. 259–61.

40. "The Corset: Questions of Pressure and Displacement," *New York Medical Journal* 46 (1887), pp. 507–16.

41. Barbour, p. 41.

42. "Bicycling for Women from the Standpoint of the Gynecologist," *American Journal of Obstetrics* 31 (1895), p. 33.

43. *The American Gynaecological and Obstetrical Journal* (1896), pp. 736–47.

44. *American Gynecology* 1 (1902), pp. 225–54.

45. *American Gynecology* 1 (1902), pp. 225, 252–253. Ellis quoted from *Auto-Erotism* (Philadelphia, 1901), pp. 171, 186.

46. " 'Urethral Labia' or 'Urethral Hymen': Pathological Structure Due to Repeated Traction," *American Medicine* 7 (1904), pp. 347–49; Kelly, *Medical Gynecology* (New York, 1908), pp. 291–98. Credit for section given in preface.

47. George W. Ward, *The American Gynecological Club, 1911–1947: A Brief History* (Privately printed, 1947). Copy in library of New York Academy of Medicine. The other two founders were George Gellhorn and Howard Taylor (senior). Incidents, p. 11; Dickinson, "With the American Gynecological Club Through Germany and Austria in July 1912," RLD-CL, pp. 7, 9, 11, 46–47.

48. "Marital Maladjustment: The Business of Preventive Gynecology," *Long Island Medical Journal* 2 (1908), p. 1.

49. Ibid., pp. 1–2.

50. Ibid., pp. 2–4.

51. Ibid.

52. Interview with Dr. Jean Alonzo Curran, September 14, 1970, Boston. Curran, in 1970 professor emeritus in the Harvard School of Public Health, was one of Dickinson's students at LICH.

53. *Surgery, Gynecology, and Obstetrics* 23 (1916), pp. 185–90.

54. Harold Speert, *The Sloane Hospital Chronicle* (Philadelphia, 1963), pp. 229–32, 238–41, 80; Donald Fleming, *William H. Welch and the Rise of Modern Medicine* (Boston, 1954), p. 94.

55. "Has the American Gynecological Society Done Its Part in the Advancement of Obstetrical Knowledge?" *Transactions of the American Gynecological Society* 39 (1914), pp. 3–20.

56. "Suggestions for a Program for American Gynecology," *Transactions of the American Gynecological Society* 45 (1920), pp. 1–13.

For answers to Dickinson's rhetorical questions, see "Simple Sterilization by Cautery Stricture at the Intra-uterine Tubal Openings, Compared with Other Methods," *Surgery, Gynecology, and Obstetrics* 23 (1916), pp. 203–14. The article describes a sterilization operation Dickinson was still actively promoting in 1950, which can be performed in the doctor's office.

Dickinson's 1908 article, see footnote 48 above, was a plea for giving birth control information to every bride. There are many instances in his case histories at Countway Library of Dickinson arguing with women to practice contraception when they were hesitant to do so because of religious belief or their husband's opposition.

Most of the case histories on which *One Thousand Marriages* and *The Single Woman* were based were complete by 1920 and Dickinson certainly knew what the general conclusions of those monographs, published in 1931 and 1934, would be.

57. "Suggestions for a Program for American Gynecology," p. 7.

Chapter 12

1. John Truslow to Dorothy Dickinson Barbour, December 2, 1960, RLD-CL.

2. Interview with Dorothy Dickinson Barbour, June 2, 1971; *Surgery, Gynecology, and Obstetrics* 23 (1916), pp. 185–90. Robert Dickinson to Margaret Sanger, November 7, 1945, MS-SS.

3. There are seven volumes of minutes from the meetings of the Committee on Maternal Health. They have been incorporated into the Robert Dickinson papers at Countway Library. Included are treasurer's reports and other manuscript reports of the committee. The minutes are arranged chronologically and little purpose would be served by quoting or making up a title for each document. These volumes are cited as CMH and a date given.

CMH, December 31, 1923. For a list of the officers and Associates of the CMH, see *A Survey and Report of the National Committee on Maternal Health* (New York, 1932), pp. 13–15 and "The Committee on Maternal Health," *American Journal of Obstetrics and Gynecology* 12 (August 1926). Reprint RLD-CL. Hereafter cited as *AJOG*.

4. "Now that conditions have changed, it is impossible to make clear the uneasiness of those days about a cold war with the law." Lura Beam, *Bequest from a Life: A Biography of Louise Stevens Bryant* (Privately printed, Baltimore, 1963), p. 92.

5. *AJOG* 6 (1923). Discussion of the paper, pp. 351–53. For Kosmak's early hostility to birth control, see "Birth Control: What Shall Be the Attitude of the Medical Profession toward the Present-Day Propaganda?" *Medical Record* 91 (1971), pp. 268–73; *Bulletin of the Lying-In Hospital of the City of New York* 11 (1917–1918); Interview with Iago Galdston, Brooklyn, New York, November 4, 1970.

6. B. P. Watson, "George William Kosmak," *Transactions of the American Gynecological Society* 77 (1954), pp. 233–34; Interview with Lura Beam, November 30, 1970.

7. "Newspaper Clippings on Birth Control, Child Birth Deaths, etc.: 1917–1941," ed. George Kosmak, vol. 2. This is a collection of items Kosmak kept from his clipping service about himself. New York Academy of Medicine Library. Volume 1 has been lost. See Kosmak's interview in the *Evening Post*, May 1933. Kosmak's conservatism as an obstetrician appears, in retrospect, to have placed him on the right side in the debate over inducing labor and the use of instruments in delivery. See, Joyce Antler and Daniel M. Fox, "The Movement toward a Safe Maternity: Physician Accountability in New York, 1915–1940." In Press. *Bulletin of the History of Medicine*.

8. Kosmak Clippings, *New York Times*, June 19, 1931.

9. "Birth Control Propaganda," p. 281.

10. "What Shall Be the Attitude of the Medical Profession toward the Present Propaganda," *Lying-In Hospital*, pp. 5–6.

11. "Birth Control Propaganda," p. 285.

12. Kosmak Clippings, n.d.

13. *AJOG* 6 (1923), pp. 351–52.

14. Ibid.

15. Ibid., 7 (1924), pp. 338–40.

16. Ibid., p. 601.

17. Summary of the Answers to the Questionnaire Submitted to the Members of the New York Obstetrical Society on the "Regulation of Conception," *AJOG* 7 (1924), pp. 266–69.

18. "Origins of National Committee on Maternal Health," RLD-CL, n.d.

19. CMH, November 28, 1925; May 28, 1924.

20. CMH, June 13, 1924; February 1, 1928.

21. Lawrence Lader, *The Margaret Sanger Story* (New York, 1955), pp. 224–25.
22. CMH, March 12, 1926.
23. CMH, March 9, 1923; May 10, 1923; January 10, 1924.
24. CMH, December 7, 1923.
25. CMH, December 7, 1923; December 10, 1925; December 11, 1924.
26. *AJOG* 8 (1924), p. 600; CMH, December 10, 1925.
27. CMH, January 12, 1926.
28. CMH, March 9, 1926.
29. CMH, December 10, 1925.
30. CMH, March 9, 1926; March 12, 1926.
31. CMH, October 11, 1927.
32. *AJOG* 8 (1924), p. 600; Dorothy Bocker, *Birth Control Methods* (Privately printed, 1924), p. 1.
33. CMH, January 4, 1924; January 10, 1924; February 29, 1924.
34. Louise S. Bryant to Norman Himes, June 18, 1931, NH-CL. Another problem was that the clinic was run by women. In 1929, Edward East, the Harvard geneticist, explained his reservations about retaining Hannah Stone as medical director of the clinic. He wrote Sanger (February 1, 1929, PPLM-SS): "It seems to me that Dr. Stone is admirably fitted to be Medical Director. . . . On the other hand, though, I think we must consider the Clinic rather than the individual. If we do that, would it be wise to appoint any woman as Medical Director, no matter what her ability is? Men, in general, do not like to work under women, even when they do not have half as much sense; and doctors are particularly jealous cattle."
35. CMH, February 29, 1924.
36. *AJOG* 8 (1924), pp. 583–604; *JAMA* 85 (1925), pp. 1153–54.
37. CMH, November 2, 1925; March 19, 1925.
38. CMH, November 10, 1925; March 19, 1925.
39. CMH, November 2, 1925, is representative of the way Dickinson handled opposition to his ideas. He cheerfully reported his participation in the Sanger conference, making no reference to the committee's earlier decision not to send a delegate.
40. "Report of the Sub-Committee to the Public Health Committee on the Medical Work and Clinic of the American Birth Control League," RLD-CL.
41. Kosmak to Dickinson, February 16, 1925, RLD-CL.
42. CMH, November 13, 1925. Sanger wrote Dickinson, "May I . . . remind you that we are under contract to Dr. Stone and Miss Johnson for the period of another year"; CMH, November 28, 1925.
43. CMH, November 2, 1925. On the Committee on Dispensary Development, see Ralph E. Pumphrey, "Michael M. Davis and the Development of the Health Care Movement, 1900–1928," *Societas* 2 (Winter 1972), pp. 38–39.
44. "England and Birth Control," part of travel notes made in 1926, RLD-CL; CMH, January 21, 1926 and December 10, 1926. Sanger's main motive in handing the clinic over to Dickinson was his promise of a license. See, Margaret Sanger to Edward M. East, May 28, 1925, MS-LC. In their negotiations it was agreed that the clinic would remain "under its present auspices until such time as the Maternity Research Council obtains a license for its operation. In the event of such a license being refused, the medical members of the Council will be obligated to withdraw their active participation in the Clinic." "Report of Conference of the Maternal Health Committee and the Clinic Committee of the American Birth Control League: November 29, 1925," MS-LC. For a transcript of the hearing before the Board of Charities, see "Minutes of the Public Hearing: January 15, 1926," MS-LC.
45. CMH, January 17, 1927.
46. CMH, January 26, 1927; Louise Bryant to Margaret Sanger, September 21, 1929, MS-LC; Margaret Sanger to Robert L. Dickinson, October 19, 1929, November 26, 1929, and December 9, 1929, MS-LC.
47. CMH, July 22, 1926. The fears of Margaret Sanger and Gertrude Sturges about the future of the Clinical Research Bureau in Dickinson's hands were in part the result

of his tendency to exaggerate the potential for medical cooperation. See Norman Haire to Norman Himes, February 18, 1929, NH-CL.

48. Hannah Stone, "Therapeutic Contraception," *Medical Journal and Record* 127 (1928), pp. 9–17. Introduction by Dickinson, pp. 8–9, cf. note 42 above. In 1925, Stone had to leave before the CMH would consider taking over the Sanger clinic. By 1927, Dickinson's praise for her was high.

Publication of Stone's report by the Clinical Research Bureau was held up on Dickinson's promise that he would get the article into either the *JAMA* or the *AJOG*. Publication in the *Medical Journal and Record* was the third choice and a bitter disappointment to the staff of the clinic. See Penelope Huse to Margaret Sanger, January 14, 1928, and Louise Bryant to Margaret Sanger, February 16, 1928, MS-LC.

49. Robert Dickinson, "Concerning Teamwork for Birth Control," Memorandum to the Directors of the American Birth Control League, March 23, 1937. Copy in NH-CL and in CJG-CL.

50. "England and Birth Control," RLD-CL. In September 1931, Sanger wrote Dickinson asking for a copy of his *Control of Conception*, which was not yet off the press. He replied (September 19, 1931), "Send you a copy? Almost the first one ought to go to you. Do you know what I would do if my Committee would sanction it?—only they won't—and that is to dedicate it to you." The book was dedicated to Charles Knowlton.

Chapter 13

1. Caroline H. Robinson, *Seventy Birth Control Clinics* (Baltimore, 1930), pp. 33–34.
2. CMH, October 11, 1927, p. 4.
3. Lura Beam, *Bequest from a Life: A Biography of Louise Stevens Bryant* (Privately printed, Baltimore 1963). The biographical details that follow are all drawn from this work and from interviews and correspondence with Miss Beam. Bryant's papers are in the Sophia Smith Collection.
4. Robert Dickinson and Louise S. Bryant, *Control of Conception: An Illustrated Medical Manual* (Baltimore, 1931).
5. Robert Dickinson and Lura Beam, *A Thousand Marriages: A Medical Study of Sex Adjustment* (Baltimore, 1931).
6. Robert Dickinson and Lura Beam, *The Single Woman: A Study in Sex Education* (Baltimore, 1934).
7. Robert Dickinson, *Human Sex Anatomy: A Topographical Hand Atlas* (Baltimore, 1930).
8. Caroline H. Robinson, *Seventy Birth Control Clinics* (Baltimore, 1930).
9. Norman E. Himes, *Medical History of Contraception* (Baltimore, 1936).
10. Cecil Voge, *The Chemistry and Physics of Contraception* (Baltimore, 1933).
11. Carl G. Hartman, *The Time of Ovulation in Women* (Baltimore, 1936); Frederick J. Taussig, *Abortion: Spontaneous and Induced* (St. Louis, 1936); Samuel R. Meaker, *Human Sterility: Causation, Diagnosis and Treatment* (Baltimore, 1934).

Many of these volumes would never have been published in the middle of the Great Depression without financial subsidies from the committee. The quality of most of them was substantially improved by committee editing.

12. Bryant had married her teenage sweetheart, a Harvard man and classical scholar, on graduation from Smith. The marriage withered. "The girl he had read the *Iliad* with now preferred the contemporary to the classical and it mortified her that a Greek scholar read Westerns for recreation . . . he could hardly believe it when she accepted a position in a Municipal Court" (Beam, *Bequest*, pp. 40–41).

A beautiful woman with a passion for quantification, Louise Bryant became Lura Beam's lover and lifelong companion. Beam scrupulously avoided discussing their sexual relationship in her biography of Bryant and in her correspondence with me. The correspondence between Beam and Bryant in the Bryant papers at Sophia Smith reflects a mature, and I believe admirable, companionship between two gifted women who played crucial parts in the success of the CMH publishing program while all the credit went to male doctors.

Bryant suffered a nervous breakdown in 1935, precipitated by Dickinson's plan to hire Gershon Legman, a flamboyant homosexual, as a CMH consultant. Beam has written of Bryant, "Her lifetime followed that of the feminists. She was therefore at liberty to concentrate upon her work, rather than upon the position of women in work" (*Bequest*, p. 1). This personal truce was irrevocable, but the professional life style it made possible was still vulnerable in a man's world. Bryant spent a year recovering from her conflict with Dickinson and never sought another executive position.

13. *AJOG* 8 (1924), p. 603.

14. CMH, November 2, 1925; *Journal of the American Medical Association* 85 (1925), pp. 1113–17. Hereafter cited as *JAMA*.

15. "Pessaries and Candles in Bladders," *JAMA* 92 (1930), pp. 286–87.

16. CMH, October 11, 1927.

17. CMH, Report for November 1924; January 12, 1926; April 16, 1926; *Biennial Report: 1928*, pp. 16–18.

18. Most of the Committee on Maternal Health's publishing program was funded by the Bureau of Social Hygiene. The bureau also paid for the Committee for Research in Problems of Sex, so the division of labor between the National Research Council Committee and the Committee on Maternal Health reflected in part the demand by John Rockefeller, Jr., that his money not be wasted on duplications. For a history of the Committee on Research in Problems of Sex, see Sophie D. Aberle and George W. Corner, *Twenty-five Years of Sex Research* (Philadelphia, 1953), and James H. Jones, "Science and Progressives: The Development of Scientific Research on Sex in the United States," Paper Presented at the American Historical Association Convention, December 1972.

19. CMH, November 23, 1928; February 10, 1928.

20. CMH, March 11, 1924, "Appendix A."

21. CMH, February 10, 1926.

22. CMH, January 2, 1931.

23. "The Birth Control Clinic of Today and Tomorrow," *Eugenics* 2 (May 1929), pp. 9–10.

24. Robinson, *Seventy Birth Control Clinics*, pp. 155–59.

25. Clellan Stearns Ford and Frank Ambrose Beach, *Patterns of Sexual Behavior* (New York, 1951).

26. Robert Dickinson and Abram Belskie, *Birth Atlas: Reproductions of Twenty-four Life-size Sculptures of Fertilization, Growth, Stages of Labor and Involution* (New York, Maternity Center Association, 1940).

27. "RLD: An Appreciation," *Briefs*, vol. 14, no. 6 (Winter 1950–51), p. 5.

28. Robinson, *Seventy Clinics*, pp. 161–62.

29. Dickinson, "Control of Contraception: Present and Future," *Bulletin of the New York Academy of Medicine*, Second Series, 5 (1929), pp. 431–32; CMH, October 11, 1927, p. 3.

30. *JAMA* 106 (1936), pp. 1910–11. There were five members of the 1936 committee; one was dropped. Four new members were added to the 1937 committee. *JAMA* 108 (1937), pp. 2217–18.

31. CMH, "Notes on Informal Meeting at Atlantic City during the Sessions of the American Gynecological Society on Possible Further Programs of the American Medical Association Committee on Contraception, May 25, 26, 27, 1936"; CMH, February 24, 1937.

32. CMH, February 24, 1937.

33. "Notes on the Round Table Meeting of December 4, 1936," RLD-CL.

34. Ibid.

35. Ibid.
36. "Report of the Round Table Discussion, October 5, 1934," RLD-CL.
37. "Notes on the Round Table Meeting of December 4, 1936," RLD-CL.
38. *JAMA* 108 (1937), pp. 2217–18.
39. August 6, 1950, RLD-CL.
40. Dickinson and Beam, *A Thousand Marriages*, p. 421. Cf. pp. 347–48, 353, 369.
41. See also Robert L. Dickinson, "Medical Notes on the Sex Life of the Unmarried Adult" in *The Sex Life of the Unmarried Adult*, ed. Ira S. Wile (New York, 1935), Reprint RLD-CL.
42. Dickinson and Beam, *One Thousand Marriages*, p. 10. "With scant reading of psychology, no formal study nor even the student's exploration into the field, the doctor regarded the patient as a whole. Posture, manner, expression and even reticence were evidence quite as telling as the uterus, the ovaries and the external genitals . . . when the patient said one thing and the pelvic findings another, then . . . he investigated until he had decided which to believe. He knew nothing about psychoanalysis, had read none of its books, had no acquaintance with the methods, knew no analyst and seems to have been skeptical about such fragments of it as are thrust into the consciousness by general reading."

For Dickinson on Havelock Ellis, see *The Journal of Contraception* 4 (February, 1939), p. 29, and especially his portrait of Ellis. He dedicated his *Atlas of Human Sex Anatomy* to "Havelock Ellis: Physician, Philosopher, Pioneer, and Prophet."

For Dickinson's response to Kinsey's early work, see Robert L. Dickinson, "Truth and Consequences: Kinsey's Version," *The American Scholar* (Summer 1948), pp. 461–68, and Dickinson to Alfred Kinsey, June 18, 1941. Kinsey Papers, Institute for Sex Research. I am indebted to James H. Jones for bringing the extensive correspondence between Dickinson and Kinsey to my attention.

43. Kinsey to Dickinson, June 23, 1941. Kinsey Papers, Institute for Sex Research.

Chapter 14

1. There is no satisfactory treatment of population studies in the United States. James H. Cassedy, *Demography in Early America: Beginnings of the Statistical Mind, 1600–1800* (Cambridge, Mass., 1969) provides a good beginning. Frank Lorimer gives a rough overview in "The Development of Demography," ch. 6 of *The Study of Population: An Inventory and Appraisal*, ed. Philip Hauser and Otis Duncan (Chicago, 1959), pp. 124–79. See also Clyde V. Kiser, ed., *Forty Years of Research in Human Fertility*, The *Milbank Memorial Fund Quarterly* 49 (October 1971). Hereafter cited as *MMFQ*.

Debate over the impact of immigration is covered in John Higham, *Strangers in the Land: Patterns of American Nativism, 1860–1925* (New Brunswick, N.J., 1963); Barbara M. Solomon, *Ancestors and Immigrants: A Changing New England Tradition* (Chicago, 1956); Oscar Handlin, *Race and Nationality in American Life* (Boston, 1957), chs. 5 and 8; William Petersen, *The Politics of Population* (New York, 1964), pp. 195–215; Kenneth M. Ludmerer, "Genetics, Eugenics, and the Immigration Restriction Act of 1924," *Bulletin of the History of Medicine* 46 (January–February 1972), pp. 59–80.

Landmarks in the post–World War II discussion of man's impact on his environment are William Vogt, *The Road to Survival* (New York, 1948); Fairfield Osborn, *Our Plundered Planet* (Boston, 1948); Rachel Carson, *Silent Spring* (Boston, 1962); Paul R. Ehrlich, *The Population Bomb* (New York, 1968).

For the best treatment of discussion of environmental problems, see Donald Fleming, "Roots of the New Conservation Movement," *Perspectives in American History* 6 (1972), pp. 7–91.

2. Cassedy, *Demography in Early America*, pp. 216–20; Gerald N. Grob, "Edward Jarvis and the Federal Census," *Bulletin of the History of Medicine* 50 (1976), pp. 4–27.

3. Francis A. Walker, "Our Population in 1900," *Atlantic Monthly* 32 (1873), pp. 487–95;

reprinted in *Discussions in Economics and Statistics*, ed. Davis R. Dewey (New York, 1899), vol. 2, p. 30. Hereafter cited as *Discussions*.

For discussion of census reform, see A. Hunter Dupree, *Science in the Federal Government* (Cambridge, Mass., 1957), pp. 277–79 and Walker, in *Discussions*, pp. 3–124.

4. Walker, "The Study of Statistics in Colleges and Technical Schools," *Technology Quarterly* 3 (February 1890), p. 4; Bernard Newton, *The Economics of Francis Amasa Walker: American Economics in Transition* (New York, 1968), pp. 1–28, 137–75. Cf. Newton's high estimate of Walker with George Fredrickson, *The Inner Civil War: Northern Intellectuals and the Crisis of the Union* (New York, 1965), pp. 201–5.

5. "Our Population in 1900," *Discussions*, pp. 33, 38, 42–43.

6. "Immigration and Degradation," *The Forum* 11 (August 1891), pp. 634–44; quoted from *Discussions*, p. 424. See also, "Immigration," *Yale Review* 1 (August 1892), pp. 124–25, and "Restriction of Immigration," *Atlantic Monthly* 77 (June 1896), pp. 822–29.

7. *Discussions*, pp. 193–95, 200.

8. R. Jackson Wilson's *In Quest of Community: Social Philosophy in the United States, 1860–1920* (New York, 1968) does not include discussion of Walker, but Wilson's analysis of the alienation of other intellectuals from the emerging mass society, an alienation that found expression in nativism, is excellent and provides a broad context in which Walker's views on immigration can be understood.

9. Peter R. Shergold, "The Walker Thesis Revisited: Immigration and White Fertility, 1800–1860," *Australian Economic Review* 14 (September 1974), pp. 168–89.

10. Higham, *Strangers in the Land*, pp. 147–48; Julius Weinberg, *Edward Alsworth Ross and the Sociology of Progressivism* (Madison, Wis., 1972), pp. 156–57; *Messages and Papers of the Presidents* 16 (New York, n.d.), p. 6984; Theodore Roosevelt, "Race Decadence," *Outlook* 97 (April 8, 1911), pp. 763–69; Ansley J. Coale and Melvin Zelnik, *New Estimates of Fertility and Population in the United States* (Princeton, N.J., 1963), p. 23.

Economists still lack a satisfactory explanation for the continuous decline in fertility until the late 1930s. While it is sometimes assumed that fertility was low during the 1930s because of the Great Depression, this theory does not account for the declining fertility of the 1920s. For an excellent discussion of twentieth century fertility in the United States and an argument that changes in economic conditions do not provide an adequate explanation for fertility trends, see Alan Sweezy, "The Economic Explanation of Fertility Changes in the United States," *Population Studies* 25 (1971), pp. 255–66.

11. D. V. Glass, *Population Policies and Movements in Europe* (London, 1940), chs. 1, 3, 4, 6–8; "Fertility Trends in Europe Since the Second World War," *Fertility and Family Planning: A World View*, ed. S. J. Behrman, Leslie Corsa, and Ronald Freedman (Ann Arbor, Mich., 1970), pp. 25–74.

12. Dupree, *Science in the Federal Government*, p. 279; John Hajnal, "The Study of Fertility and Reproduction: A Survey of Thirty Years," in *Thirty Years in Human Fertility: Papers Presented at the 1958 Annual Conference of the Milbank Memorial Fund*, Part 2 (New York, 1959), pp. 11–37; Lorimer, "Development of Demography," pp. 144–46, 155; Clyde V. Kiser, "The Work of the Milbank Memorial Fund in Population Since 1928," and Frank W. Notestein, "Reminiscences: The Role of Foundations, the Population Association of America, Princeton University and the United Nations in Fostering American Interest in Population Programs," in Kiser, ed., *Forty Years of Research in Human Fertility*, pp. 15–62, 67–84; Kiser, "The Growth of American Families Studies: An Assessment of Significance," *Demography* 4 (1967), p. 389.

13. Notestein, "Reminiscences," pp. 68–69; Warren S. Thompson and Pascal K. Whelpton, *Population Trends in the United States* (New York, 1933); Committee on Population Problems, *The Problems of a Changing Population* (Washington, 1938); "The Population of the Nation," in *Recent Social Trends: Report of the President's Committee on Social Trends* (New York, 1934; one-volume edition), pp. 1–58; Whelpton, *Cohort Fertility* (Princeton, N.J., 1954).

14. Clyde V. Kiser, "The Work of the Milbank Memorial Fund in Population Since 1928," pp. 18–20, 38–43. This article includes an excellent bibliography of fund-sponsored publications; Edgar Sydenstricker and Frank W. Notestein, "Differential Fertil-

ity According to Social Class," *Journal of the American Statistical Association* 25 (March 1930), pp. 9–32.

15. Notestein, "Reminiscences," p. 70.

16. For a representative selection from Fairchild's work, see *The Melting-Pot Mistake* (Boston, 1926), pp. 107–35. A critique of Fairchild's views on immigration is provided by Oscar Handlin, *Race and Nationality in American Life* (Boston, 1948), pp. 188–207. See also Peterson, *Politics of Population*, p. 203.

17. Notestein, "Reminiscences," pp. 71–73.

18. Ibid., pp. 73–74; Kiser, "Work of the Milbank Fund," p. 24.

19. Edgar Sydenstricker and G. St.J. Perrott, "Sickness, Unemployment, and Differential Fertility," *MMFQ* (April 1934), pp. 126–33.

A good example of the improved quality of population studies is Frank Notestein's "The Fertility of Populations Supported by Public Relief," *MMFQ* 14 (January 1936), pp. 37–49, in which Notestein debunked the irresponsible claims by some popular writers that public relief *caused* higher birth rates among the indigent. See also Helen Griffin and G. St.J. Perrott, "Urban Differential Fertility During the Depression," *MMFQ* (January 1937), pp. 48–74. A good summary of demographic thinking in the 1920s, illustrative of the persistent concern over differential fertility but expressed in better defined and more objective terms, is Frank Lorimer and Frederick Osborn, *Dynamics of Population: Social and Biological Significance of the Changing Birth Rates in the United States* (New York, 1934). The racist rhetoric of Fairchild's *The Melting-Pot Mistake* was banished from this book. The authors stressed the effects of social environment as well as genetic heritage on character formation. But fear of underman and cultural deterioration remained the central concern of the work.

20. *The Biology of Population Growth* (New York, 1925).

21. Frank Notestein believed that differential fertility resulted largely from contraceptive practice and recruited Pearl for this study in order to change his mind. Interview with Frank Notestein, Princeton, N.J., August 12, 1974.

22. *The Natural History of Population* (New York, 1939), p. 246; Lorimer, "Development of Demography," p. 161. Pearl's initial skepticism and then change of attitude can be followed in three articles he published describing his investigation of the effect of contraception on fertility. "Preliminary Notes on a Cooperative Investigation of Family Limitation," *MMFQ* 11 (January 1933), pp. 37–60; "Second Progress Report on a Study of Family Limitation," *MMFQ* 12 (July 1934), pp. 248–69; "Third Progress Report on a Study of Family Limitation," *MMFQ* 14 (July 1936), pp. 254–84.

For Hannah Stone's account of the Milbank conference, see Stone to Margaret Sanger, March 21, 1934, MS-LC.

23. Regine K. Stix and Frank Notestein, "Effectiveness of Birth Control: A Study of Contraceptive Practice in a Selected Group of New York Women," *MMFQ* 12 (January 1934), pp. 57–68 and 13 (April 1935), pp. 162–78, and *Controlled Fertility* (Baltimore, 1940); Stix, "Contraceptive Service in Three Areas," *MMFQ* 19 (April 1941), pp. 171–88, and (July 1941), pp. 304–26.

24. Lorimer, "Development of Demography," p. 160.

25. Louis I. Dublin and Alfred J. Lotka, "On the True Rate of Natural Increase, As Exemplified by the Population of the United States in 1920," *Journal of the American Statistical Association* 20 (1925), pp. 305–39; Dublin, *After Eighty Years* (Gainesville, Fla., 1966), pp. 134–41.

26. "The Excesses of Birth Control," *Problems of Overpopulation*, ed. Margaret Sanger (New York, 1926), pp. 186, 189.

27. Norman Himes, "The Vital Revolution," *Survey Graphic* 24 (April 1935), pp. 171ff.; *Medical History of Contraception* (Baltimore, 1936), chs. 13–15; Norman Himes to Guy Irving Burch, September 18, 1941, NH-CL.

28. Norman Himes to Bradley Phillips, March 22, 1937, NH-CL. For claims that the intelligence of the population was declining, see the drafts Himes wrote for his speech to the Cincinnati Committee on Maternal Health, October 11, 1934, and W. E. Brown, Medical Director of the Cincinnati Committee on Maternal Health, to Himes, October

3, 1934; Draft of speech delivered before the Maternal Health League of Michigan, February 19, 1937; News release quoting from speech given before the Fourth Annual Conference on Conservation of Marriage and the Family, April 12, 1938, NH-CL. For the attitudes of the early leaders of the eugenics movement toward birth control, see Chapter 13 above.

29. Robert Lekachman, *The Age of Keynes* (New York, 1966), pp. 130–37; Alfred Hansen, "Economic Progress and Declining Population Growth," *The American Economic Review* 29 (March 1939), pp. 1–15.

30. Gunnar Myrdal, *Population: A Problem for Democracy* (Cambridge, Mass., 1940), pp. 18–19, 22.

31. Ibid., pp. 24, 57–58, 102–3, 105. For a discussion of Swedish social welfare programs which Alva and Gunnar Myrdal helped to fashion, see Part 2 of Alva Myrdal's *Nation and Family: The Swedish Experiment in Democratic Family and Population Policy* (New York, 1941; paperback reprint MIT Press, 1968).

32. United States National Resources Committee, Committee on Population Problems, *The Problems of a Changing Population* (Washington, 1938); Irene B. Taeuber, "Fertility, Diversity, and Policy," in *Forty Years of Research in Human Fertility*, p. 217.

33. I do not mean to imply that a society can be analyzed in the same manner as a neurotic individual. Widespread concern that young Americans could not or would not have enough children to maintain population growth was, however, a dominant theme in discussion of American population and this concern was the most serious obstacle for those interested in more intensive efforts to spread contraceptive practice, especially as a matter of public policy.

Chapter 15

1. National Committee on Maternal Health, Minutes of Round Table Discussion, "The Eugenic Effect of Contraception—The Significance of the Decline in the Birth Rate," May 13, 1937, RLD-CL.

2. Ibid., pp. 2–3.

3. Ibid., p. 12.

4. Ibid., pp. 1–2, 5–7.

5. Ibid., p. 10.

6. Ibid., p. 4.

7. Ibid., p. 8.

8. Frank Lorimer and Frederick Osborn, *Dynamics of Population* (New York, 1934), p. 339.

9. On the opposition of organized medicine to modest reform proposals, see Louis Dublin, *After Eighty Years* (Gainesville, Fla., 1966), pp. 120–29, 166–72; Daniel S. Hirshfield, *The Lost Reform: The Campaign for Compulsory Health Insurance in the United States* (Cambridge, Mass., 1970); J. Stanley Lemons, "The Sheppard-Towner Act: Progressivism in the 1920's," *Journal of American History* 55 (March 1969), pp. 776–86.

10. Regine K. Stix and Frank W. Notestein, *Controlled Fertility: An Evaluation of Clinic Service* (Baltimore, 1940), pp. 23, 25–27, 58, 62–63, 103–8, 125–26.

In rural populations provided with contraceptive jelly by a nurse, there was also a high drop-out rate, but just as in the clinic sample, even brief participation in a contraceptive program was associated with lower fertility after the prescribed method was abandoned. See Gilbert Beebe, *Contraception and Fertility in the Southern Appalachians* (Baltimore, 1942), p. 135.

11. Robert Dickinson, "Expansion of Work of the Committee," CMH, April 24, 1935; "Birth Control Stalled," Memo, October 30, 1935, RLD-CL; "Are Present Birth Control Methods Satisfactory?" CMH, January 12, 1934.

12. New York, 1963, pp. 72–73.

13. Clarence J. Gamble, A Leader in the Birth Control World, unpublished bio-

graphical sketch of Doris Davidson, n.d., CJG-CL; Memo, Florence Rose to Margaret Sanger, December 13, 1932, MS-LC; Doris Davidson to Margaret Sanger, January 23, 1933, MS-LC.

14. Doris Davidson to Florence Rose, October 28, November 8, 1933, MS-LC.

15. Florence Rose to Doris Davidson, November 6, 1933, MS-LC.

16. Doris Davidson to Dr. Gehring, November 15, 1933; Doris Davidson to Florence Rose, November 19, 1933, MS-LC.

17. Gladys B. Russell to Florence Rose, n.d., MS-LC.

Chapter 16

1. A. R. Kaufman, "Address Given in Montreal on June 13, 1935 to the Annual Conference of the Combined American and Canadian National Conference of Social Work," MS-LC; "The Parents' Information Bureau of Canada," *Journal of Contraception* 3 (March 1938), pp. 54–55.

2. Kaufman, "Address Given in Montreal on June 13, 1935." See also "Report on Birth Control Activities and Procedure" and other publications of the Parents' Information Bureau, CJG-CL.

3. A. R. Kaufman to H. L. Mencken, August 10, 1937, copy in CJG-CL; A. R. Kaufman to C. S. Curtis, n.d., copy in CJG-CL.

4. A. R. Kaufman to Clarence J. Gamble, July 12, 1934; July 21, 1937, CJG-CL. Kaufman later lowered his estimate of the number of women prevented from using a diaphragm because of birth injuries or pathological uterine conditions to 25 percent. Kaufman to Randolph Cautley, May 20, 1935, CJG-CL.

5. Robert L. Dickinson, *Control of Conception* (2nd ed., Baltimore, 1938), pp. 140–49; Hannah Stone, "Contraceptive Jellies: A Clinical Study," *Journal of Contraception* 1 (December 1936), pp. 209–13; Clarence J. Gamble and Gilbert Beebe, "The Clinical Effectiveness of Lactic Acid Jelly as a Contraceptive," *American Journal of the Medical Sciences* (July 1937), pp. 79–84; A. R. Kaufman to Clarence J. Gamble, July 21, 1937, CJG-CL.

6. Dickinson, *Control of Conception*, p. 149; A. R. Kaufman to Clarence J. Gamble, May 29, 1935; March 12, 1936; July 21, 1937; Kaufman to F. T. Cook, September 7, 1937, copy in CJG-CL.

Kaufman's thesis that the attitude of the user is much more important than the method employed has been confirmed by sociological studies, most notably Lee Rainwater, *Family Design: Marital Sexuality, Family Size, and Contraception* (Chicago, 1965), chs. 7–8. The key variable differentiating ineffective from effective contraceptive practice is the amount of cooperation and mutuality between a married couple.

7. A. R. Kaufman to Margaret Sanger, October 1, October 26, 1936, MS-LC.

8. Eric M. Matsner, "The Trial of Dorothea Palmer" and " 'Pro Bono Publico': The Decision of the Court in the Canadian Birth Control Case," *Journal of Contraception* 2 (April 1937), pp. 80–83. See also the clipping related to the trial in MS-LC.

Chapter 17

1. Clarence Gamble to Mary A. Gamble, October 4, 1925, CJG-CL.

2. Most of my biographical information on Gamble is drawn from a manuscript biography by Greer Williams. The Gamble family commissioned the Williams biography. The Gamble papers at Countway do not include much material on Gamble's personal life or family background, but the Williams manuscript is an impressive study based on dozens of interviews as well as the personal papers. The version of the

Williams biography which I read was a 900-page first draft which will be considerably shortened and his pages were numbered by chapters, so there is no point in citing pages. Throughout this essay I cite the name of the chapter or section in the manuscript on which I am drawing. The working title of the manuscript is *The Cutting Edge: The Work of Dr. Clarence J. Gamble in Birth Control.* Williams, "Notes for CJG Biography, II."

3. Ibid.

4. Ibid., "Notes for CJG Biography, VI."

5. Ibid., "Richards and the University of Pennsylvania."

6. Starr remained at the University of Pennsylvania, where he established himself as a distinguished investigator and later became dean of the University of Pennsylvania Medical School.

7. Williams, "Notes for CJG Biography, V."

8. Stuart Mudd, "Sequences in Medical Microbiology: Some Observations over Fifty Years," *Annual Review of Microbiology* 23 (1969), p. 2; E. Newton Harvey, "Edwin Grant Conklin," National Academy of Sciences, *Biographical Memoirs* 31 (New York, 1958), pp. 54–91.

9. Edwin G. Conklin, *Heredity and Environment in the Development of Man* (Princeton, N.J., 1915), pp. 361–63.

10. Kenneth M. Ludmerer, "American Geneticists and the Eugenics Movement, 1905–35" *Journal of the History of Biology* 2 (1969), pp. 337–65; Hermann J. Muller, *Out of the Night: A Biologist's View of the Future* (New York, 1935) and "Should We Weaken or Strengthen Our Genetic Heritage?" *Daedalus* (Summer 1961), pp. 432–50 and "Better Genes for Tomorrow," in *The Population Crisis: Implications and Plans for Action,* ed. Larry K. Y. Ng and Stuart Mudd (Bloomington, Ind., 1966), pp. 223–47; Alfred Rosenfeld, *The Second Genesis: The Coming Control of Life* (Englewood Cliffs, N.J., 1969).

11. Interview with Stuart Mudd, Haverford, Pa., May 24, 1974. Transcript in the Schlesinger Library.

12. "Annual Report of the Maternal Health Centers," 1933, Pennsylvania File, CJG-CL.

13. Clarence Gamble, Notes for Speech as President of the Pennsylvania Birth Control Federation, n.d.; Clarence Gamble to Fellow Members, February 23, 1935, Pennsylvania File, CJG-CL.

14. James H. Bossard, "The New Public Relief and Birth Control," article distributed by the Pennsylvania Birth Control Federation and the Maternal Health Committee of Philadelphia. Cf. Bossard's article with the traditional argument for birth control by Sophia Kleegman in "Medical, Social and Religious Aspects of Birth Control." Both articles in Pennsylvania File, CJG-CL. Kleegman stressed maternal and infant health and the ideal of companionate marriage.

15. Ibid.; Clarence Gamble to Raymond C. Chapin, June 13, 1933 and Gamble to Dr. Huston St. Claire, December 8, 1936, CJG-CL.

16. Bossard, "New Public Relief."

17. D. Kenneth Rose to Margaret Sanger, February 6, 1941, MS-SS.

18. CMH, June 11, 1929.

19. The following discussion of Elizabeth Campbell is based on Chapter 10 in a manuscript biography of her sister, Edith Campbell, written by Mrs. Louis Zapoleon of Fort Lauderdale, Fla.

20. Williams, "Notes for CJG Biography, II."

21. Interview with Dorothy Dickinson Barbour, Cincinnati, Ohio, June 2, 1971. Quote from Zapoleon manuscript.

22. William E. Brown to Clarence Gamble, December 15, 1930; Gamble to Brown, February 11, 1931, CJG-CL.

23. Williams, "A Rebirth in Birth Control"; Clarence Gamble to Christine Sears, June 9, 1931, CJG-CL.

24. Williams, "Elsie Wulkop in Michigan"; Clarence Gamble to Mrs. Louis deB. Moore, April 5, 1937, p. 2, note 1 and note 2, CJG-CL.

25. Elsie Wulkop to Clarence Gamble, November 29, 1931, CJG-CL.
26. CMH, April 23, 1935.

Chapter 18

1. Clarence Gamble to Doris Davidson, September 7, 1936, CJG-CL.
2. Robert L. Dickinson, *Control of Conception* (2nd ed., Baltimore, 1938), p. 1; William H. Chafe, *The American Woman: Her Changing Social, Economic, and Political Roles, 1920–1970* (New York, 1972), pp. 188–95, 218–25.
3. "The Accident of Birth," *Fortune* (February 1938), pp. 83–114; "The Lay Press Looks at Birth Control," *Journal of Contraception* 3 (March 1938), pp. 60–61. Hereafter cited as *JOC*.
4. "Accident of Birth," p. 110; Henry F. Pringle, "What Do the Women of America Think about Birth Control?" *Ladies' Home Journal* (March 1938), copy in MS-LC.
5. "The Consumer and the Law," *Human Fertility* 8 (June 1943), pp. 48–49, and 9 (September 1944), pp. 93–94. Hereafter cited as *HF*. Chauncy B. Garver, counsel for the PPFA, to D. Kenneth Rose, June 11, 1943, MS-LC.
6. "The Accident of Birth," p. 112.
7. "Contraceptive Standards Program," Minutes of the Committee on Maternal Health, Robert Dickinson Papers, Countway Library, July 12, 1934. Hereafter cited as CMH.
8. Quinine, for example, was shown to be ineffective, and coconut oil soap did immobilize sperm.
Cecil Voge, *The Physics and Chemistry of Contraception* (London, 1933); "Memorandum to the Bureau of Social Hygiene on Progress during 1930," November 20, 1930; Louise S. Bryant to Elizabeth Devree, November 14, 1933, CMH.
9. John Peel, "Contraception and the Medical Profession," *Population Studies* 18 (1964), pp. 140–42; John R. Baker, "A New Chemical Contraceptive," *Lancet* (October 15, 1938), p. 882, and *The Chemical Control of Conception* (London, 1935).
Baker's research grants from the BCIC were provided by Clinton Chance, the British industrialist and friend of Margaret Sanger who gave her £1,000 with which she opened the Birth Control Clinical Research Bureau.
For more information on the Birth Control Investigation Committee, see Peter Fryer, *The Birth Controllers* (New York, 1966), pp. 256, 267, and Beryl Suitters and Clive Wood, *The Fight for Acceptance: A History of Contraception* (Aylesbury, England, 1970), pp. 169–70.
10. F. A. E. Crew to Penelope Huse, October 3, 1931, CMH.
11. Peel, "Contraception and the Medical Profession," p. 142.
12. Randolph Cautley to Clarence Gamble, May 30, 1934, CJG-CL; CMH, January 6, 1938. The 1938 grant to Baker was Rockefeller money supplied through the Davidson Fund.
When the CMH tried to import Volpar for experimental use in 1938, it was seized by United States Customs. (Gilbert Beebe to Clarence Gamble, November 23, 1938, CJG-CL.) There were already several good spermicides available from Holland Rantos, Johnson and Johnson, and Squibb, and American researchers concentrated on publicizing effective formulas and exposing ineffective products, leaving the development of new chemical spermicides to the large commercial laboratories.
13. Editorial, *Western Journal of Surgery, Obstetrics, and Gynecology* 51 (September 1943), pp. 381–83. Copy in CJG-CL.
14. CMH, September 24, 1936; April 2, 1937; April 27, 1937; October 6, 1938. Engle quoted from CMH, June 14, 1946.
15. CMH, November 3, 1938, p. 4; CMH, July 12, 1934. For a description of the committee's publishing program and Dickinson's conflict with Bryant, see Chapter 13.

16. Dickinson (Baltimore, 1938); *Fortune* (February 1938); CMH, July 31, 1934; "Standards Report on Rubber Condoms, March 11, 1935" and "Standards Report on the Contraceptive Jelly Industry, April 4, 1935," CJG-CL. See also, Randolph Cautley, Gilbert W. Beebe, and Robert L. Dickinson, "Rubber Sheaths as Venereal Disease Prophylactics," *American Journal of Medical Sciences* 195 (February 1938), pp. 155–63; Randolph Cautley and G. A. Fingalo, "An Instrument for Measuring the Spring Tension of Vaginal Diaphragms," *JOC* 4 (February 1939), pp. 34–37.

17. Bulletin issued by the Oregon Board of Pharmacy, September 6, 1935; Gilbert Beebe to Lewis C. Britt, November 26, 1937, CJG-CL; CMH, April 21, 1936.

18. Gilbert Beebe, "Progress Report for the Year Ending May, 1938," May 26, 1938, CJG-CL; "Prophylactic Sheaths," *HF* 5 (June 1940), p. 86.

19. "The Lanteen Laboratories, Inc.," *JOC* 4 (May 1939), pp. 116–18; "Official Action Against the Misrepresentation of Contraceptive Products," and "Action Against the Misbranding and Adulteration of Commercial Contraceptives," *HF* 6 (June 1941), pp. 90–91 and 7 (1942), p. 124; Gamble quoted in Planned Parenthood Federation of America, "Minutes of the Medical Committee Meeting," February 8, 1944, CJG-CL. For criticism of efforts to restrict condom sales to drug stores, see Gilbert Beebe, *Contraception in the Southern Appalachians* (Baltimore, 1942), pp. 187–88.

20. Clarence Gamble to Florence Rose, April 7, 1938, MS-LC.

21. CMH, April 21, 1936; Gilbert Beebe to Clarence Gamble, November 29, 1935, CJG-CL; CMH, September 22, 1937; Leo Shedlovsky, "Some Acidic Properties of Contraceptive Jellies," *JOC* 2 (August-September 1937), pp. 147–55.

22. "Standards for Contraceptive Products Adopted by the American Medical Association," *HF* 9 (September 1944), pp. 90–92; Stuart Mudd to Margaret Sanger, February 9, 1943, copy in CJG-CL; Robert L. Dickinson, "Conception Control," *JAMA* 123 (December 18, 1943), pp. 1043–47; National Committee on Maternal Health, "Minutes of Members Meeting, May 17, 1940," CJG-CL.

For Gamble's later work in evaluation of commercial contraceptives, see Christopher Tietze, *Selected Bibliography of Contraception: 1940–1960* (National Committee on Maternal Health Publication No. 6, 1960), pp. 19–20.

Chapter 19

1. Gamble and Beebe, "The Clinical Effectiveness of Lactic Acid Jelly as a Contraceptive," *American Journal of the Medical Sciences* 194 (July 1937), pp. 79–84; Beebe, *Contraception and Fertility in the Southern Appalachians* (Baltimore, 1942); Beebe and M. A. Geisler, "Control of Conception in a Selected Rural Sample," *Human Biology* 14 (February 1942), pp. 1–20. See also Lena Gilliam, "A Contraceptive Service for Mountain Women," *JOC* 3 (March 1938), pp. 56–59.

2. Clarence Gamble to the Birth Control Federation of America, March 24, 1939; "Standards Report on the Contraceptive Jelly Industry," April 4, 1935, CJG-CL; "The Effectiveness of Jelly Alone," *JOC* 2 (October 1937), pp. 182–83.

Beebe provides an excellent analysis of the economic problems of the region in *Contraception and Fertility in the Southern Appalachians*, ch. 1. The fact that Appalachia was clearly overpopulated, in contrast to the low fertility of some other regions, helped to justify a large-scale experiment that focused on lowering the birth rate in a whole population rather than protecting the health of individual women. See also Gordon De Jong, *Appalachian Fertility Decline* (Lexington, Ky., 1968).

3. Clyde V. Kiser, review of De Jong's *Appalachian Fertility Decline*, *Population Studies* 24 (1970), p. 463; J. D. Mayo to Margaret Sanger, March 5, 1937, copy in CJG-CL; Hazel Moore to Margaret Sanger, September 28, 1935, MS-SS.

4. Clarence Gamble to Agnes Sailer, November, 1933, CJG-CL; Gamble to D. Kenneth Rose, "An Outline of the Activities of Clarence J. Gamble in the Field of Contraception," January 1939, p. 2, CJG-CL; CMH, April 23, 1935; Gamble to Aunt Julia,

June 29, 1934; Doris Davidson to Clarence Gamble, March 11, 1938; Gamble to Winifred Wencke, October 16, 1935; "Memorandum of a Conference with Dr. Clarence J. Gamble, Mr. Homer L. Morris, and Dr. Raymond Squier in Philadelphia, December 10, 1935," CJG-CL.

5. CMH, April 21, 1936. The Logan County experiment is described in Beebe's *Contraception and Fertility in the Southern Appalachians,* based on his Columbia doctoral thesis.

6. Clarence Gamble to Winifred Wencke, October 16, 1935; "Memo on Miss Alice Beaman, December 11, 1935"; "Tentative Definition of Interests and Responsibilities of the American Friends Service Committee, the National Committee on Maternal Health, and the American Birth Control League in regard to the Logan Maternal Health Service," December 11, 1935, CJG-CL.

7. Eric M. Matsner to Clarence Gamble, February 21, 1935, CJG-CL.

8. CMH, September 23, 1936, March 25, 1937, January 12, 1937. Quote from April 21, 1936; Marguerite Benson to Raymond Squier, December 24, 1935, copy in CJG-CL; Clyde V. Kiser, "The Work of the Milbank Memorial Fund in Population since 1928," *MMFQ* 49 (October 1971), p. 28.

9. Winifred Wencke to Clarence Gamble, March 3, 1936; Clarence Gamble to Winifred Wencke, March 12, 1936, CJG-CL.

10. Beebe, *Contraception and Fertility,* pp. 42–51, 53–54, 132–33, 152. Only about one-third of the women interviewed accepted the jelly, but the accepters were younger and had a higher proven fertility than those who declined.

11. Ibid., pp. 37–38, 164–67.

12. Ibid., pp. 180, 185, 191–92.

13. Ibid., pp. 23, 26–27, 192–93, 199, 202–3, 204–5.

14. Doris Davidson to Clarence Gamble, February 2, 1937; Greer Williams, "The Gamble Girls in North Carolina," in manuscript biography of Clarence James Gamble.

15. Don Wharton, "Birth Control: The Case for the State," *Atlantic Monthly* 164 (October 1939), p. 464; Clarence Gamble to Miss Stevens, January 3, 1940, CJG-CL; Lydia A. de Vilbiss, "The Contraceptive Effectiveness of the Foam-Powder and Sponge Method," *JOC* 3 (January 1938), pp. 7ff.

16. Wharton, "The Case for the State," p. 463; Roy Norton, "Developmental Background of the First State Health Department Conception Hygiene Program," *HF* 5 (June 1940), pp. 65–66, and "A Health Department Birth Control Program," *American Journal of Public Health* 29 (March 1939), p. 255. Hereafter cited as *AJPH.*

17. Clarence Gamble to Miss Stevens, January 3, 1940, CJG-CL.

18. Williams, "The Gamble Girls in North Carolina."

19. Clarence Gamble to Mrs. Louis deB. Moore, April 5, 1937, "Appendix," p. 6; Clarence Gamble to George M. Cooper, February 24, 1937, CJG-CL; J. W. R. Norton, James F. Donnelly, and Anne Lamb, "Twenty-one Years' Experience with a Public Health Contraceptive Service," *AJPH* (August 1959), p. 994. The appendix to the Moore letter is an eight-page summary of Gamble's correspondence with the league office, which he prepared when his quarrel with the ABCL leadership had come to a head, and he had to explain his position to the league's board of directors. Hereafter cited as Moore Appendix.

20. George M. Cooper, Frances R. Pratt, and Margaret J. Hapgood, "Four Years of Contraception as a Public Health Service in North Carolina," *AJPH* 31 (December 1941), pp. 1248–52; Norton; "A Health Department Birth Control Program," p. 255. Also Cooper, "Birth Control in the North Carolina Health Department," *North Carolina Medical Journal* 1 (September 1940), pp. 463–67.

21. Clarence Gamble to Edna McKinnon, October 25, 1937, CJG-CL; "Origin and Development of Public Health Birth Control Services in the United States," *HF* 5 (June 1940), pp. 90–92; Norton, Donnelly, and Lamb, "Twenty-one Years' Experience," pp. 993–99; Johan W. Eliot, "The Development of Family Planning Services by State and Local Health Departments in the United States," *AJPH* 56 Supplement to January 1966, pp. 6–16.

For more information on the southern programs, see Robert E. Siebels, "Pregnancy Spacing in the South Carolina Public Health Programs," *HF* 5 (June 1940), pp. 70–73; James N. Baker, "A State Program for Planned Parenthood in Alabama," *HF* 5 (October 1941), pp. 129–33; "Child Spacing and Public Health," *HF* 10 (March 1945), pp. 16–17; L. L. Parks, "Florida's Family Planning Program," *AJPH* 56 (January 1966), pp. 117ff; "Lasker Awards," *HF* 11 (March 1946), p. 32.

22. Regine K. Stix, "The Place of Fertility Control in Public Health," *AJPH* 36 (March 1946), p. 216; Eliot, "The Development of Family Planning Services," pp. 15, 16; D. Kenneth Rose, "Report on the Situation in Tennessee with Recommendations," January 2, 1942, CJG-CL; "Transcript of a Conference Held by the Birth Control Federation of America," June 30, 1941, pp. 84–85, MS-SS.

23. Cooper, Pratt, and Hapgood, "Four Years of Contraception," pp. 1248, 1250; Norton, Donnelly, and Lamb, "Twenty-one Years' Experience," p. 997.

24. Wharton, "The Case for the State," p. 465.

25. George M. Cooper to Clarence Gamble, May 20, 1937, CJG-CL. See also the discussion following Gamble, "Contraception as a Public Health Measure," *Transactions, Medical Society of the State of North Carolina* (1938). Reprint CJG-CL.

26. Norton, "Developmental Background," p. 68.

27. Norton, Donnelly, Lamb, "Twenty-one Years' Experience," p. 995.

Chapter 20

1. Clarence Gamble to Mrs. F. Robertson Jones, February 20, 1946; Gamble to Edna McKinnon, June 22, 1940, CJG-CL.

2. Greer Williams, manuscript biography of Clarence J. Gamble, "Money"; Clarence Gamble to Christopher Tietze, May 21, 1949, CJG-CL.

3. Williams, "Money."

4. Clarence Gamble to Phyllis Page, June 1, 1936, July 18, 1936; Gamble to Mrs. Louis deB. Moore (Allison P. Moore), April 5, 1937, Appendix, pp. 6–7.

5. Marguerite Benson to Clarence Gamble, February 15, 1936, quoted in Moore Appendix.

6. Clarence Gamble to Phyllis Page, December 8, 1938, June 1, 1936, and undated letters in Phyllis Page File, CJG-CL; Lena Gilliam, "A Contraceptive Service for Mountain Women," *JOC* 3 (March 1938), pp. 56–59; Gilbert Beebe and M. A. Geisler, "Control of Conception in a Selected Rural Sample," *Human Biology* 14 (February 1942), pp. 1–20.

7. Phyllis Page to Clarence Gamble, July 18, 1936; Gamble to Page, July 23, 1936, CJG-CL; Marguerite Benson to Gamble, May 16, 1936, MS-LC. Benson's point is well illustrated by her letter of May 16. She had received a letter from supporters in Knoxville which read: "Knoxville feels deeply grateful to the ABCL for having sent Mrs. Page and Miss Davidson to them." Benson did not even know who Mrs. Page was.

8. Carmen R. DeAlvarada and Christopher Tietze, "Birth Control in Puerto Rico," *HF* 12 (March 1947), pp. 15–17ff; Clarence Gamble to Woodbridge E. Morris, October 3, 1939, CJG-CL.

9. Matsner to Gamble, November 7, 1936, MS-LC. For a blow-by-blow account of events, see Moore Appendix, April 5, 1937, pp. 4–6 and the Puerto Rico File, CJG-CL. Gruening describes his own efforts to promote birth control in Puerto Rico in his autobiography, *Many Battles* (New York, 1973), p. 200. On Gruening's efforts for the cause after he became a senator, see Part VIII below.

10. Doris Davidson to Gamble, February 2, 1937, February 23, 1937; Gamble to Davidson, March 1, 1937; Davidson to Gamble, July 17, 1938, CJG-CL.

11. "Minutes of the Board of Directors Meeting," May 14, 1936; Mrs. Louis deB. Moore to Gamble, March 10, 1937, CJG-CL.

12. Gamble to Phyllis Page, December 8, 1936, CJG-CL.

13. Cele Damon to Allison P. Moore, May 10, 1937, CJG-CL.
14. Hazel Moore to Clarence Gamble, June 28, 1937, CJG-CL.
15. Hazel Moore to Clarence Gamble, June 26, 1937, CJG-CL.
16. Moore Appendix, pp. 2–4; Undated letter written by Sarah Gamble, American Birth Control League File, CJG-CL.
17. Cele Damon to Clarence Gamble, April 1, 1937, CJG-CL.
18. Mrs. Louis deB. (Allison Pierce) Moore to Clarence Gamble, March 10, 1937, CJG-CL.
19. Clarence Gamble to Edna McKinnon, October 11, 1940; Undated letter to field workers written by Clarence Gamble, ABCL File, CJG-CL; "Milestones in Planned Parenthood," January 1948, Planned Parenthood Federation of America File, CJG-CL; J. H. J. Upham to Clarence Gamble, November 23, 1942, CJG-CL.
20. Gamble to Moore, April 5, 1937.
21. Undated letter to field workers written by Clarence Gamble, American Birth Control League File, CJG-CL.
22. Eleanor Dwight Jones to Mrs. Edward A. Norman, January 2, 1931, MS-SS; David M. Kennedy, *Birth Control in America: The Career of Margaret Sanger* (New Haven, Conn., 1970), p. 227; Margaret Sanger to Cele Damon, December 24, 1938, MS-SS.
23. "A Statement by the Birth Control Clinical Research Bureau and the American Birth Control League," *JOC* 3 (1938), p. 240; "Minutes of the Meeting of the Birth Control Council of America," June 22, 1937, p. 10, CJG-CL.
24. "Summary of Recommendations to Joint Committee of ABCL and Clinical Research Bureau," October 10, 1938, MS-SS; "National Referendum on the Name to be Adopted by State Leagues, Affiliated Committees, and Federation," April 17, 1941, CJG-CL.
25. "Minutes of the Meeting of the Birth Control Council of America," June 22, 1937; "Minutes of Special Membership Meeting," January 29, 1942, CJG-CL.
26. Clarence Gamble to Margaret Sanger, January 14, 1939; "Regional Organization Committee Minutes," January 30, 1939, CJG-CL.
27. Hazel Moore to Clarence Gamble, June 2, 1938; Gamble to Katharine Mali, February 22, 1939; Gamble to Willie C. Morehead, March 3, 1939; "1940 Annual Report, Regional Organization Department," p. 4, CJG-CL.
28. W. C. Morehead to Margaret Sanger, September 16, 1939; Morehead to Gamble, April 15, 1939; D. Kenneth Rose to Morehead, March 20, 1939. All in CJG-CL.
29. A federation nurse did continue to work for three years among the migratory workers in California. See Grace Naismith, "The Birth Control Nurse," *Survey Graphic* 32 (June 1943), pp. 26off., and "Parenthood USA" reprinted from *Look* July 14, 1942. Copy in CJG-CL.
30. Hazel Moore to Clarence Gamble, May 23, 1937, CJG-CL.
31. "Freedom of Speech," *JOC* 3 (February 1938), pp. 38–39; "Annual Report of the American Birth Control League: 1938," CJG-CL.
32. Regine K. Stix, "The Place of Fertility Control in Public Health," *AJPH* 36 (March 1946), p. 216; USPHS, "Circular to District Offices," February 1942; C. C. Pierce to D. Kenneth Rose, February 2, 1942; BCFA, "Annual Report," January 29, 1942. All in CJG-CL.

For inquiries to the USPHS referred to the ABCL, see "Birth Control Folder," Box 244, Record Group 90, Venereal Disease Division, Federal Record Center, Suitland, Maryland. Thanks to James H. Jones.
33. D. Kenneth Rose to Margaret Sanger, February 7, 1942; "Summary of Conference Held in Washington, D.C. on March 12, 1942 with Dr. Warren F. Draper, Assistant Surgeon General . . . ," MS-SS.
34. "Report of the Luncheon Meeting Held At the White House at the Invitation of Mrs. Franklin D. Roosevelt," December 8, 1941, MS-LC. On the USPHS-CB rivalry, see Martha Eliot Interview, the Schlesinger Library. The further history of the rivalry between the two agencies may be followed in Harold Stein, *Public Administration and Policy Development: A Case Book* (New York, 1952), pp. 17–29.

35. Kennedy, *Birth Control in America,* p. 266; Planned Parenthood Federation of America, "Minutes of Executive Committee Meeting," November 10, 1942; Birth Control Federation of America, "Minutes of the Executive Committee Meeting," January 6, 1942, CJG-CL; James E. Allen, "The Public Health Stake in Family Planning Health Role Challenged," *AJPH* 63 (June 1973), p. 517; C. Thomas Dienes, *Law, Politics, and Birth Control* (Urbana, Ill., 1972), pp. 267, 268; Phyllis T. Piotrow, *World Population Crisis: The United States Response* (New York, 1973), pp. 141–42.

36. Birth Control Federation of America, "Minutes of Executive Committee Meeting," November 26, 1940; Planned Parenthood Federation of America, "A Suggested Program to Finance the National Federation and State Leagues," October 1942; "Annual Report–Treasurer's Report: 1947"; "Minutes of Executive Committee Meeting," September 12, 1950. All in CJG-CL.

37. The high points of the struggle can be followed in Rose to Gamble, March 6, 1939; Gamble to Rose, March 6, 1939; Gamble to Rose, September 27, 1941; Rose to Gamble, February 4, 1942; Gamble to Rose, January 15, 1942; February 20, 1942; Gamble to Margaret Sanger, December 2, 1942; Minutes of the Executive Committee Meeting, April 21, 1942, March 4, 1941, CJG-CL.

38. CMH, September 21, 1939; *The Underdeveloped Aspects of Human Reproduction: A Research Problem and Its Needs, 1942–1946* (n.d., n.p.), copy in RLD-CL.

39. NCMH, "Minutes of Executive Committee Meeting," March 28, 1938," CJG-CL. Eastman's interest in hormonal contraception may have been inspired by Raphael Kurzrok, "The Prospects for Hormonal Sterilization," *JOC* 2 (February 1937), pp. 27–29. The idea of using hormones to control conception was, however, being widely discussed, and would eventually lead to a major breakthrough in contraceptive technology. See Part VII.

40. "Minutes of Conference of June 3, 1940, between Clarence J. Gamble and Raymond Squier"; Clair E. Folsome to Gamble, June 10, 1941; Gamble to Gilbert Beebe, April 1, 1941, June 20, 1941; Clair Folsome to Leo Shedlovsky, July 11, 1941, CJG-CL.

41. Clair E. Folsome to Clarence Gamble, May 19, 1942, CJG-CL.

42. PPFA, *Annual Report: Treasurer's Report: 1947; Annual Report: 1949;* "Research Program Begins on National Scale," *New Exchange* no. 31 (December 1947); D. Kenneth Rose, "Ten Research Projects in Human Reproduction: A Memorandum," July 16, 1948; NCMH, "Minutes of Membership Meeting," May 4, 1949, May 8, 1950. All items in CJG-CL. For a description of John Rockefeller III's attempt to solve the problems he encountered as a member of the National Committee on Maternal Health, see chapter 21. For a description of further contributions by Pincus and Rock to contraception, see Chapter 27.

43. Christopher Tietze and Clarence Gamble, "The Condom as a Contraceptive Method in Public Health Work," *HF* 9 (December 1944), pp. 97–111.

44. Tietze to Gamble, April 18, 1944, CJG-CL.

45. Gamble to Tietze, May 1, 1945, CJG-CL.

46. Gamble to Dickinson, December 4, 1933; Gamble to A. R. Kaufman, July 4, 1934; Robert L. Dickinson, "Household Contraceptives: Simple and Brief Instructions for Their Preparation and Use," October 23, 1933, CJG-CL.

47. Tietze to Gamble, May 15, 1945, CJG-CL.

48. The exception to this statement is the aid program to Ceylon begun by Sweden in 1958. See Richard Symonds and Michael Carder, *The United Nations and the Population Question* (New York, 1973), p. 98 and "Swedish Government Was the First to Provide Assistance to Action Programs," *Population Chronicle* no. 1 (August 1969), p. 5.

49. Anna L. Southam, "Historical Review of Intra-Uterine Devices," *Intra-Uterine Contraception: Proceedings of the Second International Conference,* ed. S. J. Segal, A. L. Southam, and K. D. Shafer (Louvain, 1965), pp. 3–5; Christopher Tietze, "Intra-Uterine Contraceptive Rings: History and Statistical Appraisal," *Intra-Uterine Contraceptive Devices: Proceedings of the Conference, April 30–May 1, 1962, New York City,* ed. Christopher Tietze and Sarah Lewit (Amsterdam, 1962), pp. 9–20; Robert L. Dickinson, *Control of Conception* (2nd ed., Baltimore, 1938), ch. 13, "Intrauterine Stems and Rings," pp. 225–43.

50. Dickinson, "Intrauterine Stems and Rings," pp. 234, 238–39; Discussion of Hannah Stone, "Occlusive Methods of Contraception," *JOC* (May 1937), pp. 105–6; Mary Halton, Robert Dickinson, and Christopher Tietze, "Contraception With An Intrauterine Silk Coil," *HF* 13 (March 1948), pp. 10–13; Clarence Gamble to Christopher Tietze, January 9, 1947, CJG-CL.

51. Tietze to Gamble, May 29, 1947; Bernard Berelson, "Application of Intra-Uterine Contraception in Family Planning Programs," *Intra-Uterine Contraception*, p. 13.

52. *HF* 13 (March 1948).

53. Tietze to Gamble, November 26, 1948, CJG-CL.

54. Tietze to Gamble, December 2, 1948, August 23, 1949, CJG-CL.

55. Sidney Gamble to Clarence Gamble, April 21, 1952, CJG-CL.

Chapter 21

1. For an excellent short summary of the origins of the unprecedented post–World War II population growth, see "Man's Population Predicament," *Population Bulletin* 27 (April 1971).

My use of the term "demographic transition" is metaphoric and is not intended to imply any inevitable sequence of demographic events in the modernization process. For criticism of the concept as a model of demographic change, see Robert V. Wells, "Family History and Demographic Transition," *Journal of Social History* 9 (Fall 1975), pp. 1–19.

2. Richard Symonds and Michael Carder, *The United Nations and the Population Question* (New York, 1973), pp. xiv, 34, 74; Alfred Sauvy, "Le Malthusianisme anglo-saxon," *Population* (April–June 1947), pp. 221–42; Genesis 1:26–28, quoted in *Population, Evolution, and Birth Control: A Collage of Controversial Ideas*, ed. Garrett Hardin (2nd ed., San Francisco, 1969), p. 180.

3. Symonds and Carter, pp. 37, 52; A. J. Coale and E. M. Hoover, *Population Growth and Economic Development in Low Income Countries: A Case Study of India's Prospects* (Princeton, N.J., 1958).

4. Frank W. Notestein, "Summary of the Demographic Background of Problems of Underdeveloped Areas," *MMFQ* 26 (July 1948), pp. 250, 252.

5. Raymond B. Fosdick, *John D. Rockefeller, Jr.: A Portrait* (New York, 1956), pp. 85, 137–40, 404–6; Charles W. Clarke, *Taboo: The Story of the Pioneers of Social Hygiene* (Washington, 1961), pp. 65, 67, 78–79.

6. Sophie D. Aberle and George W. Corner, *Twenty-Five Years of Sex Research: History of the National Research Council Committee for Research in Problems of Sex: 1922–1947* (Philadelphia, 1953); James H. Jones, "Scientists and Progressives: The Development of Scientific Research on Sex in the United States: 1920–1963," a Paper presented at the American Historical Association Convention, December 1972. Two excellent monographs written after Kinsey's death but based on the case histories accumulated under Rockefeller funding are Paul H. Gebhard et al., *Pregnancy, Birth and Abortion* (New York, 1958) and *Sex Offenders* (New York, 1965).

7. Marshall Balfour, "Problems in Health Promotion in the Far East," *MMFQ* 28 (January 1950), pp. 84–95.

8. Frank Notestein, "Reminiscences," *MMFQ* 49 (October 1971), pp. 78–80; Marshall Balfour, Frank W. Notestein, and Irene B. Taeuber, *Public Health and Demography in the Far East* (New York, 1950).

9. Personal Communications with Greer Williams. Williams was employed by the Rockefeller Foundation to write the history of its International Health Division. Part of his study has been published as *The Plague Killers: Untold Stories of the Great Campaigns against Disease* (New York, 1969).

10. Personal Communications with James H. Jones; Notestein, "Reminiscences," p. 79. The congressional vendetta against Kinsey and the withdrawal of Rockefeller sup-

port is covered in Wardell B. Pomeroy, *Dr. Kinsey and the Institute for Sex Research* (New York, 1972), ch. 23. Although an excellent book, Pomeroy's memoir creates the mistaken impression that the Rockefeller Foundation's abandonment of Kinsey resulted solely from outside criticism of Kinsey and the Reece Committee investigation.

11. Symonds and Carder, pp. xvi, 39, 60, 62, 65, 74–75, 118–22.

12. Frederick Osborn to author, May 2, 1973.

13. Ibid. See also *Report of the Population Council, Inc: November 5, 1952 to December 31, 1955.*

14. *Report of the Population Council, Inc.: November 5, 1952 to December 31, 1955,* pp. 30–34; *The Population Council: 1952–1964*, pp. 22, 29–33; Symonds and Carder, pp. 56, 126–32.

15. Phyllis T. Piotrow, *World Population Crisis: The United States Response* (New York, 1973), pp. 89, 93, 137, 147; Remiert T. Ravenholt, "The A.I.D. Population and Family Planning Program—Goals, Scope, and Progress," *Demography* 5 (1968), p. 562; John D. Rockefeller III, "The Citizen's View of Public Programs for Family Limitation," in *Fertility and Family Planning: A World View,* ed. S. J. Behrman, Leslie Corsa, and Ronald Freedman (Ann Arbor, Mich., 1969), p. 497.

16. Bernard Berelson, "Beyond Family Planning," *Science* 163 (February 7, 1969), pp. 533–43; cf. Kingsley Davis, " 'Population Policy': Will Current Programs Succeed?" *Science* 158 (November 10, 1967), pp. 730–39.

17. Colville Deverell, "The International Planned Parenthood Federation—Its Role in Developing Countries," *Demography* 5 (1968), pp. 574–77.

18. Frank Notestein, "The Population Council and the Demographic Crisis in the Less Developed World," *Demography* 5 (1968), pp. 556–57.

Chapter 22

1. Margaret Sanger, *Autobiography* (New York, 1938), chs. 25–26, 37–38; Arata Ishimoto to Margaret Sanger, January 2, 1938, MS-SS; T. J. Samuel, "The Development of India's Policy of Population Control," *MMFQ* 44 (January 1966), pp. 51–52.

2. Address given to Family Planning Association of Great Britain, June 2, 1956, MS-SS. See also Shidzue Kato, "History of the Birth Control Movement in Japan," *Proceedings of the Third International Conference on Planned Parenthood* (Bombay, 1953), pp. 232–34.

3. Vera Houghton, "International Planned Parenthood Federation: Its History and Influence," *The Eugenics Review* 53 (October 1961 and January 1962). Reprint by IPPF, April 1962, MS-SS; Lawrence Lader, *The Margaret Sanger Story* (New York, 1955), p. 322; *Proceedings of the International Conference on Population and World Resources, Cheltenham, August 1948* (London, 1948).

4. Dorothy Brush, "Impressions of Margaret Sanger," MS-SS. A shorter version of the story can be found in "Farewell to Mrs. Dorothy Brush," *Planned Parenthood: Monthly Bulletin of the Family Planning Association of India* 4 (February–March 1957). Copy in CJG-CL.

5. Brush, "Impressions of Margaret Sanger"; *The Brush Foundation, Cleveland, Ohio: 1928–1958* (n.d.; n.p.). Copy CJG-CL. The foundation was endowed in 1928 with $500,000, supplemented in 1942 with another $250,000 from one of Charles Brush, Sr.'s grandsons, Maurice Perkins.

6. Dorothy Brush to Margaret Sanger, May 29, 1946, MS-SS.

7. Dorothy Brush, "The IPPF Bulletin: Around the World News of Population and Birth Control," *The Fifth International Conference on Planned Parenthood: Report of the Proceedings* (London, 1956), pp. 271–272; Dhanvanthi Rama Rau to Margaret Sanger, February 24, 1954; Dorothy Brush to Margaret Sanger, November 16, 1953, MS-SS; "Report of the Allocation of Funds at Berlin Meeting of IPPF Governing Body, October 26–30, 1957," CJG-CL; Frederick Osborn to C. P. Blacker, May 18, 1959, MS-SS.

8. "Swedish Government Was the First to Provide Assistance to Action Programs," *Population Chronicle* #1 (August 1969), p. 5; Richard Symonds and Michael Carder, *The United Nations and the Population Question*, p. 98; Siva Chinnatamly, "The Family Planning Association, Ceylon," *The Fifth International Conference*, p. 294.

Chapter 23

1. Mary Halton, Robert Dickinson, and Christopher Tietze, "Contraception with an Intrauterine Silk Coil," *Human Fertility* 13 (March 1948), pp. 10–13. See also Chapter 20.

2. During the 1940s, Gamble became active in Birthright, Inc. (later the Human Betterment Association of America; since 1965, the Association for Voluntary Sterilization), but he was asked to leave the organization in 1947. He had been antagonizing the Planned Parenthood Federation of America by offering money to local birth control clinics to do sterilizations. The PPFA had refused to endorse sterilization (PPFA, "Minutes of Board of Directors Meeting," May 16, 1946). Also, Gamble continued his habit of making contacts with local sterilization groups and offering to pay for projects without securing the approval of the national organization. See "Minutes of Executive Committee Meeting of Birthright, Inc." April 11, 1947, CJG-CL.

Gamble's publications on eugenic sterilization include: "State Sterilization Programs for the Prophylactic Control of Mental Disease and Mental Deficiency," *American Journal of Psychiatry* 102 (November 1945); "Sterilization of the Mentally Deficient under State Laws," *American Journal of Mental Deficiency* 51 (October 1946); "The Sterilization of the Mentally Handicapped in North Carolina," *North Carolina Medical Journal* 9 (February 1948); "Sterilization of the Mentally Deficient in 1946," *American Journal of Mental Deficiency* 52 (April 1948); "The Sterilization of Psychotic Patients under State Laws," *American Journal of Psychiatry* 105 (July 1948); "The Prevention of Mental Deficiency by Sterilization," *American Journal of Mental Deficiency* 56 (July 1951); "Protective Sterilization in the Rocky Mountain States," *Rocky Mountain Medical Journal* (July 1949). Reprints of all articles in CJG-CL.

Christopher Tietze tried to dampen Gamble's enthusiasm for sterilization, but was not very successful (Tietze to Gamble, December 8, 1948, CJG-CL). See also, Gamble to Mrs. F. Robertson Jones, February 20, 1946, CJG-CL.

For Gamble's efforts to promote higher birth rates among the college educated, see his correspondence with C. M. Goethe (CJG-CL) and "The Deficit in the Birthrate of College Graduates," *Human Fertility* 11 (June 1946), pp. 41–47; "The College Birthrate," *Journal of Heredity* 38 (December 1947); "The Score of the Colleges," *Journal of Heredity* 43 (May–June 1952). Reprints in CJG-CL.

3. Greer Williams, manuscript biography of Clarence J. Gamble, "Dr. Koya and the Three Villages"; Clarence Gamble to Margaret Sanger, July 4, 1949, MS-SS; Gamble to Warren Thompson, June 17, 1949, CJG-CL.

4. Williams, "Dr. Koya and the Three Villages."

5. Yoshia Koya, *Pioneering in Family Planning* (Tokyo, 1963), pp. 17–20; John Y. Takeshita, review of Tenri Ota, *Datai Kinshi To Yuseihogoho* (The Prohibition of Induced Abortion and the Eugenic Protection Law), *MMFQ* 45 (October 1967), pp. 467–71. Abortion was only legal for medical indications in 1948, but the law was broadened several times. See Juitsu Kitaoka, "How Japan Halved Her Birth Rate in Ten Years," *The Sixth International Conference On Planned Parenthood: Report of the Proceedings* (London, 1960), p. 29.

6. Williams, "Dr. Koya and the Three Villages."

7. Yoshio Koya, "Seven Years of a Family Planning Programme in Three Typical Japanese Villages," *The Sixth International Conference*, pp. 304–8; "Five Years of Family Planning in Three Japanese Villages," *The Fifth International Conference on Planned Parenthood: Report of the Proceedings* (London, 1956), pp. 113–17.

8. Koya, *Pioneering in Family Planning*, pp. 25–26.

9. Koya, "Seven Years," p. 305. In 1957, having had the chance to experiment with several methods, 50 percent of the contraceptors were using condoms (12 percent only during the fertile period), 13 percent were using the diaphragm/jelly, and 10 percent had been sterilized. Clearly effectiveness or confidence in the method was a big factor in its acceptability. As Tietze had told Gamble before, "back yard" methods would not work.

10. Edward M. Brecher, *The Sex Researchers* (Boston, 1969), p. 179.

11. Williams, manuscript biography of Gamble, "Emerging Problems and the IPPF"; Gamble, "Pregnancy Rates During the Use of Contraception in India and Pakistan," *The Fifth International Conference,* pp. 145–49.

12. Dorothy Brush to Margaret Sanger, April 13, 1953, MS-SS.

13. Margaret Sanger to William Vogt, November 10, 1953; C. P. Blacker to Margaret Sanger, January 13, 1954, MS-SS.

14. Sanger to C. P. Blacker, January 18, 1954, MS-SS.

15. T. O. Griessemer to Vera Houghton, March 29, 1956, CJG-CL.

16. Clarence Gamble to C. P. Blacker, May 5, 1955, CJG-CL.

17. Dhanvanthi Rama Rau to Clarence Gamble, September 14, 1954, MS-SS.

18. Vera Houghton to Margaret Sanger, August 27, 1954, MS-SS. See also Vera Houghton to Margaret Sanger, February 24, 1955; Sanger to Mrs. G. J. Watumull, December 28, 1954, and Sanger to Clarence Gamble, December 7, 1954, MS-SS.

19. Williams, "Margaret Roots"; Rufus Day to Margaret Sanger, May 21, 1956, MS-SS.

20. C. P. Blacker to Gamble, February 11, 1955; July 27, 1955; "Conference with Dr. Blacker at IPPF, April 20, 1958"; Blacker to Gamble, May 14, 1958, July 2, 1958; September 17, 1958; October 29, 1958, CJG-CL.

21. Clarence Gamble to Mary Lasker, March 14, 1946, CJG-CL.

22. Williams, "Harvard" and "School of Public Health," manuscript biography of Gamble; June Weiss, "Clarence James Gamble; 1894–1966," *Harvard Public Health Alumni Bulletin* (January 1967), pp. 20–22.

23. Williams, "The Khanna Study," manuscript biography of Gamble; John B. Wyon and John E. Gordon, *The Khanna Study: Population Problems in the Rural Punjab* (Cambridge, Mass., 1971), pp. 1, 3.

24. Williams, "The Khanna Study"; Wyon and Gordon provide a bibliography of articles deriving from the project, pp. 381–84; grants listed p. xxii. For a critique of *The Khanna Study,* see Mahmood Mamdani, *The Myth of Population Control: Family, Caste, and Class in an Indian Village* (New York, 1972).

25. Wyon and Gordon, pp. 36–48, 141–42, 147–48; Mamdani, p. 160 and passim.

26. Wyon and Gordon, p. 44.

27. Moore's contribution to the population control movement is described in Lawrence Lader, *Breeding Ourselves to Death* (New York, 1971; paperback only).

In a letter that was widely circulated under Moore's signature, and those of Bruce Barton and Will Clayton, they wrote, "We're not primarily interested in the sociological or humanitarian aspects of birth control. We *are* interested in the use . . . which the Communists make of hungry people in their drive to conquer the earth." For criticism of this approach by Loraine Leeson Campbell (Mrs. Walter E. Campbell), who was then president of the Planned Parenthood Federation of America, see Part 7 of her oral history in the Schlesinger Library, and Mrs. Walter E. Campbell to Hugh Moore, November 30, 1956; Bruce Barton, Will Clayton, and Hugh Moore to Loraine Campbell, November 13, 1956, PPLM-SS.

28. Frederick Osborn to Margaret Sanger, April 3, 1957, MS-SS.

29. Rufus Day to Margaret Sanger, January 20, 1957; Sanger to C. P. Blacker, July 18, 1957, MS-SS.

30. Phyllis T. Piotrow, *World Population Crisis: The United States Response* (New York, 1973), p. 45.

31. *The Population Council, 1952–1964,* p. 36.

32. Interview with Christopher Tietze, New York City, April 27, 1971.

33. Transcript of an Interview with Christopher Tietze, New York City, March 8, 1973, p. 43. Interview conducted by R. Christian Johnson. Copy in Countway Library. Hereafter cited as Tietze Transcript. Minutes, "Special Meeting of the NCMH," October 30, 1957, CJG-CL.

34. Tietze Transcript, p. 1; PPFA, *Simple Methods of Contraception: An Assessment of Their Medical, Moral, and Social Implications,* ed. Winfield Best and Frederick S. Jaffee (New York, 1958).

35. Interview with Frank Notestein, Princeton, N.J., August 12, 1974.

36. Transcript of an Interview with Alan F. Guttmacher, New York City, February 23, 1973. Interview conducted by R. Christian Johnson. Transcript in Countway Library. Hereafter cited as Guttmacher Transcript.

37. Guttmacher Transcript, pp. 12–13; Tietze, "Intra-Uterine Contraceptive Rings: Historical and Statistical Appraisal," *Intra-Uterine Contraceptive Devices: Proceedings of the Conference, April 30–May 1, 1962, New York City,* ed. Christopher Tietze and Sarah Lewitt (Amsterdam, 1962), pp. 11–18; Oppenheimer, "Prevention of Pregnancy by the Graefenberg Ring Method," *AJOG* 78 (August 1959), pp. 446–54; Ishihama," Clinical Studies on Intrauterine Rings, Especially the Present State of Contraception in Japan . . . ," *Yokohama Medical Journal* 10 (April 1959), pp. 89–105; John Y. Takeshita, review of Tenrei Ota, *Datai Kinshi To Yuseihogoho* (The Prohibition of Induced Abortion and the Eugenic Protection Law).

38. Guttmacher Transcript, p. 13.

39. Tietze Transcript, p. 11.

40. Frank Notestein, "The Population Council and the Demographic Crisis of the Less Developed World," *Demography* 5 (1968), pp. 555–57.

41. Tietze Transcript, p. 16.
The anovulant pill was also becoming available during the time the IUD was developed. The Population Council did not believe the pill was the answer to their problems. First, the pill was being developed by commercial interests, specifically J. D. Searle, the company for which Gregory Pincus worked. Even if provided at cost, the pill was still prohibitively expensive. Second, the council was seeking a method that did not require "the birth control habit," that could be used in a population without high motivation to practice contraception.

42. Frank Notestein, "1966: A Milestone; Report of the President," The Population Council, *Annual Report: 1966,* pp. 11–21; John A. Ross and Oliver D. Finnegan, "Within Family Planning—Korea" *Demography* 5 (1968), pp. 679–89; Enver Adil "Pakistan's Family Planning Programme," in *Population Control: Implications, Trends and Prospects; Proceedings of the Pakistan International Family Planning Conference at Dacca; January 28 to February 4th, 1969* (Lahore, 1969), pp. 15–30.

43. Philip M. Hauser, "Family Planning and Population Programs: A Book Review Article," 4 (1967), pp. 397–414; Harry M. Raulet, "Family Planning and Population Control in Developing Countries," *Demography* 7 (May 1970), pp. 211–34. Criticism of this kind is discussed at length in Part VIII, "The Trouble with Family Planning."

44. Notestein Interview.

45. George Wilbur, "Fertility and the Need for Family Planning among the Rural Poor in the United States," and Gary D. London, "Family Planning Programs of the Office of Economic Opportunity: Scope, Operation, and Impact," *Demography* 5 (1968), pp. 894–909 and 924–40.

46. The Hastings Center Institute of Society, Ethics, and the Life Sciences, *Bibliography of Society, Ethics, and the Life Sciences,* ed. Sharmon Sollitto and Robert M. Veatch (n.p., 1973); Ronald M. Green, "Population Growth and Justice" (doctoral dissertation, Religious Ethics, Harvard, 1972); Arthur J. Dyck, "Procreative Rights and Population Policy," *Studies: The Hastings Center Institute* 1 (1973), pp. 74–82.

Chapter 24

1. L. Haberlandt, "Uber hormonale Sterilisierung des weiblichen Tierkörpers," *Münchener Medizinische Wochenschrift* 68 (1921), pp. 1577–78; Sophie D. Aberle and George W. Corner, *Twenty-five Years of Sex Research: History of the National Research Council Committee for Research in Problems of Sex, 1922–1947* (Philadelphia, 1953).

2. Aberle and Corner, pp. 9–13, 15, 23.

3. Ibid., p. 17.

4. Ibid., p. 32.

5. The "heroic age of reproductive endocrinology" is described by George W. Corner, *The Hormones in Human Reproduction* (Princeton, N.J., 1947; 1st ed., 1942), and Alan Parkes, "The Rise of Reproductive Endocrinology, 1926–1940," *Journal of Endocrinology* 34 (1966), pp. xx–xxxii; reprinted in Parkes, *Sex, Science, and Society* (Gateshead, England, 1966), pp. 14–36. See also Corner, "The Early History of the Oestrogenic Hormones," *Journal of Endocrinology* 31 (1964–65), pp. iii–xvii.
The contributions of the Committee for Research in Problems of Sex to the development of endocrinology may be followed in the list of grants and publications in Aberle and Corner, *Twenty-five Years.*

6. Albert Q. Maisel, *The Hormone Quest* (New York, 1965), pp. 34–35, 44; Corner, *Hormones in Human Reproduction*, pp. 110–13.

7. Maisel, pp. 29–37; Edward Farber, *Nobel Prize Winners in Chemistry: 1901–1961* (New York, 1963), pp. 107–10, 168–70, 171–74. The two Americans were Edgar Allen and Edward Doisy of Washington University (St. Louis), the discoverers of estrogen. Doisy shared the Nobel Prize in physiology and medicine with Henrick Dam in 1943 for isolating vitamin K.

8. Corner, *Hormones in Human Reproduction*, p. 87; Maisel, pp. 45–52.

9. Corner, *Hormones in Human Reproduction*, pp. 126–32.

10. Raphael Kurzrok, "The Prospects for Hormonal Sterilization," *Journal of Contraception* 2 (February 1937), pp. 27–29.

11. Fuller Albright, "Disorders of the Female Gonads," in *Internal Medicine: Its Theory and Practice*, ed. John H. Musser (Philadelphia, 1945), p. 966; quoted in *Human Fertility* 10 (September 1945), p. 80.

Chapter 25

1. Dwight J. Ingle provides a short essay, "Gregory Pincus," in National Academy of Sciences, *Biographical Memoirs* 42 (1969), pp. 229–70, which includes a useful bibliography. Hudson Hoagland, Pincus' friend and co-worker at the Worcester Foundation for Experimental Biology, discusses Pincus' background and education in his manuscript autobiography, Change, Chance, and Challenge, ch. 5.
Biographical material is thin in the Gregory Pincus papers at the Library of Congress (GP-LC), but there is a long diary that Pincus kept during his senior year in high school (including many poems) and some correspondence from the 1930s when he was teaching at Harvard. Included in the Library of Congress collection are many newspaper and magazine feature articles on Pincus which are repetitive but do provide some information on his early years.

2. Pincus, "Diary—1920," entries for January 7, January 20, July (n.d.), August 23, 1920; Ingle, "Gregory Pincus," p. 230.
Pincus' early development seems to have been unexceptional. He loved his parents, did well in school, and, as a senior in high school wrote much sweetly idealistic poetry. In his diary he reminisced that in grammar school, "We were the only family of Jews there and I was tortured and hooted a great deal. But pleasant days were spent

there . . . I remember in school I used to faithfully recite the morning prayer to Jesus and sing 'Onward Christian Soliders' with a fervor unequalled by any Christian present." The good memories far outweighed the bad.

3. Gregory Pincus, "I. A Comparative Study of the Chromosomes of the Norway Rat and the Black Rat; II. A Study of the Genetic Factors Affecting the Expression of the Piebald Pattern in the Rat" (unpublished Sc.D. thesis, Harvard, 1927).

4. Interview with Min-Chueh Chang, October 24, 1973, Shrewsbury, Mass.

5. L. C. Dunn, "William Ernest Castle," in National Academy of Sciences, *Biographical Memoirs* 38 (1965), pp. 51–54. For another description of life at the Bussey, see Mary and Howard Evans, *William Morton Wheeler: Biologist* (Cambridge, Mass., 1970), ch. 9.

6. Dunn, "William Castle," pp. 38–41, 45–47, 56. For discussion of Mendel and his impact on evolutionary theory, see Loren Eiseley, *Darwin's Century: Evolution and the Men Who Discovered It* (New York, 1958), ch. 8. Garland E. Allen's "Thomas Hunt Morgan and the Problem of Natural Selection," *Journal of the History of Biology* 1 (Spring 1968), pp. 113–39, provides a description of the resistance to the theory of natural selection on the part of experimental biologists, a resistance that was eventually diminished by the insights into evolutionary change provided by Mendelian concepts.

7. Loeb's research is described in W. J. V. Osterhout, "Jacques Loeb," *Journal of General Physiology* 8 (1928), pp. ix–xcii, reprinted in National Academy of Sciences, *Biographical Memoirs* 13 (1930), pp. 218–401. Loeb's place in the history of science is delineated by Donald Fleming in his introduction to Loeb's *The Mechanistic Conception of Life* (Cambridge, Mass., 1964).

8. For de Kruif's criticism of medical practice and research in the United States, see *Our Medicine Men* (New York, 1922) and "Medicine" in *Civilization in the United States: An Inquiry by Thirty Americans*, ed. Harold Stearns (New York, 1922), pp. 443–56. De Kruif lauds Loeb in "Jacques Loeb, the Mechanist," *Harper's Monthly Magazine* 146 (1922–23), pp. 181–90. De Kruif describes his collaboration with Sinclair Lewis in *The Sweeping Wind: A Memoir* (New York, 1962). See also Mark Schorer, *Sinclair Lewis* (New York, 1961), pp. 361–69. Charles E. Rosenberg's "Martin Arrowsmith: The Scientist as Hero" discusses the Loebian ideals of Martin Arrowsmith, *American Quarterly* 15 (Fall 1963), pp. 447–58. For Loeb's influence on other scientists, see Fleming's introduction to *The Mechanistic Conception of Life;* Jay Tepperman, M.D., "The Research Scientist in Modern Fiction," *Perspectives in Biology and Medicine* 3 (Summer 1960), p. 550; and George Corner, *A History of the Rockefeller Institute: 1901–1953, Origins and Growth* (New York, 1964), pp. 77–80, 166–70.

9. When Loeb taught at the University of Chicago (1892–1902), a separate department of physiology had been created for him. The division of biology into several branches reflected both the growth of knowledge and the conflicting philosophies of experimental biologists and the traditional naturalists. "General physiology" in effect meant experimental, a manipulative rather than a descriptive approach to the study of nature. More recently general physiology as a separate branch of knowledge has ceased to have much importance as the scientific animus it once represented has found expression in other specialties such as molecular biology.

Among Harvard biologists, W. J. V. Osterhout, professor of botany and coeditor with Loeb of the *Journal of General Physiology,* represented the Loebian philosophy before Crozier's arrival, but Osterhout left Harvard in 1924, following Loeb's death, to take over his department at the Rockefeller Institute.

All of the information on Crozier comes from Hudson Hoagland and R. T. Mitchell, "William John Crozier: 1892–1955," *American Journal of Psychology* 69 (March 1956), pp. 135–38 and Hoagland, *Change, Chance and Challenge,* ch. 2.

10. Pincus' publications can be easily followed in the bibliography included in Ingle's memoir.

11. Fleming, introduction to *The Mechanistic Conception of Life* p. xxiii.

12. "Observations on the Living Eggs of the Rabbit," *Proceedings of the Royal Society of London,* Series B, 107 (1930), pp. 132–67.

13. *The Eggs of Mammals* (New York, 1936); J. M. Robson, *Recent Advances in Sex and Reproductive Physiology* (London, 1934), pp. 129–30, 159, 208.

14. *The Eggs of Mammals*, p. vii; Aberle and Corner, *Twenty-five Years of Sex Research*, pp. 199–200.

15. Gregory Pincus to George L. Streeter, department of embryology, Carnegie Institution of Washington, May, 1937, no date given in handwritten copy, GP-LC.

16. It is almost certain that Pincus was mistaken in his claim to have achieved *in vitro* fertilization. It is now known that rabbit spermatozoa must undergo "seasoning" or capacitation in the female genital tract before they can activate the ovum. The live birth of a rabbit developed from an ovum fertilized *in vitro* would not be achieved until 1959, by Min-Chueh Chang, Pincus' long time co-worker at the Worcester Foundation for Experimental Biology. In 1934, Pincus probably caused the rabbit eggs to develop through accidental parthenogenetic activation. Ironically, parthenogenesis proved much easier to achieve in rabbits than *in vitro* fertilization.

Gregory Pincus and E. V. Enzmann, "Can Mammalian Eggs Undergo Normal Development *in vitro*?" *Proceedings of the National Academy of Sciences* 20 (1934), pp. 121–22; C. R. Austin, "Observations on the Penetration of the Sperm into the Mammalian Egg," *Australian Journal of Scientific Research*, Series B, 4 (1951), p. 594, and *The Mammalian Egg* (Oxford, England, 1961), pp. 119, 123.

17. May 13, 1934, sec. 8, p. 6, col. 3. See also *Time* 23 (March 12, 1934), p. 57.

Bokanovsky's process involved, of course, much more than *in vitro* fertilization. Pincus was not conducting cloning experiments. His study was a legitimate attempt to define the process of normal fertilization. The readiness with which Pincus' experiment was exaggerated into "Rabbits Born in Glass" and the mass production of identical twins does illustrate, however, the attitudes of popular writers toward scientific study of conception.

18. William Crozier to Gregory Pincus, July 28, 1934, GP-LC.

19. My understanding of why some of Pincus' results were not reproducible is based on a discussion with Min-Chueh Chang. Although he has done as much as any researcher to demonstrate specific errors in Pincus' publications, Chang is quick to point out that Pincus' mistakes reflected the inherent difficulty of pioneering in a new field. He believes Pincus' main contributions in the 1930s were the development of the technique of drug-induced superovulation and the demonstration that ova could be grown in culture and transplanted into host-mothers. Pincus misinterpreted some of the results he obtained, but he stimulated the work of others through both the audacity of his claims and by developing experimental techniques that others refined. See also Ingle, "Gregory Pincus," p. 232.

20. *The Eggs of Mammals*, pp. 108–10.

21. J. D. Ratcliff, "No Father to Guide Them," *Collier's Magazine* (March 20, 1937), pp. 19ff. See also *News-Week* 7 (April 4, 1936), p. 30; *Time* 27 (April 6, 1936), pp. 49–50; *New York Times*, March 27, 1936, p. 19, and Editorial, March 28, 1936, p. 14, and April 5, 1936, sec. 10, p. 6.

22. Ratcliff.

23. George W. Corner, *A History of the Rockefeller Institute* (New York, 1964), p. 80.

24. Quoted in Ratcliff, p. 79.

25. Ibid.

26. "An Address to Members of the University on the Birthday of President Charles W. Eliot, March 20, 1936," in *Addresses in Connection with the Tercentenary of Harvard College* (Cambridge, Mass., 1936), p. 7.

27. L C. Dunn, "William Castle," pp. 51, 54–55.

28. William Crozier to Gregory Pincus, October 20, 1934. See also Crozier's criticism of Walter Cannon, Crozier to Pincus, October 18, 1937 (both letters in GP-LC) and Crozier to Walter Cannon, August 5, 1931 (Cannon Papers, Countway Library).

29. Hudson Hoagland, *The Road to Yesterday* (privately printed, Worcester, Mass., 1974), pp. 61–62.

30. William Crozier to Walter Cannon, April 11, 1940. Cannon papers, Countway Library.

31. William Crozier to Gregory Pincus, May 10, 1938, GP-LC.
32. William Castle to Gregory Pincus, April 19, 1938, GP-LC.
33. William Castle to Gregory Pincus, April 26, 1938; Hudson Hoagland to Warren Weaver, May 24, 1938, GP-LC; Hoagland, Change, Chance, and Challenge, ch. 5.
34. *New York Times*, November 2, 1939, p. 18; November 3, 1939, editorial, "Rabbits without Fathers," p. 20; April 28, 1940, p. 8; April 30, 1941, p. 11.
The scientific articles describing Pincus' experiments are: "The Development of Fertilized and Artificially Activated Rabbit Eggs," *Journal of Experimental Zoology* 82 (1939), pp. 85–120, and "The Breeding of Rabbits Produced by Recipients of Artificially Activated Ova," *Proceedings of the National Academy of Sciences* 25 (1939), pp. 557–59; with Herbert Shaprio, "Further Studies on the Activation of Rabbit Eggs," *Proceedings of the American Philosophical Society* 83 (1940), pp. 631–47, and "Further Studies on the Parthenogenetic Activation of Rabbit Eggs," *Proceedings of the National Academy of Sciences* 26 (1940), pp. 163–65.
35. R. A. Beatty, *Parthenogenesis and Polyploidy in Mammalian Development* (Cambridge, England, 1957), p. 40. See pp. 37–42 for a summary and evaluation of Pincus' experiments.
36. "Development of Parthenogenetic Rabbit Blastocysts Induced by Low Temperature Storage of Unfertilized Ova," *Journal of Experimental Zoology* 125 (February 1954), p. 128.
37. R. A. Beatty, "Parthenogenesis in Vertebrates," ch. 9 in *Fertilization*, vol. 1, ed. Charles B. Metz and Alberto Monroy (New York, 1967), p. 433.
38. November 2, 1939, p. 18.
39. Maisel, *Hormone Quest*, ch. 3 and passim; Paul Vaughan, *The Pill on Trial* (London, 1970), ch. 1.
40. Hoagland, Change, Chance, and Challenge, ch. 6.
41. Albert Q. Maisel, "The Worcester Foundation: An Appreciation," Worcester Foundation for Experimental Biology, *Annual Report* (1967), p. 9; Hudson Hoagland to Leon Fenton, Trustee of Clark University, April 20, 1943. Copy in GP-LC.
42. Interview with Hudson Hoagland, October 24, 1973, Shrewsbury, Mass.
43. Hoagland, Change, Chance, and Challenge, ch. 6, p. 7. See also *The Road to Yesterday*, p. 80.
44. Hoagland, Change, Chance, and Challenge, ch. 6; Maisel, "The Worcester Foundation," p. 11.
45. Interview with Hudson Hoagland.
46. Minutes of Searle Research Conference, October 9 and 11, 1944, p. 16; Albert L. Raymond, Searle director of research, to Gregory Pincus, April 26, 1946. Both in GP-LC.
47. Maisel, *Hormone Quest*, ch. 4; Oscar Hechter, "Homage to Gregory Pincus," *Perspectives in Biology and Medicine* 11 (Winter 1968), pp. 358–70. See also Memo of Albert L. Raymond to Mr. Searle, "Clinical Steroid Program," May 8, 1950, GP-LC. Hechter, now professor of physiology, Northwestern University School of Medicine, was the key man on the WFEB perfusion team supported by Searle and is a good example of a young scientist whose career was advanced through work at the foundation.
48. For details of the perfusion project at WFEB, see Albert Raymond to Gregory Pincus, May 16 and December 1, 1950; Warren D. McPhee, attorney for Searle, to Pincus, November 27, 1950, GP-LC.
49. Gregory Pincus to Abraham Stone, January 25, 1952; "Report of Progress to PPFA," January 24, 1952, GP-LC; Min-Chueh Chang, "Mammalian Sperm, Eggs, and Control of Fertility," *Perspectives in Biology and Medicine* 11 (Spring 1968), p. 380.
50. This quote is taken from a letter Pincus wrote to Raymond on Stevens Hotel stationery following a meeting with Raymond in Chicago. He placed the letter in an envelope with Raymond's home address, but never mailed it. The letter is dated "Mon. PM" and internal evidence (Raymond to Pincus, November 1 and December 21, 1951) indicates that the letter was written in October 1951. GP-LC.

Chapter 26

1. Most of my biographical information on Katharine McCormick comes from "A Tribute to Katharine Dexter McCormick Presented on the Occasion of the Completion of Stanley McCormick Hall-East," MIT, March 1, 1968 (Copy in MIT Historical Collections). Especially useful were the nine pages of "Remarks" by William H. Bemis, Mrs. McCormick's attorney. Also useful were the obituaries from the *Santa Barbara News-Press*, December 30 and 31, 1967, MS-SS. In addition I have benefited from conversations with Warren Seamans, director of the MIT Historical Collections.

Katharine's older brother died in 1894 and the Dexter line died with her in 1967.

2. For discussion of the Sanger-Dennett rivalry, see Chapter 8.

The History of Woman Suffrage, vol. 6, ed. Ida H. Harper (New York, 1922), pp. 274, 276.

3. For discussion of Sanger's attitude toward other women reformers, see Chapter 10.

The History of Woman Suffrage, vol. 5, pp. 324–25, 337, 372, 442, 454, 555, 560, 600. McCormick wrote ch. 24, "War Service of Organized Suffragists" in this volume of the *History*.

4. Ibid., pp. 854, 869; Frank Lorimer, "The Development of Demography," ch. 6 in *The Study of Population: An Inventory and Appraisal*, ed. Philip H. Hauser and Otis D. Duncan (Chicago,1959), pp. 163–64; Sanger, *Autobiography*, pp. 383–84; Margaret Sanger to Katharine McCormick, October 27, 1950, MS-SS.

Aletta Jacobs' friendship with Catt is chronicled in Mary Gray Peck, *Carrie Chapman Catt* (New York, 1944), ch. 3, pp. 147–58. For discussion of McCormick's relationship to Catt and to the International Alliance, see pp. 348, 351, 352, 372, 420.

5. Alan F. Guttmacher to Friends of Planned Parenthood, February 10, 1968, PPFA-SS.

Margaret Sanger's correspondence with McCormick discussing contraceptive research begins in 1928 (Sanger to McCormick, July 31, 1928, MS-LC). They may well have discussed the question much earlier. I believe that McCormick was made acutely aware of the inadequacy of existing birth control methods by her husband's illness. As a biology major during the first heady days of Mendelianism in America, she was probably very much concerned over the possibility of transmitting Stanley's madness to posterity. And she did spend considerable time with Stanley on a Santa Barbara estate where he was kept as happy as possible for forty years. Barbara Solomon remembers that in 1960, while Solomon was director of the Radcliffe Archives, McCormick had been asked to contribute to Radcliffe College. One day McCormick burst into Solomon's office and announced that she would only give money for a Radcliffe-sponsored birth control clinic, still a shocking idea in 1960. McCormick then went into a long soliloquy in which she expressed great resentment over woman's biological burdens, denouncing not only the discomforts and risks of childbearing, but menstrual periods also. Solomon found McCormick's bitterness puzzling at the time, but after I told her of McCormick's marriage, she noted that the resentment toward menstruation made more sense. For a woman who must never have children, menstrual periods might not be a necessary part of life but a constant reminder of the barriers to equality for women. Perhaps Mrs. McCormick's periods became a monthly reminder of the cruel joke nature had played on her in the form of Stanley's insanity. While she could not abolish menstruation, she could aid the search for a foolproof contraceptive.

6. Bemis, "Remarks," p. 7.

7. Katharine McCormick to Margaret Sanger, April 27, 1937, MS-LC. See also Sanger to McCormick, July 31, 1928, January 8, 1937, April 6, 1937, September 17, 1938, MS-LC. The correspondence resumes in the Sophia Smith Collection, Katharine McCormick to Margaret Sanger, November 15, 1948.

8. Hudson Hoagland, Change, Chance, and Challenge, ch. 6, pp. 3–4.
9. Interview with Hudson Hoagland, October 24, 1973.
10. Bemis, "Remarks," pp. 5–7; Katharine McCormick to Margaret Sanger, November 15, 1948, MS-SS.
11. Sanger to McCormick, October 27, 1950. For discussion of the ill-fated attempt to fund contraceptive research through the National Research Council, see Chapter 20.

McCormick wrote Sanger on November 18, 1950, explaining: "Unfortunately our estate, which was terribly crippled by the inheritance taxes of over eighty-five percent, will again suffer from the new ones about to be imposed so I do not yet know what I shall be able to do."

McCormick was able to give Sanger $5,000 for the IPPF, and she was making an annual contribution of $1,000 to the PPFA (McCormick to Sanger, December 29, 1950).
12. McCormick to Sanger, January 22, 1952; Sanger to McCormick, February 26, 1952, MS-SS.
13. Gregory Pincus, *The Control of Fertility* (New York, 1965), p. 6; Abraham Stone to Margaret Sanger, March 1, 1952, MS-SS. Sanger had met Pincus in 1950, but their meeting was a casual one, far from the dramatic encounter described by Maisel in *The Hormone Quest*, ch. 7. Contraceptive research did not become a high priority item at the WFEB until after Mrs. McCormick's arrival on the scene in June 1953. In short, while the scientific foundation had been laid for the development of a birth control pill, that knowledge might not have been translated into a marketable product nearly so quickly without McCormick's decisive intervention.
14. Paul S. Henshaw, "Research Activities 1952–53, Dickinson Memorial Fund, Attachment II, Grants-in-Aid," Abraham Stone Papers, Countway Library. (AS-CL).
15. Sanger to McCormick, March 10, 1952; McCormick to Sanger, March 13, 1952, MS-SS.
16. McCormick to Sanger, May 31, 1952, MS-SS.
17. Gregory Pincus to Paul Henshaw, research director for the PPFA, June 10, 1953. Copy in MS-SS.

McCormick wrote Sanger (n.d., MS-SS), "I have persuaded my counsel [lawyer]—William Bemis—to come here about middle August—for a few days quiet visit—when I shall again try to wring more funds for contraceptive research from him."
18. Interview with Hudson Hoagland.
19. "Report of Progress to PPFA," January 24, 1952, p. 3; Pincus to William Vogt, April 21, 1952, GP-LC; Sanger to McCormick, September 25, 1952; McCormick to Sanger, October 1, 1952, MS-SS.
20. Sanger to Marion Ingersoll, February 18, 1954, MS-SS.
21. Sanger to McCormick, October 27, 1950, MS-SS.
22. William Vogt, *The Road to Survival* (New York, 1948), p. 280.
23. McCormick to Sanger, February 17, 1954, MS-SS.
24. William Vogt to Paul Henshaw, November 9, 1953. Copy in MS-SS; Alexander Langer to Margaret Sanger, May 5, 1954, MS-SS.
25. McCormick to Sanger, February 17, 1954, MS-SS.
26. Hoagland to McCormick, n.d. (November 1954), GP-LC.
27. Gregory Pincus to Margaret Snyder, executive secretary, PPFA, May 1, 1956, GP-LC.
28. Dickinson Research Memorial of the PPFA, July 1, 1953, "Appendix IV, Grants-in-Aid Administration," p. 8, AS-CL. Pincus had accepted this clause in 1953 (Pincus to Paul Henshaw, January 28, 1953, GP-LC), although he did point out that many of the compounds he was experimenting with belonged to the drug houses that supplied them. The PPFA was not deprived of a patentable discovery made with their research funds. Nevertheless, by receiving McCormick's money directly, Pincus skillfully avoided this question.
29. McCormick to Stone, July 6, 1954, MS-SS; Pincus to McCormick, December 28, 1955, GP-LC. See also Pincus to David Tyler, clinician in Puerto Rico, September 30, 1955, GP-LC.

30. Memorandum, Gregory Pincus to A. L. Raymond, October 31, 1956, "Ovulation Inhibitors," GP-LC. Searle's role in the pill's development is discussed at length in Chapter 27.

31. Sanger to McCormick, December 12, 1956, MS-SS.

32. See William Vogt's description of Pincus' reception at the 1955 IPPF conference in Tokyo (Vogt to McCormick, November 23, 1955, copy in MS-SS); Vaughan, *The Pill on Trial,* pp. 32–35; Robert Sheehan, "The Birth-Control 'Pill' " *Fortune* (April 1958), pp. 54, 222.

Chapter 27

1. National Science Foundation, *Technology in Retrospect and Critical Events in Science,* vol. 1 (December 15, 1968) and vol. 2 (January 30, 1969). Hereafter cited as *Traces.*

2. *Traces,* vol. 1, Figure 8, pp. 73–74.

3. National Science Foundation, *Science, Technology, and Innovation* (February 1973), pp. 6–11; *Science News* 103 (April 14, 1973), p. 238. The ten technological innovations chosen for study were: Heart Pacemaker, Hybrid Corn, Hybrid Small Grains, Green Revolution Wheat, Electrophotography, Input-Output Economic Analysis, Orgonophosphorus Insecticides, Oral Contraceptive, Magnetic Ferrites, Video Tape Recorder.

4. Carl Djerassi, "Prognosis for the Development of New Chemical Birth-Control Agents" and "Birth Control after 1984," *Science* 166 and 169 (October 24, 1969, and September 4, 1970), pp. 468–73 and pp. 941–51.

5. *New York Times* (January 11, 1967), p. 1; James H. Jones, "The Macon County Experiment," unpublished paper written while Jones was a fellow in the Kennedy Program in medical ethics, Harvard Medical School, 1972–73. For general discussion of abuses of human subjects, see Henry K. Beecher, "Ethics and Clinical Research," *New England Journal of Medicine* 274 (June 16, 1966), pp. 1354–60, and *Research and the Individual* (Boston, 1969); M. H. Pappworth, *Human Guinea Pigs: Experimentation on Man* (Boston, 1968).

6. Ralph A. Fine, *The Great Drug Deception: The Shocking Story of MER/29 and the Folks Who Gave You Thalidomide* (New York, 1972).

7. Oscar Hechter, "Homage to Gregory Pincus," *Persepctives in Biology and Medicine* 11 (Spring 1968), p. 358.

8. "Gregory Pincus," National Academy of Sciences, *Biographical Memoirs* 42 (1969), p. 237.

9. Chang, "Mammalian Sperm, Eggs, and Control of Fertility," *Perspectives in Biology and Medicine* 11 (Spring 1968), p. 380.

10. Chang, On the Study of Animal Reproduction, an unpublished talk, GP-LC.

11. Ibid.; "Mammalian Sperm, Eggs, and Control of Fertility," pp. 376–77, 379.

12. Gregory Pincus to Warren Weaver, June 5, 1950; Weaver to Pincus, October 23, 1950; Pincus to Weaver, October 27, 1950; Weaver to Pincus, November 6, 1950, GP-LC. When I asked Chang why he stayed on at Worcester, he said, "I like it here" and pointed out the section in "Mammalian Sperm, Eggs, and Control of Fertility" where one of Pincus' old professors is quoted as saying that Pincus was "very fertilizing" (p. 377).

13. Chang to Pincus, August 4, 1949, GP-LC.

14. *Report of the Population Council, November 5, 1952, to December 31, 1955,* p. 34; "Report to the Rockefeller Foundation," March 17, 1952, GP-LC; Chang, On the Study of Animal Reproduction, GP-LC.

15. Chang, "Mammalian Sperm, Eggs, and Control of Fertility," p. 380; Pincus and Chang, "The Effects of Progesterone and Related Compounds on Ovulation and Early Development in the Rabbit," *Acta Physiologica Latinoamericana* 3 (1954), pp. 117–83.

16. Pincus, Chang, E. S. E. Hafex, M. X. Zarrow, and Anne Merrill, "Effects of Cer-

434

tain 19-Nor Steroids on Reproductive Processes in Animals," *Science* 124 (November 2, 1956), pp. 890–91.

17. Chang, "Mammalian Sperm, Eggs, and Control of Fertility," p. 380.

18. Chang to Pincus, February 24, 1951; Pincus to Albert Raymond, December 16, 1946; WFEB, salary budget, March 1964, box 79, GP-LC.

19. Margaret Sanger to Marion Ingersoll, February 18, 1954, MS-SS.

20. Katharine McCormick to Margaret Sanger, July 19, 1954, MS-SS.

21. Margaret Sanger to Mrs. John D. Rockefeller, Jr., February 19, 1960, MS-SS.

22. John Rock, *The Time Has Come: A Catholic Doctor's Proposals to End the Battle over Birth Control* (New York, 1963). Rock describes his further adventures as a Catholic advocate of contraception in "Dr. John Rock at 83: An Interview," *Boston Globe Sunday Magazine* (July 19, 1973), pp. 6–8.

For criticism of Rock by a Catholic spokesman, see remarks of Msgr. George A. Kelly, director of the Family Life Bureau of the Archdiocese of New York, *New York Times*, May 6, 1963, p. 20. For criticism by a more liberal Catholic, see J. S. Duhamel's review in *America* 108 (April 27, 1963), p. 608.

For criticism of Rock's rationalization of the pill by a fellow physician and birth controller, see Robert E. Hall's review of *The Time Has Come* in the *New York Times Book Review*, May 12, 1963, p. 30.

23. For a discussion of Rock's role on the AMA's committee on contraception during the 1930s, see Chapter 13.

"Maternal Mortality: What Must Be Done about It," *New England Journal of Medicine* 205 (1931), p. 902; "Medical and Biological Aspects of Contraception," *Clinics* 1 (April 1943), pp. 1601–2.

24. "Dr. John Rock at 83," p. 8.

25. National Committee on Maternal Health, "Notes on the Round Table Meeting of December 4, 1936: Should the Newly Married Practice Contraception," CMH-CL.

26. "Medical and Biological Aspects of Contraception," pp. 1608–9.

27. Ibid.

28. Ibid.

29. Ibid., pp. 1599–1601.

30. George V. Smith to Gregory Pincus, October 1, 1937; Minutes of Searle Research Conference, December 11, 1945; Albert Raymond to Gregory Pincus, April 26, 1946, GP-LC.

31. Interview with John Rock, June 15, 1971; John Rock and Miriam F. Menkin, "In Vitro Fertilization and Cleavage of Human Ovarian Eggs," *Science* 100 (August 4, 1944), pp. 105–7.

32. "Research Activities—1952–53: Dickinson Memorial," Attachment II, Grants-in-Aid, AS-CL.

33. Paul Henshaw to Gregory Pincus, April 27, 1953, GP-LC.

34. John Rock, Celso Ramon Garcia, and Gregory Pincus, "Synthetic Progestins in the Normal Human Menstrual Cycle," *Recent Progress in Hormone Research* 13 (1957), pp. 324–25.

35. Ibid.

36. Katharine McCormick to Margaret Sanger, June 17, 1954, MS-SS; I. V. Sollins to A. L. Monserrate, November 11, 1954, GP-LC. Chemical Specialties Company, a marketing corporation owned by the managers of Syntex, supplied the drug at a cut rate.

37. Carl Djerassi, "Steroid Oral Contraceptives," *Science* 151 (March 4, 1966), pp. 1055–61. See also Vaughan, *The Pill on Trial*, pp. 16–21, and Maisel, *Hormone Quest*, pp. 121–22.

38. Gregory Pincus to Albert Raymond, May 8, 1953; Memo, Francis J. Saunders to Albert Raymond, December 8, 1953, GP-LC.

39. Memo, Francis J. Saunders to Victor Drill, December 9, 1954; Albert Raymond to Gregory Pincus, December 21, 1954, GP-LC.

40. Pincus to Victor Drill, December 15, 1954; Pincus to Albert Raymond, October 11, 1954; Raymond to Pincus, October 4, 1957, December 2, 1955, GP-LC.

41. Albert Raymond to Pincus, December 2, 1955, GP-LC.

42. U.S. Congress, Senate, Subcommittee on Patents, Trademarks, and Copyrights of the Committee on the Judiciary, *Wonder Drugs: Hearings on S. Res. 167.*, 84th Congress, 2nd session, 1956, p. 29 and passim.

43. Ibid., pp. 31–40.

44. Ibid., pp. 64–151.

45. Ibid., pp. 104ff.

46. Gregory Pincus to Albert Raymond, June 16, 1952, GP-LC; Katharine McCormick to Margaret Sanger, June 17, 1954, MS-SS; Gregory Pincus to Paul Henshaw, July 23, 1954; I. V. Sollins to A. L. Monserrate, November 11, 1954; Joanne Sanford to Gregory Pincus, May 12, 1955, GP-LC.

47. Gregory Pincus to J. G. Searle, January 29, 1957, GP-LC. Since at least 1952, Pincus had been buying stock in Searle through the company's payroll deduction plan. See for example Joanne Sanford, Pincus' secretary, to Treasurer, G. D. Searle and Company, July 21, 1952, and July 28, 1954.

48. "Remarks by Mr. J. G. Searle at Annual Meeting of Stockholders," April 26, 1958, pp. 2–3, GP-LC.

49. Irwin C. Winter to Gregory Pincus, December 29, 1958, GP-LC.

50. McCormick to Sanger, July 21, 1954; n.d. (Christmas Day, 1954); May 31, 1955; January 9, 1956; February 1, 1955; June 29, 1955; September 14, 1955; March 24, 1956; January 3, 1957, MS-SS; McCormick to Bruce Crawford, business manager, WFEB, April 4, 1958, GP-LC. Characteristically, once the pill was marketed McCormick lost all interest in supporting Rock's research. Interview with John Rock, June 17, 1971.

51. Pincus to William Vogt, August 13, 1955, GP-LC.

52. Gregory Pincus, John Rock, and Celso Ramon Garcia, "Effects of Certain 19-Nor Steroids upon Reproductive Processes," *Annals of the New York Academy of Sciences* 71 (1958), p. 677; Gregory Pincus to Albert Raymond, August 16, 1956, GP-LC.

53. The Puerto Rican trials of Enovid are described in Maisel, *Hormone Quest*, ch. 8, and in Vaughan, *The Pill on Trial*, ch. 3. Pincus provided a summary of the first two years of the experiment in "The Hormonal Control of Ovulation and Early Development," *Postgraduate Medicine* 24 (December 1958). See also Pincus, *Control of Fertility* (New York, 1965).

54. Rice-Wray to Pincus, June 11, 1956. See also "Translation from *El Imparcial*," April 21, 1956, GP-LC.

55. Iris Rodriquez to Gregory Pincus, May 8, 1956, GP-LC.

56. Edris Rice-Wray, "Study Project on SC-4642," January 1957; Edris Rice-Wray to Gregory Pincus, December 20, 1956, GP-LC.

57. Pincus, "The Hormonal Control of Ovulation and Early Development," pp. 657–59; Pincus to I. C. Winter, July 31, 1957, GP-LC.

58. Greer Williams, manuscript biography of Clarence J. Gamble, "The Pill—Mrs. Sanger's Dream Come True."

59. Ibid.; Pincus to McCormick, March 11, 1957, GP-LC; Gregory Pincus, John Rock, and Celso R. Garcia, "Field Trials with Norethynodrel as an Oral Contraceptive," *Sixth International Conference On Planned Parenthood: Report of the Proceedings* (London, 1960), pp. 216–36.
The Satterthwaite-Gamble correspondence is in CJG-CL. See also my interview with her for the Schlesinger-Rockefeller Oral History Project, transcript in the Schlesinger Library.

60. D. A. McGintry to Gregory Pincus, May 16, May 18, 1956, GP-LC.

61. Manuel Paniagua to Gregory Pincus, August 12, 1957; Pincus to Paniagua, August 15, 1957; Paniagua to Pincus, September 9, 1957, GP-LC.

62. Searle Research Laboratories, *Proceedings of the Symposium on 19-Nor Progestational Steroids* (Chicago, 1957); "Enovid: A Case History in Clinical Research," February 2, 1962, transcript of dialogue in film produced by Searle for physicians, GP-LC.

63. Robert Sheehan, "The Birth-Control 'Pill,' " *Fortune* (April 1958), p. 222.

64. Pincus to Alan Guttmacher, December 16, 1957; Guttmacher to Pincus, December 18, 1957; Pincus to Guttmacher, December 30, 1957; Katharine McCormick to Pincus, July 14, 1959; Pincus to McCormick, July 18, 1959; Pincus to Christopher

Tietze, May 5, 1959; Tietze to Pincus, May, 12, 1959; Pincus to McCormick, May 21, 1959, GP-LC.

65. L. C. Ayres to H. A. R. Bough, March 3, 1959, GP-LC.

66. Pincus to McCormick, December 15, 1958, GP-LC.

67. The pill does suppress ovulation but its effectiveness apparently depends on attacking the reproductive system at many points, so that if an ovum does leave the ovary its chances of survival are very small. The pill may also change the character of the mucus of the cervix, making the environment hostile to sperm; it may inhibit the movement of the ovum through the fallopian tubes; it may affect the lining of the uterus in such a way that it is impossible for the fertilized ovum to imbed itself; it may prevent the hypothalamus from sending out certain hormones that regulate the normal reproductive cycle.

See Paul Vaughan, *The Pill on Trial*, chs. 4–8, and "The Pill Turns Twenty," *New York Times Magazine* (June 13, 1976), p. 9.

68. Interview with John Rock, June 15, 1971.

69. Vaughan, "The Pill Turns Twenty," p. 9.

70. *Newsweek* 57 (January 30, 1961), p. 71; *Business Week* (January 21, 1961), p. 32; (February 23, 1963), pp. 62–63; (March 28, 1964), p. 32.

71. Elizabeth B. Connell, M.D., "The Pill Revisited," *Family Planning Perspectives* 7 (March-April 1975), p. 62.

72. Barbara Seaman, *The Doctors' Case against the Pill* (New York, 1969); "The New Pill Scare," *Ms.* 3 (June 1975), pp. 61–64ff; Vaughan, "The Pill Turns Twenty"; Connell, "The Pill Revisited."

73. Connell, pp. 62, 69.

Part VIII

1. *Playboy* 17 (August 1970), p. 57.

2. Kingsley Davis, "Population Policy: Will Current Programs Succeed?" *Science* 158 (November 10, 1967), pp. 730–39; Judith Blake, "Population Policy for Americans: Is the Government Being Misled?" *Science* 164 (May 2, 1969), pp. 522–29.

3. Davis, "Population Policy," pp. 737, 734.

4. For an in-depth analysis of one specific incidence of attempts by Roman Catholics to coerce other citizens into accepting their position on contraception, see Kenneth Underwood, *Catholic and Protestant: Religious and Social Interaction in an Industrial Community* (Boston, 1957).

5. June 16, 1958.

6. Interview with Loraine Leeson Campbell, chairman of the Brookline, Massachusetts, Mothers' Health Office during the 1930s, past president of the Planned Parenthood Federation of America, December 7, 1973, Cambridge, Mass., transcript in the Schlesinger Library.

7. *Birth Control in America: The Career of Margaret Sanger* (New Haven, Conn., 1970), pp. 211–12. Cf. ch. 12, "Clinical Studies," and ch. 9, "Providing Clinics."

8. Personal communication with Madeline Gray Rubin of Northampton, Mass., who is writing a biography of Sanger.

9. Interview with Howard Taylor, Jr., April 27, 1971, New York City; Interview with John Rock, June 15, 1971, Boston, Mass.

10. PPFA, *Simple Methods of Contraception: An Assessment of Their Medical, Moral, and Social Implications*, ed. Winfield Best and Frederick S. Jaffee (New York, 1958).

In the perspective of the history of the birth control movement in America during the 1930s and especially the efforts to appease the medical profession, the Minutes of the PPFA Medical Committee, January 6, 1960, are full of irony. First, the use of Emko, an aerosol vaginal foam, was approved even though it was not "ethically marketed," i.e., one did not need a prescription to buy it. Second, the committee voted to ask the

Food and Drug Administration to remove diaphragms from the list of items that required a prescription! As Dr. Mary Calderone explained, ". . . she receives many letters from patients who find that their physicians simply will not give them the time to explain the diaphragm and its use or to answer their questions." Printed instructions might serve just as well as a physician for patients experienced in use of the device. Mary Calderone Papers, The Schlesinger Library. See also Mary J. Cornish et al., *Doctors and Family Planning* (National Committee on Maternal Health Publication No. 19, 1963).

11. Greer Williams, manuscript biography of Clarence Gamble, "Clarence Gamble versus Frank Notestein."

12. Roger Bernard, "International IUD Programme—The Pathfinder Fund IUD Baseline Data," in *Population Control: Proceedings of Pakistan International Family Planning Conference at Dacca* (Lahore, 1969), pp. 163–77; Phyllis T. Piotrow, *World Population Crisis: The United States Response* (New York, 1973), pp. 129, 153, 154.

13. Frederick S. Jaffe, "Public Policy on Fertility Control," *Scientific American* 229 (July 1973), p. 17.
For discussion of conflict between IUD boosters and pill advocates, see Piotrow, pp. 97–98.

14. Gregory Pincus to Mary Calderone, October 26, 1959, GP-LC; Interview with Hudson Hoagland, October 24, 1973; Interview with Christopher Tietze, April 27, 1971.

15. Frederick S. Jaffe, "Family Planning and Public Policy: Is the 'Culture of Poverty' the New Cop-out?" in *Population Crisis: Hearings on S. 1676 before the Subcommittee on Foreign Aid Expenditures, 89th Congress, 2nd session, 1966*, part 1, pp. 195–201. Hereafter cited as *Population Crisis*.

16. Sheldon J. Segal, "Contraceptive Research: A Male Chauvinist Plot?" *Family Planning Perspectives* 4 (July 1972), pp. 21–25.

17. Jaffe, "Public Policy On Fertility Control," pp. 19–20; C. Thomas Dienes, *Law, Politics, and Birth Control* (Urbana, Ill., 1972), pp. 188–93, 245–52.

18. Ernest Gruening, *Many Battles: The Autobiography of Ernest Gruening* (New York, 1973), pp. 28, 57–58, 70–71, 103–6, 115, 200–2.

19. Piotrow, pp. 78–79.

20. Quoted in Piotrow, p. 89, and in *Population Crisis*, part 1, p. 3. Gruening, who would later come into conflict with Johnson over the Vietnam war, read every favorable comment Johnson had ever made on birth control into the record, thereby making sure that testifying bureaucrats would not forget their leader's position.

21. Piotrow, ch. 11, "The Gruening Hearings," pp. 103–11.

22. Ibid., pp. 136, 126–29, 152, 154, 181, 141.

23. Thomas Frejka, "Reflections on the Demographic Condition Needed to Establish a U.S. Stationary Population Growth," *Population Studies* 22 (November 1968), p. 388. An excellent summary of the literature debating the role of family planning in population control is Robin Eliott, Lynn C. Landman, Richard Lincoln, and Theodore Tsuoroka, "U.S. Population Growth and Family Planning: A Review of the Literature," *Family Planning Perspectives* 2 (October 1970), p. 24ff.

24. Larry Bumpass and Charles F. Westoff, "The 'Perfect Contraceptive' Population," *Science* 169 (September 18, 1970), pp. 1177–82.

25. Dudley Kirk, "Comments on a Paper by John G. Graham, 'The Relation of Genetics to Control of Human Fertility,' " *Perspectives in Biology and Medicine* 15 (Winter 1972), pp. 284–93; Frank W. Notestein, "Zero Population Growth: What Is It?" *Family Planning Perspectives* 2 (June 1970), pp. 20–23.

26. Roger Revelle, "Paul Ehrlich: New High Priest of Ecocatastrophe," *Family Planning Perspectives* 3 (April 1971), pp. 66–70; Jaffee, "Public Policy on Fertility Control,'" pp. 22–23; William H. Glazier, "The Task of Medicine," *Scientific American* 228 (April 1973), pp. 13–17.

27. "Beyond Family Planning," *Science* 163 (February 7, 1969): 533–43.

28. "Zero Population Growth: What Is It?" p. 23.

Bibliographical Essay

This work is largely based on the papers of Margaret Sanger, Robert Dickinson, Clarence Gamble, and Gregory Pincus. I have also drawn heavily on published sources in fields ranging from medicine and experimental biology to demography, sociology, and literary criticism. The following essay deals with sources that provided unique information or strongly influenced this work. A fuller list of sources is provided in the Notes.

Until recently historians have been reticent about discussing sexual behavior or values. The literature is reviewed by John C. Burnham in "American Historians and the Subject of Sex," *Societas* (Autumn 1972). Arthur Calhoun, *A Social History of the American Family* (1917–1919) is an exception to this rule. Sidney Ditzion, *Marriage, Morals, and Sex in America* (1953) is the only scholarly survey of sexual reform in America and is indexed, but lacks footnotes and a bibliography of primary sources.

Linda Gordon's *Woman's Body, Woman's Right: A Social History of Birth Control in America* (1976) appeared after this work was completed. Although we cover some of the same ground, there are great differences, both topical and interpretative, between our studies. In her treatment of the nineteenth century, Gordon chose to emphasize the ideas of a small group of radicals who advocated "voluntary motherhood." The ideal of marital mutuality was not unique to iconoclasts such as Ezra Heywood, however. It was a salient feature of the diverse Victorian domestic literature. Throughout her study Gordon ignores or denigrates the work for birth control of liberals and conservatives and exaggerates the contribution of those whose views she finds congenial. Gordon underestimates the achievements of Margaret Sanger and hardly deals at all with the activities of Robert Dickinson and Clarence Gamble, the experiments in the mass delivery of contraceptives from the 1930s to the 1950s, or the development of the plastic intrauterine devices and the pill. She treats the activities of a large number of organizations and individuals ranging from the Planned Parenthood Federation of America to the Population Council to Hugh Moore as one vast undifferentiated conspiracy in the service of political repression and American imperialism. There were considerable differences in ideology and strategy between birth controllers which Gordon ignores, allowing her own ideology to compensate for inadequate research.

PART I
Birth Control Before Margaret Sanger

Norman Himes' *Medical History of Contraception* (1936), while ponderous and incomplete, provides a valuable introduction to the nineteenth century literature on contraception and an excellent bibliography. A more readable account of the birth control movement in the English-speaking world is Peter Fryer, *The Birth Controllers* (1966). There is no one library where all of the important nineteenth century works that discuss contraception can be consulted. Norman Himes' collection of birth control tracts has been incorporated into the holdings of The Francis A. Countway Library of Medicine, located in the Harvard Medical School, Boston, and Countway's collection is probably the best in the country.

The startling regularity of the nineteenth century fertility decline is noted by Wilson H. Grabill et al., *The Fertility of American Women* (1958). The authors of this excellent survey also suggest that contraceptive practice played the key role in the phenomenon, an idea championed by Calhoun in the third volume of his *Social History*. Ansley Coale and Melvin Zelnik provide demographic data in readily digestible form in *New Estimates of Fertility and Population in the United States* (1963).

While the fertility decline is well documented, the literature explaining the phenomenon is largely impressionistic. The best behavioral studies of fertility change are Maris A. Vinovskis, "Demographic Change in America from the Revolution to the Civil War, An Analysis of the Socio-Economic Determinants of Fertility Differentials and Trends in Massachusetts from 1765 to 1860" (Ph.D. dissertation, Harvard, 1975) and "Socioeconomic Determinants of Interstate Fertility Differentials in the United States in 1850 and 1860," *Journal of Interdisciplinary History* 6 (Winter 1976). Although Himes was a sociologist, he gave little attention to the role played by changes in family structure or social values. Richard D. Brown traces the growth of a manipulative attitude toward nature in "Modernization and the Modern Personality in Early America, 1600–1865: A Sketch of a Synthesis," *Journal of Interdisciplinary History* 2 (Winter 1972). Daniel S. Smith, "Family Limitation, Sexual Control, and Domestic Feminism in Victorian America," *Feminist Studies* 1 (Winter–Spring 1973) and Robert V. Wells, "Family History and Demographic Transition," *Journal of Social History* 9 (Fall 1975) are interesting attempts to explain the fertility decline.

Informed discussions of nineteenth century sexual values are provided by Charles Rosenberg, "Sexuality, Class, and Role in Nineteenth Century America," *American Quarterly* 25 (May 1973); Ronald Walters, "The Family and Ante-Bellum Reform: An Interpretation," *Societas* 3 (Summer 1973); Carl Degler, "What Ought to Be and What Was: Women's Sexuality in the Nineteenth Century," *American Historical Review* 79 (December 1974). These essays are no substitute for primary sources, however. William Alcott's *The Physiology of Marriage* (1855) is a fascinating exposition of mid-nineteenth century sexual ideals. Good secondary discussions of the nineteenth century family ideology are Bernard Wishy, *The Child and the Republic* (1968); Kirk Jeffrey, "Family History: The Middle-Class American Family in the Urban Context, 1830–1970" (Ph.D. Dissertation, Stanford, 1972); Kathryn Sklar, *Catharine Beecher* (1973); and Calhoun's *Social History*.

The best introduction to the history of medicine in the nineteenth century is Richard Shryock's *Medicine and Society in America, 1660–1860* (1960). There is no satisfactory history of gynecology, but Seale Harris, *Woman's Surgeon: The Life of J. Marion Sims* (1950) provides a starting point. James V. Ricci, *The Development of Gynaecological Surgery and Instruments* (1949) and *One Hundred Years of Gynaecology, 1800–1900* (1945) provide a chronicle of events that illustrates the complexity of many issues misunderstood or distorted by some historians.

David Pivar's *Purity Crusade* (1973) provides a context in which the suppression of contraceptive information may be understood. Heywood Broun and Margaret Leech, *Anthony Comstock: Roundsman of the Lord* (1927) remains the best work on Comstock, while Paul Boyer, *Purity in Print: The Vice-Suppression Society Movement and Book Censorship in America* (1968) provides a broader treatment of the effort to suppress obscenity.

Alexander Skene's *Education and Culture as Related to the Health and Diseases of Women* (1889) provides a classic example of the use of medical sanctions to defend established sexual norms. Henry Maudsley's *Sex in Mind and in Education* (1874) is a contemporary survey of the debate over the effects of higher education on women. *Sexual Hygiene* (Chicago, The Clinic Publishing Co., 1902) provides insights into the attitudes of physicians toward a broad range of sexual problems, including contraception.

Norman Himes and Ben Reitman discussed Emma Goldman's role in the American birth control movement in their correspondence at Countway Library. *Living My Life* (1931), Goldman's autobiography, and Richard Drinnon, *Rebel in Paradise* (1961) provide a wealth of information on Goldman's career, but for a fuller chronicle of anarchist birth control activities, see *Mother Earth*.

Bibliographical Essay

There is no complete treatment of the changes in sexual behavior and values during the first two decades of the twentieth century, but understanding of the era has been advanced by a number of excellent studies: Henry May, *The End of American Innocence* (1959); James R. McGovern, "The American Woman's Pre–World War I Freedom in Manners and Morals," *Journal of American History* 55 (September 1968); and John C. Burnham, "The Progressive Era Revolution in American Attitudes toward Sex," *Journal of American History* 59 (March 1973). Lewis Erenberg, "Everybody's Doin' It: The Pre–World War I Dance Craze, the Castles, the Modern American Girl," *Feminist Studies* 3 (Fall 1975), explains aspects of what May called "the first years of our own time." William O'Neill focuses on one key area of change in *Divorce in the Progressive Era* (1967); and Daniel S. Smith, "The Dating of the American Sexual Revolution: Evidence and Interpretation," in *The American Family in Social-Historical Perspective*, ed. Michael Gordon, shows that there was continuity as well as change.

PART II
The Woman Rebel

Margaret Sanger left two autobiographies: *My Fight for Birth Control* (1931) and *Margaret Sanger: An Autobiography* (1938). She has had five major biographers: Harold Hersey, *Margaret Sanger: The Biography of the Birth Control Pioneer* (1938); Lawrence Lader, *The Margaret Sanger Story* (1955); David M. Kennedy, *Birth Control in America* (1970); Emily Taft Douglas, *Pioneer of the Future* (1970); Madeline Gray Rubin has completed another biography. Joan Dash has dissected Sanger's second marriage in *A Life of One's Own: Three Gifted Women and the Men They Married* (1973).

Hersey worshipped Sanger, but her rejection of him gave his work a certain critical edge, and he included long quotations from individuals he interviewed. Sanger disliked Lader's book, complaining that he made her into a combination of Joan of Arc and Florence Nightingale. Her own suggestion for a title, "Radiant Rebel," indicates that she would not have allowed a more critical work to appear at a time when she was still fighting tough battles for the cause. Lader's book lacks documentation and an index, but it is rich in detail, well written, and based on considerable research.

David Kennedy's *Birth Control in America* provides a provocative critique of Sanger. Kennedy's work is marred, however, by an animus against Sanger that is never explained. I believe that I have disproved Kennedy's claim that Sanger obstructed medical research on contraception. His claim that birth control quietly became a part of federal health policy during World War II is not true. His claims that men like D. Kenneth Rose and Robert Dickinson represented male good sense in opposition to Sanger's "anti-rationalism" can only be maintained by ignoring the human failings of those two men. Sanger's conflicts with them can best be explained in terms of legitimate policy disputes or conflicts of value. While Sanger often distorted her past to serve her own ends, her *Autobiography* is a surprisingly candid and accurate account of her career, not a classic of the genre but certainly better than most autobiographies. Kennedy's study ends in 1937, with Sanger's *Autobiography*, about twenty-five years before the end of her career (she became senile and was put into a nursing home in 1962).

Emily Taft Douglas' book reads like a second edition of Lader, with an index added. Douglas does provide additional information on Sanger's relationship with British intellectuals, and she does note Sanger's role in the development of the anovulant pill. Douglas manages to regularize Sanger's sex life somewhat, and Sanger emerges as an adventurous creature, but one that most club women can accept.

Joan Dash's essay on Sanger is mostly derivative, except for the material drawn from the Sanger-Slee correspondence at Smith. Ironically, Dash apparently failed to read Sanger's correspondence with lovers besides her two husbands. Sanger's long affair with Angus Macdonald explains some of the tensions in her marriage to Slee that Dash

441

finds hard to explain. Dash's preoccupation with Sanger's constipation illustrates the fact that Sanger's life has been subjected to intense scrutiny, largely owing to the fact that she left abundant material behind, fully aware that it would be used. To date no scholar has worked through all of it.

There are approximately 500 boxes of Sanger papers, divided between the Library of Congress, the Sophia Smith Collection, and Houghton Library. In general, institutional records (for example those of the Clinical Research Bureau) are at the Library of Congress, while the more personal and later material (after 1940) is at Smith, although there are numerous exceptions. The fifteen boxes of papers at Houghton Library are cataloged as papers of the American Birth Control League and cover the period roughly from 1920 to 1935. Records of Dr. James Cooper's cross-country tours, of Sanger's lobbying activities in Washington, and a scattering of interesting correspondence are included among the Houghton materials. The Sophia Smith Collection is currently microfilming Sanger materials at the Library of Congress. Smith also has the papers of Dorothy Brush, Sanger's friend and co-worker, and of Florence Rose, Sanger's personal secretary. The archives of the Planned Parenthood Federation of America, covering the period roughly from 1940 to 1960, have been deposited at Smith. Finally, Smith has the papers of the Planned Parenthood League of Massachusetts, an unusually rich collection that provides insights into the problems birth controllers faced in a state with a large Catholic population led by an unusually politicized clergy. The Ames Collection at Smith also contains interesting materials on the early attempts to organize a birth control league in Massachusetts.

For the interpretation of Sanger's relationship with Havelock Ellis, Edward Brecher's *The Sex Researchers* (1969) and Joseph Wortis' *Fragments of an Analysis with Freud* (1954) are most useful. Perhaps it bears repeating that Sanger was not one of those who misinterpreted Freud but one who ignored him. Arthur Calder-Marshall's *The Sage of Sex* (1959) is the best biography of Ellis, but it is marred by Calder-Marshall's condescending attitude toward Ellis and by his inability to appreciate Ellis the aesthete.

Sanger's conflict with Mary Ware Dennett is analyzed in Francis Vreeland, "The Process of Reform with Especial Reference to Reform Groups in the Field of Population" (Ph. D. dissertation, University of Michigan, 1929). Dennett makes her case against Sanger in *Birth Control Laws* (1926). C. Thomas Dienes provides an interesting interpretation of Sanger's reform role and a very useful analysis of the important court cases in the history of contraception in the United States in *Law, Politics, and Birth Control* (1972).

The Institute for Sex Research, Indiana University, has data on contraceptive practice among Alfred Kinsey's subjects, but this information has not been included in the institute's publications.

Emily Mudd's Oral History is one of a series I recorded for the Schlesinger's Library's oral history project. Other subjects were: Elizabeth Arnold, R.N.; Mary Calderone, M.D.; Loraine Leeson Campbell; Florence Clothier, M.D.; Frances Hand Ferguson; Louise Hutchins, M.D.; Mrs. Allan Guttmacher; Virginia Johnson Masters; Adaline Satterthwaite, M.D.; Julia Tsuei, M.D.; Sarah Tietze and Christopher Tietze, M.D.

The transcripts are indexed and there is a brief introduction to each which explains why the interviewee was asked to participate in the project.

PART III
Robert Dickinson and the Committee on Maternal Health

The professional papers of Robert Dickinson are now in Countway Library and are being catalogued. Included are many original drawings, Dickinson's case records, notebooks, and some professional correspondence. The collection includes the Minutes of the Committee on Maternal Health. These formal records of the committee were in the possession of Dr. Christopher Tietze of the Bio-Medical Division of the Population Council, but are now on permanent loan to Countway Library and are being incorporated into the Dickinson collection. Also included in the collection are the transcripts of Round Table Seminars sponsored by the Committee on Maternal Health to which key figures, including John Rock, Frederick Osborn, and Frank Notestein, were invited to give their views on specific topics. Unfortunately transcripts of only a few of these meetings have survived.

Most of my biographical information on Dickinson is based on two documents placed in the collection by his son-in-law, George Barbour of Cincinnati, Ohio. The documents are Incidents in a Happy Life, a 26-page transcript of Dickinson's reminiscences, recorded in December 1949, while Dickinson was visiting the Barbours in Cincinnati, and R.L.D.: The Life of Robert Latou Dickinson, 1861–1950, Barbour's manuscript biography of Dickinson, covering the period to about 1900. Dickinson's correspondence with his wife is still in the possession of Dorothy Dickinson Barbour. Interviews with Lura Beam, Dr. Jean A. Curran, Abram Belskie, and Dr. John Truslow, Dickinson's nephew, all provided insights into Dickinson's character. Dickinson was a prolific writer and his publications are unusually revealing. There is a valuable Bibliography of Robert Latou Dickinson by the New York Academy of Medicine Bibliography Department, compiled in June 1953, copy in Dickinson papers.

The concern of gynecologists over the future of their specialty may be followed in the Presidential Addresses, *Transactions of the American Gynecological Society*. An overview of developments in American medicine during the period when Dickinson was practicing is provided by Donald Fleming, *William H. Welch and the Rise of Modern Medicine* (1954).

My understanding of the conflict between Dickinson and Louise Stevens Bryant was improved by my correspondence with Lura Beam, now deposited in Countway Library, and by the Bryant papers in the Sophia Smith Collection. There is an extensive correspondence between Dickinson and Alfred Kinsey at the Institute for Sex Research, Bloomington, Indiana. There are no important letters from Kinsey in the Dickinson papers.

PART IV
The Prospect of Depopulation

Bernard Newton's *The Economics of Francis Amasa Walker* (1968) is a broader work than its title indicates, but Walker's publications, conveniently collected in *Discussions in Economics* (1899), ed. Davis R. Dewey, remain an essential source for understanding the origins of American population studies. The Norman Himes papers at Countway Library (132 boxes) include correspondence with many of the key figures in the development of population studies in the United States. Another valuable source is *Forty Years of Research in Human Fertility*, ed. Clyde Kiser, the proceedings of a conference honoring Kiser upon his retirement from the Milbank Memorial Fund staff (originally published as the October 1971 issue of the *Milbank Memorial Fund Quarterly*). Especially interesting are the papers by Clyde Kiser, "The Work of the Milbank Fund in Population since 1928," Frank W. Notestein, "Reminiscences: The Roles of Foundations, the Population Association of America, Princeton University and the United Nations in Fostering American Interest in Population Problems," and Charles F. Westoff, "Some Reflections on Population Policy in the United States." A valuable survey of the refinement of techniques in demography is provided by Frank Lorimer, "The Development of Demography," chapter 6 in *The Study of Population* (1959), ed. Philip Hauser and Otis Duncan.

The minutes of the Committee on Maternal Health reflect the pervasive fear of

443

depopulation during the 1930s, a theme neatly summarized in the transcript of the committee's Round Table discussion on "The Eugenic Effect of Contraception—The Significance of the Decline in the Birth Rate," May 13, 1937.

PART V
Birth Control Entrepreneur

There are now over 200 boxes of Gamble papers at Countway Library. Additional material has been received from Gamble's widow and is now being cataloged. The collection includes correspondence with birth controllers in practically every state and in many foreign countries. Elin Wolfe has prepared an excellent guide to the collection.

Most of the Gamble collection deals with his population interests (contraception, sterilization, eugenics). I am therefore indebted to Gamble's biographer, Greer Williams, for most of my information on Gamble's childhood, education, and career at the University of Pennsylvania. Plans for publication of the Williams biography are still incomplete, but a copy will be available at Countway Library for future scholars. Williams is especially useful on Gamble's activities in North Carolina, Puerto Rico, Japan, and India.

During the period from 1935 to 1948, experiments in delivery of contraceptive services and contraceptive research are reported in the *Journal of Contraception* (1935–39) and in its successor, *Human Fertility* (1940–48), published by the Birth Control Clinical Research Bureau and edited by Hannah Stone, and, after her death (1941), by Abraham Stone. In constructing the story of Clarence Gamble's efforts to police the contraceptive marketplace, Countway Library's complete runs of these two journals and large collection of Gamble reprints were essential. Also necessary were the Minutes of the Committee on Maternal Health and the Committee on Maternal Health file in the Gamble papers.

Gilbert Beebe's *Contraception and Fertility in the Southern Appalachians* (1942) is a classic of social science reporting. The introduction of contraceptive services into the North Carolina public health program is described in a series of revealing articles. Don Wharton, "Birth Control: The Case for the State," *Atlantic Monthly* (October 1939); Roy Norton, "Developmental Background of the First State Health Department Conception Hygiene Program," *Human Fertility* 5 (June 1940); Clarence Gamble, "Contraception as a Public Health Measure," *Transactions*, Medical Society of the State of North Carolina (1938).

Gamble's problems in working with other birth controllers can be followed in the Committee on Maternal Health, American Birth Control League, Birth Control Federation of America, and Planned Parenthood Federation of America files in the Gamble papers. Also revealing is Gamble's correspondence with Edna McKinnon, Hazel Moore, and Elsie Wulkop. Gamble's collaboration with Christopher Tietze is chronicled in the Gamble-Tietze correspondence. See also the Tietze-Himes correspondence in the Himes papers.

PART VI
Propagandists Turned to Prophets

The development of post–World War II concern over the demographic situation in the Third World may be followed in the *Milbank Memorial Fund Quarterly*, which provides an excellent source for historians interested in public health, population studies, or contraceptive research. Frank Notestein's "Reminiscences" in *MMFQ* (October 1971) is a key document. Richard Symonds and Michael Carder, *The United Nations and Population* (1973) is excellent and provides a general survey of the emergence of overpopulation as a recognized problem. Phyllis T. Piotrow's *World Population Crisis: The United States Response* (1973) is a comprehensive treatment of events in the United States by an insider and a scholar. The history of the Population Council can be gleaned from *Annual Reports.* I am indebted to Frederick Osborn for prompt answers to specific questions about the council's origins.

Beryl Suitters provides a narrative history of the International Planned Parenthood Federation in *Be Brave and Angry* (1973). International developments are also covered in *News of Population and Birth Control,* published by the International Planned Parenthood Committee. The Sanger papers at Smith include revealing correspondence with C. P. Blacker, Dorothy Brush, and other officers of the IPPF.

Greer Williams' biography provides an excellent introduction to Gamble's international activities. Yoshia Koya's *Pioneering in Family Planning* (1967) describes Japanese experiments in population control. The proceedings of the IPPF's conferences provide useful collections of reports on experiments in family planning. Gamble's conflict with the IPPF may be followed in the Gamble papers. The Sanger papers at Smith also provide insights into the attitudes of the IPPF's London office, especially the reports of C. P. Blacker and Vera Houghton to Margaret Sanger.

John Gordon and John Wyon's *The Kahanna Study* (1971) and Mahmood Mamdani's *The Myth of Population Control* (1972) provide insights into the failure of the simple methods approach in India. Christopher Tietze, "Intra-Uterine Contraceptive Rings: History and Statistical Appraisal," in *Intra-Uterine Contraceptive Devices* (1962) provides a succinct history of the IUD. I am indebted to Christopher Tietze and to Frank Notestein for candid interviews. R. Christian Johnson's interviews with Christopher Tietze and with Alan Guttmacher, transcripts in Countway Library, also provide insights into the Population Council's decision to give high priority to development of the IUD.

PART VII
The Pill

George Corner, *The Hormones in Human Reproduction* (1947), and Alan S. Parkes, *Sex, Science and Society* (1966) are excellent introductions to the history of endocrinology by two gifted scientists who can write. Sophie Aberle and George Corner, *Twenty-five Years of Sex Research: History of the National Research Council Committee for Research in Problems of Sex* (1958) is a brief history of sex research in the United States and documents the role played by Rockefeller money in the development of endocrinology. Carl Djerassi, "Steroid Oral Contraceptives," *Science* 151 (March 4, 1966), is a succinct account of the development of steroid chemistry. Albert Maisel chronicles the rise of the steroid drug industry in *The Hormone Quest* (1965).

A useful bibliography of Gregory Pincus is attached to Dwight Ingle's "Gregory Pincus" in National Academy of Sciences, *Biographical Memoirs* 42 (1969). Pincus' character and career are discussed by Hudson Hoagland in his manuscript autobiography, *Chance, Change, and Challenge,* and also by Min-Chueh Chang, "Mammalian Sperm, Eggs, and Control of Fertility," *Perspectives in Biology and Medicine* 11 (Spring 1968), and Oscar Hechter, "Homage to Gregory Pincus," ibid. Donald Fleming discusses the struggle between experimental biologists and proponents of an older scientific lifestyle in his introduction to Jacques Loeb, *The Mechanistic Conception of Life* (1964) and in "Emigré Physicists and the Biological Revolution," *Perspectives in American History* 2 (1968). Pincus' early relationship with G. D. Searle and Company may be followed in his correspondence with Searle officials and in the transcripts of Searle research conferences in the Pincus papers at the Library of Congress, which are well indexed.

The Sanger-McCormick correspondence at Smith chronicles an interesting episode in the history of women in America. William H. Bemis' "Remarks" in "A Tribute to Katharine Dexter McCormick Presented on the Occasion of the Completion of Stanley McCormick Hall-East," was made available to me by Warren Seamans, Director of the MIT Historical Collections, and provides scarce biographical information on McCormick.

Paul Vaughan's *The Pill on Trial* (1970) is a refreshingly irreverent account of the pill's development and marketing. Carl Djerassi, "Prognosis for the Development of New Chemical Birth-Control Agents" and "Birth Control after 1984," *Science* 166 and 169 (October 24, 1969, and September 4, 1970), suggests that Pincus may have seized a unique opportunity. The term "product champion" is taken from National Science Foundation, *Science, Technology, and Innovation* (February 1973). The Abraham Stone papers at Countway Library, recently acquired and as yet uncataloged, provide a record of PPFA research grants. Searle's role in the pill's development, somewhat distorted by Albert Q. Maisel in *The Hormone Quest*, is clarified by Pincus' correspondence with Albert Raymond, I. C. Winter, and other Searle employees, in the Pincus papers. The corespondence between Pincus and Edris Rice-Wray provides insights into the practical problems of clinical testing.

Manuscript Collections

American Birth Control League Papers. Houghton Library. Cambridge, Massachusetts.

Clarence James Gamble Papers. Countway Library. Boston, Massachusetts.

Robert Latou Dickinson Papers. Countway Library. Boston, Massachusetts.

Norman Himes Papers. Countway Library. Boston, Massachusetts.

Gregory Pincus Papers. Library of Congress. Washington, D.C.

Abraham Stone Papers. Countway Library. Boston, Massachusetts.

Planned Parenthood Federation of America Papers. Sophia Smith Collection. Smith College. Northampton, Massachusetts.

Planned Parenthood League of Massachusetts Papers. Sophia Smith Collection. Smith College. Northampton, Massachusetts.

Margaret Sanger Papers. Library of Congress. Washington, D.C.

Margaret Sanger Papers. Sophia Smith Collection. Smith College. Northampton, Massachusetts.

Periodicals

Birth Control Review, 1917–40

Family Planning Perspectives, 1969–75

Human Fertility, 1940–48

Journal of Contraception, 1935–39

Milbank Memorial Fund Quarterly, 1923–75

Mother Earth, 1906–17

Population Council, *Annual Reports,* 1953–75

Woman Rebel, 1914

Bibliographical Essay

Interviews

Dorothy Dickinson Barbour, June 2, 1971, Cincinnati, Ohio.
Leona Baumgartner, May 29, 1973, Cambridge, Massachusetts.
Lura Beam, November 30, 1970, Croton-on-Hudson, New York.
Abram Belskie, December 18, 1970, Closter, New Jersey.
Jean Alonzo Curran, September 14, 1970, Boston, Massachusetts.
Min-Chueh Chang, October 24, 1973, Shrewsbury, Massachusetts.
Hudson Hoagland, October 24, 1973, Shrewsbury, Massachusetts.
Frank Notestein, August 12, 1974, Princeton, New Jersey.
John Rock, June 15, 1971, Boston, Massachusetts.
Howard Taylor, Jr., April 27, 1971, New York City.
Christopher Tietze, April 27, 1971, New York City.
Dr. and Mrs. John Truslow, November 28, 1970, Biddeford, Maine.

Transcripts of Interviews in Countway Library Conducted by R. Christian Johnson
with Alan Guttmacher, February 23, 1973, New York City, and with Christopher
Tietze, March 8, 1973, New York City.

Schlesinger-Rockefeller Oral History Project Transcripts Cited in This Study
Loraine Leeson Campbell, December 1973–March 1974, Cambridge, Massachusetts.
Emily Hartshorne Mudd, Ph.D., May 21–August 3, 1974, Haverford, Pennsylvania.
Adaline Pendleton Satterthwaite, June 7, 1974, New York City.

Index

Abortion: among slum dwellers, 47-48, 81-83; role in fertility decline of, 5-6, 16, 17, 24, 28, 31, 375, 385, 390; Sanger's position on, 118-19

Ackermann, Frances, 109, 110

Act for the Suppression of Trade in, and Circulation of, Obscene Literature and Articles of Immoral Use, see Comstock Act

Addams, Jane, 58, 155

Agency for International Development, U.S., 288, 374; population control programs and, 379

Air Force, U.S., Operations Analysis Group of, 329

Albright, Fuller, 315-16

Alcott, William A., 13, 22-27, 30, 37, 389, 440

Alien Property Act, U.S., 357

Allen, Willard, 313

American Birth Control League, 108-14, 116, 123, 373, 374; Committee on Maternal Health and, 172, 174-76; Gamble and, 226, 235, 249; organizers for, 216-17, 252; state affiliates of, 231

American Cancer Society, 331

American Chemical Society, 355

American Dilemma, An (Myrdal), 209

American Economic Association, 198, 208

American Eugenics Society, 136

American Friends Service Committee, 249

American Gynecological Club, 161

American Gynecological Society, 163-67, 183, 184, 187

American Journal of Eugenics, The, 135

American Journal of Obstetrics and Gynecology, 144, 169, 244, 275, 306

American Medical Association: committee on contraception of, 306; on contraception, 52, 211, 375; on control of venereal disease, 36-37; Council on Pharmacy and Chemistry of, 245; opposition to "medical socialism" by, 213-14; Section on Obstetrics, Gynecology and Abdominal Surgery of, 186-87

American Public Health Association, 36, 110

American Social Hygiene Association, 58

American Society for Sanitary and Moral Prophylaxis, 58, 146

American Society for the Study of Sterility, 350

American Statistical Association, 198, 207

American Union against Militarism, 98

American Woman Suffrage Association, 336-37

Ancestors and Immigrants: A Changing New England Tradition (Solomon), 411

And the Poor Get Children (Rainwater), 387

Anthony, Susan B., 35-36

Anthony Comstock: Roundsman of the Lord (Broun and Leech), 440

Armour, Samuel E., 150

Association Pro Salud Maternal e Infantil de Puerto Rico, 260

Associated Charities (Cleveland), 109

Association for Voluntary Sterilization, 425

Association of Out Patient Clinics, 174

Association of Tuberculosis Clinics, 174

Atlas of Human Sex Anatomy (Dickinson), 411

Atwood, Wallace, 328-29

"Average Sex Life of American Women" (Dickinson), 184

Bailey, Harold C., 177-78

Baker, John R., 242-43, 417

Balfour, Marshall, 284-85

Barbour, Dorothy Dickinson, 405

Barbour, George, 405

Barnard, Chester, 286

Beam, Lura, 168, 409-10

Beatty, R. A., 326-27

Beebe, Gilbert, 247-51, 418

Beecher, Catherine, 22

Beecher, Henry Ward, 25

Belaval, José, 260

Bemis, William, 433

Benson, Marguerite, 258-67, 420

Berelson, Bernard, 381

Berkman, Alexander, 75, 76, 393

Berthold, Arnold, 346

Besnt, Annie, 10, 90

Birth Control in America: The Career of Margaret Sanger (Kennedy), 82, 397, 441

Birth Control Clinical Research Bureau, see Clinical Research Bureau

Birth Control Federation of America, 122, 265, 266

Birth Control Information Committee, 242

Birth Control Laws (Dennett), 101, 390

Birth Control Review, 108-10, 113, 135, 178, 395

Birthrate: concern over, x, 3-5, 17, 32-33, 40, 45, 52, 122, 198-210, 211-13, 273-74, 382-83, 287, 296, 305-7, 369, 372-73, 380-81

Birthright, Inc., 425

Blacker, C. P., 298, 300

Blackwell, Antoinette Brown, 34

Blackwell, Elizabeth, 34, 36

Blacke, Judith, 369

Blatch, Harriet Stanton, 131

Bloomer, Amelia, 71

Blossom, Frederick, 109-10

Bocker, Dorothy, 113-15, 175

Bonaparte, Joseph, 336

Boudreau, Frank, 287

Boyer, Paul, 440

448

Index

Bradlaugh, Charles, 10, 90
Breeding Ourselves to Death (Lader), 426
"Broader Aspects of Birth Control Propaganda, The" (Kosmak), 168
Brome, Vincent, 93
Bromely, Dorothy Dunbar, 212
Broun, Heywood, 440
Brown, Richard D., 4, 440
Brush, Charles, Sr., 292
Brush, Charles, Jr. 291
Brush, Dorothy, 290-92
Brush, Margaret, 109
Brush Foundation, 291, 299
Bryant, Louise Stevens, 182-84, 190, 243, 409-10
Bureau of Social Hygiene, 87, 117, 170, 242, 283; Committee on Maternal Health and, 176, 226, 410
Burnham, John C., 439
Burroughs, John, 153
Butenandt, Adolf, 314
Byrne, Ethel, 106-9

Cabot, Richard, 229, 237
Calhoun, Arthur, 5, 439, 440
Call, The (newspaper), 80-81
Cambridge University, Strangeways Laboratory of, 325
Campbell, Arthur A., 386
Campbell, Edith, 416
Campbell, Elizabeth, 235-36, 416
Campbell, Loraine Leeson, 426
Canada, birth control clinics in, 220-22
Carlile, Richard, 89-90
Carnegie Institute, 209
Carrel, Alexis, 323-24
Carson, Rachel, 411
Cassedy, James H., 411
Castle, William, 317-18, 324, 325
Catherine Beecher: A Study in Domesticity (Sklar), 389
Catt, Carrie Chapman, 132, 133, 336-37
Cautley, Randolph, 189, 244, 247
Census, U.S.: first, 197; seventh, 199; ninth, 198
Census Bureau, U.S., 380; establishment of, 203
Ceylon, 281, 285, 286; birth control clinics in, 299, 422
Chance, Clinton, 114, 417
Chang, Min-Cheuh, 344, 349-51, 430, 434
Child and the Republic, The (Wishy), 440
Child Health Act (1967), 268
Children's Bureau, 266-68
Children's Bureau, U.S., 253
China, birth control clinics in, 304
Chopin, Frederic, 136
Christian Medical College (Ludhiana City, Punjab State, India), 301
Cincinnati Maternal Health Clinic, 236-37
Clark, Joseph S., 378
Clark University, Physiology Laboratory of, 325-30
Clarke, Edward, 40, 392
Claverrack College, 71, 73
Clayton, Will, 426
Cleveland Maternal Health Association, 291-92

Clinical Notes on Uterine Surgery (Sims), 29
Clinical Research Bureau 113-28, 175-80, 265, 299, 337, 340, 373, 401, 408-9
Coale, Ansley, 440
Cochran, Thomas, 203
Coitus interruptus, 6-8, 10-11, 12, 16, 25, 27, 28, 124-26
Colgate, Samuel, 37
College Equal Suffrage League of Massachusetts, 336
Collier's (magazine), 323-34
Columbia University, Neurological Institute of, 329
Comfort, Ann, 392
Comfort, George, 392
Committee on Dispensary Development, 178, 182
Committee for Maternal Health Betterment, 233
Committee for Research in Problems of Sex, 170, 312-13, 320, 410
Committee on Human Reproduction, 339
Committee on Maternal Health, 163, 168-91, 410; American Birth Control League and, 172, 174-76; minutes of, 407; eugenics debate in, 211; Gamble and, 269-77 Logan experiment and, 249-50; Population Council takeover of, 304-5; as publisher and clearing house, 181-96; "Standards Program" of, 241-43, 246, 247
Comstock, Anthony, 37-39, 97, 107, 168, 391
Comstock Act (1873), 12, 37-39, 46, 100, 391; 1970 rewriting of, 102, 377
Conant, James Bryant, 324
"Conception: A Medical Review of the Situation" (Dickinson), 183-84
Condom, 15, 16, 32, 43, 124-26, 244
Congregational Christian Churches: Board of Foreign Missions of, 116; Board of Homes Mission of, 361
Congress Party, Indian, 289
Conklin, Edwin Grant, 231-32, 235
Consumer Reports, 240
Consumers Union, 240
Contraception and Fertility in the Southern Appalachians (Beebe), 249-52, 418
"Contraception with Intra-uterine Silk Cord" (Dickinson), 191
Control of Conception (Dickinson), 183, 185, 409
Cooper, George, 252-55, 260, 295
Cooper, James F., 116, 145-46, 174
Copeland, Royal S., 104
Corner, George, 269, 313, 315
Cowan, John, 25-27
Cox, Harold, 110
Cram, Mrs. John Sargeant, 108
Crane, Frederick, 107
Crew, F. A. E., 242
Critic and Guide (journal), 46
Crozier, William John, 319-21, 324, 325, 329, 429
Cummins, Albert A., 103
Cummins-Vaille Bill, 104
Current Opinion (journal), 55

Darwin, Charles, 153
Dash, Joan, 400

449

Index

Index

Maudsley, Henry, 40, 440
May, Henry, 441
Mayer, Dr., 189
Mayo Clinic, 331
Medical Common Sense (Foote), 16
Medical Follies (Fishbein), 144
Medical Gynecology (Kelly), 160
Medical History of Contraception (Himes), ix, 51, 385-86, 439
Medical Journal and Record, 409
Medical profession: contraception and the, 28-29, 39-45, 82-83, 101-2, 113-20, 143-48, 167-80, 184-90, 212-17, 245-46; reform and the, 143-48, 160-66, 212-14; veneral disease and the, 35-37, 58
Medical Week, 174-75
Medicine and Society in America, 1660-1860 (Shryock), 440
Meeker, Edward, 385
Melting-Pot Mistake, The (Fairchild), 204, 413
Mencken, H. L., 219
Menkin, Miriam, 354
Merck and Company, 331
Meyer, Adolf, 118
Midwestern States Birth Control Conference (1924), 117
Milbank, Alfred, 205
Milbank Memorial Fund, Research Division of, 203-6, 249-51, 282
Milbank Roundtable on International Approaches to Problems of Underdeveloped Areas (1947), 282
Mill, John Stuart, 6, 89
Mindell, Fannia, 107, 108, 399
Mitchell, R. T., 429
Modernization of Sex, The (Robinson), 398
Moore, Allison P., 263-64, 266
Moore, Hazel, 261
Moore, Hugh, 303, 426
Moral Physiology; or A Brief and Plain Treatise on the Population Question (Owen), 7, 8, 11, 19
Morrow, Prince Albert, 58, 105, 146
Mosher, Celia Duel, 32, 390
Mother Earth (monthly), ix, 47, 51, 75
Motherhood in Bondage (Sanger), 123
Mountain Maternal Health League, 260
Mudd, Emily H., 126-28, 233
Mudd, Stuart, 231-33, 245
Muller, Herman J., 233
Myrdal, Gunnar, 209
Myth of Population Control, The (Mandani), 445

National Academy of Sciences, 283
National American Woman Suffrage Association, 309
National Birth Control Conference (1921), 110, 112
National Birth Control League, 98-99, 399
National Committee on Federal Legislation for Birth Control, 121, 261, 292
National Committee on Maternal Health, *see* Committee on Maternal Health
National Fertility Survey (1965), 379
National Institute of Public Health, Japanese, 295

National Institutes of Health, 378
National Research Council, 369-70; Committee for Research in Problems of Sex of, 170, 184, 283-84, 312-13, 320, 410; Committee on Human Reproduction of, 339; Division of Anthropology and Psychology of, 312; Division of Medical Sciences of, 283, 312; sterility research funded by, 355
National Science Foundation, 346-47
National Social Workers Congress (1916), 109
National Tuberculosis Association, 146
National Woman Suffrage Association, 98
National Woman's Party, 336
Nativists: birth control and, 111, 198-202
Nehru, Jawaharlal, 289
Nelson, Warren, 362
Neo-Malthusian Congress (1900), 48
Neuroendocrine Research Foundation, 338
New Basis of Civilization, The (Patten), 59
New England Journal of Medicine, 9
New Estimates of Fertility and Population in the United States (Coale and Zelnik), 440
New Hampshire State Medical Society, 17
New Harmony *Gazette* (newspaper), 7
New York Academy of Medicine, 36, 119-20, 182; inspection of Clinical Research Bureau by, 177-78
New York Birth Control League, 109
New York Committee of Fourteen, Brooklyn Auxiliary of, 155
New York County Medical Society, 116
New York *Herald*, 59
New York Obstetrical Society, 168-71
New York Police Department, 35
New York Society for the Suppression of Vice, 37-38, 50, 97, 168, 388
New York State Board of Charities, 178-79
New York Times, 38, 170, 320, 327
New York Women's Publishing Company, 110
New York World's Fair (1939), 186
Newton, Bernard, 443
Nichols, Francis Low, 13, 25, 26, 389
Nietzsche, Friedrich, 87, 136
Nissenbaum, Stephen, 389
No Sex in Education, or An Equal Chance for Boys and Girls (Duffey), 392
Norris, George, 103-4
North Carolina: birth control program in, 252-56
North Carolina Conference for Social Service, 253
North Carolina State Board of Health, 252-56
North Harlem Medical Society, 117
Notestein, Frank, 203-6, 212-13, 282-83, 285, 287, 294, 305, 307, 381, 413

O'Neill, William, 131, 441
Office of Air Surgeon, U.S., 329
Office of Economic Opportunity, U.S., 378
Office of Population Research, xii, 203, 205, 282, 295
Ogden Corporation, 357
One Hundred Years of Gynaecology, 1800-1900 (Ricci), 440
One Package decision, 120-21, 373
One Thousand Marriages, 406-7

Index

Oppenheimer, Willi, 306
Oral contraceptives, xiii, 311-16, 332-33, 340-66, 374-77
Ortho Pharmaceutical Corporation, 250, 362
Osborn, Fairfield, 411
Osborn, Frederick, 136, 189, 205, 212, 213, 287, 305, 413; on anticommunism and population control, 303-4
Osterhout, W. J. V., 429
Ota, Tenrei, 306
Ottensen-Jensen, Elise, 290, 299
Our Plundered Planet (Osborn), 411
Owen, Robert, 6-7
Owen, Robert Dale, 7-8, 11, 19, 37, 89, 386, 397

Page, Phyllis, 258-63, 420
Pakistan: family planning program of, 304; IUDs in, 307; United Nations and, 286
Pandit, Mrs. Vijaya Lakshmi, 290
Paniagua, Manuel E., 361, 362
Papanicolaou, George, 313
Parents' Information Bureau, 220-22
Parke Davis and Company, 314-15, 362
Parkes, Alexander, 15
Parsons, Elsie Clews, 97
Paterson strike (1913), 77-78
Pathfinder Fund, 305, 374, 379
Patten, Simon, 59
Patterns of Sexual Behavior (Ford and Beach), 185
Paul, Alice, 131
Pearl, Raymond, 118, 189, 205-6, 413
Pennsylvania Birth Control Federation, 231, 234-35, 258
Philippines, birth control in, 272-73
Physicians Club of Chicago, 42
Physics and Chemistry of Contraception, The (Voge), 242
Physiology (Hollick), 30-32
Physiology of Marriage, The (Alcott), 13, 389, 440
Pill on Trial, The (Vaughan), 446
Pinchot, Gertrude Minturn, 108-9
Pincus, Gregory Goodwin, xiii, 309, 317-33, 339-45, 373, 374, 427, 430; biographical material on, 428; as "product champion," 347-66
Pioneering in Family Planning (Koya), 445
Pivar, David, 440
Pivot of Civilization, The (Sanger), 137, 400, 402
Place, Francis, 6, 89
Plague Killers, The (Williams), 423
Planned Parenthood Federation of America, ix, 122; caution of, 404; doctor's manual of, 300; funding of oral contraception research through, 332, 340-44; Gamble forced out of leadership of, 294; International Planned Parenthood Federation and, 292; membership referendum creating, 265; National Medical Committee of, 365; lay education and, 240-41; opposition to sterilization by, 425; on publicity on pill, 363; Robert Dickinson Memorial Fund of, 339; simple methods and, 374; sterility research funded by, 355
Plass, E. D., 187
Playboy (magazine), 369
Pomeroy, Wardell B., 402, 424
Popenoe, Paul, 134-35

Population Association of America, 203
Population Bomb, The (Ehrlich), 411
Population Council, ix, 287-88, 379; Bio-Medical Division of, 305; demographic and biomedical research backed by, 303; Gamble and, 226; grant Worcester Foundation for Experimental Biology by, 350-51; IUDs and, 305-8, 374; oral contraceptives and, 363, 375, 427; pressure on governments by, 294; takeover of National Committee on Maternal Health by, 304-5
Post Office Department, U.S., 37-38, 240
Pouchet, Felix, 13
Powell, Aaron, 36
Practical Birth Control Methods (Himes), 15
Pratt, Frances, 252-53
Presbyterian Board of Foreign Missionaries, 228
Princeton University: Office of Population Research of, xii, 203, 205, 282, 295; Woodrow Wilson School of Public and International Affairs of, 205
Problems of a Changing Population, The (National Resources Committee), 210
Problems of Life (S. Dickinson), 155
Proctor and Gamble Corporation, 227
Productos Esteroides, 357
Pronatalism, ix-xi, 28-29, 40-45, 135-37, 169-70, 188-90, 202-3, 207-13, 232-33, 241, 265, 370-71
Public Health Service, U.S., 253, 266-68, 348
Puerto Rico: Family Planning Association of, 359-61; Emergency Relief Administration of, 259; Reconstruction Administration of, 259, 377; testing of Enovid in, 359-62
Purity Crusade (Pivar), 440
Purity in Print (Boyer), 440
Pusey, William A., 118

Quackery, 6, 9, 16-17, 44-45, 144-46, 239-41
Question of Rest for Women During Menstraation, The (Jacobi), 392

Race and Nationality in American Life (Handlin), 411
Race Suicide, 201, 267
Rainwater, Lee, 387, 415
Rama Rau, Dhanvanthi Handoo, Lady Bengal, 297-99, 341
Ransom, Eliza, 60
Ratcliff, J. D., 323
Raymond, Albert L., 332-33
Reader's Digest, 254
Rebel in Paradise (Drinnon), 440
Reed, John, 75, 76, 78
Reitman, Ben L., 47, 49-54, 393, 440
Ricci, James V., 440
Rice-Wray, Edris, 359-61
Richards, Alfred N., 229-31
Richardson-Merrell, Inc., 348
Road to Survival, The (Vogt), 341, 411
Robert Dickinson Memorial Fund, 339
Robinson, Paul, 398
Robinson, William, 46-47, 185, 402
Rock, John, 187-89, 306, 351-59, 361, 363-64, 435
Rockefeller, John D., Jr., 86, 117, 226, 283-85, 312, 410

454

Index

Rockefeller, John D., III, 283-87, 378
Rockefeller Foundation, 117, 253, 284-88, 350, 423-24; Division of Medical Sciences of, 285; Division of Natural Sciences of, 285; International Health Division of, 284-85, 423
Rockefeller Institute, 323, 326
Roe, Humphrey Vernon, 112
Roman Catholic Church, xii
Roosevelt, Eleanor, 267-68
Roosevelt, Theodore, 201
Root Chemicals, 357
Roots, Margaret, 299
Rose, Florence, 215-16
Rose, D. Kenneth, 136, 265-71, 297, 341, 374
Rosenberg, Charles, 389, 390, 440
Rose, Edward A., 201
Rothschild, Nathaniel, 325-26
Rousseau, Jean-Jacques, 136
Rublee, Juliet, 109, 110
Rusk, Dean, 286
Russell, Bertrand, 112
Russell, Bertrand, 112
Russell Sage Foundation, 182
Rutgers, Johannes, 95
Ruzicka, Leopold, 314
Ryan, Mary, 389
Rhythm, 6, 12-14, 25, 43, 387-88, 402

Sach, Sadie, 82
"Saddles and Postures for Women on the Wheel" (Dickinson), 159
Sanger, Margaret, xi-xiii, 155, 210, 261, 275, 377; assessment of, 67-69; biographies of, 395, 396; cheap methods supported by, 222; Clinical Research Bureau and, 113-28, 401; courtship and first marriage of, 72-75, 84-85, 396; death of, 369; Dennett and, 98-105, 112, 336; Dickinson and, 46, 167-69, 176-80, 225, 235, 237, 393, 408-9; early life of, 69-72; European influences on, 89-96; first clinics opened by, 106-8, 399-400; funding of, 226; International Planned Parenthood Federation and, 290-93, 303-4; Gamble and, 298; Goldman and, 50, 81-82, 86, 95, 393; India and, 289-90; Kaufman and, 221; McCormick and, 337-45, 358, 373, 432; manufacture of contraceptives and, 239; paramedical clinics advocated by, 215-16, 218; in old age, 373-74; radical activities of, 75-88, 393; on Rock, 352; Rockefellers and, 284-86; Roman Catholic hierarchy and, 110-12, 119-20; second marriage of, 113-16, 121; social vision of, 129-39; support from women for, 371; wealthy supporters of, 108-10, 167
Sanger, Peggy, 97
Sanger, William, 50, 72-75, 77-85, 88, 97-99, 108, 395
Satterthwaite, Adaline Pendleton, 361-62
Saunders, Francis, 356
Schreiner, Olive, 131
Schering Corporation, 357
Scheuer, James H., 102
Science (magazine), 361
Science of a New Life, The (Cowan), 25, 27
Scripps, Edward, 203

Scripps Foundation for Research in Population Problems, 203
Schudder, Vida, 132-33
Seaman, Barbara, 365
Sears, Christine, 237
Selected Bibliography of Contraception (Tietze), 403
Sen, B. R., 287
Senate, U.S.: Subcommittee on Doreign Aid Expenditures, 378; Subcommittee on Patents, Trademarks, and Copyrights, 357
Seventh International Birth Control Congress (1930), 275
Sex and Education: A Reply (Howe), 392
Sex in Education; or, A Fair Chance for the Girls (Clarke), 392
Sex in Mind and in Education (Maudsley), 440
Sex in Relation to Society (Ellis), 93
Sex Side of Life, The (Dennett), 185-86
Sexual Behavior in the Human Female (Kinsey), 284
Sexual Behavior in the Human Male (Kinsey), 284
Sexual Hygiene (handbook), 42-45
Shaw, George Bernard, 398
Shedlovsky, Leo, 245
Sheppard-Towner Act (1921), 144, 268
Shryock, Richard, 440
Silent Spring (Carson), 411
Simonds, Herbert R., 114-15
Sims, James Marion, 28-29, 36
Single Woman, The (Dickinson), 406-7
Sixth International Birth Control Conference (1925), 116
Sixth International Neo-Malthusian and Birth Control Conference (1926), 135
Skene, Alexander, J. C., 40-42, 150,53, 155, 160, 440
Sklar, Kathryn, 389, 440
Slee, J. Noah, 113-16, 122
Slick, Tom, 350
Smith, Al, 396
Smith, Daniel S., 440, 441
Smith-Rosenberg, Carroll, 390, 394
Social History of the American Family, A (Calhoun), 5, 439, 440
Social Security Act (1936), 253
Socialist Party of America, 74, 77
Social Security Amendments (1967), 379
Eociology of Human Fertility, The (Freedman), 385
Sollins, Irving V., 357
Solomon, Barbara M., 411, 432
South Korea, IUDs in, 307
Spellman, Francis Cardinal, 286, 377
Spermicidal jelly, 44, 52, 114, 220-21, 242-43, 248-51, 402, 417
Spirit of the Ghetto (Hapgood), 83
Squier, Raymond, 188
Stanton, Elizabeth Cady, 25, 76
Starr, Isaac, 230, 416
State Board of Charities (New York), 118, 177-79
Station for Experimental Evolution, 134, 135
Sterilization, 135-36, 165, 406, 425
"Sterilization without Unsexing" (Dickerson), 191

455